Praise for
Don't Get Taken Every Time

"The secrets Remar Sutton brings to light are dirty but not little. A scary, readable book that will inform and help any car buyer."

—Willard P. Ogburn, Executive Director,
National Consumer Law Center

"This book reads like the best and most terrifying thriller since Michael Hudson's classic work *Merchants of Misery*. Don't even touch your computer before reading this extraordinary exposé on the new schemes and scams in the high-tech, ethically-challenged world of automobile sales in the twenty-first century."

—Patricia Sturdevant, Executive Director,
National Association of Consumer Advocates

"*Don't Get Taken* is more than a superb and witty how-to book—it's also a dramatic and absolutely scary look at the impact of the Web and high technology on your privacy, your safety, and your pocketbook."

—Clarence Ditlow, Executive Director,
Center for Auto Safety

PENGUIN BOOKS

DON'T GET TAKEN EVERY TIME

Remar Sutton is president and cofounder, with Ralph Nader, of the nonprofit Consumer Task Force for Automotive Issues (www.autoissues.org). The task force collects and disseminates information on auto fraud activities, including Internet activities, for many state attorneys general, dozens of significant national consumer groups, and eight well-known plaintiff law firms. The task force also administers "The Reality Checklist for Vehicle Leasing," a project of twenty-three attorneys general and hundreds of consumer groups. Sutton serves without compensation as task force president.

Sutton's knowledge in the automotive area comes from his own experiences as a former automobile dealer and from an ongoing eighteen-year investigation of dealership tactics and operational procedures (at times using undercover employees at dealerships), from his friends in the automobile business, from other experts he deals with, from his work with the attorneys general, and from the thousands of consumers who have written or talked with him over the years about their own dealership experiences.

Dateline NBC, 20/20, 60 Minutes, Nightline, ABC Primetime, Good Morning America, The Today Show, CBS Morning News, Newsweek, USA Today, the *Wall Street Journal,* the *New York Times,* the *Washington Post,* PBS television's *News Hour with Jim Lehrer,* and *People* magazine have all used Sutton as either a consultant, on-air authority, author, or subject.

He is also a pro bono consultant to Ralph Nader and his affiliated groups and to Clarence Ditlow, president of the Center for Auto Safety, and his affiliated groups. He is or has also been a consultant to the attorneys general of New York, New Jersey, Florida, Illinois, West Virginia, Hawaii, and Missouri.

Sutton lectured on auto fraud at the Practicing Law Institute, and for various state attorneys general offices, for the National Consumer Law Center, the Consumer Federation of America, and the National Association of Attorneys General. He has been an expert witness concerning automotive issues in many of the major class-action lawsuits in America.

Sutton's book *Don't Get Taken Every Time* (Penguin) became the "Book of Record" on the automobile buying process when it was first published in 1982. *Don't Get Taken Every Time* was published in six previous editions and became one of the few how-to books published in America to remain a best-seller for more than twenty-five years.

In addition to his work in the automotive arena, Sutton is a cofounder of the Privacy Rights Now Coalition (www.privacyrights now.com) and is the founder of the Give Me Back My Rights Coalition (www.givemebackmyrights.com). This coalition coordinates the activities of dozens of consumer groups opposed to binding mandatory arbitration in consumer contracts.

Remar Sutton is a Book-of-the-Month Club novelist and a contributor to national magazines such as *Reader's Digest* and *Sports Illustrated*. He served for ten years as a special consultant to *The Paris Review* literary quarterly and was a board member of the New York Philomusica Chamber Orchestra. Sutton currently serves as a Governor of the Trustees of the British Virgin Islands National Parks, USA, and as a board member of the Hearst Castle Preservation Foundation.

Books by Remar Sutton

Nonfiction

Don't Get Taken Every Time
Body Worry
The Common Ground Book

Fiction

Long Lines
Boiling Rock

Don't Get Taken Every Time

The **Ultimate Guide** to **Buying** or **Leasing** a Car in the **Showroom** or on the **Internet**

SIXTH REVISED EDITION

Remar Sutton

PENGUIN BOOKS

To the memory of 603

Acknowledgments

Thanks go first to Dr. Mary Abbott Waite, my cohort in many adventures for over twenty years, and to J. C. Pierce, director of the Consumer Task Force for Automotive Issues. It is a very lucky thing to have the type of trusting, inquisitive, and thoroughly pleasant working relationship Mary Abbott and I have had for all these years.

J. C. Pierce, one of the country's leading authorities on auto issues on the Internet, provided both the impetus for this book and good portions of the technical observations, knowledge, and conclusions that permeate it. "Remar, you'd really better watch what's happening on the Web," J. C. said some years ago, "it's getting scary out there. . . ." How right *that* observation was!

Dozens of consumer, technology, and legal experts have also contributed important facts, observations, corrections, and ideas to this book. I'm not going to try to mention them all, but in particular I would like to thank in no specific order, but with equal credit: Clarence Ditlow, president of the Center for Auto Safety; David Szwak, an expert on Fair Credit Reporting Issues; John Richard, director of Essential Information (Ralph Nader's umbrella organization); Jon Sheldon, director of the National Consumer Law Center; Pat Sturdevant, president of the National Association of Consumer Advocates; Ralph Nader; Garry Desjardins, Deputy Attorney General of Connecticut; Terry O'Loughlin, lead investigator in the Florida Attorney General's Office; Andrew Schwartzman, president of the Media Access Project; Tom Domonoske, Duke University consumer rights specialist; Jack Gillis, author of *The Car Book*; and A. J. Hiers, a friend and Florida automobile dealer who isn't afraid to speak his mind on both the good and bad parts of the auto business. I buy my cars from A. J.

I'd also like to thank the hundreds of consumers around the country who, each year, help me and my staff stay abreast of the lightning mutations that always make the auto business fascinating but oh so dangerous to the pocketbook.

Contents

Part Two

Battle Time   275

Don't Get Taken Every Time

A Day in the Life of Killer Monsoon

Killer Monsoon is late for the sales meeting again, the daily "ream-'em-out-and-charge-'em up" gathering that begins the day at most automobile dealerships in America. Killer's feeling fine today. He's delivering a new car to the home of a young couple who used an Internet buying service to find their dream car. The confident, nearly smug duo shopped for their financing on the Web and even used the most reputable online used-car guide to determine the "value" of their old car.

An inside look at what's happening in today's automotive arena.

The couple is happy, of course. They did it all at home. No bothersome dealerships to worry about. No haggling. And the money they saved! The couple's buyers order will show they bought the car at invoice; it will show they received the right value for their trade-in. Even the installment loan contract will show the couple received the actual rate the Web site had pegged as the best rate in the city! Killer smiles at the brilliance of the deceptions. The dealership made *thousands*. And the people never knew they'd been taken. It's Killer's best talent, giving people what they want.

The general manager is running the sales meeting this morning. Killer knows, when that guy's up this early, it's usually going to be an interesting session. And he's right. J. C. looks angry. Don, one of the sales managers, looks solemn. Killer stands by the door until everyone is seated, then strolls down the aisle, nodding, passing out "good morning"s and "how are you"s to the forty men and women settled tentatively in their seats. Several preppy-looking young men, three African Americans, a Korean, and four grandmother types sit in the front row that's reserved for new sales personnel. Behind them sits a row of parts employees and assistant service managers. As Killer passes J. C. and Don, he turns slightly toward them and curtsies, spreading his imaginary dress with both hands, a thin and innocent smile curving his lips. The rumble of laughter in the room quickly turns to silence as J. C. stands, pulls his belt up over his belly, and inhales, a snorting sound. Obviously, J. C. isn't amused.

Pressure to sell. He walks three heavy steps to the podium, grabs both edges with an intensity escaping no one in the room, and booms, "Why, boys and girls, are you so screwed up? We had fifty bumblebees* on this lot last night and you only nailed thirty-two files! We've got forty-eight salesmen in this establishment and all of you together only sent 1,148 e-mails yesterday! And you don't even have to write the damn things! *No one's* signed up to be our expert in the 'Young Consumer' chat room tonight, and to beat it all, some of you *didn't log on for last night's lowballing forum!*"

> "We had fifty bumblebees on this lot last night and you only nailed thirty-two files!"

J. C. shakes his head, "And then there's the money. We're down in new-car gross. We're down in used-car gross. *How's that possible?* Our 'upsale' of accessories stinks." J. C. sweeps his hand around the room. "And not a damn one of your financing scores is up to last week's scores. Same goes for warranty sales, and some of you SOBs are trying to discount the damn things!

* Lots of terms at car stores are peculiar to the automobile business. The glossary on page 445 will help you with those that are unfamiliar to you.

"We didn't 'spot' deliver half the deals we did write up last night. We didn't mini-pay or lease five cars! And half of you didn't 'T.O.' a soul. The *next* one of you that walks an 'up' without letting a manager grind 'em for a while is going to be on his ass out the door with 'em!"

J. C. begins to upbraid each salesperson individually, saying each name as if it were a command, looking first at the man or woman and then at the computerized Perk Board on the wall. While J. C. talks, the board literally changes as a clerk in another room updates information. It ranks every salesperson on unit sales, new and used, Internet sales, "spot" deliveries, accessory sales, service appointments that led to vehicle sales, "front-end" gross, "back-end" gross, deals financed, deals leased, and bonus cars. Killer is leading in all but one column—deals leased; he's not only "Salesman of the Year" again, but the dealership's best closer. But even the Salesman of the Year isn't immune from a lecture today.

Pausing at the end of his roll call, J. C. looks at Killer, who's slouched in his chair, eyes half closed in boredom. "Hey, Killer, wake up!" J. C. slaps the lectern. "This applies to you, too. You may lead the board with three hundred units out the door, but you've been doing too much sleeping! This time last year you had more service converts and higher warranty grosses, so either you've been dozing or you're over the hill, old man."

Killer's used to being picked on, so he doesn't flinch. "Well, J. C., I guess you'd better send me to that great car store in the sky. But before you do that, why don't you help us sell some widows, like that beat-up old Town Car? Nobody's going to sell that thing without a spiff. I get indigestion every time I see it. Maybe it's my age or something. . . ." Killer still reclines in his chair, but he's made a smart move. He's changed the subject. He's also changed J. C. into a bear again.

"Killer, you traded the damn thing in," J. C. replies hotly. "But I'm going to be nice today. We'll make that the 'credit fixer' car-of-the-day on the Web. The first person that brings me a deal on that piece of junk will get $200 in walking-around money when the sucker drives it off. I'm also paying $500 to the salesman—uh, pardon me, Internet representative—who ties down the most 'Web ups' by six today, from any of our Web sites. I want some big deposits, too, on every one of those tie-downs, none of that silly stuff. *And,* just for the fun of it, I'm paying a hundred to the first one of you who converts a credit union member."

Auto sales are big business. J. C. nods suddenly as two people enter the back of the room, causing most in the room to glance backward, then sit up straighter at the sight of God himself, Gary Oliver Davies. Until a year ago, Davies had been the sole owner of this store and a dozen other equally successful stores around the country. Then the Davies dealerships were bought by AFF, Inc. for $150,000,000—that's *$150 million!* Killer still can't believe the number. AFF (America's Family Friend Inc.) is a gigantic, diverse conglomerate.* It owns 250 dealerships—18 of them within thirty miles of Killer's store. It owns two multibillion-dollar banks and several subprime lending institutions, a media company with five television stations, fifty radio stations, eleven major daily newspapers, and three national magazines, including a magazine that bills itself as "the consumer's friend." AFF also owns portions of three popular Internet portals, a national insurance company, a real estate company, a large car rental company, a national online survey company, a branded credit card, and a chain of hardware stores. America's Family Friend itself is owned by five even bigger "specialty" conglomerates whose possessions include a television network, a major Hollywood studio, one of the largest cable TV companies in the country, a nationwide credit-reporting bureau, and finally three of the largest and most powerful Internet software developers in the world.

Very impressive. Gary Oliver Davies, a man who started as a lot boy at a used-car dealership, is a worldwide player, and he runs a lot more than 250 dealerships now. He runs all AFF's auto enterprises, including over seventy Web sites and "e-cars-to-your-door," one of the largest "buying clubs" proliferating on the Internet. The AFF dealerships cover virtually all car makes and now provide all the cars for the buying club and Web sites (click!), along with doing their regular business (brick!).

---

* America's Family Friend Inc., and other fictional businesses and Web sites in the narrative sections of this book are all registered on the Web to the author.

Now Davies is right here in the sales meeting, not five feet from Killer. Something momentous really *is* up, Killer thinks. He doesn't recognize the sharply dressed and tanned young man standing beside Davies, but Killer figured out why the guy was there the instant he saw him.

"Charles!" J. C. calls out, breaking into a grin, as he waves the young man to the podium. "Glad you could make it, son! Come on down here! And bring your escort, too, whoever that guy is!" J. C.'s comment sends a nervous ripple of laughter through the sales force—until Davies also laughs as he walks the young man to the front. J. C. shakes Davies' hand, then gives the young man a one-armed bear hug.

Tapping the power of the Internet. "You all know Mr. Davies, I'm sure. And we'd both like for you to know the man that's going to make you all a lot more money. AFF's new customer-facing Web development manager, Charles Pierce. A fancy title for a fancy brain! Charles will report directly to Mr. Davies." No one misses the importance of that statement.

Killer quickly glances around the room and sees few looks of surprise, and none of dismay. The Web has become the most lucrative source for prospects and profits anyone can remember, particularly since the dealerships had been bought by AFF. Every salesman's office was online, and every salesman was online daily. A press release had already announced that Davies was the Internet boss for all of AFF's Internet auto interests. The whole store had watched with fascination as a special "Web Central" building had been constructed just off the back entrance to Gary Oliver Davies' new suite of offices. "Man, there are some *really big* Internet things happening around here," J. C. had told everyone who asked. The low-slung, modern building held dozens of cubicles and as many offices. Rumor had it that Gary Oliver Davies himself had been interviewing lots of clever young things to occupy those cubicles.

"Good morning!" The deep, nearly gruff voice of Gary Oliver Davies pulls Killer's attention back to the podium. Even Killer straightens up an inch as Davies begins a rapid-fire presentation.

"Years ago, when I washed cars," Davies leans over the podium drawing his troops in, "I knew I could do more than make money in this damn business. I knew that sometime I'd make history. We're starting to do that today, and that building . . ." Davies points in the general direction of the new structure,

". . . that building is the engine of our weapon. That's why we're calling it WAR Central, the Web and Resources Center. It's going to control the way millions of people around the country buy their cars, because we're developing and testing every damn new AFF Web project right here, right in my first dealership. And you lucky sons and daughters will benefit from that testing."

Davies ticks off a dozen new Web-related products: very sophisticated "car clubs" targeted toward everyone and everything from sexual orientation to racial and ethnic background to intellect and age; very sophisticated prospecting tools that accurately predict which customers would buy and when, even before the customers knew that; very sophisticated "consumer" sites designed to immediately counter safety or reliability alerts from the government or watchdog agencies with soothing rebuttals from public relation flacks who sound like consumer experts but actually only regurgitate the company line.

And that was just the start! All those magical sites and products would interface with every database throughout the entire America's Family Friend empire. Subscribe to *SmartThinker,* AFF's "consumer magazine" and *boom!* a file is opened in your name, and your entire history with all AFF companies and products is poured into it. Live in Killer's telephone area code? *Boom!* your name pops up instantly on the dealership's "new prospect" page, available to anyone at the dealership. Have an auto loan with an AFF bank across the country? The loan information and an informal dealership-generated "cue" ranking your creditworthiness appear in your file, too, along with the payoff on your old vehicle, and an estimate from the Automated Appraiser program of its wholesale value.

Did you stop by one of the AFF dealerships a few years ago to use the restroom and end up test-driving a car? An informal evaluation of your creditworthiness during that visit is right there in this file available for anyone at any of the 250 AFF deal-erships, including the lot boy! Had your vehicle serviced in an-other city by an AFF dealership a couple of years ago? The "service predictor" automated program estimates how many miles you've driven since the last service visit and alerts the sales department to contact you. The sales force is too busy to contact you? No problem. Just hit the "automated dealer re-sponse system" icon and the computer generates a schedule of friendly fax and e-mail messages for you, then instantly begins to send them. The system will monitor the responses, too.

Just when consumers thought it was safe. Magic! Stunning! And all of this was to be run from WAR Central. Virtu-ally all of it is a gimmick for grabbing "ups" out of the air, Killer realizes with a smile. And it's all cloaked in the handsome re-spectability of customer service, "lifetime" relationships, and "honest customer information."

Killer continues to listen, rapt, the fingers of his right hand strumming his leg. The Web is already Killer's best friend. Killer isn't a computer expert, but he is a communications expert. He had been the first salesman at the dealership to sense the Inter-net's power to communicate. And with a fast hunt-and-peck typ-ing skill, he has learned to play it like a beautiful violin.

But now Gary Oliver Davies was talking about making it a whole virtual symphony orchestra! Killer had seen it coming. Thirty years of car sales experience told him that the earth is moving and the car business is changing in a thousand ways as it moves to add "click" to "brick." Practically all of the ways would be extremely profitable for a smart fellow like Killer. He smiles. Just when the suckers thought it was safe! The power was shifting from the consumer back to the dealer, after years of increased consumer sophistication and eroding dealer profits brought on by consumer sophistication and consumer watch-dog groups.

The tanned new guy—young enough to be Killer's son and probably never sold a car—is the earthmover, not Killer. A lesser man would be intimidated by that thought, but Killer is excited by it. The young man would need a mentor. Killer is the first person to greet Charles Pierce as the meeting breaks up and the first salesman to volunteer for "all that beta test stuff you'll be doing, I'll bet."

Killer heads for the old computer room, a converted storage space, pours a cup of coffee, drops in six sugar cubes, and settles in a chair in front of a 17-inch monitor. Rather than a screen saver, the monitor displays a smaller version of the Perk Board, where Killer again notes his top ranking.

He types in Jerry's name, a "bird dog" who loves to trade cars every six months or so. Jerry's financial life pops up onscreen: the number of cars he's bought in the last three years, the profits he's paid, the balance due on his current car loan, the estimated wholesale value of that car, and his current dealership-generated "customer value" score. Killer smiles. The guy had just enough equity to trade again now. Good ol' Jerry. He's a hairstylist at a trendy salon frequented by successful, under-forty men and women. Jerry's also one of Killer's best Web dogs. "Here, take one of his cards," Jerry will say when the topic of buying on the Web comes up in his chair. "Robert DeMarco is the senior consumer consultant at this site called YourConsumerFriend. You never even have to go *near* a dealership."

Watching the salesman work. Robert DeMarco is Killer's real name, but Killer Monsoon is what everyone at the dealership calls him, and it's an apt description, too. Killer devastates most customers. He squeezes every single ounce of profit from every customer, from the richest and most confident to the weakest and most tentative—yet leaves them feeling like he's done them a favor. Killer's famous for "bumping" one particular woman, raising her nine times, delivering her the car on the spot, and then calling her back a week later, raising her again.

By ten in the morning, Killer has e-mailed two dozen people, all sales leads from the dealership's many "prospect aggregators." Killer notices that one of the leads has mentioned she is expecting a baby. He sends her e-mail address to a Web site that specializes in consumer and health issues—and of course, products—for expectant mothers. The lady will remember Killer for his thoughtful act, and the site will remember him, too: It will pay him a small commission on everything the woman buys through that site.

Resting his eyes from the screen, Killer quickly phones a few of his old customers. As he keys in each phone number in the computer-based phone, the customer's entire history with the dealership and Killer pop up on the screen, including the birthdays of the customers and their kids. Killer likes the old-timers who don't believe in the Web. He doesn't make as much money on them; he just has more fun with them.

Killer then uses one of the sales department's digital video cameras to film a sixty-second tour of a snappy red BMW convertible, which he then e-mails to a prospect. At ten-fifteen he joins a live chat room filled with car salesmen in twenty states. The topic is "Using the Web to lower your prospect's expectations on the value of their trade-ins."

By eleven, Killer is standing close to the main entrance of the showroom. He's hot. A couple of those new sales personnel, the "floor whores," are grabbing all the unscheduled "ups" and blowing them off the lot and, even after J. C.'s tirade in the sales meeting, are letting them leave without nailing a single file! For over a year the dealership had been using a magnificent software program on first-time customers: Just scan their driver's license and *boom!* the computer opens a file on the person, automatically displaying a color picture of the driver's license, then usually a credit summary or "spending history" score from an outside source's databank, then a form for timing the ups' every move on the lot. The ups' history would be on file forever. Who didn't have time to nail a file?

"Those new people, especially that honey with the rehearsed Southern accent, don't know squat about how to control a customer," Killer's always bitching to J. C. "They're costing you money, man." J. C. knows he's right, too. One of these days J. C.'s going to kick their butts out the door.

Keeping files on potential customers. Just then Killer sees a car pull onto the lot and quickly enters the car's tag number into the computer near the front door. The computer instantly recognizes the couple from visits to two other dealerships owned by AFF—one here, one hundred miles away. It flashes their dealership "worth assessment"—they can get approved for anything—and summarizes their last two dealership visits: they are "payment" buyers, Killer's favorite victims. They refused to pay more than $550 per month, their current payment. They are also "allowance" buyers. How much they are "allowed" on their old car means a lot to them. They wanted $14,000, but the other Davies dealerships wouldn't go a dollar above $12,000. Not a problem for Killer, he's sure.

At the top right of the screen, a highlighted notation says, "Factory Portal"—the couple have surfed the car manufacturer's Web pages. Killer clicks on the portal icon and reviews the couple's visit to the site: they spent virtually all their time looking at information on the newest limited-edition four-door truck and had even used the manufacturer's site to pinpoint the exact truck sitting right there on Killer's lot. They had also used the manufacturer's "Lease or Buy?" comparison calculator. And then they clicked on the manufacturer's link to the Kelley Blue Book. Killer smiled. The Blue Book was one of the best used-car evaluation sites on the Web. But few customers really knew how to use it effectively. Killer knows, of course, just how to use it to his advantage.

Killer heads out the door toward the couple. They look nice, in their thirties, and slightly nervous. Killer pulls his tie a bit to the side. He isn't dressed like a hotshot. He is a perfect shade of gray in a gray world: slightly rumpled short-sleeved shirt covering an ample belly, a tie that's the wrong width. He also needs a haircut. Killer always needs a haircut. He is quiet, almost shy, unassuming in the most disarming way, and friendly without showing his teeth too much. If you met him, you'd instantly feel comfortable and slightly superior.

Trusting a smiling salesperson. "Hi, I'm Bob DeMarco, thanks for coming in to see us." He shakes both their hands, paying attention to them equally, watching for signs revealing which person is really in control, the decision maker of the two. As Killer talks, he glances at the couple's car. He shakes his head and smiles, "Mr. and Mrs. Baskin, you know, I've got a customer who's been looking for a car like yours. I'll bet we could get you $16,000 for it, if we could trade you out of it today." The Baskins

"This is going to be a good day." Right!

just look at Killer for an instant, trying to mask smiles. The most they had been offered was $12,000. And this man, right off the bat, is talking $16,000. This is going to be a good day!

And just think how low the payments would be with that much money for their trade!

"As long as the payment isn't too high, and as long as you can do that on our trade, we don't care what the car costs," Sara Baskin says. Killer just loves payment buyers. From that moment on, he'll never mention what the couple's trade-in is really worth. He'll just talk payments, "and after all, it's the payment that's important, isn't it folks?" They nod yes. "Well, let me ask you then—if I can give you the payment you want, will you buy a car today? Or maybe a truck? We've got some real specials on trucks this week." Just the vehicle they wanted! At the payment they wanted! Well, who wouldn't say yes to that?

Soon the three of them are sitting in Killer's office, sur- rounded by "Salesman of the Month" plaques, pictures of the DeMarco grandchildren, and several "Appreciation" scrolls from various organizations. The computer printout for a pretty silver limited-edition four-door—the very vehicle the Baskins had lo- cated by using the manufacturer's Web site—was lying on the desk right by a pad of buyer's orders and the two Cokes Killer insisted on purchasing. Both people had driven the truck— Killer insisted on that, too. After a few moments of small talk about the price of cars these days, Killer begins his quiet talk, an honest man speaking to intelligent buyers.

"Now, I know you folks were paying $550 per month on your old car. But the new one lists for several thousand more. You understand, then, that it will cost you a little more per month?"

Mrs. Baskin frowns. "Well, you know, we just don't want to spend much more. So, I don't know . . . what would the pay- ment be?"

Killer has already decided that she is the decision maker in this couple, and he begins to work on his response, turning to the computer, punching in numbers furiously. He frowns an in- stant, then punches some more keys, muttering, "Well, I know we can do better than that." Finally, with a firm nod and a smile, he looks up. "Excellent! I've got you qualified for our lowest rate. We can have you riding in the special edition today for a payment of only $725 per month!"

The Baskins turn dove-white. Sara Baskin clears her throat. "Mr. DeMarco, there's just no way we can afford that . . . I don't think."

Killer knew that all along. He was just testing. The last two times the Baskins had been at Davies dealerships, they had bolted when the numbers were too high. But they have not bolted with Killer yet. They aren't *that* shocked, either. Killer continues talking, lowering the payment in small amounts, reminding them how much money they are receiving for their old car, reminding them that all their research on the Internet indicated this was indeed the right truck for them. "Well, Mrs. Baskin, I don't really believe the boss will let me get the payment below $645 a month. If you remember how much this pretty thing costs, and remember it's our most popular model— you saw that on the Web site, didn't you?" They both nodded. "And at this price, you're actually saving over $5,700, the difference between the $725 payment you *should* be paying and the $645 payment I can get you." The two of them like that logic, and look at each other silently as Killer continues, "And don't forget that we're giving you $16,000 for your trade; that took a lot of work to accomplish, you know." Killer pauses. "I'll tell you what: I will even *make* the first payment for you two. You won't have a payment for two and a half months." Killer pauses again. "And, since you came to us from the manufacturer's Web site, I'm going to sign you up for free in our new Buyer's Club program. You'll be able to make appointments right online for lifetime free oil changes here at the dealership, and you'll receive product bulletins at the same time as the factory sends them to us. I'm proud to say our dealership is the first dealership in this program, and you'll be one of the first members!"

And so the Baskins buy the truck for $645 per month, and they're happy. They bought the highest-rated truck on the manufacturer's Web site. The first payment is paid for them, too. And they received the $16,000 they wanted for their trade-in. Now, what could be wrong with this deal?

Everything is wrong. First, the truck the Baskins had researched so carefully on the manufacturer's Web site was rated as the most dangerous truck sold in America. That information, of course, wasn't on the manufacturer's Web site. It was, however, page one on the Center for Auto Safety's site.

Second, Killer knew all along that he could have sold the Baskins the truck for their original payment of $550 per month rather than the $645 per month they ended up paying. He knew how much money—the lump sum of cash—$550 per month would really buy.

Third, Killer didn't really lower the sales price of this truck when he cut the monthly payment from $725 per month to $645 per month. He didn't cut the price one dime. Killer simply quoted the first payment based on financing for forty-eight months at the maximum interest rate. But the final payment was based on financing seventy-two months at a slightly lower rate. Killer's profit didn't go down, *it went up*.

> *What could be wrong with this deal? Everything.*

Fourth, Killer did give the Baskins a $16,000 allowance for their old car. He did it by raising the selling price of the new vehicle by three thousand dollars at the last minute. The Baskins hadn't been paying attention to all the figures on their sales contracts. Payments and trade-in allowance are all they focused on.

Fifth, there's the "free" payment. In the car business, this technique is usually called the "Christmas Club." Killer didn't reach into his pocket and make that payment; he simply added the amount of the payment to the total vehicle price, then financed the $645 payment in their contract. Killer gave them a check for $645, sure. When he turned his deal into the finance office, he simply attached a note saying, "First payment financed; cut a check to the Baskins." The Baskins would be paying that $645, plus interest, back over the next seventy-two months.

And, finally, there's the free membership and those lifetime free oil changes in the dealership's Buyer's Club. Killer will receive a $25 bonus for signing the Baskins up. The club will send lots of "product bulletins" to the Baskins: sales pitches for products and services. But it won't include the "secret" warranty bulletin about potentially faulty brakes already e-mailed from the manufacturer to the dealership's service department. The potentially faulty brakes are on trucks just like the Baskins'. The club will send lots of questionnaires, too, "mining" the prospect, er, club member for nuggets of information to arm both the manufacturer and AFF for their next sales attempt.

The club will give free oil changes, if an appointment for those changes is made through the Buyer's Club Web site. But every time a service appointment is made, Killer will be alerted to be waiting for that customer in the service department. Maybe the Baskins are ready for a used car for the kids, you know. And every time the service manager greets the Baskins, he'll be thinking of the list of other services he needs to sell them to cover the cost of the oil change and earn his bonus.

And, of course, the Baskins' name and an informal summary of their creditworthiness and their e-mail address will be sold to other "Prospect Aggregators" around the country.

Profits everywhere. Killer needs a little celebration after a nice sale like the Baskins. He makes a quick trip to the little food shop next door and downs a quick beer. Yes, sir, this is going to be a fine day.

By twelve-thirty, Killer is sitting up at the used-car department's "Credit Fixer" lot. Older cars, cars the dealership would normally wholesale or sell for junk, neatly line three rows. Killer likes the lunch hour here. Hardworking folks looking for reasonable transportation rush over at lunch hour, and many of the regular used-car sales personnel are conveniently away at lunch. A very easy time to catch an "up" in a hurry.

Killer "helps" more customers. A car pulls in before Killer's feet are up on the desk, and a couple jumps out quickly, hurrying around a small used Nissan. These folks are jumping beans, nervous types convinced they'll be taken whenever they buy. Killer is a master with this type of customer.

"Hi, folks, I'm Bobby DeMarco. Boy, I'm glad I saw you! The guys have been trying to sell that car to someone for a month. It's just not a car you want to own." The people stop walking and look at him. Here is an honest man, they think, just what they've been looking for.

They are a young couple with "no credit," the man volunteers nervously. "We're cash buyers." The type of car they purchase isn't important, as long as it's a good car with a "drive-out price" of $2,000—tax, title, and tag included. And Killer knows just the car to fit the Karlsons' budget: the ten-year-old Lincoln with the $200 bonus.

"Tommy, it's a better car than the Nissan. It's also a safer car. Did you read the story in the paper about the wife and two kids who were killed in a little car like this?" Killer looks at the Nissan as if it's infected with a dangerous, highly contagious germ. He pulls a copy of the article from his pocket. This article has switched lots of people from small cars.

Killer doesn't price the Lincoln at all. He will work that later. He takes both of their driver's licenses—"for insurance purposes, you know," Killer says, and excuses himself just long enough to scan them. In under a second, the dealership file opens with the couple's pictures placed right by a credit report showing them to be very slow payers, but payers, anyway. Killer likes the sound of that. They are also members of a local credit union. Killer doesn't like that. Credit unions often finance members who are slow payers but good members.

Killer puts them out in the old Lincoln by themselves; that's against the rules, but Killer isn't worried about that. He knows the couple will be impressed with the gesture.

In less than ten minutes, the Karlsons drive the Lincoln back to the new-car showroom and wander inside, looking for Killer. He's in his office, and as they enter, he hits a few keystrokes on the computer, noting the time the ups enter the room. It's the second time Killer's made a notation on these particular folks. The first time was when they drove out. Killer swings from the computer, makes sure the couple looks happy with the Lincoln (they do), and quickly puts a somber look on his face.

"Tommy and Allison, sometimes I want to quit this business," he says, shaking his head. "Would you believe the boss says I can't sell this car for a dime less than $5,971? That guy never gives up." Three times the amount of cash the couple have.

Before they can respond, Killer smiles and nods yes, "But don't worry, I've worked out the financing already."

"Uh, you know we've kind of got a credit problem. I was laid off, you know," the man says, "and I've just started to work again."

"Oh, that's no problem, Tommy. I'm known as 'the credit fixer' around here. We'll use your $2,000 as down payment, and I've already got you approved for the rest, at a national financing company, no less." Killer never says that the "national company" is a subprime financing company owned by AFF, and of course he doesn't say it charges 28 percent interest rather than the 9 percent interest this couple's credit union would probably charge them for the same loan. Killer could even fill out the credit union's paperwork right there at the dealership because all of Gary Oliver Davies' dealerships proudly advertise their "partnership" with credit unions. But the credit union wouldn't let the Karlsons spend $6,000 on a junker car in the first place, and definitely wouldn't pay Killer a fat commission. Forget the credit union.

Of course, Killer wouldn't have been worried no matter how bad the couple's credit might have been, because the Karlsons have $2,000 in cash. The dealership has only $1,000 in the old Lincoln. Even if the couple doesn't make a single payment, the dealership will make a thousand dollars profit. And Killer? He'll be paid his standard 25 percent commission on the entire profit—$3,900—plus the $200 bonus. Killer's mind ticks up the total commission from this single sale—$1,125. An hour well spent.

Killer likes to take a break in the afternoon. Around five o'clock each day he checks out with the switchboard, "I've got to show a car across town, honey. I'll be back by seven." He winks at her. That Killer is such a sport.

The Dead End is a noisy bar, and after two Seven and Sevens have done their job, Killer barely hears the waitress. "Hey, Killer!" Cherry nudges his shoulder, drawing him from some other world. "You may have your pager off, but they found you, anyway. Your boss is on our phone." Mr. DeMarco is not worried, however. Today, alone, he's already made his bosses over $7,000. When you're that good, bosses may yell and scream, but they don't fire you. It's one of the nicest realities about the car business. Whatever you've done in the past means nothing. It's what you do every day with the "ups" that makes you good.

Watch the "specialist" work magic on the hardest deal.

A specialist is needed at the store; that's why J. C. has called. One of the new boys has spent three hours with a guy who's on a customized mini-SUV, a bright yellow one some customer had ordered, then rejected. The new boy had already given away the deal—not a penny of profit was left on the sale of the thing. And he'd already given away the finance rate, too, was selling the money at the same price the dealership paid for it. *And* the guy didn't have a trade-in. Killer couldn't play around with that.

No problem. It takes Killer exactly sixty seconds to come to a price with the man—a price actually $700 under the SUV's true cost, and Killer agrees to the man's interest rate terms, too. The dealership won't make a dime on the loan. The new boy's eyes are wide as Killer takes a pad of buyer's orders from the desk drawer and begins to write up the deal, chatting away as he scribbles, ". . . but I've got to insist on one thing if we sell you this custom-painted SUV at this price and at this financing rate."

The man sits up. He's so smart, he's sure Killer's trying to pull something. "Yeah, and what's that thing?"

"That you don't tell a soul what you paid for it. We can't do this for everybody."

The rookie salesman chirped in, "And that's for sure! I can't believe that price."

The man breaks out in a grin and pokes his spouse in the side. "See, I *told* you," he says victoriously.

Killer continues to fill out the paperwork, as the new salesman watches wide-eyed. "Folks, I need you to sign this waiver saying you don't want our life and accident and health insurance protection plans. Our attorneys require us to get this form signed when people don't want the insurance on their payments."

"What do you mean, don't want 'em?"

"Well, you fought so hard on money, I thought you probably didn't have the money for that."

"Oh, we've got the money. What's it cost?"

"Barely a Coke a day. We can even put it on your spouse, too."

The man nods yes, his eyes going out to the yellow SUV. Sparkling, it has been pulled right up to the window.

"What's it cost?"

"Barely a Coke a day."

"We've already put kryptonic rustproofing and undercoating on it, you know. And I'm assuming you want our best extended warranty. Comes with a twenty-four-hour service feature, you know. It's on sale this month, too." The man nods yes. His mind is on the yellow beauty. And he's already showed these people he's a tough bargainer.

"And, if you want to get those insurance rates down, you should probably have our best alarm system installed, don't you think?"

"Don't you make a lot of money on those warranties and things?" the man asks absentmindedly.

"Mr. Stevens, we're here to serve you, not make money on you every time you turn around. Those days are gone."

Killer flips the buyer's order and finance contract around, watches as the man looks only at the price of the vehicle and at the interest rate, and barely cracks a smile as the man begins to sign his name. "If you can afford it, I need a deposit of $3,000, that's to show the boss you're serious, you know. If you can afford it."

Of course he can afford it. The guy's no idiot.

Sure. The dealership really did lose $700 on the sale of the SUV itself. But on the life and accident and health insurance, it made $1,800; on the rustproofing and undercoating, it made $850. The service agreement gave them a profit of $1,200, the alarm system a profit of $500. And Killer had picked up another $500 when he pulled out the buyer's order pad from the desk drawer—he just used the pad with the $575 dealer preparation charge rather than the pad with the $75 dealer prep charge. Who cares if the dealership lost $700 on the sale of the car itself? Even after that loss, the profit on this deal was $4,100, and Killer's take was just over $500, after splitting the $1,000 commission with the rookie salesman.

"You see, kid," Killer says as he walks from the sales booth, "it doesn't matter which pocket you take their money from. It just matters that we get in their pocket."

It is a satisfying way to end the evening. Killer stops by a computer in the break room just long enough to write a quick e-mail to J. C. "Boss, I only made three deals today, only grossed you $11,000. Guess I'm over the hill, huh?" With a very satisfied smile, Killer clicks the SEND button and walks from his office. He's headed back to the Dead End, where a couple of times each week other "Internet consultants" from other dealerships and buying services around the city meet to share a laugh and a fun story or two about the Internet's wonderful impact on their lives and paychecks.

Chapter 1

What's Happening to the Automobile Business?

The Bad News

If you find your introduction to Killer and his world startling, and find the implications of some of these tales chilling, welcome to the Brave New Automotive World. Though the corporate and personal names in Killer's Day and throughout the narrative portions of *Don't Get Taken Every Time* are fictional, the scenarios are fact.

As Killer and his friends are happily going to show you, every aspect of the auto industry has been ripped apart, reinvented, interconnected, and energized in a titanic battle to "nail" you—"acquire" you—for life. The battle is constantly changing and evolving, too. Even if you just use your computer for e-mail and think the Web has to do with real spiders, every aspect of your contact with any part of the auto business from now on is going to be affected by this battle.

In just a few years, the stunning fusion of technology, databases, the Internet, and Very Big Business has turned the disparate, fragmented, slightly old-fashioned, often shady auto business into the trillion-dollar blue-eyed baby many in the investment world want to kiss. As traditional dealership-based business, often referred to as "brick" commerce (representing actual stores), continue to incorporate the vast resources of the

Internet, called "click" commerce (for the mouse), the ongoing changes hold disquieting implications for your legal rights, your privacy rights, your safety, and last, but certainly not least, your pocketbook.

In this battle, everybody is using the same seductive weapon: the mantra of "lifetime relationship-convenience-service-honest consumer information." And "everybody" really means *everybody*.

At the turn of the new millennium (not so long ago as it seems), when the "new economy" hype was booming, auto manufacturers were racing to establish "strategic alliances" and "affinity relationships" with Internet companies. Ford teamed up with Yahoo! and General Motors linked up with America Online (AOL), which was riding high with the AOL–Time Warner merger. The Internet offered the auto business a new way to capture customers.

"We want to develop an ongoing relationship with vehicle owners throughout the entire lifetime of their ownership," Former Ford CEO Jac Nasser said when he announced Ford's "strategic alliance" with Yahoo![1]

"We'll work together to assist consumers throughout the entire ownership cycle," said a General Motors release announcing its "strategic alliance" with AOL.[2]

Then came the dot-com bust. Hundreds of auto-related Web businesses and Web sites went bust, too. Among those that survived, ownership and relationships changed as fast as musical chairs. Exclusive alliances vanished and new strategies emerged. What hasn't changed and won't change is the goal of all the players in the auto business to acquire you.

Web-based advertising is the big hook now. The vast majority of profitable Web sites, including auto-related Web sites, make their profits on advertising. These include those "consumer-facing" sites that claim to offer "reliable consumer information." Manufacturers and dealerships know that at least three-fourths or more of new car shoppers will use the Internet to research vehicles that interest them or fit their needs. More used-car shoppers browse the Internet than the local newspapers or penny shoppers. So companies compete for high-profile advertising space. Their biggest targets these days are search engines like Google, Yahoo! or MSN.

Not only do manufacturers and dealerships pay big fees to have their ads and links come up on top of the "sponsored links" when you do a keyword search on almost any search engine, but they also spend big bucks working with online marketing gurus to "optimize" their Web site designs and "buying" keywords so that their Web sites will pop up at the top of the links a search engine reports from a "natural search." Manufacturers and dealerships also advertise or form business relationships with "third-party, independent" automotive sites.

Once you click on a link or go to a Web site, the "customer relations management" program—CRM to insiders—is the name of the game. The goal is to turn you from a "lead" to a "sale." And after you are sold, they want to keep you for life. The marketer of one CRM software program promises dealers that their "solution" both helps dealers sustain "strong lifetime relationships" with customers and provides tools that automate the sales and customer follow-up process, "mine customer data" for targeted marketing campaigns, and track the return on the dealership's investment. Automotive CRM consultants have also devised sophisticated programs that do such things as help dealerships identify consumers' nonverbal cues so that the sales personnel can better target the individual customer's "hot buttons."

To carry out their marketing plans, individual auto manufacturers and dealerships alike have multiple Web sites, geared toward different customers. Depending on the company, the number of Web sites can range from dozens to hundreds. Some may not carry any obvious clue or logo that identifies the sponsoring company. The Web sites may offer special features to get you to browse further or perhaps register with your name and e-mail address. Or maybe there are car clubs, bulletin boards, chat rooms, or other "services" to tweak your interest.

Some manufacturers now offer "co-branded" credit cards that typically provide "rewards" that you may use toward the purchase of a new vehicle. That's nice, you think. But did you know that co-branded credit cards may give the manufacturer the legal right to assess your credit regularly without checking with you further. Credit card issuers have the privilege to do so.

And knowledge about your credit is the single most important negotiating tool for a seller of cars.

Third-party auto-related sites, even the best and most reliable, also have become economically intertwined with carmakers and car sellers. Edmunds Inc., for years hated by the dealers because they provided consumers the true inventory cost of new cars, now serves as a lead aggregator for dealerships, generating more than 400,000 consumer-submitted leads monthly for dealers according to their Web site.[3]

Autobytel.com, which provides editorial content on autos to such consumer portals as Yahoo!, AOL, MSN, and Earthlink, also sells marketing, advertising, data, and customer relations management programs to dealers, including a CRM program called Web-Control® (interesting name).[4] In the shakeout time since the great dot-com bust, Autobytel.com has become the owner of a number of consumer sites including Autoweb.com, CarSmart.com, Car.com, AutoSite.com, Autoahorros.com, and CarTV.com.

"Well, what's wrong with all of that?" you may ask. "What's wrong with any of these companies sending me helpful information? Isn't the Web a great place to gather information? And aren't all those buying clubs and car services a lot easier to deal with than the pressure-cooker boys down at the dealership, anyway?"

There's a lot wrong here, if you're not wary—that's what this book is about—and it starts with the mantra of "lifetime relationship-convenience-service-honest consumer information." With the exception of relatively few sites, this mantra uses Alice in Wonderland definitions, which are the opposite of what they appear, and old-time auto industry code words that hide their true message: "spend more money." The mantra "lifetime relationship-convenience-service-honest consumer information" also masks the true agendas of the companies and Web sites that mouth it.

"Thanks! I needed that!" Convenience has always been an automotive buzzword. "Oh, it's more 'convenient' for you to finance here at the dealership than to have to call your credit union," a finance person may say, for instance. True, perhaps. But what the finance manager forgot to tell you about was the cost of that convenience. In a test project in Austin, Texas, University Federal Credit Union analyzed the finance contracts of 607 members who had chosen the convenience of dealership financing rather than taking the time to call or visit their credit union. This group of members seemed to have thought, Just how much could convenience cost, anyway? Well, for these 607 people, the cost of convenience was $1,200,000. That averages $1,976 per person. Would you be inconvenienced for an hour or two to save that kind of money?[5]

And that $1,976 wasted was the needless profit the consumers had paid on just the finance aspect of the vehicle-buying trans- actions. How much do you suppose they may have wasted in other parts of the transaction? In the Brave New Automotive World—where you can conveniently finance online in thirty sec- onds, conveniently sell your old car online in minutes without leaving your house, and conveniently have that shiny new char- iot delivered to your home with a ribbon tied around it!—a gullible and unwary shopper is going to throw away a lot more than $2,000.

Convenience has one more meaning for the auto industry that involves your pocketbook. Although all those clubs and Web sites may wish to forge a lifetime relationship with you, their even stronger goal once they've "tied you down" (their jargon for getting a deposit) is to sell you very fast. "Turn a five-hour trans- action into a one-hour transaction!" says TargetLive.com's top online trainer.[6] That's more convenient, you see. "Three clicks to a sale!" is another hymn of Web-based automobile marketing.[7] Sell them in three clicks of the mouse—a very fast transaction, and in the auto business, speed almost always leads to wrecked budgets and worse.

"Service? So that's what service is!" Service is the second part of the New Automotive World's mantra. Selling extended warranties that cost $150 for $1,900 is presented as "service" at some dealerships and buying clubs. Charging you $495 to regis- ter your car, when it only costs $7, is considered a service by many dealerships and online sites. Offering to "happily take your old car in trade" is a "service" with almost all online buying sites. Oops, they forget to mention that's where you may be ripped off the most. Offering to finance your car is presented as a "service" by just about everybody. Actually, financing is a big profit center for dealerships and the financing arms of auto manufacturers.

"Service," whether it is smoothly mouthed by a dealership employee or is an online catchphrase, carries hidden meanings in the auto industry. Consider it a caution light, not a green light.

"Just the friend I was looking for. . . ." The new automotive mantra's promise of "true consumer information" is generally an illusion if you're dealing with a "commercial" Web site—a site that benefits financially in any way from the information it provides you. General Motors, for instance, may send you an e-mail about an official recall concerning your vehicle. Good for them. The manufacturers are required to contact you during an official recall, and e-mail contact is certainly cheaper than mail contact. But the manufacturers aren't going to send you an e-mail inviting you to read their e-mails to dealers that discuss the many "secret warranties" the manufacturers are offering at any time.

A Toyota or Honda dealer may be nice when they offer to call you up or e-mail you about an upcoming service visit. But they aren't being nice when they review your entire history before that visit, review your credit, then assign the dealership's best salesperson to talk you into buying when you're perfectly happy with your old car.

And neither AOL, MSN, or Yahoo! nor the best online buying services in the world is going to do any better. If it's a commercial site, they're going to leave out what you really need to know, refrain from criticizing their "affinity partners," or create information that looks consumer friendly, but isn't really. In the world of big business, "true consumer information" is an elusive reality. You won't find much of it on commercial sites.

"Well, okay. If you think the mantra is an illusion, what is the Brave New Automotive World's true agenda?" The true agenda has two objectives: First, to "data mine" your life—to gather every possible bit of information about you, then refine that information. Second, to make you so comfortable in that ongoing, supposedly consumer-friendly relationship that you throw caution away and open your pocketbook wide. "How do you disarm that customer?" an online trainer on TargetLive.com asks enthusiastically, after talking about the importance of establishing an ongoing relationship with customers. "How do you turn them into a sale? It's all about that sale! All about making money!"[8] And to do that, a business has to make its Web site "sticky." Only customer loyalty or a deposit certifies "stickiness."

The battle to nail your file before the next combatant can nail it is happening as you read this. And it doesn't matter if you've never surfed the Web, it doesn't matter if you have decided to drive your current vehicle until the wheels fall off, it doesn't matter if you never go near a dealership, it doesn't matter if you service your own car. It doesn't even really matter if you own a car yet or are even old enough to drive!

It goes beyond auto dealerships. You are probably going to be nailed from the moment you visit an auto supply store, apply for a bank loan for that big-screen TV, change your insurance company, enter an "Auto Buffs" chat room, use a credit card, use a relocation service when you move to another city, or subscribe to some consumer magazines.

You are, of course, fair game if you like surfing the Web. Your file is going to be nailed by lots of folks if you log on to any auto-related Web sites such as manufacturers' home pages, dealers' pages, used-car sites, finance sites, leasing sites, or budgeting sites; even if you log on to some of those "yellow page" sites. And, sisters and brothers, you will most certainly be nailed if you visit any dealership—or even call a dealership on the phone!

"Okay, I'll take all that abuse, as long as I don't have to deal with a dealer or go near those places." That's what most people feel and that's why the Internet is chockablock with "direct" auto services, services that supposedly cut out the dealership. And that's the really funny part of the Brave New Automotive World.

The Grim Reality No Buying Service Wants You to Know: Dealers are intimately involved in every Internet and buying service transaction

The Web site and buying-club hype about "independence" from dealership influence is a myth. Why? Direct vehicle sales between the automobile manufacturers and Web-based "buying services" or brokers of any kind do not exist. All buying services and brokers must buy their vehicles directly from dealers. And because the dealers control the flow of vehicles, they in many ways control the buying services and brokers.

The Dealer's Stranglehold on Vehicle Internet Sales and Pricing

Thank your state legislatures for allowing dealerships to prevent meaningful competition on the Internet. State automobile franchising laws, heavily lobbied for by the dealers, have always required that brokers must buy their vehicles from dealerships, not from the manufacturers directly. Those laws are being beefed up as you read this to make sure dealerships now also control every aspect of the manufacturer's relationship with you on the Internet.

In addition to preventing manufacturers from providing direct financing to consumers, many laws may also prevent the manufacturers from posting the average sales price of each model. This information can give consumers a realistic guideline when negotiating to buy.

Finally, the laws may require that manufacturers not withhold leads from a dealer generated in the dealer's marketplace. What's the practical impact on you? If you click on a manufacturer's site, the manufacturer now can be required to send your information to a local dealer. So much for your privacy there.

Would-be independent brokers have failed to change these practices. Although independent auto brokers have tried to attack these laws, they have failed to get them changed. Nor have the manufacturers—who would dearly love to sell to you directly, to open stand-alone service departments, and generally to buy back all their dealerships—given up on this fight.

The impact on you? When you buy or lease a car online or through a buying service, that car is coming directly through the dealership's own Web site, coming from a "broker" who buys it from a dealership and sells it to you, or coming from a "direct" Web service that owns its own dealerships. Any way you drive it, a dealership and its particular slippery, misleading profit gimmicks will be involved in the transaction.

Many dealers see nothing wrong with a misleading gimmick or two, either. Consider Mark Phillips, manager at a Ford dealership in Arizona, who matter-of-factly shared this story a while back with *Automotive News*. After receiving a price quote from the dealership on a Mercury Cougar, his customer decided to check that price with Ford's "e-price" on the Web. "The e-price was $400 less than what we had originally submitted to them," Phillips was quoted as saying, "so we *dropped the cash on their trade by about $400.*"[9] (emphasis added) The net result of that drop? By "lowballing" the customer's trade-in, allowing the customer $400 less than it was really worth, the dealership completely canceled the $400 savings for the customer. And thank you, ma'am or sir, for shopping on the Internet!

So it's worse if you're trading in your old car. Even at a "direct" site that sends someone to your house and hands you a check for your old car, you are dealing with the same used-car wholesale dynamics and used-car "road hogs" who have made the wholesale used-car business a bit slimy to the touch for years.

"Well, hasn't the involvement of big business and high-tech companies made the auto business a safer place for the consumer?" It's done the opposite in my opinion. The job of big business is to boost its stock price, not hold your hand. Big conglomerates don't invest in the auto business as a public service. They've taken to it because they smell money. Don't you think most big business hotshots reading the tale of Ford manager Mark Phillips and his $400 "lowballing" of a customer will chuckle at the deceptive ploy rather than cringe?

And the high-tech involvement? The cutthroat, crash-and-burn, light-speed nature of Web-based entrepreneurship makes

Killer's worst action seem positively saintly. People and companies that deal in gigabytes of information in a nanosecond, that reach millions of "acquired targets" and "delineated affinity pods" in a thirty-word e-mail directive sent simultaneously to thirty thousand employees, that deal in billions of dollars in potential profits at the touch of a SEND button aren't generally too concerned about you as an individual. Think about the last time you dueled on the phone with a computer; think about the mindless, smug, invulnerability of that recorded voice. The mentality that believes you deserve that now rules the auto business.

To make a bleak sky a bit darker, many of the latest owners and partners in the Brave New Automotive World have absolutely no street-level experience in the auto industry. So what do these newcomers do? They hire the most successful street people in the auto industry. Who are the most successful people? Generally speaking, those who do the worst things to your pocketbook. What do the new rulers of the auto business want from these executives? To duplicate the most profitable tactics the executive used against the customers at one dealership so that they can be used at hundreds of dealerships to grab thousands of dollars from vulnerable consumers. As you read this, some of the worst (for the consumer) car sales personnel in the world are speaking live to legions of new, young, enthusiastic auto employees on Web sites and buying clubs and large automobile dealership chains around the world. None of those sales personnel are speaking about ways to help you fill your piggy bank, only theirs.

Those are the people who send you those nice e-mails and make you feel so comfortable when you're shopping for a car on the Internet.

"If it's really that bad, won't the media tell me about this nationally? And won't my local newspaper and television consumer reporters cover local abuse?" In the past, most of the serious fraud and abuse in the car business, even though it might involve the manufacturer or some other national company, happened at the local dealer level. And the fraud was widespread. Check with your State Attorney General's Office or Consumer Affairs Department if you have any doubt.

Auto sales and services complaints have ranked near the top of the top ten for years. And all the time dealers have been crowing about their newfound professionalism and concern for the customer.

But how many times have you seen your favorite television station's consumer reporter cover shenanigans at local new-car dealerships? How many articles on dealerships ripping off local consumers have you seen in your local paper?

In the past you haven't seen much of that coverage, if any, because local auto dealers have always been the local media's biggest source of advertising revenue. Just look at your paper or count local dealer commercials on television. Dealers running full-color, full-page ads and snappy television commercials aren't exactly shy in their response when the local media does go after their bad tactics. In fact, dealers are vicious, relentlessly demanding, and fast in their wolf-pack response to even the smallest criticism by the local media.

"Pull our advertising!" is their first knee-jerk response. In Washington, D.C., a local network affiliate lost $250,000 in dealer advertising in a week when it ran a hard-hitting exposé on tactics at one dealership chain.[10] Around the country, dealers continually pull their local advertising at even the hint of a negative story.

"Fire the reporter!" is the dealers' second knee-jerk response. Can that really happen? Are dealers that vindictive and powerful? Ask Silvia Gambardella, former consumer reporter at WCCO Television in Minneapolis, Minnesota. Silvia was fired twice for her continuing consumer reports on local auto dealers, after the dealers pulled over $1 million in advertising from the station.[11]

"Shoot the messenger!" is the dealers' third knee-jerk response. In the middle of a live "How to Buy a Car" radio interview in Louisiana, I was physically pulled out of the studio by the station's very nervous general manager and pushed out the station door. For twenty-four hours the station ran on-air "apologies" to local dealers, each apology saying how wonderful the local dealers were, and each apology attacking me personally.

Why on earth would a station do such a thing? The local dealers ordered them to. Can the station get away with that? Usually, but not this time. With the help of the Media Access Project in

Washington, D.C., we went after the station's license and eventually forced the station to run on-air apologies to me and pay damages to a Louisiana consumer group. Can dealers get away with their actions? Of course. The dealers weren't sanctioned in this case, the media was. The day after the settlement, it was business as usual at the dealerships and radio station. And you can bet inviting me for a return how-to-buy-a-car seminar won't be part of "business as usual."

If you don't think this stifling dealer attitude prevails in your market, talk to your local consumer reporters. All of them will know a dealership war story to pass along informally. And most of them will tell you there's just no margin in bucking the system. The best investigative reporters have to make two decisions when they consider a story: (1) Can I get it on the air? and (2) Will the grief the story brings me be worth the effort? When it comes to covering local dealer problems, the answers are usually, no, you can't get it on the air, and, no, it isn't worth the grief.

And even if you cover the story at the network level, the dealers will make sure that story never runs again. A few years ago I was the expert on a one-hour *Dateline NBC* special on the car-buying process. The special "swept" the ratings, won an Emmy, and caused quite a commotion around the country. *Dateline* normally repeats shows like that. "But not this one," a network executive told me, "It won't run again. The network affiliates saw to that." The network affiliates, of course, live and die on dealership advertising.

In the national and local media, censorship and self-censorship ("I just won't suggest that story") permeate any thought of covering negative auto issues. As one of my favorite sayings goes, it's always darkest before it gets even worse. In the past, reporters or shows like *20/20* only needed to worry about offending their advertisers. Today, they have to worry about offending their parent company, which now probably owns a very lucrative piece of the auto business itself or has a very lucrative "affinity relationship" with the auto business. Some time ago, CBS, for example, announced a "relationship" with AOL that would feature CBS News online. Did that relationship bring with it any form of censorship? The day the CBS/AOL affiliation was announced, a leading and powerful CBS reporter called me and said, "Well, I guess I won't be suggesting that AOL story tomorrow morning."

Media giant Cox Enterprises owns newspapers, major television stations, radio stations, and twenty interactive media companies. They provide cable television and Internet service to millions of people. For years, Cox has owned the highly profitable Manheim Auto Auctions for used cars, a business primarily directed at automobile dealers. Now their auto businesses include AutoTrader.com, a selling site for used vehicles. (And the media giant through its subsidiaries is in the finance, warranty, and insurance business—sometimes murky places in the automobile world.) Do you think any Cox reporters or on-air talents would further their careers if they suggested a story on the potential conflicts of interest Cox might face because of its automotive business ventures?

And these are just two examples. If you think the coverage of auto abuse was rare in the old days, just watch what isn't happening now. We are in the Brave New Automotive World of infotainment news, not serious investigative automotive reporting.

"Okay, my dependable consumer group will protect me from harm." There are hundreds of magnificent groups with thousands of committed consumer staff members who will do all they can to help you make the right decisions in the auto transaction. And many of these groups will do all they can to alert you to major abuse and help you seek redress if that abuse happens anyway.

But the consumer movement—from the Consumer Federation of America to the Center for Auto Safety, from the Media Access Protect to many of the attorneys general offices around the country, and to Ralph Nader himself—doesn't have the time or resources to adequately keep up with the terrifyingly rapid and complex Internet-related abuses happening in the auto business.

"There probably hasn't been a time in which consumers face more risk in a financial transaction," says J. C. Pierce, director of the Consumer Task Force for Automotive Issue's Web evaluation project. "It's like a parakeet trying to survive in a hurricane."

"So, are you really saying that most of these people are crooks?" No I'm not, as we'll see. But the nearly blind faith some consumers put in the accuracy of Web-based shopping has already cost tens of thousands of consumers untold thousands of dollars. Do you, for instance, think all those online services that list the invoice "cost" on a new vehicle provide you the accurate cost? If you believe that, and relied on that "cost" figure to make an offer on a vehicle, you may have thrown away a pile of money. Simply appearing on a Web page does not necessarily make information accurate.

The Brave New Automotive World has also created some enormous ethical and legal issues and has probably already wreaked havoc on some of your credit and privacy rights. Some of the worst problems aren't technically illegal, either.

For instance, you make an innocent call to a dealership one spring day simply to sign your kid up for the softball team the dealership is sponsoring. Do you really like the idea that your call can automatically generate a file on you—can "nail" you? Would it bother you to know that the guy who cuts your grass but also works weekends at the parts counter at a local dealership can read through your credit report and loan application for fun during his lunch break at the dealership? Both things are happening right now. If a dealership has ever pulled a credit report on you, the parts man or anyone at that company can legally peruse your credit file. Credit reports are pulled for companies, not for individuals such as the finance manager, and loan applications are part of credit files.

In the past, this possibility hasn't been a serious problem except at the most unethical dealerships. Though your credit file may technically have been open to any employee, the finance manager's office had the only real access to it. But at most dealerships now, particularly at the big dealership chains, your credit file is readily available to anyone from any dealership computer. And many dealerships have installed freestanding computers throughout the dealerships to make customer "intelligence" more readily available to all employees, including parts department employees.

All the "customer relations management" programs I mentioned earlier, for instance, allow employees to pull up with a few clicks customer information including pictures, contact history, buying history, and credit history. With caller ID, just a phone call from you can open your file on the dealership's computer. Programs automatically send out e-mails, prompt call-backs to you, and log each of your phone calls or Internet visits and the times of the same. The programs even schedule all those nice, "personal" follow-up letters.

Probably illegal but not tested in the courts yet is another troubling reality in the Brave New Automotive World. For example, credit reports aren't supposed to be shared between companies, even if the companies are owned by the same parent company or same person. A Ford dealership generally can't legally share your credit report with a Chevrolet dealership down the road. But what if the Ford and Chevrolet dealership are under the same roof? What if they share the same finance manager? What if a company that owns three hundred car dealerships with three hundred separate finance departments incorporates those three hundred separate finance departments into one corporation? Can three hundred dealerships now share your credit report?

For instance, companies certainly can't sell your credit report. But can a megachain of automobile dealerships sell a list of their "highly preferred customers"—those with perfect credit scores and credit histories—to others? Conversely, can that same chain sell or share its list of persons who were declined credit to subprime lenders or to their own subprime used-car operations?

And just what is happening with all that "intelligence" those Internet sites are collecting on you? Who decides what is confidential and ethical? Who decides if you have "customer value," and does that rating by itself constitute a credit rating subject to fair credit reporting guidelines? Because these issues continually develop with the speed and ethical blindness of the Web, the privacy, legal, and ethical problems in the auto world will continue to grow for a long, long time and should concern you. Some of these questions are beginning to be tested in court, but any clear outcomes legally can and will take years.

With some exceptions, most of the persons and companies running the Brave New Automotive World are like most of us, ethically and workwise. If we were working on their side, we'd probably do many of the same things. Do you own any stock in Microsoft or Yahoo! or some other high-tech company? Do you root for that stock to keep climbing? Except for your own car transaction, if you owned stock in an automotive business, wouldn't it be best for you if that business hires the toughest salespeople and fights for every penny of profit they can find?

Honestly, if you were a local reporter, would you cover a car story in your hometown if you knew it might cost you your job? Would you cover a story like that every week?

If you were a car salesperson, would you automatically cut the price of every car to the absolutely lowest amount your dealership would take, or would you try to make a little money? If a customer offered you a $2,000 profit, but you knew you were authorized to take as little as a $200 profit, what would you do? Your commission on that $2,000 would be at least $500. Your commission on that $200 profit would be $50. What would you do?

The Worst New Development: BMA Clauses Everywhere. The Brave New Automotive World is terrifying even when you're dealing with the "good" guys, and now even they have reason to turn into bad guys. Until recently, if you had a serious problem with a dealership or with a vehicle (like buying a lemon), you could always turn to the court system to help you. You don't have that option anymore at most dealerships. Since the last edition of this book, the vast, vast majority of dealerships in America have inserted "binding mandatory arbitration" clauses into all of their paperwork. BMA clauses, as they are called, forever take away your right to use the American court system if you have a dispute with a dealership or manufacturer. Find out a dealership literally stole money from you? Forget going to court. Find out a dealership employee stole your credit card numbers and ran up thousands in bills? Forget going after the dealership!

Binding mandatory arbitration clauses have taken away your one stick in the battle to keep dealerships fair and honest. You need to know more about this issue, incidentally, since these clauses are in virtually every agreement you have right now— from credit card statements to your telephone bill. When you take a break here, head to www.stopbma.com and see what hundreds of consumer groups say about this truly terrifying development.

Is There Any *Good News* Out There?

If you're big on the concept of yin and yang, you know what's coming now: For all the negative realities we've been talking about, the Brave New Automotive World offers an equal amount of positive realities for the adventuresome and wise. For all the real and potential abuse the Internet has brought to the auto industry, it has also certainly brought the cure for that abuse, and much more. No one in their right mind has to pay much profit on a vehicle anymore, thanks to the astonishing competitiveness that the Web has opened up in comparison shopping. A very careful person can actually shop finance rates online and find the best rate if they know how. For the first time, it's potentially easy to find the exact used car you want without leaving your home. Finally, you can really research vehicle safety and reliability issues thoroughly without spending weeks of your time. At home, in your own sweet time, you can be the master of it all, fight your way through the quagmire of misinformation, gather the right information to help you make wise and seasoned decisions, and save yourself thousands and thousands of dollars in the process. You just need patience and ammunition for that fight.

You provide the patience, and this book will provide the ammunition. That ammunition includes the Don't Get Taken Every Time Web site, www.dontgettakeneverytime.com. The site works with this book and provides updated news about online automotive information plus breaking auto news that might affect your safety or your wallet.

The Don't Get Taken Every Time site is a "cookie-free" site, too. It won't track your every click or share your vital statistics with anyone. (Our site host does use a "session cookie" that is erased when you log out. It doesn't identify you or your computer but helps provide overall figures about site use that we can use to improve the site.)

Want to Stop Other Sites from Tracking You While You Explore the Brave New Automotive World (or Anything Else) Online?

You can control some of the invasions of your privacy online. Read the sidebar "Should You Disable Your 'Cookies'? And Other Tips for Safe Surfing" below, before you begin to use the Web. Then go ahead.

Killer is waiting for you, as we take a look at the people you're going to be meeting—whether in person or behind the scenes—as the battle for your personal pocketbook begins.

Should You Disable Your "Cookies"? And Other Tips for Safe Surfing

"Cookies," in basic lay language, are files installed on your hard drive by other computers somewhere out there on the Internet in order for these other computers, wherever they are and whoever may be running them, upright person or not, to get a handle on you and your life. In addition, lots of companies may be using spyware (they call it adware) or keystroke loggers to track where you go on the Web, what you see, and how long you stay. The keystroke loggers can even pick up data you enter (including personal financial information).

In the opinion of companies or just about anybody who benefits financially from cookies or spyware, you are a lucky person indeed to have these voracious, relentlessly incessant, and nonblushing little creatures set up house in your private space.

A cookie's humble purpose in life, says one chirpy article, is to tell the server [the stranger's computer] that you have returned to that Web page. This soothing, made-for-a-child explanation is roughly equivalent in its disclosure to a cat burglar saying, "What I do, really, is to just go into places."

I much prefer explanations from people who aren't making money on me when it comes to the significance and potential danger of cookies—folks like those at www.junkbusters.com, one of my favorite sites. JunkBusters gives you the real McCoy on computer privacy, and I heartily recommend that you visit that site before checking anything else out. I also recommend that you check out another great organization, the Privacy Rights Clearinghouse and their Web site, www.privacyrights.org. They have good information on cookies, spyware, and other cyberinvaders.

"Imagine that your television remote control informed stations the second you switched to them," JunkBusters says on their home page. "Imagine that the queries you type are probably being logged and analyzed." Then imagine that the cookies that made most of this possible (called "persistent cookies") remained attached to your identity for years, even if you change computers, perpetually sneaking away with some of your most cherished possessions, including your privacy and your personal interests. Folks, that's really what cat burglars do, metaphorically speaking, in the real world.

"Don't let them use your browser as a tool of surveillance,"[12] says JunkBusters, and, wow, do I agree with that sentiment. If you agree with me, either turn your cookies off entirely ("disable" them) or make them visible. If you see them, you can at least decide which strangers will be tracking and, in all likelihood, selling information about your habits and private interests. (Please note that if you bank online, pay your bills online, or shop online, those organizations will need to set cookies to enable your account and their security functions. Sure is a complex world.)

Cookie Monsters (those folks that send bad versus good cookies to your computer) chuckle at all this concern, of course. "We don't share information," they seem to say collectively, "or at least we don't share it without permission. Or, if we do share it with permission, it's with people we trust like our moms . . . well, maybe like our mother-in-law's new boyfriend . . . er, you know we're not really responsible for what other people do with all those goodies about all those strangers out there. Now while you're here, can I tap your brain? I'm particularly interested in that time three years ago you visited that "sex without love" Web site. . . ."

You have probably already seen the impact of this on your privacy. For instance, have you ever simply dragged your cursor over a Web site without opening it? Maybe you visited a lending site momentarily, found out the site was pushing subprime loans, then left the site without even clicking on it. You don't have to click on a Web site for a cookie to be installed. Days later, you find an unsolicited piece of mail from some other subprime lender in your e-mail box. Welcome to Cookieland with Spyware.

"Without the consumer's thoughtful permission, the process of identifying the virtual user has begun," says Michael Firmin, a computer and investment expert in Great Britain. "The cookies normally remain residents indefinitely, continually updating and notifying their creator of your latest activities."

Don't be a part of that rather chilling process unless you are comfortable with its potential downside, particularly as you begin to use the Web to research your auto interests. The auto industry has a history of running over privacy rights at high speed—and that was even before the advent of high technology and computers. Starting years ago with Ralph Nader (General Motors' private detectives followed him) up through right now with untold numbers of dealerships and dealership chains, the auto industry remains the Godzilla of privacy monsters.

If you worry at all about this, spend a few useful minutes researching your privacy concerns and how to address them without losing the usefulness of the wonderful World

Wide Web and Internet. Remember that the great Wizard of Oz was only a bad guy until he was unmasked by the sweet and innocent Dorothy.

Go to www.privacyrightsnow.com, cofounded by me to give you a quick look at some of the best privacy groups and Web sites. Meanwhile, here are a few places to start:

- Go to www.junkbusters.com/cookies.html and to www.privacyrights.org. As spyware has gained in popularity for surveillance, JunkBusters has not updated its information on cookies as regularly as it once did, but its basic information on how to disable your cookies is good. The Privacy Rights Clearinghouse gives you real-time information on unfolding privacy issues, including cookies and spyware.
- If you use Windows, go to www.microsoft.com/info/cookies.htm. This site, after trying to convince you to leave their sweet babies alone, gives you clear instructions on how to throw cookies out with the bathwater.
- All browser controls have improved. Popular browsers include Internet Explorer (IE), Firefox, Opera, and Safari for Macs. You can change your browser settings to show cookies, block cookies from third-party sites, and allow you to control them. Look under the SECURITY or PRIVACY tabs (sections) in your browser, or look in the HELP function.
- Simply type "disable cookies," "control cookies," or "remove spyware" in your search engine, and you'll find literally thousands of other sites on this issue.

Part **One**

Forearming

So, You're Determined to Skip the Dealership Entirely and Buy or Lease on the Web?

Killer and his pals probably have you thinking that way, right? Well, it can be an expensive way to think.

First, you *can't skip the dealership*. As I discussed in chapter 1, dealerships are directly or indirectly involved with *every Web site:* Dealerships sell every new car sold on the Web. So, don't think you're pulling an end run on the dealers. They've pulled one on you.

Second, for many people, dealerships themselves are definitely the cheapest and best places to buy or lease.

If you have an open mind, we'll give you the information to help you decide what is best for you, dealership or online buying service. But if you've already decided to not even *think* about dealerships and their role in the car-buying process—much less visit a dealership—fine. This book will lead you quickly through online buying and leasing, starting on page 295.

However, if your goals are to save *serious* money, to get the most for your trade-in, to get the best vehicle for you and the best financing for you, then—keep reading. The in-depth education you're going to get with Killer and his friends will give you the power to understand and control every aspect of an online transaction.

What's the smartest stance for you right now concerning any auto transaction? Slow down and read on.

Chapter 2

Inside the Dealership Family

Killer and His Family

"I mean to tell you, I was going to *give* her the car, just for one night on the town, and a good-night kiss . . . or something, you know," Ted said with a shy grin and a shrug. Ted was very new but he already had the reputation as the biggest ladies' man at the dealership. He seemed like a good guy, too. But Killer couldn't force more than a weak smile at the story. The stunning young woman—was she really old enough to drive?—had looked just like Killer's youngest daughter. It didn't escape Killer at the moment, either, that he was old enough to be the father of all but one person sitting around him.

The guys were in their favorite "break room," the cleanup shop located behind the service department. On cold and wet days like this one, everyone seemed to head back there. It was a good place to hide from the boss, J. C. It was also a good place to hide the community bottle. Buzz and Ted were there. Forrest DeLong was there, too.

Even Kip had joined the sipping party this day. He was the dealership's lease renewal manager, a quiet guy who never really seemed to fit in comfortably with the off-color joking and constant stream of four-letter words that constitute many in-house discussions at automobile stores. Kip's reassuring manner was just right for his job.

Ted took the bottle next and sweetened his coffee. He was maybe twenty-two, had moved to town several months earlier, and had just completed the dealership's intense training agenda, which included forty hours of "live" training at BallisticImpact.com, the "closed" Web site visited only by sales personnel at the 250 America's Family Friend dealerships. His first live customer had been the pretty young woman, lured to the dealership by AFF's FirstTimeBuyersClub.com Web site.

Ted wiped his lips with his right thumb and began to talk. Maybe it was the juice. Half-and-half at eleven-thirty would untie any tongue.

"Well, guys, let me tell you something. I am trained and tuned. I'm ready for all those big commissions they've been telling us about! I'm ready for some customers! And I'm *ready to be their friend for life!*" Everybody but Forrest DeLong laughed at that, and no one laughed harder than Killer.

"From what they tell me at the Dead End, Ted, you're also ready to chase every tail that flies by," Killer said. "I hear you're a lot better Girl Scout than Boy Scout."

"Yes, sir, I plead guilty," Ted grinned. "After watching some of the old geezers standing around here all day moaning about us new guys and grousing about all the training, I've got to have some recreation." Ted stopped short, embarrassed. "Killer, I didn't mean you or Kip, you know. You guys may be old, but you don't act it . . . uh, you know what I mean."

Forrest DeLong, who hadn't laughed much at anything this morning, didn't laugh at this, either. "Ted, let's see how long you stay so chipper—just wait till you have to put up with all the crap around here."

"What do you mean?"

"If the flakes don't drive you crazy—God, I hate those damn computer geeks who think they know it all!—if they don't drive you crazy, then it's J. C. or Don. I don't think they know any other words than 'send those e-mails, boys,' or 'get on the damn phone, boys,' or 'let's see some deals, boys.' Why don't they just record all that bull, play it over our earphones during 'computer hours,' and go off and play golf with Davies?"

"Sure," Buzz added, "Davies doesn't even talk to his *girl-friend* anymore, much less his wife or his managers. He's too busy 'consulting' with the corporate big boys. He's not going to get his pinkies dirty around us."

Killer raised his hand. "Now, wait a minute. I don't want to hear any of you damn guys talking about my dealer. I want you to know, he speaks to *me*. Of course, that was before he made $150 million. And he called me Bill. Then he got confused and called me Will." Killer started laughing. "Maybe I'll give him one of my cards the next time we meet. As a matter of fact, I think I'll ask him to *pay* for my cards the next time we meet!"

Killer had hit a nerve. Forrest spoke first, "Hey, Killer, I was going to ask you about that. I don't mind paying for my cards, but, hell, I hear they're lowering our demo allowance again."

Everybody came to Killer for the real scoop on what was happening at the store, and Killer liked that. "Yeah, for some people," he said. "But it's not that simple. He's tying your demo allowance to your Web work—score high there, and it's free. Score low, and your thumb is going to be out hitching." Killer looked at DeLong and shook his head, smiling. "And from your Web scores, I'm betting on your thumbs."

Killer's words lit a short fuse in DeLong. "Like hell he'll fool with my demo! I'll be damned if I'm going to hang around this place and put up with that. Hell, there are a lot of other stores in this town." His outburst brought a laugh. In spite of different names, all but three of the new-car dealerships inside the city limits were owned by America's Family Friend.

Types of salespeople. DeLong's hot head was probably one of the reasons he was a vagabond in the business, spending one or two months at one dealership and then lighting across town or down the road at another. But he wouldn't be missed. There would probably be a hundred DeLongs at this one dealership in the next twenty-four months. The Forrest De-Longs of the world still make up the vast majority of automobile sales personnel, and they may sell and lease lots of cars in aggregate, but they are always low men on the scale of respect.

At the opposite end of the scale was Kip, a retired high-school teacher. Killer called him "Professor." Kip had been at the store for five years and had always worked as the lease renewal manager. He seldom was part of the pack, and rarely took a drink with the guys, either. But at this particular moment, he performed an important function for the meeting of the Half-and-Half Club. Hearing the door open as they were talking, he silenced the group with a "shhh," then stepped quietly around the corner. He returned double-speed. "It's J. C.!" he whispered. Everyone quickly lit up cigarettes, hoping perhaps the smoke would cover up the smell of Jim Beam.

J. C. sauntered around the corner and ambled toward them, as if he were simply taking a Sunday stroll. No one spoke as they stood there, waiting for the explosion. J. C. just looked at them, his lips parting enough to make a smacking sound—like some wild animal's anticipation of the bite to come. "Well, boys," J. C. looked from man to man, no expression betraying his thoughts. He looked at Killer last. "I sure could use some of that half-and-half—my coffee's cold."

It was an unexpected comment. But that's why most of the guys liked J. C. He was a real bastard at times, but just as the guys were ready to write him off, he would say or do something like that. No one could really figure J. C. out. No one cared at the moment, though. They all sat on the floor, their feet pulled up, bodies in a semicircle.

Buzz broke the ice. "Well, J. C., if you'd send someone for marshmallows, we could have a campfire."

"Hell, yes," J. C. said. "Tell you what, we could get a van and go to my cabin, take the computers, and sell as many cars there as here today." J. C.'s statement didn't really seem like a cut—it sounded more like the truth. Business had been lousy, real lousy for the last two weeks, even on the Web, and no one had gotten more heat than J. C. "Boys, I'll tell you what. I think all the ups have just packed up and left town, or blown up their laptops. I talked with some of the other stores a while ago, and none of them are doing any business."

The nature of the business. It's the damnedest thing about the car business. Even with the colossal changes the Internet has brought to the business, even with Web surfers hitting auto sites twenty-four hours a day, customers either buy in droves, filings to the magnet, or they don't buy at all. After a few years, people in the business accept that fact. Or, at least, the employees do. But dealers like Gary Oliver Davies had never accepted it, and God knows the megachains like America's Family Friend don't accept it.

The coffee thermos was sitting on empty and the Jim Beam down to a third when the new kid, Ted, asked, "J. C., I know this sounds dumb, but everything really is changing in this business, isn't it? I mean, that's not just a line they gave us in training?"

J. C.'s eyes widened, "Son, let me tell you, the *air you breathe* is even changing in this business. You're going to have some *real fun* here, if you stay out of trouble."

Ted continued. "On the Ballistic Web site, when I was training? All those hotshots say we new guys can be making fifty a year, if we follow the program. Is that bull?"

J. C. grinned and reached over and gently patted Ted's shoulder. "Son, be patient. How many customers have you closed? One? Why, you're sitting in the room with one of the guys right now who makes more money than *I* do at this damn store!" J. C., of course, didn't mention the million-dollar bonus he'd received last year. He was just talking about pure salary. "Killer!" he continued, "tell this boy what you made last year."

Killer blushed just enough to look modest and shrugged, "Hell, J. C., I've had better years than the last one. But I made $270,000, which isn't bad, I guess." You can bet on that. Killer was in the top 100 salespeople in the country—out of 300,000 people. He continued, "And, hell, it took me fifteen years and a lot of work to get to that. And I spend nearly $25,000 a year on things for my regular customers, too. Plus, I really *do* work, you know." He smiled and started to speak again before any of the guys could stop him. "And, yes, I do sell *lots* of cars at the Dead End. I'm thinking of setting up an iMac there."

Smart move. Killer's visits to the favorite automobile watering hole were one of the worst-kept secrets in the business. But Killer really didn't want the conversation changed to that subject. He had just started a tale about how the business *really* used to be when Don Burns, one of the new-car managers, came hustling around the corner.

Don showed no surprise but started talking quickly. "Excuse me, fellows, but there are some ups on the lot. And J. C., Davies is calling from his plane. He tried to beep you. I told him you were in the Web room in a meeting." It was a good breaking point in the camp meeting, and the group stood up and, almost in unison, reached in their pockets for the nice little bottles of Binaca mouth freshener. J. C. started laughing as he pushed down the little nozzle and turned toward the door. "Well, boys, if you'll excuse me, I've got to call my broker. It looks like Binaca stock is going up again."

It had been a nice morning, and the guys headed back to the showroom single-file. "Hey, Buzz." Don Burns walked up behind him, pulling him back a little as the others went on. "Buzz, I hate to tell you this, but there's another process server in the showroom. I told the man you were out, but he says he's going to wait for you. Since J. C.'s in a good mood, do you want me to ask him to talk to the man? If he can't put him off, maybe J. C.'ll pay him."

Buzz looked just a tad upset—nothing really monumental in a process server, he thought. Car people were pretty used to people like that. As a group, even the new breed of car sales personnel aren't exactly known for their good credit ratings. "No, but thanks," he said. "Hell, I might just as well add this to the pile. Thank God J. C. doesn't care, though. At least it's in the family."

Buzz was right, too. It's one very, very big family now.

Who's Who Inside the Dealerships

Baitfish. The feeding chain in the Brave New Automotive World leads to some very big fish, but it starts with the baitfish, the new floor salespeople at your friendly neighborhood dealership. The baitfish who waits on you could be a young college dropout, a successful salesperson from another field, or a young ex-con. One of the nicest things about the auto business is its ability to forgive the past. If you want to be a salesperson in the twenty-first century, and if you're clean-cut, filled with enthusiasm, and sincere-looking, your past won't matter. As a matter of fact, if you drink too much, or are hiding from the police, or have a couple of wives or husbands, that's okay, too. All that matters is how efficiently you can sell cars!

But be warned that baitfish have a very high mortality rate. They are constantly gobbled up by stronger salespeople or quickly disillusioned by the stark realities of the car business: long hours, little money, lots of deception (on both the salesperson's part and the customer's part), and unrelenting pressure to sell again *right now*. Nevertheless, even baitfish have been rigidly trained in the "new" automotive etiquette of selling service before the sale, and most have been trained in how to turn your Internet research against you, if you've used it carelessly as your research tool.

Floor whores a.k.a. lot lizards. Just above the baitfish are the "floor whores," salespeople who have survived by learning to pounce on the first person who walks in cold, without making an appointment. The floor whores aren't liked by any sales personnel—they don't work for their ups. But they are tolerated by any dealership because, even today, the vast majority of people who buy cars buy them from local dealerships without making appointments. So, the floor whores serve an important role in the food chain.

Geek masters. Smart dealerships aren't simply using their regular sales force to close sales started on the Internet. They've learned that Web shoppers are often a different breed: interested in copies of invoices without an argument, not at all interested in being bounced around once they've arrived at the dealership, and more trusting of a shy bookworm than a stereotypical salesperson. That's why sales forces are sprouting computer-friendly types carefully trained to look like order takers rather than salespersons. Are they easier to deal with? Definitely. Will you get a better deal from one? Seldom, if ever. The Geek masters practice sleight-of-hand better than the old guys, making their profits on silent add-ons and misdirection.

Specialists. "Specialty" sales personnel are even more important. Do you speak fluent Korean in a city with a large Korean population? Sign for the hearing impaired? Don't mind dealing with persons with physical handicaps? Don't mind catering to the gay community? Like to hang with military personnel? Specialty sales personnel, even rookies, have an easier time in the auto business because their particular skills aren't easy to duplicate or replace.

The old masters. Way above these previous types in the food chain are the old-timers like Killer. The old-timers have dealt with every type of customer: the easy ones, the suspicious ones, and the crooked ones. They are professionals in the sense that years of selling have provided them a steady flow of repeat customers who have always dealt with them and always will. "You know," an elegant and seasoned old salesman told me in San Francisco, "some people *enjoy* paying more." These successful old guys have taken to the Web with a vengeance, too.

Salespeople don't get much respect. Except for the likes of Killer, the "house" (the dealers) do their best to keep sales types from knowing about goodies like factory incentives, which generally make the bosses more money but not the sales force, or shower the bosses with fancy trips. Dealers don't tell salespeople about "write downs," used cars that have been lowered in value because of their condition or time on the lot. For years the dealers didn't even tell their sales forces about "holdbacks," extra profit built into each car invoice designed to look like extra cost. Now, everybody knows about holdbacks.

Despite all the hoopla about the new-car age, and despite all the lip service given the word "professionalism" in the car sales arena, dealers still think most salespeople are cheap to replace. Although they may very occasionally smile at them or visit a sales meeting, most dealers hold the men and women who make them their fortunes in disdainful contempt.

What do salespeople earn? It may be hard to believe, but no matter what type of salesperson waits on you, that person probably isn't getting rich selling you or anyone else a vehicle. Most dealerships pay their lower-level sales personnel 15–30 percent of the "front end gross," the actual profit on the sale or the lease of the vehicle itself. The percentage goes up as the gross profit on the vehicle goes up.

Or, rather, they pay 15–30 percent of the profit above the "pack." What's that? Let's say the actual cost to the dealer of your average Expenso Gargantula is $16,500. But when the dealership's title clerk prepares a computerized stock card on that car, the invoice price is coded as $17,000. This $500 "pack" added to "invoice price" is supposed to help the dealer pay his overhead. In reality, it's just another way to keep from paying the salesperson his or her due.

Many dealerships used to encourage their salespeople to show this pack figure to recalcitrant customers. "Here, Mr. Jones, that's the actual cost of the car. If you will pay me a $400 profit over that figure, the car is yours." Presto, the house has just made $900 rather than $400. Now that most dealerships claim they are putting actual invoice costs on their Web sites, "packs" are even harder to see, often because they are masked in other charges.

Virtually all dealerships also pay their sales personnel a percentage of the profits from the sale of financing and life and accident/health insurance. Most pay a flat fee for warranty sales, and virtually all pay "spiffs" (walking-around money—cash bonuses) during special promotions and sales. But even with all the spiffs and percentages and flat fees, the average salesperson at dealerships doesn't make much money. You won't find many run-of-the-mill car salespeople making more than $30,000 a year for a seventy-hour week. But who said life is fair?

Managers. Above the sales personnel are the sales managers, supervisors who crack the emotional whip to keep the sellers working. These days, floor managers truly "manage" every deal. They're like the cameras in casinos, monitoring everything you do and say. Almost all floor managers are former salespeople who draw good salaries and hefty percentage overrides from their sales forces. Many of these folks are in the midst of traumatic changes in their responsibilities because of what new technology and the Internet have brought to the closing booth. Many old-time managers are being pushed aside by hotshot salespeople who thrive on new technology.

Web "managers." Dealership Web managers generally don't require much auto experience and generally don't manage sales personnel. They manage you—the potential customer. Web managers know that you feel much, much more comfortable and in control communicating with a dealership via e-mail rather than talking to a salesperson on the phone or in person. And they know you feel some measure of anonymity and privacy on the Web.

The Web manager's job is to keep those comforting thoughts flowing as he or she begins to work you: Send an e-mail to a smart dealership Web site and almost before your e-mail is opened the dealership computer has searched its files to see if your name's already there. If not, a file is opened. Want to e-mail questions back and forth for a few days? The Web manager has hundreds of canned responses to choose from, all designed to lead you to the one momentous milestone on which the Web manager's job depends: the tie-down—getting a deposit from you online. Even a hundred dollars. Even if it has to be "refundable." If the Web manager has tied you down, you are now an acquirable target worth everybody's attention. That's why the best Web managers are as valuable and talented as Killer in their own ways.

The semi-big cheese—the general manager. Above the baitfish and lot lizards and managers are the general managers like J. C. who feed and tend to the crops of money that flow quickly in and out of the parts departments, the body shops, the finance and insurance offices, the new and used sales and lease departments, and the wholesale car and truck departments.

Though Gary Oliver Davies wouldn't admit it, his best talent is hiring the likes of J. C. Hollins. J. C. is a fairly unusual type to be in the car business, especially as a general manager. He is college educated, from a family of professionals, and much more sophisticated in his personal tastes than most managers. He is also a good man, the type of person who thinks nothing of lending his men money, even a guy he's just fired. J. C. is comfortable with people on the "outside," people not in the car fraternity, mixing well with just about anyone. He belongs to Rotary, coaches his youngest son's Little League team, and goes to church, too.

But in the car business, J. C. is known for one talent: he is a troubleshooter. That's why Davies hired him away from another dealership some years ago, in the midst of a long sales downswing. J. C. was used to people like Davies calling him in the slow times. He'd also heard the same sob story over and over again: a small dealer who grew rich, started to play, and forgot to tend his store. Hell, J. C. had known the problems before he'd asked the questions, but he had asked them anyway.

"Well, Gary, you say there's water on your used-car lot. Just how much?"

"Hell, I don't know—I just know that we can't wholesale a damn one of our cars." Davies had approximately $500,000 worth of used cars at his store—the actual dollar amount his people had appraised the cars for when they took them as trade-ins. If those cars valued at $500,000 can be wholesaled for only $460,000, he's got $40,000 in water. Water is an obsession with dealers—it's lost money just as surely as if someone took the same amount of money from their pockets. The problem develops when appraisers put more than wholesale value on a trade, or when someone's hand is in the till.

"Well, what about your R.O.s?" Repair orders, usually written in the service department or body shop. "If you're losing a lot of money in the body shop, have you checked the R.O.s?"

"No," Davies said. That was before the time of truly computerized R.O.'s, and Davies didn't have the time to have someone sift through old repair orders. "No one would be stealing in the body shop, anyway. The manager back there is an old friend of mine."

J. C. would want to know more about that later, but right then he wanted to know a little bit more about the used-car operation. "Gary, I know you say you've got water, but are your people wholesaling cars, anyway? Are they even breaking out of any of them?"

"Hell, no! Every used car we wholesale is at a loss. I think we sold three cars last month at what we had in them. The rest were all losses."

The phone conversation had lasted no more than twenty minutes, but J. C. smelled at least two rats. He was also very interested in the dealership's deposit procedure when new cars were sold. "Tell me, what type of receipts do you give your customers after the business office is closed?" Davies wasn't sure but believed that the night manager simply wrote them out a receipt.

"Gary, there's just one thing more. How did you hire your present general manager, did you know him or what?"

"Listen, the guy is not a crook. He just doesn't seem to know what's going on around here," Davies retorted.

Following the money. J. C. thanked the man for the call, and added, "Oh, Gary, I want to tell you one thing. I don't think your general manager is the only one who doesn't know what's going on. And if you hire me, you can be damn well sure I'm going to fire whoever needs firing—including your buddy in the body shop. Now, do you want to do business on that basis?"

His last comments are probably the reason that J. C. and Davies are business associates, not friends. Davies really didn't have a choice in that conversation, however, for the waters at his store covered more than the used-car lot. Mr. Davies had made two classic mistakes as he climbed quickly up the dealer's ladder—he had hired friends and at the same time stepped away from the daily operations of his business.

When J. C. took over the Davies store, it took him less than a week to find three sets of sticky fingers. His first morning there, he'd invited the used-car manager out for a cup of coffee. The guy was too nervous in the beginning, and J. C. had seen the nervousness increase considerably when he casually mentioned, "It's funny, I noticed that you wholesale a lot of cars to the same people regularly. I sure would like to meet those people." The guy set his cup down with a shaky hand.

J. C. just smiled at him. "And I also noticed that you sell a lot of trades to some of the salesmen every now and then. I didn't know Mr. Davies allowed any curbing here." "Curbing" refers to the practice of salesmen buying nice trade-ins from their own stores and then selling them privately. It's a nice way to make a few bucks.

Sticky fingers at the dealership

The guy just sat there, his hand over the coffee cup and eyes anyplace but on J. C., who continued: "You know, I once had a guy working for me that you might be interested in. This

SOB. would have a nice used car come on the lot, maybe a car that was worth $6,000. Nine times out of ten it would be a real pretty car, too, one that makes a nice resale piece. But, no, this guy would call up some wholesaler—as a matter of fact, he would usually call up the *same* wholesaler—and he'd sell it to the man for $6,000. But damn, this was a funny thing—he would always tell the man to give him a check for $5,500 and the rest in cash. I never could figure out where that $500 went, either."

J. C. paused just long enough for the words to press down on the guy a little more. "And, do you know what else he'd do? I guess he did this just because he was generous or something— well, that same wholesaler would come by the used-car lot with some sled worth $1,500. The hog would want to sell it to us for about a thousand, too, but my friend would pay him $1,900 for it. Hell, we'd be stuck with the tub *and* $400 in water. Well, any- way, one day I talked to the wholesaler myself, and do you know what? The bastard said *he* only got $1,700 of that money—he'd given the rest to my friend."

J. C. didn't say anything after finishing that little story. Instead, he just sat there drinking his coffee. In a couple of minutes, the man sitting across from him simply said, "Well, what do you want me to do now? I've already spent the money." He had, too. All $325,000.

The body shop skim was just as easy to find. When a body shop foreman needs parts to repair a car, he simply fills out a parts ticket and sends that ticket over to the parts department. Each part is "charged out" to the ticket. The part is also listed on the repair order attached to the windshield of whatever car is being repaired. In theory, the parts listed on the R.O. should al- ways be on a parts ticket also.

But Mr. Davies' old friend, the body shop foreman, had a much better idea: he would contract to do private repair work at his house, check the parts out from the dealer- ship, list them on a legitimate repair order in the shop, and then have free parts for his home repair work. J. C. caught that quickly, just by comparing the new parts on a few repaired cars with the parts listed on the car's R.O. He readily found a car with an old windshield that should have had a new one.

Cash flow rules the dealership.

Another nice way some folks try to make money on the sly is simply to tear up repair orders. J. C. had that problem at another store he'd managed. It was a real sweet operation. The service cashier would wait for some customer to pay cash for repair work, then put the cash in her pocket rather than in the register and quickly destroy the repair order.

All of these little tricks are not too hard to catch in a tight store operation. But that had been the problem with Mr. Davies' store—nothing had been tight. J. C. was one of the best specialists in the business because he never trusted a soul and always watched the little things.

"I'll tell you what," he was fond of saying, "if you watch the pennies, the dollars will take care of themselves."

A good general manager or sales manager at a car store needs years of on-the-job training simply to understand what is happening at his store. And J. C. Hollins is a good example of a good general sales manager. He understands that a store is like a giant sieve: Regardless of how much is poured into it, there are literally hundreds of little places where profits can be drained away. There's the salesman who promises a set of floor mats to close a deal and neglects to tell his manager. That's $70 off the top. Or the lot boy neglects to check the coolant in a nice trade-in, and a $4,000 piece of merchandise quickly needs a $1,500 engine overhaul. These all add up.

And then there's the cash-flow problem. Even in the most profitable dealerships, cash flow is a daily challenge and headache. Like the Wade deal. The Wades paid $17,300 for a hardtop that cost the dealership $16,000, a modest profit. But the Wades had a one-year-old trade-in that was worth $9,000 in real cash. After subtracting that $9,000 from the dealership's selling price of $17,300, the dealership received a check from the Wades for $8,300. The dealership then had to pay off the "floor plan" on the new car, $16,000.

On paper, the store made a $1,300 profit, sure. But in cash-flow terms, they had to pay out the difference between $8,300 and the $16,000 owed on the car's floor plan. Until the Wades' trade-in is sold, the dealership will have a net cash *loss* of $7,700. There's an old axiom in the car business that selling lots of cars with trade-ins can break a dealership.

And, finally, there's the personnel problem. After the experience of supervising a staff of car salespeople, most sales managers and general managers can relate really well to the den mother of a Cub Scout pack or, more appropriately, to the house mother at the Lotsa Whoopee Frat House down the road from Worldly Wise University. This Animal House attitude partially accounts for the rambunctious nature of salesmen as a group. J. C., for instance, has received more than one call from the local gendarmes to bail out a salesman. He's always firing guys for not selling or for "skating," stealing another salesman's customer.

J. C. doesn't resent all these problems, either, because they are a given in his job. A general manager in most stores doesn't have the luxury of stepping back from his business as his boss does. He is on the firing line each day, taking flack from his dealer, the customers, the guys in the service and parts departments, and the new- and used-car sales folks. He's dealing with the factory, trying to resist their rep's weekly cajoling to buy a few more of this or that slow-moving car, to order more tilt steering wheels, and to shape up things like the restrooms and the general condition of the used cars.

He's worried about the "floor planners," the people who come by without notice to be sure each new car's "mortgage" is paid on the day the car is sold. Automobile lending institutions, who loan dealers money to floor-plan their stock, don't like dealers who sell their collateral (the cars) but neglect to pay off their loans.

Each moment of his waking day, the general manager is also watching the Perk Board. Dealers don't want success every month or quarter. They demand success—selling—every hour. J. C. knows this and doesn't begin to feel upbeat until customers' names start lighting up the board each morning. If by noon the list isn't long, he begins to growl to the sales manager. If by two the list is still short, he'll call a special sales meeting. If by five the deals are still short, he'll call another meeting. "Now, God damn it, *no one* is leaving this place until I see some paper," he'll tell the troops.

It's the J. C.s who make a car store tick. You may not see them much, may never meet one, but they are there, pulling the strings, orchestrating the four-wheeled ballet of buyers and sellers.

On the throne—the dealer. At the top of the whole dealership pecking order are the dealers. Dealers come in several types.

Many dealers are the "old gang," the self-made men who worked their way up from lot boys, pioneered many of the worst practices in the auto business, gobbled up a dozen or so dealerships, ruining a lot of people financially in the process, and now cruise the Caribbean on their megayachts. These guys generally sell out to bigger fish, or leave the day-to-day operation of their chains to individual store general managers, like J. C., or their sons or in-laws.

Many newer dealers at the great chains have little or no direct auto experience. CPAs, former bank presidents, or former officers of auto manufacturers, these guys are the "number gnomes" who couldn't care less about cars, individual sales, or a lonely customer, but care a lot about image, numbers, and "replication," making auto transactions at every level reliably repeatable.

But the most interesting dealers today are those like Gary Oliver Davies, Killer's boss. He's a lot boy alumnus like the other old guys. And he could surely spend the winter playing on his ninety-foot Magnum speedboat off the coast of Tortola in the British Virgin Islands, fly there on his Falcon Jet, and sleep at his new mountaintop villa overlooking Brewer's Bay. But Davies would drop dead of boredom if that's all he did. This man has to be working, and working on a big, big scale.

Like the problem he's discussing on the phone with a bigwig at America's Family Friend corporate headquarters outside Taos, New Mexico. Those damn consumer people are after AFF again! They've filed a big national class-action lawsuit on a stupid privacy issue, and they've got a newspaper *and a television reporter* interested in the case! Gary Oliver Davies snorts at the effrontery of the suit. This is a man who has a DVD of the film *Patton* in his office. Lawsuits bring down stock prices. Davies owns lots of stock options now. This is war! Only one person can save AFF's 250 dealerships from defeat. And that one man is not shaking in his Belgian loafers.

Davies drops his feet from his custom teak desk, leans forward, and barks one final comment in the direction of his speakerphone. "Hey, don't worry about those damn do-gooders," he says to the bigwig at AFF, "I'm smarter than those bastards—that's why I've got a jet and those wimps fly tourist!"

Davies punched the "off" button and looked around his office, so new, the rare Ibo wood's wonderful aroma made the office feel alive. Every inch of every curve on every piece of furniture, paneling, and molding glistened, and nowhere, *nowhere* could you even see a joint or a wood plug.

On the far wall, three large, flat plasma computer monitors nearly filled a center panel. The monitors displayed steady-cam pictures via Internet sites from three AFF dealerships: the left screen was tuned to the showroom of a large dealership across town; the center monitored the "Tower" of another dealership (where the managers "worked" individual deals), and the right screen broadcast a picture of a young couple in "the box," the new experimental closing room right there at Davies' home dealership. And Killer was talking with the young couple! Davies laughed. What consumer group had an office like this? What consumer group could win against Killer?

Always looking for more profit in the bottom line.

For an instant Davies started to turn on the microphone in the box to enjoy Killer's performance. Instead, he turned back to his own monitor and began paging intently through the monthly financial statements for the eighteen dealerships within a thirty-minute drive of his office. These were Davies' home dealerships, his babies, and the test sites for every new project eventually rolled out to AFF's other stores.

He flipped to the statement for Davies Motors, his first store, right where he sat, and began to dissect the statement. It is a complicated form, encompassing hundreds of categories on everything from "selling gross, new and used" (the monthly gross from new and used departments left after paying variable expenses such as advertising, used cars, repairs, and commissions) to "service sales per service order."

This dealership was doing mighty fine, he thought. By itself, before write-downs of used cars, it would make $3 million net this year. Not bad. Then, as he focused on the lease section, Davies grimaced. Leasing profit, after peaking at $4,400 per unit a couple of years ago, was now down to $2,800. Those damn consumer people again. Ten years ago, leasing had been a license to print thousand-dollar bills because consumers didn't have the foggiest notion how to negotiate a lease. Back then, all of Davies' dealerships were leasing vehicles at *110 percent of MSRP* (manufacturer's suggested retail price)! If the manufacturer's window sticker said $20,000, they leased it for $22,000—a car the consumer could have bought for just $18,000! Back then you turned what would have been a $800 profit on the sale of that car into a $4,400 lease profit! And then those damn consumer people started educating customers about leasing, started suing people like Gary Oliver Davies himself. And, right there on the financial statement was the result: The dealership was leasing vehicles now for 89 percent of MSRP, and the profit was *zilch,* only $2,800.

Davies picked up a dart and hurled it across the room into the center of the custom dartboard hanging by the door to his office. "But 'half-a-payment' will take care of that little problem," he muttered as he turned back to the screen. "Just make half your payments for the first year, folks! We'll make the other half!" Only fools fell for it. But that's why it would succeed, Davies knew.

As he hit two keys, a combined report on the eighteen used-car operations at AFF's eighteen local dealerships popped up on the computer screen. Davies operated all the used-car operations like one big lot: four full-time appraisers worked all eighteen used-car locations. Each carried wireless palm-size computers tied directly to Web databases of used vehicles. At least two appraisers had to agree on the "number," the wholesale value placed on any customer's trade-in. On oddball vehicles, just by dialing a code in their cell phones, the appraisers could page any of a dozen "road hogs" who specialized in buying odd vehicles. The road hogs would put "buying figures," sight unseen, on the vehicles before the customers even knew their vehicles were being appraised.

Every used vehicle at every lot had a bar code on the windshield's bottom left corner. Any manager could scan that code and instantly see the vehicle's cost, a summary of the vehicle's condition, and the minimum price the dealership would take for

it. That price could be changed on any of the thousand used vehicles at any of the lots in an instant by Davies himself from his
computer, or it could be changed from the used-vehicle inventory supervisor's office in the building adjacent to Davies' office.
Davies had "invented" this control system and was now installing it in all 250 AFF dealerships. What worked for tomatoes
at the supermarket worked just as well for lemons on the lot!

The windshield bar code also told how long the vehicle had
been in the used-car inventory. That detail for all used vehicles,
summed up on the report on the computer screen, drew Davies'
stormy attention. "Damn!" Something really bad! He dialed a
pager number using the keyboard, then punched in "99." Getting the page, Timothy Raxalt, the used-vehicle inventory supervisor, sprinted to the office. No employee, however busy, ever
delayed. Davies didn't page people often, and when he did, the
reason was invariably unpleasant.

Davies was talking before Raxalt had a chance to sit. "How
many times do I have to tell you about ninety-day cars?" Ninety-
day cars, "widows," generally had something wrong with them.
Or at least the customers and sales personnel seemed to think
so. They walked around them. Davies wouldn't have it! "I want
you to bring all the ninety-day cars from all the lots *right here!*"
he yelled. "Write them down again. Then, I want you to get with
the boys and have a 'Used-Car Carnival,' and *I want those cars
gone at retail or you can go with 'em.*"

Raxalt hadn't seen Davies this hot in a month. But, right there
on the report, the figures showed nearly $2 million tied up in
ninety-day cars that weren't selling. Idle money is dead money
in the car business, and there would be no dead money in a
Davies operation.

Raxalt didn't argue. It didn't matter that a third of those cars
were still on the lots because Davies had insisted on their high
appraisals for trade-ins of his pals—sailing buddies and bankers
and a half-dozen local pro football players. "Look," Davies continued, "I pay you to do your job. And *this*"—he pointed to the
screen—"isn't doing your job!"

Raxalt was settling in for a long, long, tirade—he'd heard
them before—but was saved by the soothing sound of Davies'

secretary over the computer speaker: "Mr. Davies, they're waiting for you in the broadcast room. Your presentation on Web site opportunities. . . ."

From habit, Davies looked in the mirror mounted on the wall to the left of his desk. His hair, including the newest inserts, looked just fine, his tan just right. He straightened the Armani tie just a bit. And all those 250 managers of AFF's dealerships sitting in front of their computers needed his wisdom. He turned to Raxalt. "Well, go to work!" he said as he stood and headed to the broadcast room, "I've got some money to make!"

Who Are the People Behind Those Web Pages and Online Services? And What's Their Modus Operandi?

There are thousands of automotive Web sites and online services, from the manufacturer's sites to handy hubcap sites, to sites run by individuals interested in telling you about their pet Mustang coupe. Most of them are fun to visit, some of them are surprisingly useful. You can spend an easy afternoon or two putting the word "auto" with any other word in your search engine and reviewing the sites found—and you should. Throughout this book we take a look at sites in detail as you need specific information. But here's a quick overview of the players by category:

Dealer-Controlled Sites and Buying Services

Behind even the best Web page or online service are the same types of people facing the same pressures and ethical problems that dealership employees face. They, of course, may even *be* the exact same people, as I said in chapter 1. Many dealerships, like America's Family Friend's 250 dealerships, put up multiple "Sucker Sites" to soothe you with consumer cyberspeak while the dealership Web managers and sales personnel and geek masters analyze your available credit information, dissect your life, then work you like any other "up," or worse.

The holy grail. The great gimmick is to create the illusion you're not dealing with a dealership. "We have to stop them before they go to a service," says an online trainer at TargetLive.com, a training service for dealership sales personnel. "We have to emulate buying services." TargetLive.com even recommends emulating the online security of many buying services. "Have a secure site because it *looks like a little more confidential site,*" the trainer says. (emphasis added)

"Independent" Internet Buying Services Such as CarsDirect.com

These companies act as brokers for you. They find vehicles at dealerships, buy them from the dealerships, then sell them to you. Generally, you don't have to visit or talk to dealership employees directly unless you choose to.

- **Who's sending you e-mail?** Usually, computer programs developed by the owners of the site or their consultants who've designed their customer relationship management (CRM) system. Generally, the sites are run by persons with auto-related experience.
- **Who are the "consumer service advisers" or counselors?** Sales personnel, not true "counselors." A few are former auto salespersons.
- **What happens to your trade-in?** They are typically appraised by the site's "select" dealer network, which means you risk getting "lowballed," being given far less for your trade than what it's worth. Buying services often use terms such as "facilitate your vehicle trade" or "assist with your trade-in." These phrases are simply dealerspeak for "appraise your old vehicle like a dealer would any other customer's vehicle." You're not going to receive more for it simply because a buying service is involved.
- **How do they make money?** Generally, such buying services add the equivalent of a broker's fee of $200–$500 to the sales price, and at times they are paid by the dealers to buy from them.

The one definite goal of all nondealership sites: The nondealer folks want your money as badly as any dealership wants your money. There's absolutely nothing wrong with that. But it does mean you have to be wary of their promises. For instance, all these sites offer financing, and all tell you how "convenient" (there's that dangerous word again) and reasonable their financing is. Some sites even acknowledge that you should compare rates or offer to help you compare rates, but none of them says what you really need to hear about financing: *If you don't shop financing and shop it beyond the sources they offer, you probably won't get the cheapest rate.* You could throw away *thousands.* And "shopping," as we'll see, means more than using an online rate-shopping or comparison service.

"Prospect Aggregators" Such As Autobytel and Its Subsidiaries

These sites are also known as "lead aggregators" or "third-party lead generators" by dealers and automotive insiders. Although most of these sites today provide lots of consumer-oriented information and tools, their ultimate role is linking consumers with their affiliated dealers in order to sell vehicles. Autobytel, for example, now owns and operates several such Web sites including CarSmart.com, Autoweb.com, Car.com, and AutoSite.com. Prospect aggregators work closely with their dealers and at some point in the transaction usually put you in direct contact with a specific dealer.

Any automotive Web site that offers to provide a price quote from a dealer or seller, even if the rest of the site is primarily informational, is serving as a lead aggregator. For example, Yahoo! Autos, MSN Autos, AOL Autos, and Edmunds.com offer quote services that connect you with local dealers.

All the sites will assert that their dealer affiliates must meet strict criteria, often based on the dealer's customer satisfaction rating (CSI). Such criteria sound good, but here's the problem, in my opinion: Dealerships regularly manipulate their CSI ratings. Even a dealership with a truly outstanding CSI rating has a perfect right to try to "lowball" you on your trade-in, and even the best dealership probably has a Killer Monsoon on its team.

There's also another problem: Although these third-party sites are "independent" in the sense that they are not generally dealer owned, they have divided loyalties. For example, consider these two statements from Autobytel about the purpose of its Web sites and services:

- From Autobytel backgrounder on Car.com: "Autobytel Inc. ... is one of the largest online automotive marketplaces, empowering consumers to make smart vehicle choices using objective automotive data and insightful interactive editorial content. The result is a convenient car-buying process backed by a nationwide network of dealers who are committed to providing a positive consumer experience." The statement goes on to assert that Autobytel's many innovative marketing, advertising, data, and CRM products for dealers "are designed to enable dealers to offer a premium consumer experience."[1]

- Autobytel's wording of its purpose has a bit different slant in its press release announcing BMW's adoption of one of its products: "Autobytel Inc., ... a leading Internet automotive marketing services company, helps retailers sell cars and manufacturers building brands through marketing, advertising, data, and CRM products and programs. . . . This automotive research and buying network [their Web sites] reaches millions of car shoppers each month as they make their vehicle buying decisions, generating billions of dollars in sales for dealers."[2]

Is there a lot of good information on Autobytel sites and other reputable automotive sites that generate leads for dealers? Certainly, there is. But the smart consumer never forgets that such sites have a vested interest in promoting sales and satisfying their dealer networks, whose dollars support the companies through buying the ads and marketing products and paying for the leads produced when car buyers request quotes or other information.

- **Who's sending you e-mail?** As a rule, you'll receive e-mails from both the aggregator and eventually the specific dealer.
- **Who are their "consumer advisers?"** Salespeople, not true advisers. Since most prospect aggregators' survival depends on good dealer relationships, you're not going to find much criticism of their "approved" dealers from a prospect aggregator's consumer adviser.
- **What happens to your trade?** Usually, the specific dealership "takes it off your hands." Again, you are subject to usual dealer "lowballing."

Manufacturer-Related Sites Such As GMBuyPower.com and FordDirect.com

You're certainly not going to find sales personnel at a GM site recommending that you buy a Ford, or vice versa, though it might be better for you. These manufacturer-related sites are simply "prospect aggregator" sites with a point of view based solely on what automotive product or line each site is selling. Such sites usually deliver you to the dealer by sending you to the dealer's Web page or "Internet coordinator." Killer is the "Internet coordinator" at twenty sites, so be forewarned.

Sites That Deal Exclusively in Used Vehicles

Some of these sites will sell you a used car, some will buy your car, some will even guarantee the *value* of the car you're buying or selling. Potentially, some of these options are very useful. But many of them are also a snake pit of potential problems, and others are virtually worthless. Even the best of the sites frequently involve old-time used-car types, involve lots of fine print, and thrive on the "lowball" aspect of the used-vehicle business.

I'll go into more detail about this in the sections on how to determine the wholesale value of your present car (your trade), how to sell your car yourself, and how to locate and buy a good used car.

Sites That Offer Only Financing or Loans

Some sites offer to "shop" your credit and give you a menu of potential financing sources. Other sites offer only their own financing, and, of course, these sites always claim they are the "best" or "easiest." Other sites will supposedly help you if you may have credit problems. But none of these sites will tell you to shop their best rate at your credit union (or bank), and many charge too much for fees and related items.

Most of these sites also offer loans on many things other than vehicles such as boats and home equity loans. Most of the staff members are not from the auto business.

"Where do these sites make their money?" The "comparison" sites are paid a commission by the company that eventually finances you. The "Agenda" sites, which are those offering their own financing, simply sell you the money for more than it costs them. Manufacturer-owned finance companies such as GMAC or Ford Motor Credit normally sell money only to dealers. As a consequence, their Web sites eventually pass you along to a dealership finance manager—oops, I mean "financial adviser" or "business manager"—who loves to resell it to you at a fat profit. Whatever the name of the dealership person you are passed to, remember they are simply very high-paid and skillful sales personnel.

Information-Driven Rather Than Product-Driven Sites Such as Edmunds.com, a Leading Car-Pricing Site

Many of these sites offer excellent information on pricing and products, and responsible sites such as Edmunds post clearly written privacy statements, if you take the time to read them. But virtually all of these sites are now in cahoots with dealers in some manner. Edmunds, for instance, says it guards your privacy, and it does if you don't interact with the site much. But in its privacy statement, Edmunds also alerts you that it is not responsible for the privacy policies of its affiliates. Its affiliate sites include manufacturers who share information with dealers.

- **How do these make money?** They normally charge affiliates a fee and at times make a profit on sales linked to their sites.

Now that you've met Killer's family of people and services in dealerships and those active in automotive sales on the Internet, it's time to look at how they play the sales game.

Chapter 3

Where's the Money? Understanding Automotive Sales Tactics and Realities

It's Time for Some Very Good—and Some Very Surprising News: Even the worst dealership will cut its prices for vehicles, financing, and fees to the bone, if you know how to ask. That's certainly not true of most Web sites.

In combativeness and in pure, raw competition, whether it's at a dealership or online, the automobile business, in all its forms, makes the forces of Attila the Hun look like a group of butterfly collectors running through the fields in their safari shorts, squealing, "It bit me, it bit me!"

Sales personnel at dealerships froth at the mouth each time some customer says, "Well, there's a car just like your car just down the road," or says, "Well, the e-price I got on a Web site was cheaper than that." These sales managers know from long experience that the fickle nature of customers rivals any teenager's loyalty to the latest fashion. Web managers at online sites age quickly each time their "customer response times" get longer and longer. Those Web managers know if they don't sell you quickly, you're gone. Some customers have actually bought cars below cost thanks to this rivalry for your attention.

Car dealerships, more than Web sites, survive this siege mentality by adhering closely to the "bird-in-hand" theory: A definite $200 profit, right now, today, is much better than some vague chance of selling the car to someone for a $1,000 profit tomorrow. The axiom is gospel even in a strong "seller's" market, and this reality presents the informed customer with the best opportunity to buy or lease a new car at the lowest possible price.

That fact in itself is not the answer you need, however. Neither dealerships nor Web sites survive, much less prosper, by selling you a car or truck. The vehicle is simply the starting point. Dealerships and Web sites today make their money from "add-ons" like warranties, fees, financing, and with fancy footwork with your trade-in. You will have lost the battle for your pocketbook unless you understand this.

"Are Web sites and other buying services as likely to bargain as dealerships themselves?" If you are dealing with a dealership Web site, you might be able to bargain online because you're dealing with the same eager seller trying to sell to you before someone else does. But if you are dealing with a buying service or other Web site that removes you from all contact with the dealership, you probably won't be able to bargain. That is a key attraction for many of these sites: They give you one price, and they imply bargaining isn't necessary. And *that's* generally not good for your pocketbook.

"So, does dealing with the dealership make the most sense?" Yes—if your nerves can stand it, and if you know *how to deal in person* with the sales personnel. Take the Webbs. They could have purchased a car very cheaply *if* they had managed their salesman correctly. The Webbs had shopped prices on the Web and had also been to three dealerships, writing down carefully each discount and list price on the three cars that interested them, before they came to Davies Motors. They really liked the car Forrest DeLong was now showing them. "Forrest, if you'll sell me that car for $18,500, we'll buy it," Carl

Webb asserted. "We're tired of looking and I'm tired of dickering. I am going to buy a car today."

Forrest looked at the stock card price code and figured the guy's offer as a $400 deal. There was no trade to sweeten the deal. He didn't really like the couple; they were too sure of what they wanted and what they would pay. Why the hell should he sell a car and make a hundred bucks, his share of the $400?

"Carl, you may buy a car today, but you're not going to buy it for $18,500, at least not this car." Forrest just sat there, a bundle of frustration and impatience. The Webbs didn't know enough to insist that their offer be submitted to the manager, so they left the showroom, walking past J. C. as they headed to their car.

Oh, God, Forrest thought, *that* was a mistake. I should have T.O.'d them. He was right. J. C. was at his desk in a second. "Why the hell are those people leaving without talking to someone else!" Forrest backed up two steps at the hot tone all the guys knew too well.

"The guy wouldn't pay over a $400 deal, and I knew you wouldn't take that, J. C."

"How did you know that? You don't know *what* I'll take. Did you hear what I said about letting people walk?" DeLong shifted his weight to his right leg, but said nothing.

"Son, you're not long for this world if you keep this up," J. C. said as he walked away.

He was right, too. DeLong won't last long in the car business—he's too independent, likes to work his own deals, to decide for himself when the profit is right. You may have met his type before, the guy who never has a boss. Car stores don't want this kind of person working for them for a simple reason. If your salesman is bossing his own deal, then he is your adversary, the person you must conquer in the battle for money.

"Adversarial" Selling

Because customers are more wary in an adversarial setting, the dealerships developed a nice psychological ploy to remove the adversarial relationship between salesperson and customer. The technique involves large doses of the words "they" and "we." "They" represents the house, the bosses, the greedy people who must approve a salesperson's deal. "We" represents the customer and salesperson allied against the mean bosses.

If Forrest DeLong had been using this system in dealing with the Webbs, he would have said, "Mr. Webb, I don't think *they* will accept $18,500 for the car, but why don't *we* write it up at $18,500, and then I'll go in there and fight for *us*. Remember, I don't make any money if you don't buy a car." The Webbs now have a friend, someone on their side against the house. It's a nice system, and while no dealership likes to sell cars for a $400 profit, they will probably do that *if* the customer can't be raised.

There is one small catch to this system, though. Would you know a small profit if it bit you? Perhaps you could just ask your salesman, "Am I really getting the best price?" while gazing trustingly into his eyes. Accepting his answer would be as wise as entrusting your goldfish to the cat.

Well, Just How Honest Are Car People?

Whether in the showroom or on the Web, if you define "honesty" as telling the simple truth—for instance a yes or no answer to a question about car safety or mechanical reliability or profit—you won't find it in the car business. The same goes for most businesses that survive on sales. If you expect statements such as "Folks, we have another customer on this car if you don't take it now" to be truthful, you're going to be disappointed. If a Web site sells a car ranked lowest on a safety scale, you can't expect the site to use a "pop-up" to pass along that tidbit on their opening screen. (Would you, if you had to make your living selling it?)

Honesty in the car business is always defined like this: "What answer will give us the biggest profit right now?" If a seller has to bend the absolute truth a little, that's just fine if the profit rises.

I call this little trait "convenient truth," and it generally precludes any chance of a dealership or a commercial Web site giving you a helpful answer about anything unless that answer helps the seller.

The sin of omission also makes the auto industry the house of the *one-sided truth*. Why tell a direct lie when you can simply leave out the bad part?

"How is the transmission in that used car?"

"Fine," says the salesperson or Web adviser—the truth. But since you didn't ask if the air conditioner worked, the person certainly doesn't volunteer that it's broken.

And what responsibility does all this depressing news place on you? The responsibility to know the answer to every question before you even think about approaching a dealership or give any Web site a "tie-down." And if you don't know the answer? You've come to the right guide. This book is going to walk you through the various steps in the total buying process. It's going to show you how to manage every salesperson you encounter at a dealership, or online, at various stages of the shopping, trading, negotiating, buying, and financing process. It's going to show you how to get the objective information you need to make sound decisions at every step.

And your education begins right now with an inside look at the tactics and ploys automotive salespeople use to sell cars and trucks. They know that everyone has a "hot button," and they are trained to find and use *yours*.

The Salesperson's Greatest Talent

Killer was back in the service department, standing next to one of the young kids who spent his days taking care of the used cars. The kid was removing a worn tire from the left rear wheel of a car Killer had sold the night before. Killer had taken the car to the state inspection station just an hour earlier. He'd promised his customer the car would pass inspection, and the damn thing had failed because of that tire. The kid slipped it off the car and jacked up the left front wheel of another used car, removed the tire and transferred it to Killer's car. It was a good tire, one that would pass inspection quickly. And it would just as quickly be replaced with the worn tire before Killer delivered it to the customer. Killer smiled. Those damned inspection people were just too picky, he thought. And not nearly as smart as they thought.

Killer was heading to his car for a little midafternoon visit to the Dead End when his pager beeped, then displayed an "Auto-Minder" appointment message from the new AFF automated appointment program. Loren's appointment! He'd forgotten that one of his oldest customers had scheduled a service appointment. AutoMinder's job was to prompt Killer to "accidentally" bump into Loren in the service area. Killer walked toward the showroom, stopping first at a computer terminal in the parts department to review Loren's file and latest credit report. The old man's file contained a "pop-up" that simply said "Max, Max"— very good credit, very good profit potential. His payoff flashed, too, right beside the "probable value" of his current car. Everything was "go" in this scenario, though Loren didn't know it.

Killer first went to his demo and set the FM dial to 99.9, then headed to the customers' lounge, acting like he barely noticed the older man sitting right by the soda machine.

"Hey, Loren, what are you doing back here?" Killer asked enthusiastically. Before the poor guy could answer, Killer smiled, grabbed the guy by the arm and said, "Hey, Loren, come with me. I want you to hear something sexy." The two of them walked back to the employees parking lot. Killer opened the driver's door to his demo.

"Loren, just rub your hand over this carpet and tell me what that reminds you of." Killer walked around to the passenger side of the car and sat in the front seat. Loren sat in the driver's seat and took the keys without a second thought.

"Here, feel the padding over your head," Killer said, as both men pressed their hands hard against the ceiling. "And, Loren, push that button by the door and lean back."

Loren stretched his body as the seat automatically reclined, his eyes closed, a relaxed "ahhh" exiting his mouth. "You know, Bob, all I need is a TV and a beer!"

Killer laughed. "Hell, Loren, you've got those at home! What you need is this car. Now, get up and let's take a drive." At the instant the car started and 99.9 began to play country, Loren, grinning ear to ear, turned to Killer and said, "Its on my favorite station! This must be my lucky day!"

Killer just loved technology! Loren's file had included a notation listing the radio settings on Loren's last trade-in. Music to sell old men cars by! He sold Loren the four-month-old demo at full list in thirty minutes and convinced Loren to give up his old car for a thousand less than the dealership would have paid for it, using a wireless PDA with online used-car values to seal the figure. Thank you again, technology! Killer waved the old man off in the new car and turned again to the salesman's parking lot to pick up a new demo. The Dead End was calling.

Smell that leather! *Titillation* is the car salesman's greatest talent. Any good dealership car salesman is the master of tactile excitement, the mark of a good pimp. Salesmen are incessantly drilled in the power of tactile selling, and for good reason. You, for instance, may know someone who enjoys looking at *Penthouse* or *Playgirl*, but wouldn't that person have more fun if those pictures were replaced by real people? A smart pimp knows that. Sure, pictures are nice, but lovely temptation often makes reason fly out the window, along with the pocketbook.

Smart car salesmen use tactile excitement in many ways. They want you to feel the padding, caress the leather, slam the doors, glide the moonroof silently open and shut, listen to the ten-speaker digital stereo, take the GPS system for a spin. They want you to do anything that will make you fall physically in love with one specific car. Privately, the salesmen and managers take a slightly less romantic view. Cars are referred to as "hunks of meat," "lead," and "potatoes." They serve only one purpose: as decoys for the ducks, the surest lure for monetary reward.

Just stick your hand in the screen! Many Web sites offer an excellent "touchy-feely" tour of vehicles. If your computer is up to the task featurewise, you can take 360-degree virtual tours of the interiors, drive along a highway, tune radios to your favorite stations, do everything but clean under the seat.

Tour break! If you want to stop reading and have a little fun right now, go to any auto manufacturer's Web site and tour their vehicles online. Don't buy, just look! And don't forget any site you go to is going to "nail" you—open a file—if you haven't disabled your cookies. (Some sites may require cookies for you to view the video.)

The Salesperson's Favorite Targets

The nice old lady drove up in a plain brown sedan. A widow who had never purchased a car before without her husband, the woman was nervous. She had a right to be, too. Many sales personnel prey on women not used to the deception of selling environments and particularly older people who are often trusting of kind manners. And Buzz was very kind.

He was the first person to reach her. "Hello, ma'am, I'm Peter Kiever, but everyone calls me Buzz." He smiled. "Thanks for coming in to see us."

The nervous woman quickly fell under the spell of this "nice man," as she referred to him. Buzz was patient. He spent two hours with the lady, never pressuring. The "ma'ams" flowed from his mouth like honey from a bear's lips. He could afford to spend time with her. After all, Buzz knew that sweet old ladies don't like to argue, want to believe that niceness is honesty, and invariably buy cars from people who *are* nice.

Inexperienced women buyers and older people. These groups are just two of salespeople's favorite types of customers. First-time buyers are really popular, too, especially the young first-time buyer, a person who breathes the heaviest when first sitting behind the wheel of a car. Innocence, enthusiasm, and a trusting nature make the selling process so simple.

Poor people. Have a slim pocket? Nice! Many poor people are also favorite targets because they tend to feel inferior or insecure the moment they walk on the lot. "What do these folks know about wheeling and dealing?" is the car salesman's attitude. And then there are the people who think their credit is marginal (whether it actually is or not). If you're one of these types, keep thinking negatively, please, and your salesman will sense that your main concern is not getting a good deal but getting financed. Car salespeople make much more money on you thanks to that insecurity.

The salesperson's newest favorite target: computer geeks. Are you planning to buy on the Web because you feel safer there? Feel more in control? Do you believe the people and information on the Web just seem more reliable? Think the transaction seems simpler? Oops! *You are a prime target for every Web site.*

So, who's the best target for any car salesperson?
Anyone who assumes that nice people will sell you a car for less. Next to a water moccasin, a nice friendly car salesperson, in your face or online, is probably the most dangerous thing in the world *because* it's so easy to trust that person.

Profits, Not Profit

As we mentioned, the actual negotiation for the sale of an automobile is one of the many ways dealerships and Web sites have of fleecing you honestly, although most of the time the sale of the vehicle itself is the least profitable part of the transaction. Killer knows that better than most salesmen, and therefore he likens an automobile dealership's need for other profit sources to a rapidly flowing river. The river is never filled by the random raindrops that fall every now and then, but rather by the small streams of water that pour into larger streams, each one adding to the massive flow of the river. So the dealership fills with money.

Gotcha! Think of your friendly salesperson as playing a game with your pocketbook. Lurking around every dealership corner, waiting for you behind pop-ups on your computer screen, is some item or service that will grab just a little more money. Most of these extra profit sources are not presented to you at dealerships until you've signed your name on a "buyer's order" or "purchase agreement." Your salesperson probably just asked you to "Okay these figures," which sounds much better than "sign the binding contract here, sir."

"At *that* price, I'll take the rust!" Consider, for instance, the "protection" packages I mentioned earlier. Such packages usually include "etching," (a theft-protection gimmick), rustproofing, undercoating, "glazing," and "fabric protection." This fine package is usually sold by the "after-products" manager, the "business manager," or the "financial counselor"—dealerspeak for specialty salespersons grabbing for extra dollars.

The products themselves are cheap. Rustproofing and undercoating usually cost the dealer no more than $75. Fabric conditioning about $5. Glazing about $5. Etching your windows to scare away thieves (right) about $10. But what do the dealers want to charge you for them? One of the biggest and toughest dealership chains in New York charged $1,995.00. Most dealerships try to charge you $500–$900. And we haven't even addressed the fact that you probably don't need this extra "protection" at any price.

"I'll take the tricentennial warranty, please." And then there are the extended warranties or service agreements. You probably don't need these, either (more on that later), and you certainly don't need them at rip-off prices. If the extended service agreement is provided by the manufacturer, it might cost a dealer $375 for the average vehicle. If the agreement is from an independent warranty company, it probably cost the dealer $75. But most dealers try to sell these service agreements for $800–$2,800.

"Gotcha!" on the Web. The nature of buying and financing over the Internet makes it necessary for the good Web sites to ask you about major cost items before they send you paperwork. The charge for an extended warranty, for instance, would have to be included on the actual paperwork. You may be paying too much for the item, but at least you've agreed to do that.

But some sites deliberately add previously *undisclosed* items to your paperwork or deliberately change the terms of the sale and hope you'll sign the paperwork anyway. These sites know inertia and impatience are in their favor. If you don't agree to the higher figures, you have to wait another day while fresh paperwork arrives by snail mail. What should you do if this happens to you? Accidents don't happen much in these situations. I would cancel the deal and find a more reliable service.

Supply and Demand

This old bugbear of the economics student is the reason the identical vehicle can vary in selling price between two dealer-ships and between two "auction" sites on the Web. If a dealer has only one of the hottest-selling cars on his lot, you won't buy that car cheaply from the dealer, and neither will anyone buy it cheaply on the Web. But if the same dealer has fifty slow-selling models, he'll give them away at cost, if need be, and happily offer them to Internet buying services.

You will be happy to know the law of supply and demand is still a savvy consumer's best friend, as you'll see.

Killer Monsoon's Favorite Selling Techniques

It was Saturday night, the last night of the store's "Beat the Clock" sale, and Killer picked up one of the last cold chicken legs on the table at the end of the showroom floor. A few customers were still sitting in front of the big board that listed every single car on the lot. Believe it or not, some customers sat in front of a large computer monitor that displayed the on-line picture of the board—right by the actual board! You gotta love those geeks, Killer thought. If they saw it on the Web, it was fact!

Each hour of the past twenty-four hours, one of the salesmen had been assigned the honor of "marking down" the cars $100. Two busy salesmen in the Web room had the same honor for persons e-mailing in their bids. Many of the cars still listed on the board had bright red stars beside them, indicating "bonus cars." "Beat the clock and buy a bonus car, and we'll give you a free digital video camera!" the ads and Web banners read.

People actually believe that baloney, Killer thought, as he watched a man who had been sitting in front of the board hour after hour finally jump and yell, "I'll take that one, the one with the $3,000 discount!" Killer burped. Chicken sales weren't his idea of selling cars. Sure, it was a good technique for the suck-ers, but anyone can sell a car to a sucker.

J. C. walked up to the board and taped a SOLD sign by stock number 224. Killer laughed to himself. Not one single customer in the room knew that the car hadn't been sold at all. J. C. just didn't want to sell it at such a big discount. During the entire twenty-four hours, no one had received a camera, either. The salesmen would say, "I'm sorry, folks, but at *that* price, we just can't sell you a car and give you a video camera, too." The line worked every time, for every "giveaway"—bicycles, video games, computers, vacations. During Killer's thirty-five years in the business, he took pride in having never given away a single premium yet. Screw the showbiz, Killer thought, as he slipped out the service door and headed to the Dead End.

Have you ever driven by an automobile dealership and seen a giant "tent sale" in progress, balloons flying high in the air and clowns running around? All car stores like to create a carnival atmosphere, promising fun and prizes, and generally intoxicating the customers with an air of excitement. And why shouldn't they? Car people have learned from experience that the average customer doesn't want too serious an environment during car negotiations. This is fun! What's to worry about?

The Web sellers listened and learned. That fantasy—lots of fun and no worries when you buy or lease a car—has driven the design of virtually every Internet selling system. Look objectively at any of the auto sales-related Web sites. They emphasize utter simplicity, instant decisions, a gee-whiz attitude, and an aura of complete safety. But in reality the sites create danger for you because they are misleading. Behind every Web platitude or promise is a salesperson with a smart sales technique.

Have you ever been the victim of any of the following techniques at a dealership? Would you like to know how many of the same techniques "work" you on the Web?

"Will You Buy a Car Today at Some Price?"

It's a salesperson's most important question. The answer determines whether or not you are going to be an easy sale. If you say "yes," the salesperson will probably start salivating, especially if you're in heat over one particular car. If you say "maybe," the salesperson will be extra nice and probably even volunteer to show you the "best deal" of the day. As the salesperson talks to you, he or she will be looking for your "button"—the one psychological element that will turn you into a buyer today. If you say, "No, I'm not buying today at any price," the salesperson will in all likelihood put you out on a "ball," an impossibly low price, on the one car you've shown interest in. You would be surprised how many people come back in, too, and then let the same salesman raise them another $2,000 for the same car.

Be honest when someone asks you this question, but couch your honesty in self-protective terms if you are dead set on buying a car, a specific car, that day. Try something like this: "Yes, I may buy a car today. But I am going to buy it from the dealership that lets me determine how we negotiate."

One of the most important defensive techniques you can learn to use with car people is the ability to *be negative in a nice way*. Don't let that thought make you uncomfortable, either. Would you be passive and mushy if someone were lifting your wallet? Of course not. Well, in effect that's what a good salesperson is trying to do.

How this works on the Internet. Web sites usually ask you up front if you're a buyer and when you plan to buy. Indicate "no" until your homework is done. Remember that some sites will try to force you to say yes by requiring a deposit before they will really negotiate with you. "Getting an online deposit," says a TargetLive.com trainer, "is a great way to create 'tie-downs.'"[1]

One quick warning. *Never, ever* buy a vehicle on your first visit to a dealership or a Web site.

"If I Can . . . , Will You . . .?"

The Fillmores were walking around the new-car lot with Killer, past the plush, expensive models and the stingy little sedans, too. They had asked for Killer because Mr. Fillmore worked with one of Killer's bird dogs.

"Mr. DeMarco, these are all pretty cars, and I'd be lying if I said I didn't want to own one, but all of these things are too rich for my blood. I'm a poor man, you understand."

Killer chuckled, looking straight into Fillmore's eyes. Killer knew everything about Fillmore's credit, and his buying habits, thanks to the customized "lead-tracker" report the dealership's computer had automatically pulled when Fillmore had called the dealership. He was about as poor as Killer.

"Why, of course you are, sir. And I appreciate your concerns about money. It's ridiculous how much cars cost these days. But let me ask you something. If I can sell you this designer sedan"—Killer pointed to an expensive beauty ten feet away—"for a price and payment that is reasonable to you—if I can give you *more* than you think would be fair on your trade—Mr. Fillmore, if I can do that, will you buy it today?"

How do you answer Killer's question? Of course, most of us would buy a car if the payment was reasonable and if we felt we were getting more than our trade was worth.

"If I can . . . , will you . . . ?" is not a fair question, however, because normally if you will, they won't. The question is simply a nice way to confirm to any salesperson that you will buy a car if you *think* you are getting more than your due. The question can also lead you into deep waters quickly. For instance, once a salesman has determined that you don't want to pay over $500 a month for a car, and that you consider $375 per month an easy payment to make, he automatically knows you are a buyer if he can find a car you like that will fit that payment. So why shouldn't you be happy if he can? *Because you might be able to buy that same car for $325 a month, if you bargain.*

How this works on the Web. Services that say "Tell us what you'll do and we'll find a seller to do that" are really using the "If I can, will you" approach. If they want a deposit before you have a definite agreement on the price and terms, don't give it. If they won't deal with you without a deposit, don't deal with them.

The Sincere Salesman-in-a-Contest Ploy

If every car salesperson went on a winning trip each time he or she said, "Ma'am, this car will send me over the top," there would be no more car salespeople in America—they'd all be away on trips. Sure, there are contests. Dealerships place bonuses for salesmen on the most new or used cars sold or leased, the largest gross (profit) per car, the most "add-ons" sold, the highest number of financed cars, and so on. Dealerships and manufacturers also employ contests to sell slow-moving cars. But these contests and bonuses don't necessarily mean you're going to receive a better deal. Don't fall for the sympathy routine; negotiate even harder with these contest fellows. After all, if they are really going to win a trip or extra money, they can afford to make a little less on you.

The "I'm Salesman of the Month" Routine

Do you think that nice salesperson with the picture on the plaque was picked for service to humanity? No, salespersons of the month are generally picked because they make more *profit* for the dealer than the other sales staff.

The "I'm a Trustworthy Salesman" Ploy

Web sites just ooze this aura. "We're not like those guys!" But they are. Because most customers are naturally suspicious of car salespeople, smart sales personnel, wherever they may be, know that they *must* gain your respect if they're going to sell you a car. There are lots of techniques for doing this, too. If Killer is talking with a customer who seems determined not to buy a car that moment, he'll look the person straight in the eye and say, "You know, I'm really glad you're not buying today. Quite honestly, the house is holding out for too much profit today. I can save you a lot of money if you'll come back tomorrow."

Sometimes Killer will close a deal with a large front end (the profit on the new car) by telling the customer, "Folks, don't ever quote me on this or the boss will fire me, but you *will* get a little better financing rate if you go directly to the bank down the street. I'll be happy to call the loan officer for you." Isn't that nice of Killer? What he doesn't tell the folks about is *his* relationship with the loan officer—Killer gets paid a fee for each person he refers.

And then, there's Killer's best line for used-car buyers. You're looking at a used Toyota when he walks up and says, "Sir, I wouldn't recommend that car to you. It really isn't a very good car. Let me show you something else." What do you think of Killer? Do you instinctively trust him? After all, he *was* being honest with you. Perhaps. He may be telling the truth, but because he is so well trained in a favorite technique of used-car selling, he is usually simply gaining your confidence for the kill: that six-month-old clunker with a cracked head sitting in the back lot with a bonus on it.

"Setting You" on a Car: The Demo Ride

A good salesperson will always insist that you drive the car you like best. That's the salesperson's most important job, getting you behind the wheel of that car. They'll probably insist that the whole family go, too—kids and a spouse can quickly become a salesperson's best friends.

Of course, it's important that you drive a vehicle before you buy it. Play with all the buttons, feel the nice seats, and enjoy the ride. But don't let your adrenaline take control: be cool, be objective. Don't fall prey to the salesperson's spiel, and be prepared for the salesperson to "reinforce" you. Reinforcement is a nice technique that goes something like this: "How does the ride compare to your present car, Ms. Smith? . . . It's a quiet car, isn't it? . . . How do the seats feel? Aren't they comfortable, just like a boardroom chair?" The saleswoman saw you drive in, the smoke belching from the rear of your rusting minivan. She *knows* you've got to like the solid feel of the car, and she *hopes* you'll like all the goodies enough to smother your objectivity. Demo rides allow you to gather hands-on intelligence about a specific vehicle. Don't let it bamboozle you into throwing your intelligence out the window with your pocketbook.

How the Web handles test-drives. If you're dealing with a "Prospect Aggregator," you'll be given a test-drive at the dealership they eventually send you to. If you're dealing with a broker, you may not have an opportunity to drive the exact car you're thinking about buying or leasing.

- **Is that bad?** Probably. You need to know if you fit in a particular car, if you like the way it handles.
- **The solution:** Rent a car like the one you're thinking about getting for a weekend. Weekend rates can make that a fairly cheap and most pleasant way to gather intelligence.

"We Can Allow You This Much with a Difference of This Much and a Deferred Payment of This Much. Now, Just Sign Here." The Old Confuse-Them-and-Control-the-Sale Ploy

Confusion is the salesperson's best friend. After a day's shopping at several different dealerships, most folks hardly remember their own names, much less understand the offers and counteroffers whisked before them. Sales staffs use confusion to keep you from buying a car at another dealership. They *imply* that enormous savings are waiting for you on your return. They tell you about the customer who has been waiting for a trade-in just like yours, hoping you'll fall for that classic line.

Confusion is also used in more specific ways. For instance, if you are a "payment buyer," smart salespeople will continually quote you only payments, conveniently forgetting to mention the trade-in allowance or discount. If you are a "difference buyer" (if you care only how much difference you must pay between your old car and their new car), they will try to convince you that "allowance" (how much they *say* they are actually giving you for your trade) is more important than difference.

Your defense. Don't tell a salesperson that you care only about your payment. Don't tell him or her that you care only about the difference in price between your old car and that pretty new four-wheeled thing. Those are expensive ways to deal because you'll be lost in the confusion. The only things that count are what your car is really worth in wholesale dollars, what their car actually costs, how much profit you are willing to pay, and which financing costs the least. I'll show you how you can determine each of these things.

Justifying the Sale

These days, all of the major automobile manufacturers have on-line presentations designed to teach salesmen how to overcome customer objections. One good series is called "Justifying the Sale," a nice euphemism for making nickels look like quarters. Robbie Miers, a new saleswoman at Davies Motors, a sharp kid who enjoys talking with Killer, is sitting at the feet of the master, Coke in hand, listening to war stories. The topic is overcoming objections.

"I remember the time this know-it-all came into the dealership so set on exactly what he wanted on a car that the other salesmen gave up," Killer said with an amused smile. "I bet four of them twenty each I could sell the guy, and I did."

Robbie sat there in anticipation. Killer just looked off in space. "Well, come on, what did you do?" she asked.

Killer started laughing, a belly laugh. "Hell, I did just the opposite of what I'd done with the customer before him! God, this business is fun. Well, anyway, the first guy had wanted a specific car, but not in red—the color of the only model we had. So I pulled up the 'Car Appraiser site' and showed him the 'add' notation for bright colors. Then I put him on the phone with the used-car department. The guys up there told him red is the most popular resale color and would bring him more money in trade.

"Then, this second guy came in—the one none of the guys could sell—and he just had to have a light-colored Gargantula GL. We had only a black one. So I told him how much light colors rust, and that black cars had less rust than any cars, and I had him talk to the guys in the body shop. He bought it!" Robbie smiled. Killer was better than any chat room on the Web.

Killer was not lying to either one of those customers. He was telling the selective truth. Bright colors are more popular at re-sale time. Black cars do rust less than light-colored cars. As a matter of fact, most of the techniques used by salesmen do have some ring of truth in them. Consider these examples: Do you think you'll keep your old car for now? "Just think what you'll save on repair bills!" You can't afford the quoted new-car pay-ment? "Why, just finance for a hundred months! You can pay the loan off early when you have a little extra money." Do you want to think about the deal until tomorrow? "Why? You said you liked the car and the payment. If you buy the car today, I'll even give you a free undercoating."

So, how do you make any sound judgment with all these semblances of truth flying around? It's easy. If you need to jus-tify what you are spending or what you are choosing, if you have doubts about what you are doing, STOP THE TRANSACTION. Go home if you're at a dealership. Sign off if you're online. Don't try to think in the midst of confusion.

How Web sites handle "justifying the sale." Many deal-ership Web sites and virtually all large buying services and clubs have stock e-mail messages for any question or objection that you might conjure up. How can you know if you're getting a customer answer or a canned spiel? Send an odd question, such as "Does that model come with a bathtub option?"

"Ahh, This Is the Beauty of a Trade-in You Mentioned?" The Ploy of Bringing You to Their Reality

Killer was standing by an up's trade-in. The young woman had ridden to the store earlier that morning with a friend. It was a cool Saturday in October, one of those days that seem to draw every looker in the world to car stores, and the two friends had planned to kill some time looking over all the snappy new models lined up at the dealerships along "Dealer Row." Killer normally has little patience with these "bumblebees," the people who light at one store just long enough to draw a salesperson from the showroom, waste fifteen minutes of his or her time, and then fly off to the next candy store. As a matter of fact, he never paid any attention to the type. But Gary Oliver Davies himself had been on the warpath that week. "I want a salesman at every single up's car before the door is open," he yelled. "Hell," Killer mused, "I guess his damn boat needs a new engine."

One of the young women had even exhibited a reasonably serious case of car fever, enough to garner Killer's attention. Trish Dunaway had now returned to the store with her trade-in. But Ms. Dunaway's battle-worn car looked nothing like the glowing description presented to Killer that morning. "Mr. DeMarco, I want to tell you my car is one of the prettiest four-year-old Saturns this side of the Mississippi!" Trish had said with obvious enthusiasm. Killer was used to statements like that. Everybody who came in the store seemed to have no problem at all believing their trades were things of beauty, even if fenders were missing, seats were torn, and large pools of oil quickly formed on the pavement each time the junkers rolled to a stop. But over the years Killer had developed a really nice technique for handling this "blind love." And he was just about to unleash it on Ms. Trish Dunaway.

"Ms. Dunaway, this does look like a mighty nice car. You know, my youngest daughter has one pretty much like it. . . ." Killer continued to talk and started working his way slowly down one side of the car, something like two steps, before stopping to continue his story. Each time he stopped he'd look at the car again. If a small dent was within reach, Killer would simply rub his hand over it and continue walking, talking all the time. When he was standing by the hood, he pulled out a large handkerchief and vigorously rubbed the worst area of faded paint; then Killer ran his finger along the windshield molding, right to the large rust bubble in the corner. Ms. Dunaway, of course, was seeing these little problems for the first time. Like most of us, she had become used to the pimples. But Killer never once mentioned the little problems with the car as he stood by the driver's door.

"You know, I may have a customer for your car. Why don't we take a spin around the block?" Killer said brightly. Trish Dunaway didn't really like the idea—the brakes weren't too good really, something she kept meaning to fix, and the worn-out shocks bounced the car up and down in a good imitation of a camel loping across the desert. But how could she say no? After all, this was supposed to be a really "nice" car. They headed down the road, Killer jabbering away, seemingly not in the least aware of the lope or the brakes. He did run his hand over the torn armrest and do his best to push the ashtray in—the thing kept falling down, as if it were trying to talk. But words weren't really necessary. Trish Dunaway was getting the message. The dreamboat just wasn't that great, after all.

Or that's at least what Killer wanted her to think. Smart car people will do their best to "educate" you about the value of your trade before they try to sell you a car. It's a smart move, one you can't refute very easily. If you don't know the real value of your trade *before* you trade it in, you will lower its value in your own mind every time a salesman points out its weaknesses.

How the Web tries to steal your trade. We're going into this in detail later, but for now, know that Web sites are even worse when it comes to giving you true value for your current car. For many sites, stealing your trade—giving you less for it than its true wholesale value—is the most important profit ploy that the site will use on you. It's called "reality management."[2] "You must lower their expectations on what the car is worth," says a TargetLive.com trainer. "Use the Kelley Blue Book to set up boundaries to lower their expectations."[3] The trainer goes on to add a telling truth: "It's much easier to set the level of expectation online than in person."[4] He's in effect saying, "Since customers feel safe on the Web, it's easier to give them less than their vehicles are really worth."

"Give 'em the lowest . . ." Another technique used by some Web sites and sales personnel is to check the value of your trade-in on three or so different online services, but show you only the site with the lowest value.

The "Other Customer" Ploy

You're sitting in the salesman's office, and you want to think about your offer until tomorrow. "Folks," he says, "there *is* someone else interested in that car. The people are expected back here at five. If you really like that car, why don't you just give me a small deposit to hold it for you?"

Don't do it. Clear that glaze from your eyes and say no. You are spending thousands of dollars, and there are thousands of cars out there, too. You will invariably get a better deal and be more comfortable with your purchase if you wait a day.

But let's assume you follow this advice, only to return the next day and find your dream car gone. Don't be upset; car people know the disappointment you feel usually means you won't buy anything from them, and so they'll bend over backward to make you an even better offer on another car. Some smart buyers use this technique deliberately; they pick out a car and wait for it to be sold to someone else, when they really wanted some other car on the lot.

The Old "Lease 'Em a Car Instead" Ploy

Salespersons invariably use this ploy because they can't make enough money on you at a certain price and know for sure they'll make a lot more if you can be switched to leasing. Your response should be a quick and friendly no. Unless you've studied our sections on leasing, say, "I'm not leasing a car today, period."

"Lease 'em rather than sell 'em" in its honest guise is bad enough. But, unfortunately, its dishonest version is much more prevalent and has become the subject of state attorney general investigations and thousands of lawsuits. This version of the ploy is more accurately called "Lease 'em a car and let them think they're buying it." It's used particularly with older folks already confused, exhausted, and devastated by dealership tactics, and also with others who seem like easy marks. The salesperson simply begins to discuss leasing terms without calling them that, has a contract drawn that says it's a lease, and quickly rushes the exhausted customer through the signing process without giving them a chance to read all the papers. What makes this tactic particularly cruel and obnoxious is that the first document the buyers are usually asked to sign is a sheet saying, "I have read all of these pieces of paper, and understand them."

This tactic is used thousands of times each month in America, and many consumers don't know they've leased rather than bought for months. And unfortunately, even if they discover the switch in a day, until recently, consumers have had little recourse to have it overturned because they've signed the papers. But you will be happy to know that this tactic may be changing as lawsuits are filed again and again.

So what do you do if you find a dealership has pulled this ploy on you? If you discover it before you sign anything, get out of there. Don't accept so much as a free cup of water from them. And tell your friends to stay away, too. If you've already signed the papers, but haven't left the dealership yet, don't leave. Force them to revoke the contract that day. Then leave. If they won't cancel it, call an attorney or your local help lines.

The Very New "Sell 'Em a Car But Make the Terms Like a Lease" Scam: The Return of Balloon Payments

This tactic is the reverse, in a way, of the previous scam. In many ways, the bloom is off the leasing rose because the average profit on a new-car lease continues to fall every year. Five years ago, a lease might return 120 percent of the sticker price. Now, it barely returns 90 percent. Why? Consumers became tired of being ripped off by vague leasing contracts, tired of paying inflated "wear and tear" clauses, tired of those ridiculous lease profits. Leasing laws got tougher, too.

So, what did the car folks do? Reintroduce "balloon" payment financing. What's a balloon payment? Briefly, it's loading the majority of the loan payoff into the last payment. You know, forty-seven payments of $179 and one final payment of $23,000. You'll find out more about them in chapter 16. Right now, just remember you don't want one unless you clearly understand a balloon loan's pros and cons.

These ploys are just a few of the tactics and techniques that car salespeople are trained to use to sell you a car today at a deliciously high profit. But they are just the beginning of the sellers' feast if you're not careful. Every salesperson at every dealership is working these ploys within a particular *selling system*. Showing you how the most popular selling systems work to generate profits for the dealership at your expense is the subject of our next great adventure on the road to happy driving.

Chapter 4

Dealerships' Favorite Selling Systems on the Showroom Floor and on the Web

"At last, you've found a friend you can trust," he said as you opened your wallet. "Now, why don't you let me hold that for you. . . ."

Earlier I told you about the adversarial selling approach used by virtually all dealers, in which the salesperson is positioned as your friend against the nasty bad guys, the salesperson's bosses. The general system itself is misleading because the salespeople are only pretending to be on your side to use that appearance against you.

Largely because of the Internet and the advent of huge national dealership chains, dealers have now refined adversarial selling for use in their stores and will continue to do so. Adversarial selling, therefore, is the foundation of a number of specific selling systems popular with dealerships throughout the nation. Versions of these systems are used on the Web, as we'll see. Here's a look at the most devilish systems. Be forewarned: at times these systems are combined, too.

The T.O. System

The gold standard, the T.O. (turnover) system, has been around for over twenty years and is still the most popular way for a dealership to take your money with a slightly menacing smile and an unhealthy dose of confusion and exhaustion.

Let's say you've spent two hours at a dealership. You've found the car you like, one of those special-edition Expenso Gargantula Majesty Hardtops you have always yearned to own. Your trade-in has been appraised, and although you are not really sure what they want to pay for it, the offer must be pretty good since the salesman keeps suppressing a giggle every time the figure is mentioned.

The monthly payment they've quoted you doesn't seem that bad, either. Sure, it's twice what you pay now, but the dealership's "financial counselor," who came into the office with the salesman, showed you that, really, it's *lower*. "Yes, it's $6 a day more, but that's only twenty-five cents an hour. And you'll probably save that on gas, once gas gets up to $6 a gallon." You know, *that* type of logic.

However, you are tired and a bit confused, and you have been trying to leave for a little R & R. The salesman has even lowered the price to keep you there; he's also told you about his children and his sick mother ("She's a real saint, I tell you."). But still you want to leave. The salesman excuses himself and returns with his "team captain," who wants to dicker some more. Still you resist. Pretty soon he leaves, and now the dealership chaplain drops in for prayer. You buy the car. After all, you had to, just to get out of there.

You have been the victim of the T.O., the "fresh face can do miracles" theory. *Don't* put up with that. Don't feel guilty for leaving—it's not really a prison bust-out, though you may feel that way. Smile, shake hands, and say good-bye until tomorrow.

The Four-Square System

If you go to a dealership that uses this system, get out of there. In my opinion, "four-square" selling is dishonest and designed solely to confuse you. Why deal with a dealership this sleazy?

Four-square works like this: The salesperson either draws a cross on a blank sheet of paper, creating four squares on the page, or pulls out a "worksheet" with four squares on it. The salesperson then asks what payment you want to make per month for a car and writes that figure in the top left square without arguing. You feel pretty good.

Then the salesperson asks how much you want for your old car. You know it's worth $4,000, but you say $8,000. That figure is put without argument in the top right square. You're beginning to feel real good.

Then the salesperson asks what you want to pay for the car itself. The window sticker says $23,000, and you, as a joke, say $13,000. The figure goes in the bottom left square. Your heart skips a few beats. Are you a tough negotiator or what?

Finally, the salesperson asks you to sign that simple piece of paper and fork over a fat deposit, which you promptly do. Who wants to miss a deal like this? You sit back and smile. The salesperson disappears for a few minutes.

When the salesperson returns, the fun begins as you are "worked" on each square *as if they are not interrelated*—as if the price of the car doesn't affect the payment; as if the value of your trade doesn't affect the payment. You wanted to pay $300 a month? They scratch through that and put $700. You jump. They scratch through that and put $645. You jump, they continue to write slightly lower figures and scratch through them until you quiveringly agree to a payment.

Then they begin to work on the value of your trade. You said $8,000, but they now scratch through that figure and put $1,800. You argue them up slowly, every new figure written in the square, every old one scratched through. Next they "work you on the square" to determine the actual selling price of the vehicle.

Who can make sense out of all that chicken scratching? No one. That's the point. And why does the four-square system always come back and ask for an impossibly large amount of money for the vehicle or offer you virtually nothing for your trade? To *condition* you. If a payment should be $325, but the seller keeps asking for $700, then a little less, then $645, you'll feel pretty good when they get down to $400, won't you? But on a sixty-month contract, you'll have just paid at least an additional $4,500 in profit. Thank you very much.

Some four-square dealerships will keep you there for hours playing this game, and worse. At a dealership in California, the staff kept a deaf-mute customer at the dealership for eleven hours playing hardball. The customer eventually sued the dealership for mental anguish. And do you know what one of the dealership principal's felt about his staff's actions? "If you think *that* sales team was tough, you should see our really tough guys in action!"[1]

The Note System: Killing You with Kindness

Many people have caught on to the T.O. and four-square systems. The moment another smiling person enters the office to ask for more money or the moment the square appears, they become more savvy consumers. That, of course, doesn't please the dealers.

Enter another slick and misleading sales ploy. Rather than send other salespeople in to talk with you, the note system simply sends personalized notes to you from the sales manager. Usually five notes, all very friendly. And though each note asks for more money, their wording is so sincere it's hard to argue. For instance, note one may read: "Dear Mr. and Mrs. Smith, thanks for coming in, but we unfortunately can't meet your price. If we come down $500, could you come up $500 and let's meet in the middle?"

You agree, and note two appears. "Dear Mr. and Mrs. Smith, thanks so much. We appreciate your help, but the customer we had for your old car has already bought something else. Can you help us with another $300? We hate to ask, but some folks are coming to see that car within the hour." You pay the $300. Then note three appears: "Dear Tom and Sally (the invisible man is now your friend), we are so close. We're going to have to call the boss on this one, but if we move a little, could you help us just a little? Sam."

You give. These people seem so sincere. And the fourth note comes: "Tom and Sally, just another $21.63 and we can do it! Sam." Why, of course you pay. Boy, can you drive a bargain. And then the fifth note arrives. "Now, just remember you can't tell anyone what you paid." Right. You'll tell everyone, won't you?

The note system seems so nice, but it has a couple of flaws. First, the notes weren't written for you. The wording was taken out of a notebook, and the notes themselves were probably written up in quantity at the sales meeting. Only your name had to be added.

Second, a salesperson is required to give you all five notes *even if you agree to pay the highest maximum profit before you get the first note!* The salesperson still must try to raise you again and again.

And the last two notes? The one asking for $21.63 is simply to make you *think* you're bargaining (more on that in a minute), and the final "don't tell your friends" note is designed to make you do just that. What's the gist of the note system? *It's fantasy. Don't fall for it.*

The Note system and Internet selling. If you think about it, virtually all online selling is "note" selling. The responses you receive via e-mail from even many small dealership Web sites have been carefully researched; their effectiveness has been verified in discussion groups and online surveys. Web shrinks have toyed with them. The result: Many Web responses are worthless. For instance, you e-mail a Web site's Internet coordinator: "I just heard that the Expenso Gargantula I wanted has faulty brakes." The Internet coordinator at smaller sites, or a computer at larger sites, keys on four words: "Expenso Gargantula," "faulty," and "brakes." A pat response in the computer flies back to you, "Gargantulas have advanced four-wheel disc brakes. You can read about our excellent brakes at www.BuyaGargantulaBut DontPlanToStop.com." The Web site gives you P.R. puff about the brakes, but doesn't address your question of safety, even

though the safety issue may be constantly discussed at Gargantula's product meetings.

The Tower System

Generally used at very large dealerships and always used in
conjunction with another system, the tower system intimidates
the salesperson more than the customer but still provides maximum control over you. At these dealerships, a "control tower,"
which can be an actual tower like an airport control tower or
simply a centrally located platform area, houses managers
whose only job is *to watch you* from the moment you arrive on
the lot, at times with the help of surveillance cameras. If a salesperson doesn't reach your car immediately, a pager or cell
phone dispatches one; if you start walking toward your car to
leave, a cell phone dispatches a "runner" to stop you. Tower
systems are based on physical intimidation and control and are
becoming awfully popular these days. If you find yourself at a
"tower" dealership, tread carefully.

One-Price, No-Hassle Systems

"No hassle" or "no dicker" prices are wildly popular on the Internet and are becoming popular at dealerships. Touted in the
press, and pointed to by dealers as a sign that the car business
is becoming a friendly, downright pleasant racket, er, business,
"one price" has become a hit with just about everyone. And in
theory, one-pricing should work: You either like the price of the
car and buy it, or you don't like the price. What can go wrong?

Well, where shall we start? To begin with, this gimmick—and
that's all it is—takes away your natural defense mechanisms. Because there's no hassle, you relax and enjoy your visit to the
dealership or Web site. You feel particularly comfortable when
the salespeople tell you they are paid a flat fee on each sale.
"Folks, that means, since we don't work on commission, we
don't mind at all if you pay a small profit," they say nobly. They
of course forget to mention that they normally *are* on a bonus

plan based on gross profit—which means they *are* paid on commission. Prestidigitation at its best!

Both dealerships and online services know your guard is down. And in the car business, that's always the time to strike. First, they make a nice profit on the new vehicle itself. That's not really that bad, either. So what if you pay a measly $500 to $1,000 more for the car than if you had carefully bargained for it?

But then the real fun begins. You already know what's next, if you've been reading attentively: They try to steal your trade from you. If you're at a dealership, they look you in the eye and say, "Hey, we don't hassle you, remember? That's what it's worth, friend." You say yes, and, *bam,* accept $4,000 for your car rather than the $5,000 it's worth. You've now paid $2,000 more than you would at a "normal" dealership where your guard and trading skills are up.

And then the salesperson, smiling, takes you to the finance office to talk financing and add-ons—all done without a bit of negotiating but with lots of laughter on both sides. In the finance office they put you on a high interest rate, blithely talk you into double insurance, and perhaps even tack on $35 a month for the radon-detector package. That's usually a wax job. Let's see, they made an extra $1,700 on the financing and $2,700 on the add-ons. In total, that brings their profit on one sale up to a little over $6,000 if my math is right.

Do you see why more dealers are giving no-hassle selling a run for your money? "The test was hugely successful," says one megadealer CEO, Scott Smith, commenting on their test of one-price selling in the Houston area. And how did Mr. Smith judge success? "The store had some of the largest margins I have ever seen for a domestic franchise—6.6 percent net profit (as a percent of sales)."[2] *That's* why they've switched to this system, not because they want to be nice to you. And not, as some dealerships are saying, because their manufacturers require them to. They don't.

"Wait a minute—6.6 percent net profit doesn't sound like much profit at all. Who can survive on that?" Anybody on the earth. Dealerships use a very misleading way to determine net profit, as we'll see on page 202.

So, don't worry about the dealership's profit, and don't fall for one-price, no-haggle dealerships. Be as protective of your pocketbook there as you would be at any car operation, on the Web, or in person.

One-Price selling on the Internet. If you're dealing with a one-price Web site, they do the same thing, only more subtly. Their computers *learn* where the "price breaks" are—the level at which you begin to resist paying more. I'll bet that online selling prices will keep edging up over time, too, if Web buyers keep saying yes to Web prices without negotiating.

Trade-ins on the Web. When you deal with an online service, your trade-in is treated like any other trade-in. Whether you go to a "preferred" dealer or a "selected, professional" appraiser comes by your house, they'll give you as little as you'll take, and do it without a guilt pang. These "Web appraisers" also have a learning curve. As they repeatedly see consumers unwittingly taking less for their trades than the trades are worth, the appraisers will offer even less.

Financing and fees add-ons. On the Web, all prices, rates, and terms are presented as if the figures were carved in mood rocks.

"Yo-Yo" Selling or "Spot" Delivery

You're going to face this highly deceptive scam at almost all dealerships and a variation of it at some Web sites. This particular scam has become the subject of more customer lawsuits against dealers than any other particular dealer fraud, according to an informal poll of the four-hundred-member National Consumer Law Center auto fraud e-mail group.[3]

The salesperson looks you in the eye and points to your old car as he speaks. You half listen as you watch dealership personnel moving all your belongings from your beat-up old nine-passenger minivan to that glimmering two-passenger convertible. You have seven kids, but the dealership has convinced you the kids will fit in the trunk. They deliver the pièce de résistance: "Folks, we know you," the salesperson says (of course, he doesn't say, "we know you because we have a gigabyte of intelligence on everything including your underwear size"). "And we're letting you take that car home right now! We're drawing up the contracts right now, too, *at the figures you wanted!*"

Zowie! Well, what's wrong with that? You've been thinking the kids can hitchhike, anyway. So you start signing papers, laugh at the salesperson's final joke, and drive home happy in your dream machine. You stay happy, too—the kids bike to school—until the phone rings in about a week: "We've got a little problem," the sales manager invariably says. "We couldn't get you financed for the full amount (or, we made a mistake on our paperwork), but don't worry. All we need is another $3,500. And we need it today. Oh, and your payment is going up $75 a month." You notice the edge to the manager's voice.

Well, what do you do? You don't have the money, so you nervously tell the manager you'll bring the car back and get your old car back.

"Oh, you can't do that," the manager says. "We sold your old car. Now, when are you going to bring us the money? Have it here in twenty-four hours." His tone is a little colder.

"Uh, well, I can't get the money. And it's the dealership's fault, anyway," you say. They told you the loan was approved. And if they made a mistake, whose fault is that?

Completely your fault, in both cases. "Hey, didn't you read our rescission and mistake release?" the guy asks. You know, the forty-eighth thing they asked you to sign, that page in ant-size print filled with confusing legalese?

"Uh, no, I didn't read that very carefully. The salesperson said it was a formality."

"Well, I'm sorry you didn't read it. We'll need that money by tomorrow or I'm afraid we'll have to report this car as stolen."

What do you do? Don't Worry! The dealership has a plan to save you. If you can't come up with the money, they'll borrow you the money from a small loan house, or borrow you a bigger down payment from a bank, or help you call your favorite uncle. And when you go to sign all the new paper-work on your new loan, you'll notice the interest rate is up and the months you'll pay are longer, too. What you won't see directly is the dramatic increase in profit on your deal for the dealership.

All that financial horror happened because you fell for "spot" delivery and became a "yo-yo" sale: They threw you out in the car and pulled you right back in. So, how do you stop that? *Never* take delivery on a vehicle during your first visit to a deal-ership. And *never* take delivery when you're financing at the dealership if you are asked to sign *any* documents that imply your deal isn't absolutely final.

So how do you make sure you're not signing a yo-yo con-tract, since the legalese may be hard to find? Have the business manager write the words "This contract contains no writ of rescission clauses" on your copy of the contract and keep that copy filed away.

"Yo-Yo" Deals and "Spot" Delivery on the Internet. Spot delivery is the goal of most Web sellers. They want you to buy instantly, finance instantly, and take delivery *right now* (i.e., "on the spot"). There's nothing illegal about that, but speed never al-lows you to think and seldom allows you to compare. As a con-sequence, you pay more and/or don't get what you really want.

Online yo-yo sales happen regularly only with truly unethical sellers. Prevent it from happening to you by making sure *none of your paperwork defines any part of the transaction as* **"condi-tional."**

"Credit Doctor" Scams

Ever worried a bit about your creditworthiness? Been late for a payment or two? Ever had a credit problem? Maybe not, but many people have those concerns. And if they have, they have probably been drawn to the enthusiastic ads that say "No Credit? Bad Credit? *No problem!* Come see us: The Credit Doctor!" Just about every dealership, big and small, is running a version of this ad, and similar banners are beginning to flood the Web.

Though the purveyors of "credit doctor" promotions like to pretend they are doing a public service by helping out those who've had problems, the truth is unfortunately exactly the opposite. Dealerships and Web sites have learned that people who worry about their credit don't argue about their deal: the more you worry, the less you argue, and the less you argue, the more the seller makes. And where the profits are, the sales machines are always relentlessly at work, regardless of the damage to the customer.

You may be inclined to skip over this section. Don't. It gives you a mirror reflecting the true face of many car people.

"Here, let me operate without anesthesia." That's why practically all dealerships and most Web sites have developed special sales techniques and assign full-time "credit doctor" sales personnel to those of you who have or think you *may* have a credit problem. Let's say you've been ten days late six times and thirty days late one time on your car payments during the last thirty-eight months. You've been at your job six years, have at least one credit card with a $6,000 limit, and have lived in the same apartment for four years. You don't know that lenders actually love it when you are ten days late (they get an extra fee!). You are probably still an "A" credit risk. Yet you remember those times you were late on your payments, and assume the tardiness has probably given your credit report a scarlet letter. You consequently decide to ask for the credit doctor when you arrive at the dealership or check the "I've had a credit problem" box on the Web site. Being honest and asking for help is going to be good for you, right? Because you may have had a little problem, they'll help you find the best car for the least money, right? Wrong. Very Wrong.

Letting any seller know that you *think*, or *worry*, that you may have a credit problem is like letting a vampire know you think you're bleeding from your jugular. At that moment, you are targeted for the worst predatory sales techniques in the auto industry, starting with a vicious little game called "maxing out," which can be defined by this objective: "What is the maximum amount of profit we can squeeze from this sucker? Can we get some money from a credit card? Can we get an uncle or friend to borrow from a small loan house?" (Some Web sites actually pay you a bonus for finding a relative to borrow money for you.)[4]

If you're at a dealership, the credit doctor may encourage you to "fluff your credit statement"—to lie on it. In a nice irony, *you* are committing a felony if *they* persuade you to fluff your report by saying, for instance, "Oh, don't put down you've only been on the job six months; put down four years. They'll never know." If you eventually are caught at this little exaggeration, that same dealership person will say, "Well, here's where they signed saying the credit report was accurate. So, take them to jail, not me." Guess who broke the law here? You. You are responsible for the accuracy of your credit application, not the dealership. The credit doctor just scammed you into lots of trouble.

And then the credit doctor pushes you toward the "old maid" cars that no one else wants to buy, or, more typically, to the junk. Then you're put on the highest interest rates, even though you qualify for a lower rate. Then you're sold the "sucker" options or services that no one should buy.

Internet variations on subprime selling. Most legitimate Web sites offer some form of credit doctor help. Some sites even ask you to "rate" your credit. If you rate it as less than perfect— even though you, in reality, may have perfect credit—these sites push you to more expensive financing sources that pay them bigger commission. **Fair Warning:** If a site offers to give you an instant loan based on a "preliminary" credit assessment, run from that site.

The Advent of Major Automobile Dealerships Designed Solely for Subprime Borrowers

Can anything get worse than credit doctor schemes? Yes. The real, ugly underbelly of the American automobile business is the advent of sleek automotive sales operations aimed at the "subprime buyer," the term for buyers with poor or nonexistent credit.

For decades every town has had "buy here, pay here" lots, usually sleazy, run-down lots that made you want to wash your hands before you even touched the front doorknob. Only the most desperate buyers went to these places. But in the nineties, both major automobile dealership chains and major lending institutions began to look at the profits made by some of these fleabag operations. The dealers and lenders smacked their lips at the profits made off the unfortunate customers who had fallen for their credit doctor scams. "How," they thought, "can we make more money like this?"

One solution was the creation of subprime used-car operations with snappy names like CarsYouBet.com or Wheels for You! Clean, handsome showrooms were staffed with clean-cut, apparently helpful sales personnel. Their Web pages looked saintly in their innocence. From the look of it, a poor consumer had found a good place to do business.

But how deceiving those looks were. Although there may be a few dealerships and subprime financing companies that actually strive to help the poorer customer, the consumer movement, through involvement in many class-action lawsuits, is getting below the well-scrubbed surface of these chains and lenders and finding a messy reality.

Dump the junk. Many of these chains simply serve as dumping grounds for a new-car dealership's junkers. Cars placed on these lots generally receive cosmetic work to make them look good but virtually no mechanical repair. "If the cars were any good," one person said in a deposition, "we were told to put them in the shop and then put them on our regular used-car lot. If they were junkers, we were told to drive them directly to the junk chain." One large subprime chain tells its dealers to try to buy cars that cost no more than $1,000, and then resell them for at least $3,500. The normal markup on a used car is virtually never more than 50 percent in the most ridiculous of circumstances. The recommended markup at this chain is 250 percent.

Race is an issue. Some of these chains (and even some major national "prime" lending companies) are targeting African Americans and other minorities for especially tough sales tactics.

"What? You want to *drive* it?" At some subprime lots, customers are seldom allowed to drive the vehicles. "Oh, we don't have insurance for that," the sales personnel are trained to say.

"Oops, the rate went up. Hope you don't mind." Major financing companies are charging three to *ten* times more interest on these exorbitant vehicle prices than even the riskiest customers need to pay. And the sellers' reasoning for these excessive interest rates is often a little skewed.

"It's your fault the rate is high, you know." These sleazeballs always say that the high interest rates are necessary to cover the losses brought on by irresponsible customers. Out of the other side of their mouths, however, these very same sleaze merchants brag to their investors and creditors that the risk is *less* with subprime borrowers. Take what the owners of a subprime chain in the northern United States said about their tactics. In a statement prepared for their bank (and discovered during a lawsuit), the owners say that their losses are indeed *very low* compared to others in the subprime business. According to the owners, they were experiencing default levels of only 12 percent. Additionally, the owners claim a "relatively low level of exposure in any individual contract." These nice folks' exposure was only 30 percent of the loan amount. When you finance a car, the credit source usually requires no more than 20 percent as a down payment. But the poor people who dealt with this company paid on average *80 percent down*.

"Did we say it would run?" Many of the cars sold at these operations don't run a *single month* without breaking down. Because the cars don't usually have meaningful warranties and because the customers have already had every penny taken from them in the negotiating process, customers are unable either to repair their vehicles or to continue making payments.

Their cars are immediately repossessed and resold. Some of these vehicles have been sold, repossessed, and resold *six times in one year.*

"We know it only cost $500, but you still owe us $7,000." Many of the unfortunate customers of these chains are being sued for astounding "deficiencies." One junker car worth $500 was sold four times in less than a year; the price for each sale was $7,000. Every time the vehicle was repossessed, the unfortunate owner of the moment, though he or she had driven the car less than a month, was sued for the full $7,000 of the original loan. In one year, a $500 junk vehicle had returned a $28,000 *profit for the dealer.*

"Can It Get Any Worse Than That?" Well, we could invent a way to put a computer on poor people's cars so the cars won't start if the suckers are late on that weekly payment! What we'll do is require the suckers to bring their payment in each week and give them a weekly code to keep the car running!

Who, on earth, would do something like that? Lots of dealers. Ask Mel Farr, the former Detroit Lions running back, who owns twelve dealerships and has tested these devious little gadgets. Mel said he's helped poor people by installing these devices before he financed a vehicle.[5] Some of the customers thought otherwise. Aside from the pure indignity of such a system, attorney Ken Hylton's two clients, in a lawsuit, claimed their vehicles stopped on the freeway because of the contraptions. Try explaining that to the cop! "For Mel Farr to cast this as a means of helping people move up and out of poverty is just absurd," says Hylton.[6]

"Well, What Should I Do If I Think I Have Credit Problems? How Can I Protect Myself?" First, stay away from credit doctors and CarsYouBet.com type dealerships and Web sites. Find out your true credit status before going any further. Don't use Internet sources to determine your credit rating, either. As we'll see later, credit reports pulled from Web sources can be highly inaccurate, and they are not the same credit report a bank or dealership pulls.[7]

By federal law, you now have the right to get one free credit report annually from each of the big three credit bureaus: Equifax, Experian, and TransUnion. You may order your free reports on-line at the official Web site (www.annualcreditreport.com) or make your request by toll-free phone call to 877–322–8228. These are the *only* ways to get the official free reports. Other online offers are either commercial or scams—and there are lots of scams.

This consumer-oriented credit report will still be a bit different from that received by a bank or dealership. If you have a relationship with a bank or credit union, they may be able to help you evaluate your creditworthiness. You can also go to my article "How to Review Your Credit Report . . . and Correct It When Necessary" on www.dontgettakeneverytime.com. If you have credit problems, slow down. Talk to a credit counseling service. Better yet, talk to your credit union if you belong to one. Virtually all credit unions provide free advice and are very helpful with credit counseling.

Finding help. Bad credit or no credit, you have a right to sensible advice and a good deal. Just don't listen to the "good deal" boys at the dealerships. Look in your Yellow Pages for a local office of one of the legitimate, nonprofit credit counseling services such as Consumer Credit Counseling Services. Make sure you select one of the nonprofit agencies that offers free help.

Welcome Centers

This is another technique now used with every customer at virtually all dealerships. The moment you arrive on the lot you're escorted to the "welcome center," where a very nice person scans your driver's license, asks you to sign in for their daily contest, and gets you a cup of almond cream coffee with a tofu topping. As you sip the fresh brew, the dealership computer rummages through your life looking for weak spots. Should you go along with this? If you are truly just looking, don't register for anything that requires you to give your address, phone number, or Social Security number. If you are getting serious about buying, at some point you will obviously need to identify yourself.

Getting a Deposit

"Folks, I just need to get that deposit to show my boss you're serious." You'll hear that line at most dealerships, and it's about as truthful as "I never receive spam online." You see the deposit request on Web sites, too, usually with the soothing phrase "fully refundable" attached to it. Every vehicle salesperson, whether sitting in the "box" with you or online, lives for the moment you pull out a credit card or roll of bills or checkbook. If you're at a dealership, the favorite "deposit" is simply to "hold" a credit card and your driver's license. Likely as not, the available spending limit on your credit card is checked just for fun, too. Don't forget that deposits online are made by using a credit card, which opens you up for an easy credit check.

The significance of paying a deposit isn't what you think it is. If you're at a dealership, you probably think a deposit means the dealership has agreed to sell you a vehicle at a certain price. To the dealership, it doesn't mean that at all. It means you can't leave as they begin to pressure you, confuse you, raise you.

If you're online, the "fully refundable" deposit is supposedly meant to show you are a serious buyer, and the "fully refundable" phrase is meant to wipe away all your worries. If you can get it back, what's the problem? Here are four:

- **"Your call will be answered in either three minutes or two days, and we won't tell you which. But we will play a polka while you wait. Have a good day!"** The first problem with online deposits is that it isn't always easy or quick to get your deposit back if you gave it online. Even if the Web site willingly agrees to the refund, it can be a couple of months or longer before you receive the "credit." And if the deposit isn't credited back by then, how much fun will you have getting *that* straight?
- **"To tighten the rope a bit, please hit the SEND button."** The other reason hasty online deposits are bothersome is that they are a classic dealership ploy, known online by the catchphrase "tie-downs." When you hand over a little money, you become "sticky"—you'll keep coming back to

that site as long as they have your dough. Deposits also put you under the microscope since you have gone from a "hit" (a visitor to the site) to a buyer.

- **"A $7,000 deposit will be just fine."** These days no one asks for a $50 deposit, either. Most dealerships ask for one-third down. Do they think most customers will actually pay that? No. But if they ask for $7,000, they know you'll be embarrassed to offer $50. And, of course, the more of your money they have, the less likely you will be to leave.

- **"It's really an investment, you know."** Some dealerships have become laughingly creative in their references to deposits and even to monthly payments, referring to deposits as "initial investments" and to monthly payments as "monthly investments."

"What 'Unauthorized' Credit Report? You Authorized It When You Used Our Restroom."

Dealerships and online services hotly deny they ever pull a credit report without your permission. They *have* to say that, of course, since it is against the law to pull an unauthorized report. But virtually all dealerships have pulled unauthorized credit reports for years, usually under the guise that "we have to do that to let you test-drive the car. Insurance regulations, you know." That, naturally, is a lie.

"What's wrong with a dealership pulling an unauthorized report?" First, it gives the dealer an unfair negotiating advantage. Second, it starts in motion a process that can literally *lower your credit rating*. After pulling the unauthorized credit report, the dealership usually fills out a loan application in your name and sends the application to different loan sources such as banks, manufacturers' captive lending institutions (GMAC, Ford Motor Credit, etc.), and so forth. And then *those* loan sources pull a credit report on you. All without your knowledge. In credit scoring, a large number of "inquiries" about your credit actually lowers your score.

FTC cracks down. The pulling of unauthorized credit reports became so abusive and widespread that most credit reporting agencies changed their guidelines so that a large number of inquiries about an auto loan will not necessarily lower your credit rating. The Federal Trade Commission also recently issued clear, specific guidelines designed to stop abuse. The guidelines state the following:

- A customer must "initiate a purchase" and "request dealer financing" before a credit report can be pulled.
- A customer's "request to test-drive a vehicle" does *not* "initiate" a business transaction.
- A dealership *cannot* pull a credit report solely for the purpose of negotiating with you.
- A customer's questions about prices and financing do not necessarily indicate an intent to purchase or lease a vehicle. Therefore, the dealership cannot pull a credit report because of these questions.[8]
- Each violation is punishable by a $2,500 fine.

"Well, I guess *that* stopped the dealers in their tracks! Right?" Not at all. First, dealers generally don't need to pull a credit report anymore to know whether or not you're a good credit risk. That information, in summary form, is probably already in the computer file the dealership has already opened on you. Second, you almost certainly gave written permission for a credit report if you signed *anything* at the dealership. The permission request may be hidden away, but it's there.

Well, what can I do to protect myself from being hurt by all this?"
- The moment you enter dealership property *always* tell your salesperson, "I do not authorize you to run a credit check on me."
- Don't give your Social Security number to anyone at a dealership, unless you are requesting financing there.
- If a dealership requires a copy of your driver's license before you can test-drive a vehicle (a sensible precaution on their part), always tell the salesperson, "I do not authorize

you to open a file on me using information from my driver's license." This may not stop them, but it alerts them that you know what's going on.

- *Look before you sign anything.* If you are simply test-driving, or shopping with no intent to finance at the dealership, insist that any credit check authorization clause be stricken from the document you sign, and insist on a copy of that document.

How will dealerships react to this? Since many dealerships still rely on the trickery of deposits and credit checks to control you, some may actually say they won't sell or lease you a vehicle. Fine. Get out of there, and tell your friends to stay away, too.

But do you know what will usually happen when you stand up for your rights? The dealership will back down and do it your way. They want your sale, and even the worst dealership will usually do it your way if you control *them,* rather than allowing them to control you.

The Web and credit checks. Web sellers and financiers are usually good about asking clearly for your permission to pull a credit report. What they're not clear about is telling you whether or not, and *how,* they may share that information with others. For instance, if you are turned down for an online loan, does that company have the right to sell your name to loan companies that deal in subprime loans? Web sellers also don't generally disclose what information, other than a credit report, they may gather on you.

Documents online and in the mail. If you find an objectionable clause either online or in forms sent to you by an online company, you're going to have a very hard time getting the objectionable clause removed. If you don't like the clause, don't use the company.

Gimme *More* Money! The Raise

All dealership selling systems other than "one price" stores use "the raise." The philosophy here is simple: Always get more money. Even if the customer has agreed to pay MSRP, the full sticker price; even if the customer can't afford more money. Always ask for a *lot* more than you think you will get, too. If you want another $200, ask for at least twice as much.

We mentioned a specific type of raise, the odd raise, earlier: You sign an order, give the salesman all your credit cards, and sit there while he goes off to see the manager to "fight for you." Of course, the guy really just goes for a soda. He doesn't bother the manager at all, but returns with a smile on his face.

"Folks, we're so close! If you can just help me a little bit, $135.39, the boss will go for it." Well, of course you'll do that. These guys are down to the pennies, and the guy's salesman of the month, anyway.

Smart salespeople almost never ask for even amounts of money; they ask for those odd amounts that imply (falsely) a good deal. Don't fall for it.

There is a catch-22 in the whole "bumping" syndrome. Some customers actually want to be "bumped," or raised. If the house should take their offer without arguing, the customers feel they must have made a bad deal. Yet, many dealerships won't try to bump people who have agreed to very low grosses. A customer that close in his offer may leave if he's bumped.

One thing is sure, though. Dealerships just love to bump people who are on high-profit deals on the first offer. Why? Managers feel that anyone dumb enough to agree to a high profit will probably be dumb enough to be bumped.

Do not be patient with raises. Tell your salesperson you won't budge when he goes to get your offer approved.

Raises on the Web. Raises are harder to achieve on the Web: You can simply quit communicating with a site that tries to raise you above an agreed-upon price.

Lowballing

You're at a dealership and you've stuck to your guns. You haven't been able to get your offer approved or perhaps you simply don't want to make an offer on the Expenso today. As you're walking from the showroom, the salesperson makes one last try. "If you will come back tomorrow, I'll try to get that car for $500 less than the figure you mentioned." Or she says, "I think I can get you $500 more for your trade-in if you come in tomorrow."

Don't go home and celebrate. You've just been lowballed, "put out" on a price they just know will bring you back tomorrow. Most people who are "put out on a ball" will invariably spend hours arguing with salespeople at other dealerships, saying, "But the other folks have said they will give me $500 more." These customers exhaust themselves trying to buy or lease a vehicle from a ball figure and finally return to the first dealer the next day, only to be told, "Gosh, I'm sorry, we had a customer on your trade-in that would have allowed us to give you $500 more. But he bought something else just before you got here." And would you believe that most people, from pure frustration, will actually pay the $500 simply to end it all?

Why not take the offensive with the salesperson who makes you a ball offer? If what she proposed really would be a fantastic deal, grab her by the arm and head for her sales manager. Tell them both you'll buy the car right then and there for that figure, and if you can't, you'll never darken their door again.

Every dealership and every Web seller has a selling system. Simply recognizing that system puts you way ahead of the average customer and quickly impresses a salesperson.

Chapter 5

A Look in the Mirror: Know Yourself

Buck and Samantha Allgood pulled back onto the expressway, one of those perimeter highways that ring large cities and seem to sprout automobile dealerships on any unoccupied parcel of land. Samantha was writing on a PDA.

"You know, I really liked that minivan and think it was just about the right list price. The seats are good, too, high enough for me, and practical with the kids. I'm so glad we are actually driving the van we like the most! That rental one didn't have seats that nice at all." She entered another notation on the PDA. "And I like the way their Internet representative didn't try to pressure us. His Web coordinator was nice, too."

Buck smiled and nodded his head, biting on the end of his pipe in some salute that seemed to signify a very amused yes. "Honey, those men were run-of-the-mill salesmen if I've ever seen any, so don't fall for the fancy new titles. But," he added midpuff, "I think the 15 percent discount was good. *Consumer Reports* said those smaller vans have about an 18 percent markup. So 3 percent profit would seem fair to me." He looked in the mirror twice, turned his head just to make sure the lane was clear, and headed slowly up the ramp to the next dealership on their list.

The Careful Buyers:The Allgoods

Buck Allgood is the comptroller of a small company located just twenty miles from the city. Samantha teaches the youngest kids at a Montessori school. They are thoughtful, unemotional buyers who trade cars only when the repair bills come too quickly and irregularly on their present car. They are not in the least in love with automobiles. Their Saturday visits to three dealerships have been preceded by several weeks of careful study on the Web.

The type of vehicle they hope to purchase is no casual choice. For the last three weekends, they have picked up a rental version of each vehicle that interested them and used it for the weekend. Their shopping method was good, too: After finding a couple of vans on the Internet that fit their specific needs, they visited the dealerships that stocked those specific vans, drove them, discussed price, and then went home for the night to think objectively over the individual deals. Neither of these people feels that any "Internet coordinator" can pull the wool over his or her eyes. Both are wrong.

Living the Good Life:The Chases

Al and Allison Chase live north of town, in one of those new subdivisions with big artificial security gates that are supposed to look imposing but in reality seem pretentious. The Chases are not wealthy, but they would like people to think that at least they're getting there. Their home has two large stone urns by the front door. The flowers that used to bloom there have slowly withered from neglect. "Honey, I've just been so busy," Allison continually tells her husband. Allison Chase is very involved in the lesser social scene—you know the type.

"Well, damn it, what do you think *I* do? Whose work is it that lets you be that busy?" Al invariably snaps back. The Chases fight quite a lot, usually over money. As a matter of fact, they seem to spend what little time they have together either fighting or silently watching their new high-definition television in their media room. Like the new TV and most things they "own," this newly finished room is financed—in this case with a second mortgage. The Chases drive two cars: a three-year-old Lincoln

Navigator, the type predominant in the suburbs these days; and a large, very clean, high-mileage luxury hardtop, one of those cars that seem to blink "we are rich" while passing lesser cars and people. Both cars are financed, but Al Chase has determined that, yes, he can trade in the hardtop for one of those new sporty Gargantulas, the type that is supposed to improve your sex life. They will buy that car and receive an excellent deal in anyone's book. They will receive excellent financing rates, too. But that new Gargantula will spell the end of the Chases' solvency not too far down the road. They don't know that yet, though; they won't, until it's too late.

On the Way Up: The Estrums

The youngest of our couples, Phil and Sue Estrum seem to possess qualities shared by both the Chases and the Allgoods. They are upwardly mobile, solvent, happy with each other, and in love with those physical possessions they can honestly afford to buy. The Estrums usually trade cars every year, in the midst of new-car introduction time, or perhaps a month after that time. "I always wait until they've dropped their prices some," Phil tells the few young couples they know in their condo overlooking the river. "And, do you know what? Our payments didn't go up a 'nickel' the last time we traded!"

The Estrums are proud of their car-trading ability and of the new car that reigns proudly in their garage. "We never spend a dime on repairs, either. I tell you it pays to trade every year." This nice couple can afford to trade cars every year. In the course of their lifetime, however, they will throw away $300 a month, year in and year out, because they buy when and as they do.

"In the Bucket" and "Dipping": The Problem with the Chases

Three guys and Robbie Byers, in a sporty long dress, were flipping pennies for Cokes, the four of them standing around the Coke machine, one that looked just like a machine from the

1960s but was in reality a souped-up computerized model. The staff joked it pulled a credit report with every Coke pulled. The machine dispensed plastic bottles shaped like the original Coke bottles, too. Davies thought the old-fashioned look conveyed a down-home image to customers.

All stores in the America's Family Friend chain had nice touches like old-time soda machines. In the service lounges, Davies had even added semi-enclosed computer kiosks that allowed service customers to play games, surf the Net, perhaps visit sites they wouldn't visit at home. Of course, links to AFF Web sites were highlighted on the welcome screen. Charles Pierce, AFF's Web manager, just loved to "browse the cookies" at night of customers who had played on the computers in the service lounge. The information at times could be very useful, and many times would be funny. Charles had taught Killer how to browse the cookies, too.

Selling the Chases. Killer's attention went to the coin. "Heads," he called as Dolores "Lorrie" Cheatum, one of the store's "business managers," tossed the shiny coin into the air and snagged it. Lorrie was sixty and silver-haired. Everybody wanted to adopt her as their grandmother. But in reality Lorrie was the store's top finance, insurance, warranty, and add-on salesperson.

"Tails." Cheatum grinned as she lifted her palm from the back of her hand. "You buy."

"Shoot," Killer said, dropping a coin into the machine as the other guys grinned. "At least you owe me a favor now, honey. Get that Chase deal bought. I got no gross, but I know you'll take care of that if you can get the two of them financed." Everyone chuckled, a respectful laugh of sorts. All the sales staff liked Lorrie—they called her "Magic." She was a miracle worker who could get just about anybody financed, and she would put half of them on "the chart," a nice high interest rate with lots of insurance added on.

Upside down. But Lorrie had a problem with the Chase deal: the guy was in the bucket. He had a trade-in worth $10,000, but he owed $12,000 on it. Sure, his credit was okay, but the guy was a "hand-to-mouth"—every cent he made each month was already obligated to payments, and he didn't have a cent of the $4,000 "down stroke," the cash that would be needed to make up the difference between the $36,000 the finance company had agreed to finance on the new car and the $40,000 Chase would owe on the new car.

"Killer," Lorrie said, "I'll tell you what. If I get him dipped today, you buy me a drink tonight." Killer took Lorrie's hand and kissed it in a grand gesture. "You get him dipped today, my dear, and I'll buy you *two* drinks."

The dip will be the proverbial straw that breaks Al Chase's financial back. When he comes into the store to pick up that shiny new car, Killer will have him sign the normal papers and contract obligating him to 84 payments at $525. He will then pull out another batch of paperwork titled "America's Family Friend National Bank," the second-mortgage company recently formed by the conglomerate that owns AFF. Chase will now sign papers for an additional $6,000, be handed a check, and immediately sign it over to the dealership. He has been dipped. He now owes $36,000 plus interest on one new contract for a car that will be worth $29,000 tomorrow. He also owes $6,000 plus interest on the few pieces of household goods that weren't already mortgaged. With interest, Mr. Chase owes over $53,000 on that car. In four months, when the sap realizes he can't handle those payments, he will come back into the dealership and ask them to buy his car back.

Sure, the dealership will buy it back—for $25,000. But because the "payoff," the net amount owed on that car, will be nearly the same amount he financed and because the payoff on the dip is still the same amount, Mr. Chase won't be able to sell his car. Or, rather, if he sells it, he'll have to pay the dealership the difference between its $25,000 value and the $35,200 payoff. He'll still have the $6,000 loan, too.

But why would the payoff on both loans be almost the total amount financed if Chase has made four payments on each? Surprise: The first year or so payments don't reduce the loan much, they reduce the *interest*.

Avoid dip routines like the plague. Because financing institutions are going to rip your knickers anyway, don't fall for the dip routines, even though car salespeople have such wonderful ways to make them sound sensible. Listen to Killer as he sets up a nice old couple for the kill: "Mr. and Mrs. Carnes, as I told you, the payment on the car will be $525 a month. But what I didn't tell you is that you will pay $525 for only two years. The remaining two years, you'll pay only $375 per month."

Killer smiles, and the couple smiles, too. "Mr. DeMarco, that sounds just fine, but how do you do that?"

Killer smiles again. What a helpful guy. "Folks, what we are going to do is borrow you $3,000 from one company for two years, and only finance $18,500 through the other company. Then, if you get some extra money, you can pay off the small loan sooner. I like to do this for people because it means they owe less on their car. And it's no trouble, really. You'll just need two payment coupons each month, rather than one."

Are you laughing at these suckers? Are you saying to yourself, "Well, I'm not in the bucket, no one will ever dip me?" Don't laugh until you check your payoff. If you are like the vast majority of people, you will probably find out you owe more on your car than the actual wholesale value of the car. Even if you owe a couple of hundred less than the wholesale value, don't smile. Unless you owe at least a thousand less than your car's wholesale value, you are sitting in the bottom of that wet, slimy bucket.

And more people with excellent credit are climbing "in the bucket" (going "upside down") every day because finance institutions now regularly finance up to 100 percent of a vehicle's *sales price*. Used to be, they would finance only "invoice," or what the vehicle supposedly cost the dealership. That has changed. And the change isn't good. Why? You will always, *always* owe thousands more than your vehicle is worth.

Exactly how does a car store or a Web site know how much to dip you? What determines the amount of money financed on any car, new or used? On a new car, it's simple. If you are reasonably strong, if you have a good credit record, virtually all financing institutions will loan you the invoice price of any new car, and many will finance the sales price, as I mentioned. If the total price you want to finance is more than the lending institution's lending limit, the amount over the limit is the "dip."

What if you want a used car? In the past, financial institutions would normally lend you no more than the "loan value" of the vehicle. That's changed. Now, many institutions will finance the actual selling price of the used vehicle.

How to stay out of the bucket. For now, whether you plan to purchase a new or used vehicle, remember that financing a vehicle either at or above invoice or at or above loan value on a used vehicle is the way everyone gets in the bucket in the first place. As we discuss later, you will always want to finance less on any car than the financing source will lend you. If you do that, you really will be able to laugh at all the other suckers.

Singing the Blues:
The Trouble with the Allgoods

Just about the time that Killer delivered the Chases' car, Buck and Samantha opened the door to their car and headed to the showroom. The Allgoods had made their decision: They would not buy on the Web; they would buy directly from a dealer. And they would buy today. Killer walked up to them. "Hi, folks, can I help you?"

"Yes, we'd like to see Mr. DeLong, the Internet representative we saw a few days ago. We told him we'd be back today." My God, Killer thought, some "be-backs" that actually came back.

"Ma'am, I'm sorry, Forrest is off this afternoon. But I'd be glad to help you. Of course, should you buy, the credit would go to Forrest." The Allgoods looked at each other. Well, at least they'd asked for the guy; it wasn't their fault he took the day off. Sure, Mr. DeMarco could wait on them.

You must remember that the Allgoods are the careful shoppers. The previous night, they had pulled the actual invoice of this car from the dealership's Web site, checked those figures against an even more accurate invoice price purchased online from *Consumer Reports,* and finally figured out to the penny the cost of the minivan sitting just outside the showroom door. That morning, before driving to the dealership, they had used the Web to "shop" rates one more time and had even called their bank to check on the latest financing rates. The bank was cheaper. They had also checked the value of their trade on a Web site. The site showed the average wholesale value of their current car to be $2,200.

And then they had called the bank back. "You can expect to see us later in the afternoon. We'll be putting $2,000 down and only want to finance the van for twenty-four months." Allgood placed the receiver down, feeling just fine. Their budget would be a little strained with the short payment period, but it would be worth it. Think of the interest they would save!

Setting the Allgoods up for the kill. Killer had the Allgoods in his office. He liked these people, and he talked at length to them about the careless types who bought so many cars. "Yes, let me tell you, it's refreshing to see people who are thoughtful buyers." Killer took the keys to their trade and excused himself. "Folks, I'll be back in just a few minutes."

He drove their car behind the used-car offices and yelled to Timothy Raxalt, the used-car manager. "Hey, Rax! Come take a look at this car, will you?" The two of them looked over every inch of the car. Each part of it was clean, and the trunk was cleaner than most front seats. Sure, there were a lot of "nickels," small dents from rocks, but for a six-year-old car, this one was a cherry.

Working the used-car department. "Well, what do you think, Rax? It's a hell of a lot more than an average car." Killer was beginning to work the guy. Good salesmen also work the used-car department. Rax flipped open a handheld computer, pulled the wholesale figures on cars like this one directly from a real-time Web page, and quickly shook his head.

"Yeah. These things are real hot this month," Rax said. "I'll tell you what. See if you can trade it for a quarter [$2,500]. If you get close, call me, and maybe I can stretch it a little."

Killer looked shocked. "What do you mean a quarter? You couldn't buy a car like this at the sale for three if you tried all day."

Rax walked around it again. Without saying a word, he called one of the other full-time AFF appraisers in the city, then turned back to Killer. Rax wasn't going out on a limb on that car without some backup, but he'd gotten that. "Killer, if you can trade for the car at $2,800, trade for it. Bobby says it's worth it."

Stepping into trouble. Mr. Allgood had his PDA filled with notations, lying out on the desk when Killer returned. "Mr. DeMarco, so that we won't waste your time or ours, let me review the figures that will be acceptable to my wife and me." Killer sat down and listened thoughtfully. "We have figured the cost of your new van at $16,500. We think a 3 percent profit would be fair to both of us. And I know that my car is worth $2,500. Can you sell us the van with those figures in mind?"

Killer's expression was solemn. "Mr. and Mrs. Allgood, I believe the manager would agree to a 3 percent profit on this van; that may not be a problem. But I'm sorry, your trade-in is nice for its age, but it's not worth $2,500. We have been trading in cars like it for around $2,000."

"Only $2,000!" Allgood was angry. "I know my car's worth more than that. The bank said at least $2,200."

Gotcha! That's what Killer wanted to hear—what the guy really thought he would get for the car. "Mr. and Mrs. Allgood, let me explain the problem. Your car is six years old. Since you are familiar with financing, I'm sure you know that six-year-old cars cannot be financed at most institutions. Even if they can, twelve months would probably be the maximum time it could be financed. That makes it very hard for us to sell the car, since most folks don't pay cash when they buy." Allgood nodded. That made sense.

"Here, let me show you something," Killer said, turning the computer screen on the desk so the Allgoods could see it. Killer quickly pulled up a Web site with the title "DEALERS ONLY. Highest Wholesale Averages. Last 90 Days." He scrolled down to the section for six-year-old vans like the Allgoods' and pointed to the "clean" figure: $2,000. Killer, of course, did not mention that two of his own wholesale boys had said the Allgoods' van was worth $2,800. He didn't tell them the Web site with the $2,000 figure was a "sucker" site that always had low figures on virtually every vehicle. He simply said, "Mr. Allgood, the bank uses those out-of-date books to tell you the value of your car, and that is a disservice. There"—he pointed to the screen, "*that's* what dealers are paying right now . . . but I'm going to talk to our manager and fight for at least a *little* more money for us. I want to make this trade as badly as you folks!"

Killer headed back to the used-car lot. Killer was having fun with this. It was time to work Rax again. He turned up the enthusiasm and charged in the office, "Hey, Rax, I am so close to a deal. Listen, if you'll give me four more, I'll do it. Man, we need this car, I've got someone that will buy it in a minute." Rax started to object. "Wait a minute! If you don't want to put the money in it, just let me take it around town a little. I know I can get $3,200 for it. Rax, you can't put too much money in a car like this."

Killer was probably right, though Rax was nervous. But Killer had dug him out of holes before by selling worthless cars for huge profits. He shook his head. "Okay," Rax said. "But I want you to dehorse the guy. Send him home in your demo tonight. Tell him we need to have the car right now." Rax didn't need to tell Killer that. He never lets people ride when the deal is sweet; they might decide to shop some more.

Done deal. The Allgoods were still sitting there, and both of them watched Killer as he entered the office, a smile on his face. "Folks, we did it! I told that guy we needed help, and he finally agreed. I've got you $2,200 for the car!" The couple shifted in their seats, looked at each other, and then said yes.

The Allgoods paid their 3 percent profit. Plus they gave away their $3,200 car for $2,200. Killer's total gross on the deal was the 3 percent, $450, plus the $1,000 in gross his deal gained by underallowing the Allgoods on their trade.

What did the Allgoods do wrong? They believed in Web sites and books to determine the value of their car. *The only way to really know the value of your trade is to shop it.* No Web site, no used-car buying service can do that for you, either. But chapter 6, "Know your Present Car," will show you how to use those books and services to really know its value and, as importantly, show you how to use them to give notice to the other side that you are used-car savvy, not stupid.

The Newest Toy:
The Problem with the Estrums

Many people just love to buy a new car at intro time. They rush to the closest car store on show day or rush to a popular Web site and invariably pay thousands of dollars more for the honor of being the first kid on the block to own the latest version of the ultimate car.

Take Mr. Estrum, for instance. Phil Estrum barely graduated from high school, but he was smart and ambitious. He entered the insurance field when he was twenty-one; he studied, listened, polished that smooth tongue of his, and became a successful salesmen in five years. He's proud of his profession, too, not something, he felt, that many car salesmen could honestly say. Phil began trading cars every year his third year in the business, and the new one he bought last fall was his tenth.

One of Killer's regular customers. Of course, Phil had dealt with Killer all ten years. After all, he knew from friends that Mr. DeMarco was the top salesman at the store, and Phil likes to deal with the top people in everything. The Estrums had an appointment with Killer one night at eight o'clock. Killer was coming in on his day off, something he made sure the Estrums knew. He even had a little present for Mrs. Estrum, one of those nice large spray bottles of Chanel, which he planned to give her before talking about the new car. Killer knows his psychology. He also knows that other salesmen are always very easy prey for car people, especially when they are "peacocks," the first-kid-on-the-block-with-the-new-toy type of folk. And the Chanel cost Killer nothing, anyway. He'd received it as a gift from the "Expectant Mother's" Web site owners. The customers Killer had referred there had spent over $1,000.

Their meeting evoked one of those reunions of long-lost brothers and sisters, with Killer kissing Sue and grabbing Phil

Estrum's hand in a double grasp. "Come on!" he yelled. "I've got the car over here." It was sitting by itself, away from the other cars and any other distractions that might lessen the moment of unveiling. The car was newly serviced, polished to mirror brightness. The interior lights were left on, too, spreading a nice friendly glow over the contours of velour and leather.

The Estrums drove off alone in that pretty thing. Killer told them to take a nice long cruise, even stop for a drink on the way back. He would have the papers together when they returned; he'd "even have all the figures filled in. That's okay, isn't it, Phil?"

Phil laughed, a repeat of last year's laugh, and the year before that. "Sure, Bob! Why don't we not argue this year!"

"Phil, don't be so rough on me this time! I nearly got fired last year when you finished with me!"

Instead of heading back into the dealership as they drove away, Killer quickly slipped into his demo and swung out toward the Dead End. After all, it was his day off. And it was going to be a day to celebrate, too. Phil Estrum does negotiate each time he buys a car, and he got a good deal. He also received a fair price for his trade. Two things, however, were working against him, as always. Because he just must drive one of the first cars out each year, he's accepted the fact he'll pay some premium for that honor. Killer has reinforced that thought many times, too, reminding Phil that "these cars are impossible to get at intro time, you know that. And don't forget that you will be driving a current-year model for twelve months, not just the seven or eight months you'll have if you wait. Your car will be worth more when you trade."

What's wrong with this deal? The logic is fragile at best, but it works every time on people who want to be convinced. If Phil is determined to trade cars each year, it doesn't matter *when* he trades; it does matter that he trade at the same time each year. Phil could buy the same car in January and normally save $1,500 to $3,000 over an intro deal. His trade wouldn't be worth less the next time around, either, *if* he traded in January again.

Phil's other problem is his own ego, his surefire conviction that "any man who is good at dickering over life insurance is good at dickering over cars." Phil has forgotten that he always oversells insurance to car salespeople *because* of that same logic: Car salespeople are just so sure of themselves as negotiators that they think *they* know how to wheel and deal with their local insurance salesmen.

Maybe Killer and Phil deserve each other, after all.

Facing Our Foibles: The Problem with All Car Buyers

Maybe you've glimpsed someone you know in some action of the Chases, Allgoods, or Estrums. Maybe not. Different personalities, they make different mistakes. But they share one failing: they don't know their own weaknesses. They haven't explored all the important questions. We will.

How Naive Are You Really?

A customer's false pride is a salesman's best friend. The Chases thought they could afford a newer, sportier car, but failed to understand their financial situation. The Allgoods were *sure* they knew how to get the best price for their trade-in. Phil Estrum just had to have a new car at intro time and really believed *any* good salesman could handle car hacks. Car people just love customers like these folks; they feign respect for them and laugh with them, and then laugh *at* them when the commission slips are handed out. You will be richer if you know your limitations in the automobile arena.

Are You an Impulse Buyer? Impulse Buyers Are Favorite Targets

***Nothing* is more impulsive than Web buying.** The dream of every automotive Web seller is to turn a complex, multi-thousand-dollar transaction with huge long-term implications for your credit, your solvency, and your sanity, into a *one-hour, three-click* *sale*. I'm not exaggerating, either. "Three clicks and they buy, that's the goal!"[1] an online trainer cheerily teaches. "When a person clicks on a loan and lease comparison, have a pop-up say 'click here to finance!' Have the customer adjust their down payment, adjust the interest rate, then 'sign here, the car's yours!' Turn that transaction into a one-hour transaction!" No wonder everybody wants a piece of e-commerce.

The danger's as great if you're impulsive at a dealership. Several years ago, a carrier was unloading a bright red $40,000 sports car in front of the largest Gargantula dealership in town. A lady screeched to the curb in her equally elegant sedan. "I want it! I want it!" she screamed. The salesmen fought among themselves for five minutes, trying to decide who would "help" this lady. Finally, a slightly bloodied young man made his way to her side and walked her into the office. The lady wanted a discount of $1,000, and the salesman said no. She agreed on the spot to pay the full price. She then decided to trade in her car. It was appraised at a true value of $9,000. The salesman offered her $7,000, and she said no. The salesman left the office, supposedly to show the car to someone else, and the lady ran after him yelling, "I'll pay it!"

The Core Principle: Don't give away your bargaining power. The lady who just had to have that red sports car paid $4,000 more than she needed to because she had given away her bargaining power. Now we all know you are not going to be that dumb. Never let your enthusiasm show. Never say things like, "It's just what we've been looking for" or "I love that style" (or color, or whatever).

What Should You Buy?

If you are not going to give away your bargaining power, you need to begin by answering honestly some important questions about yourself, your car wishes and requirements, your lifestyle, and your financial situation.

Need Versus Want

The people came into the store a few minutes before closing time. They had just finished their shift at one of those local doughnut shops that make their fare from scratch, and the salesman didn't have to look too hard to see the light touches of flour on their clothes, the tired eyes, and the strained smiles of folks who work hard for a living. Two jobs, really. They both worked at the doughnut shop from 9 A.M. to 6 P.M., and then worked as security guards from midnight to 4 A.M.

Killer was off that night, and a rookie salesman just happened to be walking on the lot as they drove up.

Dreaming of an elegant ride. The couple's old car was as tired as they were. And they were nervous. It was a fortunate thing that an inexperienced salesman was waiting on them—at least it was fortunate for Davies Motors because these two very poor-looking folks wanted to look at an expensive and sporty car. Any experienced salesman would have asked them a few qualifying questions and quickly left them for some other salesperson. After all, how many doughnut people can buy a car that costs twice their yearly income?

Ted, the new guy, hadn't learned to be that sophisticated in his questions, though, and he happily showed them the special Pearl-Wide Limited Edition two-door that stretched low and sleek by the showroom. The Nelsons had never owned a new car. They had four children of their own and a couple of foster kids no one else would take because of their problems. They had a nice, very small house back in the woods. "It's not very fancy, but we're proud of it," they told Ted, the hesitant and defensive nature of their words betraying great discomfort merely at standing on a lot filled with $60,000 cars.

Ted came into Don Burns's office quite casually. "Hey, Don, I've got a deal on these folks." For a new salesman he was a very thorough fellow, and he handed Don a neatly filled out buyer's order, showing a $5,400 profit and an equally neat credit application outlining the financial life of the couple.

The deal looked too nice. The only people who let themselves be taken this badly were always people with bad credit. Don didn't even take the time to enter their name in AFF's credit rating system. Fully expecting to find the rookie salesperson with two flakes, he walked back into the closing booth with Ted and struck up a nice, friendly conversation with the Nelsons.

"Mr. Nelson! I wanted to personally thank you for coming into the dealership today. And I compliment you on your taste in cars—I drive one just like it. By the way, don't you folks work at the doughnut place just down from the courthouse?" Of course they did, Mr. Nelson happily volunteered.

"And I noticed on your credit application that your last car was financed with the Beach Bank. Do you by any chance know Sid Oliver, the chief loan officer?" Yes, they knew him well, Mr. Nelson volunteered with enthusiasm. Don began to take a bit more interest in the couple. People with bad credit don't act enthusiastic when they talk about their loans.

"Well, Mr. Nelson, since this is a pretty expensive car, though it's worth every penny, I think it will help your loan application if we indicate that both of you would like life *and* accident and health insurance on the full amount of the loan. And I think we'd better call this to our *own* financing source. They're much more used to handling cars like this." Why, of course they wanted the insurance. And Don could finance the car wherever the dealership wanted to finance it, "as long as we get the best rate, you know." Of course.

Maxing out the loan. Don immediately e-mailed the dealership's file on the Nelsons' deal to the America's Family Friend subprime in-house financing institution. Within a few more minutes the F&I (finance and insurance) branch manager called back, hesitating just slightly as he spoke.

"Don, you know we could do this loan with our other company at about half the rate?" the guy said. "These people may have never had a payment this large in their life, but they pay everything like clockwork, and they're stable as hell."

Don knew the people would qualify for the cheaper rates at AFF's bank. He also knew the contest for the most monthly loans financed through AFF's subprime company ended in a week. A thousand bucks in walking-around money to the winner in each state! "Let's keep 'em with you," Don told the manager.

"Well, are you really going to keep all that insurance on them? Jeez, that's laughable." Don wanted the insurance on them, too. His commission on the insurance alone would be nearly $1,000. Why, of course, the couple needed the insurance! A $5,400 profit was nice on the deal, but the F&I total profit would be nearly that large. "And besides," Don volunteered, "anyone that works that much might get sick. They need that income protection, too."

A dream come true—until reality strikes. The Nelsons loved that car, caressed it daily, and drove it proudly to work for seven months. But in the first week of that month, Mr. Nelson had appendicitis and missed his paycheck for two weeks. The insurance Don had so happily sold them didn't cover that gap in their income, either, since the insurance didn't begin to pay until the fifteenth day of any illness.

Mrs. Nelson was diagnosed with ulcers a month later and had to miss work for two weeks, too. Ted, the salesman, brought them both to Don's office shortly after that. "Don, we really appreciate all you did for us. But finances are a little tight right now, and we were wondering if you could buy our car back. We'll buy something else from you, of course, that's a little bit more reasonable."

Don shifted in his chair. How could he buy it back? They owed $16,500 more than the car was worth. He found some quick way to hedge—"Luxury cars have really dropped in value, you know"—and excused himself.

Within two weeks they were back again. "Don, please help us. We just can't make the payments. Please do something."

Back to the real world. Don Burns was not totally devoid of heart. Behind the dealership, close to the garbage dump, was a five-year-old station wagon with a broken windshield. The car had been sitting on the lot for over two years after a major wreck and a poor repair job, and had been slowly dying. Besides the broken windshield, the block was cracked a little, and three of the tires were flat. The paint had turned one of those gray-brown colors that is the sign of years of neglect, and dust had settled comfortably on the seats and dash. That car had been written down to nothing. Each ninety days its economic worth lowered, until the moment the comptroller had walked into J. C.'s office and said, "Well, you've got one free now, J. C."

But the wagon did have some value to a small loan house. Don placed a call to the local office of a favorite dip house and quickly arranged a loan for $6,000. He also called the loan manager at the Nelsons' bank and borrowed them another $5,000 on their signature. Banks are very lenient with their regular customers and seldom check credit bureaus or automobile lending institutions if a person pays them regularly. He called another dip house and borrowed the Nelsons $1,500 on their household goods. Most of those goods were already mortgaged, but dip houses don't really care about that, and they listed a couple of bicycles, the old furniture on the back of their porch, and their clothes as collateral.

Don and Ted also worked on that station wagon for the Nelsons. They put on a better set of used tires, replaced the windshield, and actually replaced the block. The car is still running now, and the Nelsons are maybe a little bit happier. Their payment is lower, too. That nice luxury car cost them $1,345 a month. They pay $771 on the five-year-old wagon—the total of their three payments.

If trading cars is something you don't *have* to do, don't do it unless you know you can always sell your car for more than you owe. If you can afford the nicest, smartest car on the block, by all means, buy it, if the vehicle or the mere act of buying it gives you pleasure. Just make sure then that you're strong enough to pay for the damage up front, not down the road.

What Can You Really Afford to Pay Per Month?

The soul of this book, if you think about it, is *budgeting:* that means not unnecessarily wasting your time, your money, or your wits. Most people unfortunately don't budget a car payment. They find a vehicle they like, take the payment the computer spits out as if it's gospel, then rearrange their budget and perhaps eating habits to feed that payment for the next four to seven years. "You know, pinto beans are good for you three times a day," any finance manager will be happy to tell you.

There are better ways to determine a payment you can afford:

- **Think about your current payment.** Can you afford to pay more? How much more? Or, should you be paying less? How much less?
- **Take 15 percent of your gross pay or 20 percent of your take-home pay** as a good payment guideline, if you're solvent, if you're paying your bills on time, and if you're stable in your job.
- **Use a budget calculator.** There are a number of these available online or you can buy budget calculator software programs. Some budget calculators let you input your income and debt and then calculate a payment that you supposedly can afford based on your debt and income. Other calculators let you input the payment you can afford and then tell you how much money the payment you can afford will actually buy you. Both calculators are enormously useful, if they are "honest"—programmed by budget experts, not salespeople. Later we'll give you a great Web site that has both calculators online, and both are honest.

A funny—make that chilling—observation about online budget calculators. *Many Budget Calculators at Commercial Web sites are not "honest."* Virtually every car seller and every car finance company, including the worst subprime sellers, now have budget calculators. But many of these companies unfortunately entice you to use calculators that *destroy* your budget rather than help you protect it! For example, most credit counselors at credit unions recommend you spend no more than 15 percent of your gross pay or 20 percent of your take-home pay on a car payment. For instance, if your gross pay is $2,700, you shouldn't spend more than 15 percent, or $400, on a car payment.

But one budget calculator from a major national lending company—part of a company whose dealers sell both new and used vehicles—used to recommend that you spend *40 percent of your gross pay on a car payment,* or, in our example, *$1,080 per month!* Why would a well-known and respectable financing institution use a budget calculator that recommends a payment more than twice the payment that budget counselors recommend? It's show business, folks! That budget calculator's job is to entice you to buy more car, not to objectively help you budget.

But if your budget can stand only a $400 payment, what happens to you when the payment is over $1,000? Well, that's *your* problem, folks! The Web site puts a small disclaimer on their calculator saying it may not work for everyone. Ergo, you are ruined and they are off the hook.

Calculators can be "loaded" to achieve any objective. If your business is only financing vehicles, you want your calculator to charge a higher interest rate. If your business is just selling used vehicles, you want to provide a calculator that gives you, the seller, the most money out of that payment. If you both sell and finance, you want everything to be high. High tech makes this so-o-o easy! "You can 'engineer' a calculator to do anything you want it to," says a trainer at TargetLive.com.[2]

In reality, you can "engineer" a calculator to do only one of two things: calculate an honest, mathematically sound answer based on sound data, or calculate a dishonest, mathematically unsound answer based on "loaded" data that pushes an agenda, such as selling cars.

"So, what's the message about payment calculators?" Stay away from commercial budget and payment calculators. Also stay away from calculators that won't let you input the *payment you can afford* and then tell you how much money that payment will buy you. That concept is called "loan cash," and you'll learn lots about it in chapter 8.

New Versus Used: What's Better for You?

Medora and Taylor Espy had come to the dealership planning to buy a $15,000–$20,000 used four-wheel-drive SUV. They always purchased serious off-road SUVs that were about three years old but still suitable for serious off-road camping expeditions with the couple's dogs.

The Espys are in their midthirties, a very laid-back twosome who have lived together for eight years, plan to get married this fall on their farm, and seldom do rash or wasteful things. However, their rational thinking was disturbed this day because there was a new-car sales contest in progress for the guys at Killer's dealership, and our Salesman of the Year needed just one more new vehicle to get those five nights at the Wynn Resort in Las Vegas, Killer's idea of real class.

Of course, Killer didn't get the Espys by accident. He'd been looking regularly at the "tracker" reports of visitors to the dealership's online listing of off-road vehicles. The Espys had "hit" the site three times in three days, always asking for a listing of used off-road vehicles rather than new. They had also "cruised over" the site five times without even opening the site—AFF's very sophisticated "Stalker/Vision"[3] Web monitor could see those "stealth" visits. The couple were restless, Killer thought; they wanted that off-road baby right away.

The dealership unfortunately had no late-model used offroaders at that time. But a very expensive new SUV in stock just happened to be at the top of the bonus chart that would send Killer to Vegas. Mr. DeMarco very quickly decided that the Espys should be driving a new off-roader. But "Internet coordinator" DeMarco's e-mail to the couple had not mentioned new or used, it had simply said, "I think we have the four-wheeler you have been looking for." The e-mail was a stock one in the computer's memory. "I think we have" e-mail responses to any query never mentioned new or used. The objective was to get an "up" tied down to the dealership, then a smart salesperson could sell the up what that salesperson or dealership needed to sell, new or used. Technology!

Killer's opening moves. Killer met the Espys at their car, a Toyota 4Runner parked just between the new-car storage lot and the used-car lot, and quietly started laying out his most effective new-car sales pitch. Killer already knew a lot about these strangers. Minutes before they arrived, he had used the "Tell Me" search engine on the America's Family Friend DataMerger program that used information drawn from cookies to look at their shopping habits, and they were indeed "crunchy." They shopped Lands' End regularly, had recently ordered "natural" vitamins from an AFF subsidiary, donated to their local Animal Rescue Fund, and voted the Green party. These two were definitely whale huggers, Killer thought with a smile as he began to work them.

"Mr. and Mrs. Espy, we do have a nice used 4Runner coming in this afternoon. But let me ask you something," he said, while walking slowly toward the rugged new Expenso DuneKrusher five-door. Killer knew the people would walk with him; they always did. After all, who wants to appear rude?

"Would you consider buying a new SUV, one with a warranty, one that no one has abused and that will be much more economical to operate? Would you consider that, if you could drive it with no more debt than a used one and with a payment that's even lower than a used one? Oh, and with that purchase, we donate a portion of our profits to Greenpeace."

Both of the Espys had started to interrupt Killer the moment he mentioned a new vehicle, but he just kept talking. By the time he'd presented his irresistible logic, they'd stopped walking and looked at each other. "Mr. DeMarco, just how are you going to do that?" Espy shook his head just enough to flick his ponytail and smiled ironically at Killer.

Killer laughed. "Now, Mr. Espy, I can do it, but that wasn't the question. Would you consider a new off-roader under those circumstances?"

"Well, if you're telling me I'll owe less on a new car than a used one, and that my payments will be less, I guess I'd be interested. I don't think you can do that, though." Mr. Espy looked both skeptical and hopeful—who wouldn't rather drive a new car?

Killer unlocked the driver's door of the army-green DuneKrusher and sat down, one button unlocking the passenger doors, cracking the windows a bit, and tilting the moonroof. "Mr. and Mrs. Espy, sit down for a moment and let me show you a few things."

Without hesitating the Espys got in the vehicle. It's a nice psychological trick: Don't ask people to do things, assume they'll do them—most people do. Killer pumped the pedal twice, starting the double air conditioners at the same time, talking quietly as he sat there.

Medora Espy made the first really positive statement. "My, it smells so good. Why does it?" She was giving the first buying signal. Killer looked at Taylor Espy's shirt pocket—there were no cigarettes there.

"That's the smell of a car with no cigarette smoke or spilled beer on the seats, Mrs. Espy."

"Oh, really, I like that. You know we never let people smoke in our cars."

"That's a mighty good thing, ma'am. You just wouldn't believe the things our used-car people have to do to make some cars clean." Both Espys nodded without realizing it.

"Mr. Espy, do you know a road around here that's really rutted and bumpy?" They were pulling out of the lot as Killer spoke. He hadn't asked them if they wanted to go for a ride; he'd just assumed they would.

"Well, there's that road that goes out to the mill—it's closed now, but it's a nice one." Killer was conveniently already heading in that direction as Espy opened the glove box, then ran his hand down the side of the seat.

Killer said, "You know, these seats are orthopedically designed, and the rear seat has been angled differently this year—better support there, too. Mrs. Espy, how does it feel?"

She laughed. "Well, I'll tell you one thing, it's more comfortable than *our* backseat!" This was another buying signal.

As Killer headed down the road, he suddenly steered the right wheels off the road, two wheels traveling on the pavement and two along a rutty shoulder. The Espys lit up. "How do you like *this* for a nice ride? I'll bet you couldn't do it in your Toyota."

"That's really something," Medora Espy said. "Do you do this with everyone?" Killer always does. It's not that a new vehicle really rides better than an older one, but that normal people don't suddenly drive off the road too much. The Espys weren't thinking that, of course. They were just impressed with the ride.

Then the four-wheeler stopped unexpectedly, and Killer walked around to the passenger side and opened the door. "Mr. Espy, I thought *I'd* ride a little, if you don't mind." Taylor Espy might not have wanted to drive the car right then, but what was he going to do, tell Killer to walk back around?

This was the turning point in Killer's sell job. Getting Espy into the driver's seat was the most important thing Killer needed to accomplish to sell that car—more important even than getting a deposit. Very few of us can resist the exhilarating pleasure of driving a new car, especially when we are quietly thinking, This car can be mine for less money than a used one. But it's not a logical statement, is it? Read on.

Killer normally doesn't take people to his office when he's planning to show them a lot of figures. He takes them to the "box," the small room with a window overlooking the lot. The Espys were sitting on either side of him facing that window, the new army-green DuneKrusher conveniently visible. "Before we talk figures, Mr. and Mrs. Espy, I want to ask you just one thing. Do you really like this specific vehicle? Do you like it better than any used vehicle you've ever owned?"

"Yes, we like it very much, but there's the money problem," Taylor Espy answered.

"Well, then, let me ask you this: Will you buy it if it makes financial sense to buy it?"

The technique is called an "early close." A "yes" means the car is sold, and the Espys said yes.

Killer drew a vertical line down a sheet of paper, putting the list price of the new SUV, $39,800, in one column and the "asking price" of an imaginary three-year-old, $20,000, in the other column. Where did he get that figure? He'd asked the Espys what they had planned to spend on a used SUV. He then deducted $6,000 from both figures. "Let's just assume that your trade is worth this, folks. It's what older 4Runners like yours have been coming in for."

Killer paused for a minute for any reaction, but there was none. Good, he thought. We won't have to argue about their trade. It was a very safe way to find out what the Espys thought their car was worth. If they'd jumped, Killer would have said, "Now, that's what the *average* car like yours has been bringing. I'm sure when we have it appraised, yours will be worth more."

The pitch. "Now, just for comparison's sake," said Killer, "we're going to forget that you owe anything on your present car. I believe you said the payoff was $800, and since you are paying $1,000 down, we don't really need to be concerned with your payoff." That sounded logical, Mr. Espy thought. "Now, we have a balance on the new DuneKrusher of $33,600 and on a used one of $13,800. Used cars, as you know, especially when they're three years old, can generally be financed for only three years. And we're required to finance at a higher interest rate, too. If you were to finance $13,800 on a used one for three years, your payments would be . . . " Killer began to type quickly on his keyboard, dropping in the highest interest rate, the one that was really never used, then dropping in premiums for life, accident, and health insurance on them both. "Let's see, the payment would be about $707 a month." The Espys, stunned, said nothing.

Killer continued talking. "As you know, there really are no inexpensive used cars anymore. Now, on the new car, we have a balance of $33,600. We usually finance new cars on seventy-two months and, of course, finance them at a lower rate. Let's see what your payment would be." This time Killer figured the payment on the "discount rate"—what the dealership actually paid for money for the loan. He seldom sold cars at that rate, but this time he was taking no chances. Killer conveniently neglected to add insurance to the payment. "There! Your payments on the new car will be only $548 per month."

What about those extra three years? Answering the customer's objection. "Yes," Mr. Espy said quickly, "but we're paying three more years than on a used car."

"That's right. But remember, you would probably be trading in the old car in thirty-six months, anyway. Then you'd be making more payments, probably on another used SUV. Isn't it better to be making payments during those last three years on the SUV you have babied for the first three years? And what will you have spent on service on the older vehicle? On tires? Unexpected breakdowns?" At this point, like the Espys, you're probably thinking: Honestly, don't I deserve this? And who can argue with that payment!

The Espys took delivery in an hour. The payment was just a little higher than the $548 figure that had been discussed, however. "Folks, I'm embarrassed to tell you this, but I completely forgot to figure your life and health insurance payment when we were talking. It's my fault, and I'll understand if you don't want to take the car. But all that protection is just a Coke or two a day." They took the insurance. Killer also hadn't mentioned the seven-year bumper-to-bumper warranty. That wasn't even a Coke a day! The two items raised the Espys' final payment to $655, and added $2,500 profit to the deal, too.

Killer gave Medora and Taylor Espy each a DuneKrusher Windbreaker as a driving-off present. The cost to Killer? Fifteen bucks apiece. Not a bad investment for five free nights in Vegas!

What happened to our crunchy friends? First the Espys fell prey to the logic of numbers that lie too easily. Then they accepted Killer's figures on the potential used car they were looking for without once questioning their accuracy. Then they believed the used-car values that Killer pulled up on the screen. And, finally, they took delivery of that handsome DuneKrusher *on the spot.* Wouldn't it have been better to wait a day, defuse, and think?

Don't for a minute think the Espys are unhappy, though. They will love this car for every year they own it. They just ended up paying $7,200 more than necessary to buy it.

New cars in general are the worst investment you can make with your money. In fact, ninety-nine out of a hundred new vehicles will drop *40 percent in value* the day they're driven home. For instance, let's say you buy a stripped-down Expenso Minutia, the cheapest car in the Expenso line. The MSRP (manufacturer's suggested retail price—the sticker price from the factory, craftily bonded to the vehicle's window with kryptonic glue) is $11,000. The true cost of this particular Minutia including the holdback profit[4] is $8,600. Deduct from that the "freight" charges for transporting that Minutia to the dealership. Our Minutia's true cost to the dealer is now $8,200. Now deduct the many funny dealer charges such as "preparation," "advertising," and "gas and oil." The true cost of your Minutia—the replacement cost for the dealer to buy another one, for instance—is now $8,000.

The week after you take delivery, your Ouija board tells you to immediately trade the Minutia back to the same dealer. Since you live next to the dealership, the Minutia only has fifty miles on it. The car is virtually new. But because it has now been "titled," the vehicle is technically *used*. And the dealer knows he can order an officially *new* car exactly like it from the factory for $8,000. You paid $11,000. But why should the dealer even give you $8,200? He shouldn't and he won't. So, what will the dealer in all likelihood give you? Try $6,400—60 percent of its MSRP—or less. That's about like my stock market record.

The Very Good News: The right used vehicle wisely bought can be a great thing for both your wallet and your driving enjoyment. And America is overflowing with great, late-model used vehicles. Plus, the Internet offers you a tremendous opportunity to find exactly the used vehicle to fit your needs. The proliferation of companies with a Web presence allows you to sell your old wheels online and examine hundreds of thousands of used cars from the safety of your laptop. Using these services, you can bid on used cars, put warranties on them, and of course finance them. If you've never considered buying or leasing used, you should, unless you have money to burn. Of course, to protect yourself you've got to know how to do that the right way. We'll make you a pro in the used-car arenas—online and off—in chapters 12 and 14.

American Versus Foreign: Is There a Meaningful Difference?

Foreign car manufacturers still bill themselves as makers of the best chariots available. Specifically, for a very few vehicles, this is consistently true. We'll show you how to find those vehicles and review them online. But generally, I believe that the myth of foreign superiority is just that—a myth—particularly since "foreign" and "domestic" don't really exist anymore. All the "American" manufacturers either own or are owned significantly by foreign manufacturers. Everybody knows Toyotas are now made in the U.S. of A. Everybody assumes DaimlerChrysler is finally bringing more quality to all those snappy Chrysler products. Such marriages have made all the children pretty much alike, and that is good.

But, if you hold grudges, there may be one reason to consider American-made vehicles, if you can find one, over a vehicle made by a purely foreign manufacturer. During all those years when foreign cars were the only sensible answer for sensible people, the import manufacturers and dealers were ripping off your pocketbook on a scale greater than anything Detroit would ever attempt. They saw no reason to ever, ever give the customer a break. The most popular foreign cars were often sold for *more* than list price. A $15,000 car, for instance, would have a little item like this added to the dealer sticker (more on that later): Added Value Package $1,500.

Do you know what's included in that package? *Nothing*. The dealer had just decided that his car is worth an extra $1,500. One dealer in California became so cocky he also added an *additional* $1,500 charge and blithely labeled it "DVF." Sales personnel, of course, weren't supposed to tell customers that DVF stood for "dealer vacation fund."

The practice of inflating the already handsome asking price of certain cars became so widespread that many consumer groups, even now, are bringing suits against individual dealers and manufacturers.

Will You Be "Trading Down"?

"Trading down" doesn't mean buying a car from a dealer located on the wrong side of the tracks. Rather, "trading down" is a term used to describe buyers planning either (a) to trade their newer car for an older one or (b) to trade their very expensive luxury car for a basic, stripped model. It can also refer to buyers trading very big cars for very small ones. Regardless of what situation the term refers to, the process is always expensive.

People who want to trade a newer car for an older one usually can't afford their current monthly payments. They're paying dearly for buying without budgeting, something we won't let happen to you. The same is true for people who want to trade down to a less luxurious car. The people in both situations face the same obstacles.

First, because your newer or more luxurious car was so expensive when you bought it, your payoff on the car is usually very high (and its wholesale cash value relative to the lesser car you want to purchase may be high). This hurts you, but, more important, it hurts the dealer, too, because such a car requires a dealer to pay cash from *his* pocket to deal with you. Dealers therefore give you relatively less for your trade if you owe a lot on it.

Second, another obstacle when you trade down is your incorrect belief that your nearly new car is worth a lot of money. But, remember the 40 percent depreciation in the first day we talked about a few pages ago? Well, your car just keeps on depreciating. At the end of two years, it's probably not worth 50 percent of its new-car sticker price. But dealers know you are going to expect thousands more than that. You're going to be hard to trade with and much harder to make a nice profit on. You're not a popular customer in this instance, either.

Finally, there's the most obvious and depressing reason you're unpopular with dealers if you are trading down, the reason why salespeople wince when a customer mentions the possibility. For most of you, it means you're in the bucket, you owe more than your car is worth. You can't even give the thing away without handing over a pile of cash with your wheels.

Before you decide to trade down, read carefully the sections on "retailing" your own car beginning on page 172. Your best chance in a trade-down situation is to do just that.

Things That Impress and Terrify Salesmen: Traits You Can Cultivate

In addition to arriving at an understanding of your wishes and your realities relative to cars, you can develop some personal attitudes and behaviors that will work for you and not against you in the whole car shopping-negotiation-and-buying transaction. Let's start with the attitude you should adopt from the very first, whether you are just browsing some car sites on the Net or have dropped by a showroom.

Taking Control and Staying in Charge

On the Web. Charles Pierce, customer-facing Web manager for all 250 dealerships in the America's Family Friend chain, stared at his 20-inch plasma monitor. For a man who was a consummate technogeek, Charles was both handsome and charming, even in his e-mails; never at a loss for words. But right there on the screen, in an e-mail from some woman that Charles had already identified as a highly qualified prospect to buy today, were questions that stunned his busy hands into action. "It's a good thing this is just a beta test," he muttered as he looked at the message again:

Before I go any further, tell me specifically

1.   Have you opened a file on me because I have browsed your site?
2.   Do you already have any information stored on me in your data banks other than my name?

3. Do you have any information on me from any other dealings I may have had with your dealership chain?

4. Specifically, do you have any credit information on me from any source, including information on my buying habits?

5. I do not give you permission to gather either credit information or other data on me without my specific written permission.

Who did this woman think she was? Where did she get those questions? And did she really think he would answer them in writing? Lord! Were there going to be many customers out there like her?

On the showroom floor. Forrest DeLong was losing patience with his prospect, too. She was just too damned flighty: liking a small car and then a large car, in love one minute with a four-door and then wanting to drive a two-door. And now she was trying to change her mind again, just as he laid the buyer's order in front of her. Dammit. This type of bird was even worse than the other one he'd had less than six hours ago, the man who didn't like anything. Never once showed an ounce of enthusiasm for anything on the lot! At least that guy bought a car from him. It wasn't much of a deal, less than $200, but, hell, Forrest didn't think the guy was even interested. And the guy had made it damn clear that he didn't really need to buy a car from here, anyway. At least it was a sale, Forrest kept telling himself.

Even Killer is in trouble today. It must have been the moon, Killer thought. His first customer, sent to him by a bird dog, was nice enough but just wouldn't fall for any of Killer's lines. "Now, Mr. DeMarco, let's just keep this sweet and simple," he'd say. "If you want to sell me a car, and I am really going to buy one in the next two days, let's get my car appraised before we go any further."

"I'm afraid I can't tell you what it's worth until we know what you're trading for," Killer had responded with an amused smile. But his ploy didn't work. The man raised his hand in a "stop" gesture and continued, "That won't work with me, Mr. DeMarco. I've already shopped my car at three places and know pretty much what it's worth. And I'll be *real* interested in seeing how close your guys are."

Under protest, Killer drove the car to the used-car department and nearly dropped his teeth when the guys there said they'd already put a figure on the car the day before, a strong one.

And after agreeing to the trade figure (how could Killer argue?), the man then proceeded to bargain like he knew what he was doing. Killer was on the phone to Allen, his bird dog, as soon as the guy drove out. "Hey, Allen, do me a favor and send that type of guy to someone else, okay?"

Some people get good deals on cars by accident, some get them by design. The woman whose e-mail stunned Charles Pierce was determined to let whoever might be examining her life know that she was not going to be fooled or controlled by a Web site and its anonymous salespeople. Forrest DeLong's customer did buy a car that day, a quick, easy deal, because she was the indecisive type. Killer's man got a good deal because he'd certainly done his groundwork.

These customers succeeded because they understood the things that really impress and terrify car salespeople:

1. Wariness on the Web

The Web-based sellers in particular thrive on the cockiness of knowing that their average customer doesn't have the vaguest clue what happens beyond that customer's keyboard. Ignorance has always been the false bliss of car transactions. The Web-based sellers have focused on that ignorance and tried very hard to romanticize the online transaction, making it appear to be what all frazzled and nervous car shoppers want: safe and fair. But in reality, the Web-based sellers thrive on rote response driven by statistics, canned sincerity, and inflexibility. There's no such thing as too many concerns, here, so don't be afraid to voice them.

Keep up that wariness when you visit the dealership in person, as well, particularly when it comes to unauthorized credit checks or giving deposits.

2. Indecision

If you are the indecisive type, you may be a lucky car shopper and a very lucky car buyer. No matter what their flowery mission statements, salespeople are not really interested in long-term relationships. They need to sell you a car right now! On the Web, the pressure on salespeople is like the pressure on day traders in stocks—it's impersonal, relentless, and dangerous to the salesperson's future. So turn that pressure to your advantage: Be indecisive, even after you sign a buyer's order at a dealership or receive the Web paperwork in the mail. Don't be shy about stopping the transaction, changing your mind, and looking for your exit opportunities.

3. Lack of Enthusiasm

You are taking a 360-degree virtual tour online or are actually standing by the one and only new car in the world you think you love. It's the perfect color, it has all the right options, including color night vision and an "Aspen Air" automatic nasal spritzer. Your instinct is to kiss it right then and there, then click the AGREED button or take it home that instant.

Don't. Tell your salesman how much better you like some other car down the road. Send a DECLINE message to the Web site.

Lack of enthusiasm is one of the easiest things you can do to protect yourself in a car negotiation. Put yourself in a salesperson's place for a moment. That person spends days talking or e-mailing countless people who spend the salesperson's time but don't spend money. "Thank you very much, I'll be back" is the salutation most salespeople hear relentlessly, and consider the bane of the business, because 90 percent who say they will be back, won't.

It's vital, then, for a salesperson to sell you the first time you step foot on his lot. That's why almost all dealerships and all Web sites have specific, tough procedures to make sure you don't disappear too quickly. *All* training manuals for sales staffs make that point vehemently, as this quote from a popular manual shows:

"Customers will not be *allowed* to leave without talking to management." (emphasis added) Most salespeople are also told that breaking this commandment will cost them their jobs. So, how does a salesperson feel if you're not enthusiastic, if you can't find one single car you really like, if you do nothing but talk about the *really* nice car you saw down the road or on another Web site, and the really nice price the other folks gave you? One of the first axioms every car salesman learns is "Be-backs won't make you any greenbacks." There is nothing stronger in your favor than that fear.

4. Nonromantic Attitudes

However hard you work at your car-buying skills, you know that you aren't going to win every battle. So why should your eyelids flutter with the romance of it all? Why should you use caps in an e-mail? Let the salesman know you consider a car or truck a necessary evil, not your paramour. Let him know you have better things to do with your time. Tell him straight out your romantic qualities concern your pocketbook only.

5. Patience

Patience is sort of a summary trait, isn't it? But even if you have done your homework, and even if you forgot to hide your enthusiasm and let "Well, I really do like it" slip out of your mouth before you can catch the words and pull them back, patience will save you. Here's the one rule worth repeating at this stage: *Never buy a car on the first visit to a Web site or a dealership.*

6. Impatience

You'll need just as much of the opposite of patience, too! The worst dealer sales tactics survive because of the niceness and timidness of customers. Dealers and Web sites use your good manners against you. They believe nice people just don't get up and walk out, or sign off without so much as a good-bye. Nice doesn't mean dumb. Walk out or sign off pronto if the sale becomes bothersome.

Steel Boots Prevent Shot Feet

No one wants to shoot themselves in the foot, but most car buyers do just that during an auto transaction because they don't really understand either their own motives or the dealership's gimmicks. If you've survived reading and absorbing even a part of this chapter, you've just cinched on some pretty bulletproof shoes in the ongoing battle to prevent self-inflicted wounds in the automotive battlefield. Now, how about some more armor?

Chapter 6

Know Your Present Car

Do Three Wrights Make a Wrong?

Jim Wright III, called Trey, was born in the 1960s when his dad, Jim Jr., was twenty-three, a new car could be bought for $2,000, fenders looked like rockets, and the auto business was in a gold rush: Dealerships minted money. It was a time when everyone was in love with cars and few people had the vaguest idea what mystical formulas constituted the buying and financing process. But, who cared? It was certainly a more informal business then. Cars didn't have "sticker prices." At one moment, a brawny Pontiac Firebird might have a list price of $2,000, and the next moment a price of $3,000. *Caveat emptor,* let the buyer beware, was the auto industry's most appropriate motto.

Financing was downright fun during those years, too. Most stores were still "recourse" operations: Each dealer would have to guarantee payments to lending institutions on every car sold. If you lived in a small town and happened to know someone who worked at a dealership, credit applications just didn't exist. A quick call saying, "Yes, these folks are good people," carried much more weight than any impersonal sheet of paper that bared your financial soul to the world.

Used cars were still the stepchildren of the automobile business back then. Dealerships would take your car in trade, but would usually whisk that old thing off to some used-car lot down on the other side of the tracks. Or they'd sell it to a "road hog," probably the father of some road hog who frequents American's Family Friend dealerships today. Not many self-respecting persons then seriously considered buying used cars.

Jim Wright Jr. certainly felt that way, particularly with new baby Trey to transport, and particularly when you consider what he was driving. Given to him by his father, Jim Jr. drove a nine-foot-long black English Ford with stunted mechanical wings that popped up from the door jambs for turn signals. The thing looked just like a quarter-size London cab. At a time when a Chevy Malibu had 400 galloping horsepower, the boxy English Ford had twenty-six. Not a car any self-respecting twenty-three-year-old would drive.

Jim Wright Jr. wasn't sure he had the money for a new car, but what was the harm in looking? He and his wife, Gloria, drove that English Ford to the Chevrolet dealership, the one with the fancy new showroom overlooking the intersection of every important road leading to town. The shimmering new Chevys were lined up in front of that showroom like a chorus line of Vegas showgirls all dressed up in sexy colors. There wasn't a black car in sight, much less anything square with little wings.

Dancing at the very center of that line was the most beautiful thing young Mr. Wright and his wife had ever seen: a candy-apple-red, two-door Malibu Sports Coupe with a wraparound windshield! Now, here was the car for an up-and-coming young family!

Jim Wright was surprised how easily that car became theirs. The man who talked with him barely mentioned the boxy Ford. "Oh, we'll take it off your hands," he said, adding in the same breath, "and your payments on the new one are only going to be $70 a month! *And* it's got a balloon." That all sounded like a dream! The Wrights said yes, didn't mind it when the salesman at the last minute talked them out of $400 in cash (the Wrights' only savings) "to pay the fees," and drove home ecstatic. Their paperwork would be mailed to them.

That candy-apple-red Chevrolet was the beginning of Jim Wright Jr.'s education in the car business. About six weeks later, a young couple on Elm Street bought a Chevy just like it and just happened to mention to Jim Wright Sr. that "$2,500 isn't much money for something like this." Mr. Wright looked at them for a second before speaking. "You say $2,500? Well, it can't really be the same car as my son's; he paid $3,500 for his."

Not too many days later, young Jim saw his old English Ford sitting on a shabby used-car lot on the outskirts of town. BUY HERE, PAY HERE! an enormous sign proclaimed. The lot wanted *$1,100* for his old car. How could it be worth that? Had he given it away to the Chevy dealer? And then there was the "balloon." Jim's dad was the one who saw it on the contract when it finally arrived. The installment loan contract called for twenty-three payments of $70. And one final payment of $2,000—the equivalent of about $8,000 today.

Jim Wright Jr. drove the Malibu for exactly twenty-three months and then had to sell it to the dealership for a $1,600 loss. He had no choice. Neither he nor his dad could afford the balloon payment. He had no choice when he bought a used car from the shabby "Buy Here, Pay Here" lot, either. The bank wouldn't finance him right then. For $50 a month, the Buy Here, Pay Here lot sold him the black English Ford with the stunted wings. Just $50 a month for thirty months.

Getting it right. In three years, on his twenty-eighth birthday, Jim Jr. bought his second new car. He didn't trade his old car this time, moreover, but sold it himself. He and Gloria put away their emotions as they shopped more than one dealership. Regardless of what any previous dealership had said, Jim told them, one and all, "Your price is too high."

The Wrights finally bought their car from the same dealership and salesman who had nearly ruined them before, but at the right price this time. They didn't finance at that store, either, but took the time to shop their financing options at several banks. The Wrights have bought eleven cars since then. Their cautious nature has saved them over $50,000, and that cautious nature has been passed on to their son and daughter-in-law, Trey and Dana, as we will see.

The Previous Sections of This Book Haven't Exactly Added to the Romance and Mystique of Auto Transaction, Have They?

They may have convinced you to sell your computer and skateboard to work rather than drive. And it may not make you feel any better to know that most of the same techniques and half-truths used in the auto business are used by most salespeople, whether they sell washing machines or cemetery lots.

It's really hard, however, for an appliance salesperson to inflict great damage on your pocketbook. And I doubt if you've ever daydreamed about shopping for a newer and better mausoleum slot. We only do that with our toys, and very few toys have the potential to ruin you as quickly as your car. That's why this book is designed to inoculate you from unbridled enthusiasm the next time your natural urge compels a trip to the local car store or a cyberjourney to those sexy car sites on the Web.

The More Things Change, the More They Stay the Same

In one sense, everything has changed in the car business since the 1960s, though you can see few of the changes, and very little of the change is good for the casual consumer's pocketbook. In another sense, *nothing* has changed in the car business since the 1960s:

- Credit applications aren't really needed anymore because sellers already know everything about you, including your sock size.
- Ruinous "balloon" payments are back with a vengeance. In a riotous irony, GMAC now calls their balloon payment

scheme "SmartBuy," when, for thousands who have already used it, it is a dumb buy.

- Your trade-in is your budget's Achilles' heel again. If you're not wary, dealerships and online services steal them left and right.
- The actual price of a new car doesn't mean anything once more. Anybody will give it away for no profit if they must just to hook you on the extras.
- Once again, in the Brave New Automotive World, few customers have the vaguest idea what mythical formulas constitute the buying and financing process.
- To the utter joy of the industry, the excitement is back in the car business!
- And caveat emptor rules again.

What dangerous realities! But you can manage those realities if you think Zen, not zaniness. You are not too busy to do this correctly.

Doing It Right in the Brave New Automotive World

After all, if Trey Wright and his wife, Dana, both in their forties, have the time and patience to learn the tricks of the Brave New Automotive World, you do, too. Dana edits books and doesn't even balance her checkbook. Trey is a senior account executive at the biggest ad agency in town. He's on the road four days a week and tries to hit the hotel health clubs while he's on the road, but instead ends up hitting the bar for a single drink to relax.

Four months ago, Trey and Dana took delivery on a really nice Gargantula YouthSeeker, and they were just as excited about picking up that shiny beauty as anyone in the world. What's even nicer is the Wrights' feeling about that car right now. They haven't had a moment of buyer's remorse. Not a second of doubt has plagued them, and I daresay none will. These people love cars in the most irrational way, but they have learned to keep that emotion far away from any decision-making process. The Wright family, by lucky trial and error, through the years has learned just what *you* need to know, and it revolves around four questions:

- What is your old car worth in actual wholesale dollars?
- What does their car cost?
- What is a fair profit?
- What is the cheapest and most advantageous financing?

If you listen to the pitchman in the Brave New Automotive World, all those questions can be answered in a millisecond with nary a worry. If you believe that, you don't need to be reading this book.

So, what is your time worth? Our way of buying or leasing is going to take you thirty hours in total, probably. Not one hour, as many Internet sellers and dealerships fervently hope. But our way might save you $4,000, or, as car people are fond of saying, "$4,000 *or more!*"

Do you work more than thirty hours (about three days) to take home $4,000 after taxes? If you do, keep on reading as this chapter shows you how to determine the right answer to the first of those four important questions: *What is your old car worth in actual wholesale dollars?*

Making Your Current Car Worth More

If you listen to the other side, the value of your current car is a set amount. Just look it up on the Web! That expensive fantasy is designed to enrich the other side. Remember that the trade-in is one of the main profit centers for dealers, brokers, and buying services. Your old car actually has a unique value based upon

- its condition,
- its popularity at the moment in your local area,

- the market needs of the wholesaler who is considering buying it from you (does that wholesaler already own too many vehicles like yours, for instance?),
- the sophistication of the appraiser, and,
- most important, upon your individual car's "aura," to use a nice, crunchy term. How does the car strike the potential buyer? That aura can impact your old car's value immeasurably, and that aura can be enhanced by a bit of elbow grease.

Sending the car to the stylist. Trey and Dana Wright know all about aura. These two aren't exactly fastidious about their cars. Under the front seat of one, for instance, is a vintage collection of crumpled Boston Market containers, one coat hanger, a couple of pens, two unlit cigarettes, a Nicorette gum foil cover, one sock, half of a Southeastern United States road map, a toll receipt from the Florida turnpike, matches, and a very dirty rag used frequently to wipe condensation from the windshield. On the whole, a good imitation of the city dump. The dashboard is littered with the everyday needs of busy people, and the trunk contains enough forgotten merchandise to supply at least half of the Salvation Army's annual Christmas drive.

"Dana, will you look at this!" Trey had been rummaging under the seat when something soft and mushy stuck in the springs caught the attention of his hand. It was a baked potato. "I *knew* we'd ordered four potatoes! Now how the devil did it get under there?"

"Who knows. Maybe the seat was hungry." Dana was standing by the back door counting the change, over $14 worth of nickels, quarters, and pennies. "You know, I think money multiplies back there. We should pull this seat out more often."

The Wrights' cleaning exercise was not a frequent ritual, but it was a regular one. Every few years at car trading time, they spend a day working on every inch of the car—a task they aptly refer to as "sending the car to the stylist." Trey removed the ashtrays and soaked them, then he used a brush on every single piece of chrome, including the ones most people don't look at too often, such as the ones around each wheel opening. He cleaned the hundreds of little road tar specks that dotted the entire bottom third of the car body.

They also used a brush on the grill. The damn thing was always a final resting place for careless bugs. Every single inch of the car's interior was scrubbed with a brush, too, including the headliner. Then all four doors were left open for hours. All in all, the Wrights' cleaning job would rival any scrub nurse's efforts at the local hospital.

But is all the cleaning worth it? Can a clean car really be worth more than a dirty one? Absolutely. A clean car implies something significant to road hogs and other used-vehicle appraisers. Car people, like most of us, assume that people who really take care of the way their car looks also take care of it mechanically. That is a very dangerous assumption, but use it to your advantage. Whether you're planning to sell your car or trade it (or even give it to charity for a tax deduction), make it gleam like new. Make the trunk spotless. If you have a little tear in the backseat, fix it yourself, or throw a pair of very dirty socks on it.

Does your old car have minor mechanical problems? Is the A.C. on the blink because the fuse is blown? Replace the fuse. Used-car appraisers can be very lazy, and may assume your compressor is bad, regardless of what you tell them. A fifty-cent fuse can cost you $1,000 at appraisal time.

How's the paint? Don't repaint your car if the paint is dull or scratched. Appraisers and potential customers generally believe freshly painted used cars have been in fender benders. That new paint job could cost you $500 or $1,000. Do touch up nicks if you have a properly matching paint. Do buff dull paint. You'll be making hundreds of dollars an hour in wholesale value.

Is Your Old Vehicle a Popular Vehicle?

If it's reviled, who cares? Your objective is to get the most hard cash for it, regardless of its popularity. Because a smart appraiser's objective is to tear down your car, you would be smart to know whether it's really popular or not.

So, how do you know if your current wheels are hot or cold? Generally speaking, the popularity of your old car mirrors the popularity of the current year's model: If new Toyota Camrys are zooming off the showroom floors, for example, used Camrys are usually popular, too.

What's Your Car's Mileage?

Higher than "average" miles will lower the value of your old vehicle, as every appraiser is going to tell you. "Average" is usually 15,000 miles per year. But you have some control over how much your miles impact value. Were they mostly freeway miles? If so, state that.

"Can't I just have those miles cut back a bit?" You can, if you like jail and a lawsuit or two. Killer remembers fondly those years way back when there were no cars with high mileage. When some nice customer would present Killer with a car showing sixty or seventy thousand miles, he would quickly drive it back to the service department, singing all the way, and yell out, "Hey, Harry, This damn thing has a broken clock!" Within the hour the car would reappear showing 12,841 miles.

Used-car sellers will tell you federal mileage statements brought an end to the friendly old clock-fixer's occupation. But, unfortunately, that is *not* the case. Digital odometers make rolling back miles virtually undetectable. And the very nature of the Internet makes Web businesses a great dumping ground for "clocked" cars and worse. Because it's hard to sue over many online transactions, and harder at times to even find out the name of the company or person to sue, unscrupulous sellers of troubled vehicles are flocking to innocuous-looking Web sites. Megadealers are sometimes taken in by these scams, too, because they purchase used cars sight unseen over the Web and spend very little time checking on the history of those vehicles.

Protect yourself from "clocking." You can help stop "clocking" and protect yourself from future liability by making sure that the correct mileage on your car is recorded on a mileage statement when you trade, sell, or otherwise dispose of your car. Keep a copy of that statement. If your old vehicle's mileage is altered by any future owner, your copy of that statement can help nail the guilty party.

Computing Your Old Car's Wholesale Value: *Everybody's* Got a "Value" for You

Whether you plan to trade your present vehicle or sell it outright, *you could lose thousands* if you don't move cautiously in determining your present vehicle's value. Remember, your old car is the true battleground for profit in the car business now, not the price you pay for the new car.

Because, as we noted earlier, consumers can now find out to the penny what a new car cost and what the factory "invoice price" is, car people aren't making as much profit on the new car. Such clarity helps savvy consumers. As a result, everybody in the car business—virtually to a company and to a salesperson—is now focusing on your old car as the most important profit center.

Since the used car you are driving now doesn't have an invoice cost like a new car, it's hard for you to pin down its true value. But car people can pin down that value. The job of the car person is therefore simple: to determine your car's true wholesale value, then give you less than that amount for it. This practice is called "underallowing" or "lowballing," as you hopefully know by now. "Lowballing" is specifically defined as giving you less for your vehicle than the appraiser has determined it is worth. For instance, if an appraiser gives you $4,000 for your old car, but lists it as an asset worth $5,000 on his company's final statements, you have just been lowballed $1,000. Some people might call that stealing. But the practice is so widespread that the initials "O.A./ U.A."—overallowed/underallowed—are printed on the internal transaction documents (the ones you don't see) of virtually all used vehicles purchased in America. That includes vehicles traded in at dealerships or on the Web.

Lowballing your trade is a stealth objective. Of course, you don't see this extreme interest in lowballing your trade. Dealerships and Web sites are doing their best to convince you that your old car is incidental to the transaction, a bothersome detail. And its wholesale value? You will seldom hear that word used, though it is the one value you must know. "Wholesale value" is the amount of money that a person or company will pay for a car that they intend to *resell* at a higher retail price. Wholesale value is a very specific term in the business. It's the figure "on the books" for every used car at every used-car seller. It's usually entered in your transaction's "deal jacket" right before the "O.A./ U.A." ledger entry.

"May I suggest . . . ?" Rather than using the clear term "wholesale value," a dealership, Web site, or salesperson may refer to your old car's worth as a "suggested value," "market value," or "trade-in value." I personally think many of those using these nonspecific terms are doing so to isolate themselves from future lawsuits concerning theft of consumers' money by lowballing. But whatever the term and the reasons for using it, the dealerships and Web sites tell you not to worry about determining your old car's value. "It's easy to determine a suggested value, folks! It's risk free! Just listen to us, or look at the figure on the Web site and you're done!"

Take Killer's approach to lowballing. Killer would drive your car up to the used-car manager's office and work him for the highest appraisal possible, like he did with the Allgoods in the last chapter. Let's say your car is a hot number, one that has quickly climbed in wholesale value during the past couple of weeks. The appraiser places a wholesale value, such as a cash value of $5,000, on your trade. You aren't told that figure, of course.

But you think you know your old car's value. When Killer returns to his office, you casually pull out your Web-enabled cell phone, dial directly to the Kelley Blue Book used-car value site, and flip your phone around to show Killer the latest online value for your car. Technology rules! Unfortunately, you don't know that even the best online wholesale services can't keep up with highly localized market trends. Kelley's value is therefore behind Killer's market and assesses your car at only $4,500. You inform Killer in no uncertain terms you'll not take a penny less than $4,500. Because the car is worth $5,000, you've already lost $500 on your old car, and Killer hasn't even started working you.

Killer turns your technology on you. On his monitor, he pulls up the same Web site you used and begins to read out interesting footnotes not easily read on your phone screen: "Deduct for no power windows, deduct for body damage, deduct for cloth interior, deduct for nonfactory equipment, deduct for wear and tear . . . ." Who determines what "body damage" is? If you've ever leased a vehicle, you probably know that body damage is very loosely defined. Who determines what "wear and tear" is? The person making the determination. The Killer types. Within five minutes Killer has used your own sword to slice your throat a little deeper, and you accept $4,000 for a car that the dealership has determined is worth $5,000. Thanks, they needed that!

Even low-tech dealerships try to lowball you. Don't feel any safer if the dealership is using a "book" to determine your old vehicle's value rather than a computer, or if you actually have a copy of a "black book" or "blue book" yourself. That's a sign of a sucker. A fellow drives into the lot with his own copy tucked away in his pocket and tells the salesperson, "Now when you have my car appraised, just be sure those fellows know I've got my *own* copy," patting his pocket in pride. Don't worry. The salesperson will tell his appraiser, "Hey, Mac, we've got another sucker here with a bible."

Books, like online used-car valuation sites, are simply the *average prices* for which particular cars have been selling. These prices are important to lending institutions because most institutions lend money on this "book" value, usually 80 percent of the book value of any particular car.

The problem with books or used-car Web sites. Even when used honestly, books and Web services can't write checks. Just because your car's value is listed at x dollars doesn't mean anyone will actually pay you x dollars for it.

You have absolutely no defense for lowballing other than knowing your old car's true wholesale value. Your car's wholesale value will seldom change during any negotiation or sales transaction. A case in point: When a salesperson tells you he or she will *allow* you more money in trade, it does not mean the wholesale value of your car has changed. The salesperson is simply taking some of the profit built into the price of the car you are trying to buy and adding that to the wholesale value of your trade. For example, you are looking at a new car with a markup (a gross profit) of $2,500. You're trading a used car with a true wholesale value of $2,000. If the salesman says, "Ma'am, I'll allow you $2,400 in trade," he has "overallowed" you $400, cutting his profit from $2,500 to $2,100. But the wholesale value of your car has never changed.

The *wholesale value* is the lowest dollar amount your car will be worth in any reasonable time period. It is the amount you know you can get for your car at any time during that reasonable period, which is up to a week usually. The *retail value* of your used car is the wholesale value *plus* the profit a person hopefully will pay to buy the car. Remember, the retail value is what you *hope* to receive for the car, and you will never, never receive that figure unless you sell your car yourself.

How to Determine the Wholesale Value of Your Car

All successful used-car operations—whether they are affiliated with a new-car dealership, sell solely on the Web, or are the worst subprime used-car lot in the world—are continuously looking for "fresh meat," new pieces of merchandise. All of these operations purchase used cars outright from wholesalers, from brokers, and from individuals like you.

The only way you will get the maximum wholesale dollar for your old car is to take advantage of the industry's hunger for fresh meat. You're going to have to learn how to play the bidders for your car against each other. That means you are going to have to play road hog for a day and *market your car.*

If you want an approximation of your old car's whole-sale value, skip to page 166. We'll show you how to use various online services to develop a good estimate. Be warned, however, that even the best approximation could be off by 10 percent or so. If your car is really worth $15,000 wholesale, that variance means you might unwittingly decide it's worth $13,500, let's say. The result: You throw away $1,500. That's fine if a day off is worth that type of money to you. But if $1,500 matters, keep reading. You need to determine wholesale value like Trey Wright and Dana.

Shopping for Wholesale Value the Wright Way

By two o'clock in the afternoon, Trey and Dana were riding down the road in their shiny car. "Damn!" Trey's eyes took in the polished hood and spotless interior. "Honey, I don't even think we should trade it! The car looks better than the day we bought it." It was running nearly as well, too. Trey had put the car in the shop just a few days before for some minor repairs. A couple of badly worn hoses had been replaced, the EGR system checked, and a new distributor cap put in—just about all the repairs needed, $270 in all. The expense was worth it, though, because the Wrights planned to spend the afternoon trying to sell the car. Or, rather, that's what they wanted the car people to think.

The first lot they pulled into was one of the oldest used-car operations in the city. The lot also specialized in cars that were just a few years old, like their car. The moment the engine stopped, Trey started acting nervous. After all their "fishing trips" in past years, he was the one who always nearly folded.

Asking for a price. Dana laughed. "Trey, for God's sake, they're not going to shoot us or anything; now just calm down. Do you want me to do the talking?"

"I'm fine, I'm fine," he said in a voice tinged with both irritation and amusement. "Now, just settle down." Dana bit her lip trying to keep another laugh down, as a young salesman walked to their car. Even after seventeen years of buying cars, the Wrights never had become really comfortable when it came to shopping their old car. The money made it worth it, though.

Trey told the guy what salesmen call the "basic truth"—just enough of the story to accomplish their objective. "Hello. My wife and I have been thinking about selling our car outright, and I was wondering if you guys might be interested." Why was he nervous, damn it? The guy looked at the car for a few seconds and said, "Well, we do sometimes, but that's usually handled by another man. Can you hold on a minute?" The guy headed inside, and both of the Wrights breathed out slowly and deeply.

Is the hassle worth it? "I always wonder why we go through this," Dana said. "After all, we always end up trading our old one in, anyway."

Trey shook his head. "Honey, we're going to trade it *only* if we can get as much money as one of these places will give us. And"—he looked at the two men heading toward them—"these people may end up with our car, anyway. The dealership may sell it to them. We just don't want the dealership to steal our car, and shopping it is the only way to know its real value, here, today."

"Howdy!" the older man said as he reached the car. "I understand you folks want to sell your car."

"Well, we're thinking about selling it if we get enough money. It is a pretty nice car," Trey said in a slightly defensive tone.

The man took their car for a spin and was back in a few minutes. After a moment in his office, he came back to the Wrights who were walking around the lot. "Folks, you do have a pretty nice car, and I can tell it's really been taken care of. Would you sell it to me if I paid you $11,500?"

Trey thought the figure sounded pretty good but didn't say so. "Well, I'll be honest with you, we've been offered $13,500 for it." Trey did not say that the offer of $13,500 was jokingly made by their son, fifteen, with a savings account at the credit union containing an impressive $36.48. The "other customer" ploy, the Wrights had learned several trades before, worked as well for the customers as it did for dealerships.

The used-car guy's face furrowed in thought for a moment before he said, "Well, I'll tell you what. We might stretch it to $12,500, but that would really be the limit. Would you take $12,500 for it?"

"We might. But, as I told you, we've got a better offer, I think. Will you hold to that figure for the next few days?" The guy really didn't want to hear that. He needed the Wrights' car on his lot. As a matter of fact, he needed all the nice cars he could find. "Yes sir, I will hold to that price for a few days, maybe a week. As long as the car is in the same condition, you know."

The next step. They were on the road to a second dealership quickly, and now Trey's nerves were fine. "See! I told you this was worth doing! Only the phony appraisal sites said our car was worth a dime over $11,000!"

"Yes," Dana said, "but it would have been nice if the phony sites really stuck with their figures. Like the one that 'pre-evaluated' our car at $16,000!"

"Right. That turned out to be a dealer site just trying to sucker us down to the dealership and then cut the appraisal. I'm glad we only fell for that once. And who cares? We really did just make $1,500! Did you hear me get that used-car pro to go up on his price when I 'worked' him?"

"You're really good at this, and so calm, you know," Dana said, which made them both laugh.

"Right! Now, let's see what the other places say."

The next used-car operation they visited wasn't buying cars from individuals right then and didn't even seem to appreciate the question. The third place put the same figure of $12,500 on the car. The fourth stop, at the used-car operation of one of the largest new-car stores in town, yielded a figure of $11,000. And Trey couldn't raise them, either.

A Saturday of modest tension visiting used-car lots had, in cold hard cash, made the Wrights $1,500. By shopping their car, they learned the difference between the Web sites' recommended wholesale value and a real wholesale offer on the car.

The Only Sure Way to Know the Wholesale Value of Your Old Car: Become a Road Hog for a Day

You can do this!

It really is the only sure way to know your old car's value. Using books and Web sites, as we've seen, can't determine your car's value accurately, and places you at risk. So, let's do it right:

- Prepare your car for "showing." Clean it up and clean it out.
- Drive it to three different car lots around the city. Go straight to the used-car department of a new-car store and also to a big independent used-car lot or two such as the national chain CarMax or an established local lot.
- Tell the crew you want to sell your car and that you are not interested in trading. Be firm with them; let them know that you really might sell if they give you enough money. Tell them you are going to decide where to sell it within a few days. Tell them you want a *definite, firm* offer.
- Gather at least three bids in this way.
- **The highest bid is your individual car's true wholesale value right now.**
        List the wholesale value
        of your car right here: _____

Your wholesale value will be good for a week or so, and it will make you a lot of money! Stay tuned.

I Still Want to "Shop" the Wholesale Value of My Old Car on the Web: What Are My Options?

In this section, I will show you how to find and use some of the various types of Web sites that offer appraisals and the relative merits and pitfalls of each. Virtually all of these sites, as of press date, will give you their "appraisal" for free. But remember that change on the Internet is rapid.

Individual Dealer Web Sites

General usefulness in determining your old vehicle's true wholesale value online: Virtually none.

True intentions of these sites: To sell you a vehicle right now.

How to find a local dealership site: Search using "car dealership" plus your nearest metro area for a broad search. For a narrow search, use "car dealership" plus your smallest city.

> *For the most up-to-date site listing and our comments on these sites, go to www.dont gettakenevery time.com*

Some dealership sites simply send you to pricing sites, such as Kelley Blue Book. Most dealer sites imply they will tell you the "value" of your old car online. They will indeed tell you a "value," but it probably won't be your vehicle's true *wholesale* value. In all likelihood, the value dealerships give you online will be *higher* than your old car's true wholesale value. Why would they do that? To "hook" you: To get you to the dealership, to "box you in" (put you in a closing booth), and/or to "tie you down" (get a deposit). After they get you to come in, the dealership finds a reason to tell you your old car isn't at all worth what the dealership has "suggested" online. This technique of pretending to offer more than a dealership plans to really offer you is called "highballing," and it is the opposite of "lowballing."

Dealerships get away with such deception online by playing with words. For instance, a very typical dealer site will happily give you an Internet trade-in pre-evaluation. What is a "pre-evaluation?" Nothing! It's a weasel phrase. On another page of this Web site, the dealership insists that you grant the right to have your vehicle "evaluated" by "authorized dealership personnel."

That means they don't have to stick to their pre-evaluation figure at all.

Online appraisals can put you at risk. Interestingly enough, *you* are forced to stick to *your* word with dealer sites like this one—under the threat of legal action if you're wrong. This site, which is typical of thousands of dealer sites, requires you to "certify" that the information you have given them on their on-screen questionnaire is "correct and complete." Included in that certification are questions such as this one about your vehicle: "Is your transmission in excellent, good, fair, or poor condition?"

Well, are you a transmission specialist? I doubt it. Are you ready to "certify" your old transmission in a specific enough way to differentiate between "excellent" and "good"? I hope not. But these folks are asking *you* to be the expert here, not them. And in the process, you are creating a potential liability for yourself down the road if you later decide to trade or sell your vehicle to this dealership.

This site also asks you to certify answers to seemingly innocuous questions such as "Would you recommend this vehicle to a future customer?" Well, would anyone trying to sell his car say no to this question? Of course not. But by certifying that you recommend this car, you again may be creating liability should a future owner of your old car have problems with it. And that liability is only a click away. By simply returning the dealership's pre-evaluation form, which is useless in helping you determine the real wholesale value of your old car, you have signed your name and certified your statements.

How to handle online dealer appraisals of your old car. If there is any chance at all you may eventually sell or trade your car to the particular dealership whose Web site you are using, then refuse to give an online certification of anything, including your age. Either insist that the dealership, without any obligation on your part, send a person to you to appraise your vehicle or go to the dealership in person. Some sites will send someone to you—just ask them in an e-mail. If the site sends someone, insist upon a written wholesale offer on your car, but don't accept it on the spot. Use it to find a better offer, and also feel free to try to "up" their offer: negotiate a little bit.

Established Used-Vehicle Market Guides Online

Examples: Kelley Blue Book and Edmunds

General Usefulness in determining your specific vehicle's wholesale value: Useful as a beginning guideline only.

The main problem with these sites: If you read it, you believe it.

To Receive a Free "Appraisal":

Kelley Blue Book: www.kbb.com

Edmunds: www.edmunds.com

The Web sites for these services use simple, clear instructions and online forms. The forms ask for great detail about your present vehicle. Give it to them. This detail determines the relative accuracy of each site's appraisal. Both sites are generally very accurate in providing *average* values of vehicles. They cannot provide you the specific wholesale value of your car, however, since these are "averaging sites."

While these services are legitimate and, in my opinion, still the best online guides available free to consumers, they have also become prospecting tools ("lead generators") for automotive sellers or partners of sellers. For instance, both sites offer new car quotes from dealers. As you surf the Web, you will also discover that other automotive sites, including buying services and Internet service providers offer "price guides" provided by either Kelley Blue Book or Edmunds. The auto channels of Yahoo!, MSN, and AOL, for example, offer used-car values by Kelley Blue Book.

Other Automotive Sites That Will "Appraise" Your Vehicle

Examples: Too numerous and varied and change too quickly to give reliable examples.

General Usefulness in determining your specific vehicle's wholesale value: Useful as a beginning guideline only.

The main problem with these sites: Most ultimately are dealer-referral services.

If you enter "used car appraisals" in your favorite search engine, literally hundreds of sites will pop up. Some may be as informative as the established used-vehicle evaluation sites mentioned earlier. Others, however, may be virtually useless. For example, one site offers to give you a "trade-in" value only if you enter the make and model of the new vehicle you will be shopping for. Red flag! A used car's true wholesale value is unrelated to what vehicle (if any) you plan to purchase. Other sites give you only retail prices for used cars, which is not very useful for determining wholesale value.

What many such sites have in common, however, is that they have strong dealer relationships. Expect many of the dealer-related sites to attempt to push you into buying *right now* rather than simply appraising your car. If that happens, ignore the pressure. Use the site only for appraisal purposes at this time. Also, if any sites ask for "certification" of any data you provide, refuse to give it.

Car Depreciation Calculators

Example: www.dod.mil/mapsite/cardep.html

General Usefulness in determining the true wholesale value of your vehicle: Worthless but interesting.

This type of calculator was developed by the Department of Defense Military Assistance Program. It's simple and therefore not worth much when it comes to determining wholesale value. These calculators can't write checks, don't factor in vehicle condition, don't consider current market conditions, and don't consider vehicle make or model. But if you gravitate toward simplicity, you'll like this. Some sites have adapted this approach so that you enter a make and model. But these details still won't give you an accurate wholesale value for the vehicle.

Time to Calculate Your Equity in Your Car's Wholesale Value

Once you've shopped your car or evaluated its approximate wholesale value online, it's time to calculate how much value—called equity—you have in the car.

**What's the final
wholesale value?**
List it right here: 1. _____

**Now, what do you owe
on that vehicle?** For now,
count the remaining
payments, and multiply.
Put that amount here: 2. _____
(If you owe nothing, put zero.)

Now, subtract 2 from 1
and put that figure here: 3. _____

                                                       Your equity in your car

If number 3 is positive, that's what your car's real net worth is in cash to you. If number 3 is negative, you join a very large crowd: You're in the bucket. You owe more on your vehicle than its wholesale value.

If you trade your car, you're going to need at least this much cash as a down payment along with your trade. Or, if you're very smart, you'll do your best to retail your car for enough profit to pay off your "bucket." You can read about selling your old car yourself on page 180.

Why Fool with Your Old Car at All? Give It Away as a Tax Deduction!

Donating your vehicle to a worthy cause makes sense only if your car is paid for. Dozens of charitable groups in your area will be happy to come to your house and even pick your car up, if you're feeling benevolent. New IRS rules for such donations went into effect in June 2005. If the organization sells your vehicle, then you may deduct only the "gross proceeds from the sale." The charity provides the appropriate forms letting you know that amount. If the group uses the vehicle in the work of the charity, then you can deduct the "fair market value" of the vehicle as long as the value does not exceed the private party sales price listed in a used-vehicle pricing guide such as Kelley Blue Book. Again, the charitable group will typically supply you with the appropriate forms. You can learn more about vehicle donations from IRS Publication 526 "Charitable Contributions" (www.irs.gov).

Tip: You will need to itemize your deductions on your state and federal tax returns to take advantage of your donation. If you're not currently using the long form, consult your tax adviser about whether or not the donation justifies switching to itemization.

If you know for a fact you're going to trade your old car and not try to sell it yourself, you can skip ahead to page 188. If the potential of making an extra thousand or three on your old car matters—and is worth some hassle—read on.

Should You "Retail" Your Car Yourself Rather Than Trade It In? Well, It All Comes Down to Time and Money Again

Services on the Internet have made retailing your current vehicle a lot easier, and less expensive, too. For instance, do you owe money on your car? Paying off that money and getting a "clear" title to present to the person who buys your car used to be a real hassle. Online services can handle that for you now. Or do you owe money on your old car and have a buyer willing to pay top dollar for it but is unable to come up with the cash? Online services can handle your payoff, make him a loan, *and* handle his paperwork. Found a buyer a thousand miles away who is willing to buy sight unseen? That transaction can be done online.

Selling your old car yourself is still no picnic, and everyone wants to tell you his or her opinion is right. Web sites primarily associated with dealerships (the vast majority of automotive Web sites), and of course our friend Killer, will tell you selling your own car is worse than a permanent case of hives. Their arguments are persuasive, at least to the weak of heart. On the other hand, Web sites that make money telling you how to sell your car yourself will tell you it's easy! Their arguments are persuasive, if you don't know the creepy behind-the-scenes machinations focused on you as you try to become a Web seller and have never "asked for the sale" before.

Both points of view have truth in them. Here are some thoughts for you as you decide:

Avoid Moose Heads—Advice from Killer About Selling Your Car Yourself

The Grays were in to discuss selling their car themselves yesterday. The Grays have a splendid, racing-green BMW convertible with tan leather seats piped in green. The immaculate runabout is the only sexy thing associated with this timid couple, and a very easy set of wheels for even the most mild-mannered person to sell.

Mr. Gray works in the accounting department of the last remaining girdle factory in this part of the country, and Mrs. Gray is a homemaker. This couple's involvement in the business of buying and selling anything has been limited. Mrs. Gray was in charge of the cake sale at the Parish Hall, but even that little foray into the business world was embarrassing to her. She would blush when someone asked the price of the finest chocolate layer cake and apologize profusely as she took their money.

Mr. Gray's expertise is at about the same level. He loves to visit garage sales but has yet to bargain for anything, including the magnificent moose head now sitting in his garage. Mr. Gray didn't want the thing in the first place, but an enthusiastic neighbor—Killer—had convinced him. "At this price, Albert, you can't afford *not* to buy it. These things are going up in value every year. And look at the points on it! Why, people will think you're the great white hunter! Now, do you want to take it with you or can I drop it by the house later today?"

Can't you trust a friend in the business? The Grays were sitting in the office with Killer. They had finally decided to buy a new car after at least two months of discussion and probably wouldn't be buying then, ". . . but, Bob, we know you. It's so important to know someone when you buy a car, don't you agree?" Killer just loves these folks. Almost every sentence ended in a question requiring confirmation—Little Red Riding Hoods seeking comfort from granny wolf. Of course, Killer happily told them just what they wanted to hear.

"Albert, you are more right than you know. You just wouldn't believe the horror stories in this business." Killer neglected to tell them most of the stories were about him. "Now, have you folks decided on any particular type of car this year?"

"Well, no, as long as it's sporty. We just felt the time had come to get a new one. Bob, you have so many imports, what do you think would be an *exciting* car for us?"

Killer had died and gone to heaven. "I'd like to show you a couple of cars. But before we do that, why don't I run your car up the hill and have it appraised? It'll just take a minute or two."

The Grays rustled in their chairs, and Albert started to speak, a slight stutter betraying his nervousness. After all, they didn't want to hurt Killer's feelings. "Uh, Bob, we think we're going to sell our car ourselves this time. Mr. Merit, my supervisor at work, says it's actually much more profitable to sell one's trade-in directly. Is that right?"

Killer's objections. Killer chuckled, shook his head slightly, and spoke in a hushed tone of confidentiality. "I *wish* that were true, Albert . . ." He paused, as if the words were just too horrific to be spoken in polite company. "But *that—selling your own car*—takes you out on very, very thin ice." The Grays probably had visions of pulling up Jaws while fishing through the ice with a light line, and they sat there, stunned and immobile, as Killer continued. "The used-car business is a very complicated business, filled with people who like nothing better than exploiting nice folks like yourself. Just the other day I read about a couple that sold their car to some stranger, only to find that the man's check was worthless.

"And then there were the Smiths, customers of mine who sold their old car to friends. The car broke down within a couple of weeks, and because there was no warranty on the vehicle, the Smiths' friends decided to sue them. What makes that story even sadder is the fact that the Smiths received only $100 more than I would have given them in trade."

Killer stopped just long enough for these heartrending words to register, then continued. "And, of course, there are the practical problems. What price would you ask for your car? What if the person who wants to buy it has a payoff on his old car? How would you handle that? And who is going to make all those trips to the Department of Vehicle Registration and prepare the affidavits?" His description of the paperwork sounded more like a visit to the emergency room of a public hospital than the title office.

"And, Albert, do you really want to have perfect strangers contacting you night and day?"

Each thought chilled the Grays to the core. My God! How could they have been so stupid? Albert spoke with the conviction of the born-again, fire and brimstone crackling in every word. "Bob, of course you are right. It was just a thought, anyway. And I'm sure you'll get us the maximum dollar in trade, won't you?" Uh-huh.

What's More Important? Your Time or Your Money? The Case Against Killer

Trying to retail your old car is an adventure, to put it mildly. But if you face the hassle and succeed, you will probably get 10 to 20 percent more for it retail than you will by wholesaling it. If your old car is worth $10,000 wholesale, for example, you will probably be able to retail it for $11,000 to $12,000. You pocket an extra thousand or two. If your car is *really* cheap—says its only worth $1,000 to $2,500 wholesale—you can probably *double* your money by retailing it.

The Moose Head Man's boss, Merit, nearly did. Albert Gray's boss. Dave Merit had done his homework. He had determined his old car's true wholesale value by shopping it. Merit's car wasn't a nice car, either, simply adequate transportation, a practical second car for a young family. His highest wholesale offer on the tub was $4,000 in cash.

Arriving home after shopping the car, Merit grabbed his oldest son and headed to the iMac. Within an hour they had surfed five different Web sites that let consumers sell their own vehicles, including a site that promised to do all the legal paperwork if the car actually sold on that site. "Niceservice!"

But Merit did not list his car with any Web service just yet. He simply wanted to see the "asking" prices other people were seeking for six-year-old Chevys like his. Lying next to the computer were local "swap" newspapers and a copy of the *Family Friend's Morning Journal,* owned by Killer's dealership's parent company. The papers were open at the classified used-car ads, where Merit's son had circled the asking prices of vehicles similar to theirs.

Merit laughed at some of the asking prices. "Well, I'd say those people have the right idea for sure. They certainly aren't shy when it comes to asking for the moon." A few of the individual ads had asking prices below the $4,000 Merit knew his vehicle was worth wholesale. But some individuals advertising on the Web sites were asking the moon for cars like his. One was asking $8,995. But the average asking price of similar vehicles both on the Web sites and in the classified ads was about $6,000, which was $2,000 more than Merit knew his car was worth wholesale.

Setting an asking price. "If the highest ad we've seen was for $8,995, and the average price people are asking is $6,000, we'll go in between. Let's price ours at $6,900. And we'll write a better ad than those online ads, for sure." Merit just wanted to be in the ballpark—not too high or low, but in good dickering range. Since he knew his old car could be sold wholesale to the used-car operation that put the $4,000 bid on it, Merit would have $2,900 to play with. If he actually sold his old wheels for $6,900, he would make $2,900 more than his wholesale bid! Even if he just retailed the car for $4,900, he would be making nearly $1,000 more than if he sold it to the wholesaler. It took

Merit five full days of work to take home $1,000 after taxes and deductions. It took him three weeks to take home $2,900. The potential savings of retailing their car was definitely worth the time.

Merit put his worksheet away and put the business of selling out of his mind for the day. Two answers were enough for the moment: He knew what his car was worth wholesale, and he knew the asking price he would build into his ad.

Next steps. On Friday, Merit placed several phone calls. The first one was to his bank. "Okay, you say the payoff on my car is $879.23?"

"Yes, sir, and that payoff is good for ten days. After that time it will go up slightly."

"Well, thanks very much. Now let me ask you something. I'm planning to sell the car to an individual. Just what do I have to do to get you people to release the title on the car?"

"Just come to the bank with that individual. Please have him bring a certified check made out to you for the total sales price. We'll cash that, pay off the car, and give you the difference and the title while you're here."

That sounded simple enough. "But what about the sales tax? Don't we have to pay sales tax on this?"

"You don't have to worry about that. The buyer pays the tax, not the seller. The person buying your car simply takes your bill of sale to the tag office. He pays the tax when he has the car registered in his name. And, sir, there are services listed online that will do all of that paperwork for you."

Placing the ads. Merit then went online and placed identical ads on his local "Shopper's" free online site, on one national "Sell Your Own Car" site, on the "classifieds" site for the local newspaper, and then also listed it with a site that for a fee guaranteed to handle all the payoffs and all the paperwork on a vehicle. On two of the Web sites he even scanned in a reasonably good picture of the old Chevy. His ad was simple: "Chevy Malibu. Low mileage. Clean, one-owner car. Serviced regularly. $6,900, no trade. Call 9–5 weekdays, 10–6 weekends. Individual." The ad contained all the important information, including the fact that an individual was selling the car, not a dealer. Many people are convinced that cars can be bought less expensively from individuals, and Merit knew that.

Handling prospective buyers. Merit's first response was a phone call, not an e-mail. It came as he walked in the door Saturday afternoon. "Hello, I was calling about your online ad about the Chevrolet."

"Yes, sir, what can I tell you about it?"

"Well, sir, my name is Robert DeMarco. I'm a new-car salesman here at Davies Motors just down the road from you. But I have a customer that's been looking for a used car like the one you described in the newspaper."

"I'm sorry, I'm not interested in trading my car. Thank you for calling, anyway."

"Sir, before you hang up, can I ask you what you'll be driving when you sell your car?"

"Well, I will be buying a new car."

"If I could give you more than $6,900 in trade on a new car, would you consider talking to me? I really do have someone looking for a car like yours, and perhaps we could kill two birds with one stone, as they say."

Smart car salesmen are always doing this. They simply sit down during slow times and either call or e-mail persons who have placed ads. And the salesperson invariably has some customer just panting to own a used vehicle just like the one advertised. It's a very effective technique.

"Well, Mr. DeMarco, I appreciate your call, but I'm really not interested right now. I will be happy to write your name down, though. Thanks very much for calling."

Scratch the first phone call. Hell, that call had really been more productive for Killer. He at least found out that the guy was going to buy a new car. Killer will call Merit back in a few days.

The next three responses were e-mails. Each of them asked questions, which Merit responded to online. But these three people simply disappeared into cyberspace. They did not respond again. Merit was beginning to think this car-selling idea wasn't so good after all.

The fifth response was a phone call. It didn't come until the next evening, but it sounded a little more promising. The woman asked a few questions, then made an appointment to see the car that night. She never showed up.

Negotiating the test-drive and sale. Finally, on the third day, a man actually appeared at the prescribed time at the Merit residence. He was nice enough and didn't act nearly as nervous as Merit. After all, this was the first time Merit had ever done anything like this. Merit's hand would have passed for a cold fish as he grabbed the guy's palm. There was another man with him, too, or rather an eighteen- or nineteen-year-old kid, who walked around the car as Merit talked. The kid looked under the hood, opened the driver's door, and peered in without sitting.

"Why don't we take a drive?" Merit volunteered. He climbed in the backseat and sat there quietly as the older man pulled out of the driveway. Merit didn't even recognize the buying signals the two of them were giving out.

"Hey, Dad, it's got a CD player." His father didn't seem to hear that. He was busy spreading himself out in the front seat, right arm resting comfortably on the seat back, left hand lightly holding the wheel. The man had a slight smile on his face.

As the car pulled back in the drive, Merit searched for some appropriate words. Hell, he didn't have the slightest idea what should be done next. "Well, Mr. Johnson, how do you like the way she drives?"

"I like it. It really seems like a pretty nice car. But I just don't know about the price. We looked at another car yesterday that was $1,000 less than yours."

Merit didn't have the presence of mind at the moment to ask the man if the car was the same year and model, much less if the car was as nice as his. But the guy had given him a clue. "Well, Mr. Johnson, I honestly don't want to sell the car for much less than $6,900." Merit made a good statement without knowing it. He didn't say he *wouldn't* take much less; he simply said he didn't want to. "But you said the other car you looked at was $1,000 less. Are you saying you would pay $5,900 for this car?"

Johnson sat there behind the wheel for a few seconds and said, "Well, I might. But I would like to show it to my wife before saying yes. Would it be okay if my son and I drove it over to the house?"

Merit didn't like the sound of that. Regardless of how nice the people looked, he really didn't like the idea of strangers driving away in his $4,000 piece of merchandise. "Mr. Johnson, I would be happy to do that, but my insurance company just won't let me. Why don't I follow the two of you home. I'll be glad to do that."

"That'll be fine." Johnson's reaction made him much more comfortable. Merit is a pretty good reader of people, and an indignant show of impugned honor would not have impressed him.

Mrs. Johnson liked the car and liked the price, too. They decided to buy it. "Okay, I guess we'll take it. Now what do we do?"

Closing the deal. Merit had trouble thinking for a moment. All he could visualize was the $1,900 he was earning for perhaps twelve hours' work. Even after the cost of the newspaper and Web ads, he'd still be netting over $1,800. "Well, Mr. Johnson, if you could give me a deposit tonight, I won't show the car to anyone else. And then tomorrow, if it's convenient, we can go to my bank to get the title. If possible, you do need to be with me, since those people will notarize the title for us."

"How much money will I owe you, $5,900 even?"

"Yes, you'll have to pay the tax yourself. And you'll need to bring a certified check with you. My bank says that's necessary."

"Well, I'm planning to finance the car. Maybe I'd better get the serial number tonight, and I'll call the credit union in the morning. I think they'll make the check out to me, but if there are any problems, we can talk on the phone during the day." Merit said his good-byes and headed home. He was excited!

Call Me Merit. No, Call Me Killer Junior! How to Retail a Vehicle

Here, step by step, is the technique that you can use to successfully retail your car.

1. **First, use the wholesale value of your car as a start.**
   Write that amount here: _____. Since you know you can receive this from a dealer without any more work, don't accept wholesale from a consumer.

2. **Then, determine the minimum you will accept from an *individual* for your old vehicle.**
   That minimum amount should always be determined by adding together your wholesale value plus your estimated expenses plus a profit. You may spend thirty hours selling your car, and you'll probably have $200 in advertising and transfer expenses.

   At the *absolute minimum* I recommend you accept wholesale plus $700. For instance, if your car is worth $4,000 wholesale, don't accept less than $4,700 plus taxes and fees. And don't go down to that figure quickly during the negotiation process. We'll show you how to handle the dickering.

   The minimum you will accept for your car: _____

3. **Now, choose a Web site as your primary advertising tool.**
   Even if you don't have access to the Internet at home or at work, I recommend that you advertise on the Web. The exposure is tremendous, the effort is minimal, and the cost is incidental. Rope a Web-wise friend into helping you, use a computer at your library if possible, or rent Internet time at some place like Kinko's. *But don't place an ad yet,* just choose a site.

   Enter "used-car classifieds" in your search engine. Hundreds of sites will come up. I suggest you review a number of sites and select one free site and one pay site. Key thoughts in choosing those sites: Choose one that allows your ad to

   For a current list of used-car classified sites, along with our comments, visit www. dontgettaken everytime.com.

run a very long time and one that includes your vehicle in many different listings. Before choosing a site, however, be sure that you carefully read the site's privacy policy and terms of use. Reject any site that has an inadequate privacy policy or no policy at all. Reject any that seem to require more personal information than necessary. **Note:** Most sites allow dealerships to list cars, too. Some sites tell you if the ad is from a dealer; others don't.

Tip: As you review Web sites, page through their listings for cars like yours on those sites. Make a list of the "asking" prices of similar cars. We'll use these figures to help set your own asking price.

Asking prices of similar vehicles:

_____

_____

_____

_____

Here are some examples of the types of sites you will want to surf:

- **Established national classified sites.** Three examples include AutoTrader.com, Cars.com, and CarsDirect.com. All offer several options with reasonable fees.
- **Free classified ad sites.** Entering "free auto classified ads" in your favorite search engine will produce a number of Web sites, both national and regional.
- **Classifieds/Web site of local media.** Your daily newspaper and weekly freebie papers if you live in a metropolitan area usually offer print/Web combined classifieds.
- **What about online auction sites such as eBay Motors and Yahoo! Auction?** Such sites are popular, but I don't recommend selling your vehicle on an auction site, except perhaps if you have considerable experience with both using online auctions and selling your own vehicles. Even with the ability to set a reserve,

controlling your price may be more difficult. Also, an auction site is not an advertising site but a *transaction* site. You must complete your sale within the auction site and by its rules. For example, you may be obligated to complete the sale if your reserve price is met. You can usually correspond with a bidder but typically cannot meet them for a vehicle and buyer assessment. Sites may also require that you list the vehicle identification number (VIN) of your vehicle, which is a help to buyers but may also expose you to VIN cloning and fraud. If an online auction appeals to you, do your homework thoroughly and proceed with caution.

Choose two sites and list them here:

_____

_____

4. **Now, set an "asking" price for your vehicle.**
Remember, you can always take less, but it's hard to ask for more!

Your "asking" price should be in line with asking prices for other vehicles similar to yours. For instance, if the cars like yours had asking prices online of $4,995–$6,995, don't ask more than $6,995 unless you can easily justify the higher asking price in an ad.

An added attraction *that makes your old car more attractive:*

- **Do you have an extended service agreement on this vehicle?** Is it transferable? If so, the remaining warranty transferable to the new owner is worth money. Find your paperwork and do a little research. If the warranty is transferable, determine how many months of coverage are remaining. We'll use this information in our ad a little bit later.

- **Should you consider offering an extended service agreement on your old vehicle, even if you don't have a warranty?** It might make sense and doesn't have to cost you a dime. Go to www.dontget takeneverytime.com for an up-to-date list of warranty companies, or use your search engine to search "used-vehicle warranties." Choose a warranty company that has a product that covers your age, make, and model vehicle. List the price of the service agreement here: _____. Later, we'll show you how to use this in your ad.

Reality check: You've already determined the minimum you'll accept for your old vehicle. List that figure here again: _____
Now list your "asking" price: _____
Put your potential "profit" here: _____
Is the potential profit at least $1,500? If it is, you've probably set a pretty realistic price. Nice!

5. **Think about the reality of paperwork and payoffs. Why not let someone else do it?**
    When you sell a vehicle yourself, you are responsible for transferring the title and doing other paperwork required by your state. If you have a payoff on your old car, you are responsible for paying that off and securing the title for your old car. Buyers want to give personal checks, but you don't want personal checks. Unless you're ready for a lot of odd paperwork, we recommend you use an online escrow service for this. You may spend up to $200, but it's worth every penny. And you pay nothing if you don't sell your vehicle and actually use the service.

    Most of these services will also certify that your old vehicle has never been totaled in an accident—another nice selling point for your ad. Generally speaking, these services won't do the final piece of legwork in your transaction: You'll still have to go to your tag office, but the service will prepare your paperwork and even give you the address of the title office you need to visit. Take time now to do a little surfing in the escrow world, and then choose the service that appeals most to you. Print out their explanation pages.

Choosing an Escrow Service

Fake escrow services, unfortunately, are a leading Internet scam. The problem is so widespread that it is very difficult to select a legitimate escrow service from an online search. One of the leading national escrow services, however, is www.escrow.com. It offers a useful step-by-step process to using escrow during the car buying or selling process. It also has a good section on on-line auto sales and escrow fraud.

Should you wish to locate another escrow service, please research the service using independent resources and follow these tips:

- Never use an escrow service recommended by the buyer (or seller, if you are buying).
- If you receive e-mail or money transfer instructions outside your escrow account, chances are almost 100 percent that the site is a fraud.
- Remember that fake escrow services often have very slick sites that display stolen "security" logos such as VeriSign or TRUSTe. Don't assume it is legitimate; verify the site's participation at VeriSign, TRUSTe, or the Better Business Bureau. Run a WHOIS check on the site at register.com to verify that the site has been in business for more than a few weeks or months. Fake sites typically switch identities often.
- Real escrow services will have a physical location (street address) and a working phone number. Check them out. Check the company registration with the appropriate state office. Call and talk to a person, not voice mail, at the phone number. Send an e-mail question; if you get no answer or a canned answer, reject the service.

6. Create your core ad.

Any Web sites you choose will probably have several vehicles listed similar to yours. So why would anyone read your ad versus the others? Or, more specifically, what can you do to make people want to read your ad and respond to it rather than to someone else's ad? In car ads, buyers are attracted to price and dependability. For instance, these phrases usually draw attention:

- Priced under retail
- Well maintained
- Service records available
- Single owner
- Kept in a garage
- 12,000-mile warranty

Depending upon your Web site, feel free to use a little poetry, too. For instance, "We maintained this car like an airplane, respected it, and want a nice new home that will respect it."

Other key ad pointers:

- Always include the phrase "no dealers." Many salespeople surf these sites looking for victims. Remember that a dealership will only pay you wholesale for your old car. The object of all this work is to get you retail.
- Always include the phrase "no trades." You have enough to do just selling yours.
- Decide if you want all your responses initially to come by e-mail. If so, your ad should instruct respondents to include their phone numbers and the best time for you to call them.
- If you are placing your telephone number in your ad, include the hours you will be available.

Other Ways to Advertise Your Car

Put a sign in the window. The car window, that is. You'll need to put a phone number or e-mail address and the price. This method of advertising a vehicle has been around since Roman times (really) and still works occasionally.

Post your car on your company's bulletin boards or community Web page. Dealing with a buyer at your own company can be easier than dealing with a stranger.

Traditional "classified ads" in your newspaper. If you're dealing with a big newspaper, you'll probably get an Internet listing along with your regular ad. Follow the same guidelines we listed for Web ads in writing your newspaper ad.

"Shoppers." Free local newspapers are usually very effective in generating leads, and many list your ads on their Web sites. Look for shoppers in your grocery store, in small markets, and at the dentist's office.

Your Hour on the Stage

Most people don't try to sell their own car because they are unsure of their selling skills or just plain shy. That's fine. But you can do this, shy or not, with no selling skills. Just think of that big pile of money you're going to make and what you can buy with it! To make all that money, you don't need to be as sneaky as the gang at America's Family Friend, either. But you might want to know the sneaky things they're doing to get you to finance with them. So, read on.

Chapter 7

Dollars and Non-Sense: Or, What You'd Better Know About Financing, Even If You Pay Cash

The Parallel Worlds were operating on this deal perfectly, and Buzz knew he had earned it. The "ups"—named Crenshaw—had been "jumping beans," nervous at first, on the alert for auto scams. He didn't deserve that again! They had been "hobos" on the computer scan, too, virtually invisible. A search of their tag number initiated when they drove up hadn't pulled up any databases, much less any credit database. A search of America's Family Friend's other company databases hadn't pulled up anything, either! These jerks didn't even buy a magazine owned by the company.

Buzz knew this because his pager had vibrated less than three minutes after the Crenshaws drove onto dealership property. "No data," it said. The Crenshaws had watched Buzz read the pager. And oddly enough, it was the first time Buzz, who had just finished three weeks of "sensitivity training" at America's Family Friend Institute, felt real comfortable in this deal. He observed that the Crenshaws were comfortable with technology. And they looked like nice people looking for someone to trust.

"Folks, you could do me a big favor if you'd let me talk you into a ride in one of our new cars—even if you're not interested in buying. I'm in a contest, you see. So would you help me?" Buzz smiled modestly at the couple.

What could be wrong with that? The Crenshaws were just having fun dreaming this afternoon; they weren't really planning to buy. Trent Crenshaw folded first, betraying himself with a sheepish grin. Gin Crenshaw folded at the sight of it. Of course they would like to take a short drive.

Buzz started walking toward a plain-Jane hardtop, which he noticed had caught their eye, and then paused just long enough to look spontaneous. "Oh, folks, our insurance company requires proof you have a driver's license. We have to get a copy for the files. Is that okay?"

Trent Crenshaw thought about that, then said yes. I mean, anybody ought to have a license to drive, right? Buzz didn't even go into the finance office with their licenses. He walked less than twenty feet to a handsome red British-style public phone booth, stepped in just long enough to slide each driver's license through a small scanner mounted there by a normal wall phone, grabbed a spiral-bound notebook labeled "Guests," and headed back to the Crenshaws.

"Folks, sign the guest book, please, or the boss will shoot me."

A stealth move to check credit history. Buzz flipped over several pages of signatures, each page labeled "Guests," and handed the notebook to the Crenshaws. The notebook, nearly homey looking, was a brilliant touch. So low-tech and nonthreatening. And indeed the pages contained only signatures, no addresses or phone numbers. It was like signing a guest book at a wedding! Buzz did not bother to point out the last page of the Guest Book. On this page, hidden in a thousand words of very tiny type, was a disclaimer that stated in part, "By signing this authorization log, I acknowledge that I have read this page, and understand as a part of negotiating to purchase and finance a vehicle, America's Family Friend Financial Services may need to inquire into my creditworthiness, and because I have entered into negotiations to purchase and perhaps finance a vehicle, AFF is authorized to do so." The Crenshaws signed, of course. The harmless-looking logbook had just conned them into authorizing the dealership to snoop extensively into their credit history and private lives. Buzz placed the log back in the phone booth and turned his mind to the test-drive.

Exactly three minutes and fifty-one seconds had passed since Buzz scanned the driver's licenses. And what a productive time that three minutes and fifty-one seconds had been for the dealership. At the instant of the scan, an "alert" started blinking on Chris Stretch's screen in the aptly named Money Room, a special computer center tied to all 250 AFF dealerships and powered by AFF's high-tech Matchmaker Optimal Proposal Software (MOPS) program.[1] The MOPS system had nailed the Crenshaws—it pulled up reams of credit information and scored their credit. These people were "A/B," very good, but not perfect. Chris liked that. A weak point for use in later negotiations, he thought as "A/B" began to blink on his monitor. As it blinked, MOPS instantly submitted a loan application based on the Crenshaws' credit to the sixteen "preferred" AFF lending institutions. Three of the institutions were owned by AFF. All sixteen institutions then pulled their own credit reports on the Crenshaws, electronically scored their risk characteristics, and approved them for a loan. Though all sixteen had approved them, the amounts of money each lending institution would finance, and the interest rate and number of months each institution would finance, varied. Each institution had flashed their approval and loan terms to AFF.

Planning how much to make on the customer. From the moment the Crenshaws' driver's licenses had been scanned at the dealership, this entire process had taken *one second*. Before the Crenshaws had opened the door to begin their test-drive, sixteen lending institutions had pulled their credit reports, dissected their credit lives, and in varying degrees approved them for a loan. No human being had been involved.

The blinking alert on Chris Stretch's screen signaled that a human being was now needed in this transaction. Stretch hit the OPTION button on his monitor and watched as the loan terms of the sixteen lending institutions instantly appeared on a single screen. Rather than in alphabetical order, the MOPS system listed the Offers to Finance in "Aggregate Profitability" order. The order was based on the "ideal transaction scenario" designed by AFF. The scenario itself was designed to take every factor into account to determine which financing institution's terms would make AFF the most total money on the Crenshaw transaction.

MOPS was magnificent! It could juggle the thousands of combinations of all the following variables to make picking the fattest deal for AFF a snap:

- **How much total car would each institution finance?** "Total car" was the cost of the vehicle plus dealer profit on the vehicle itself. One institution approved the Crenshaws for $25,000, plus tax, tag, and title. Another agreed to finance only $20,000. Fourteen other offers were in between those numbers.

- **How much total financing profit would the financing institution pay AFF on the deal if the Crenshaws bought a new vehicle?** The profit varied less than $1,000 among the sixteen lenders. But the choice wouldn't be that simple. The institution that would pay the *least* finance profit on a new car was also the company that would allow AFF to make the *most* profit on the sale of the vehicle itself.

- **How much total financing profit would the financing institution pay AFF on the deal if the Crenshaws bought a used vehicle?** The profit varied $5,000 among the sixteen lenders approving the Crenshaws. But the institution willing to pay the home-run $5,000 in finance profit would finance only $21,000 on the Crenshaws' purchase— $4,000 less than another lender would finance on the purchase.

- **How many months would the lending institution finance the Crenshaws?** Longer months *always* mean higher profits for the dealership—unless the lender charged more money for longer months. Used cars usually meant fewer months. One company "conditioned" the months they would finance on the amount of the Crenshaws' down payment.

- **What was the "add-on cap" for each institution?** Add-ons described any item or service added to the amount of money to be financed on the Crenshaws' vehicle. Add-ons usually did not add value to the vehicle, but added risk to the lender because they had to lend more money without more collateral. That's why not every institution would allow AFF to "sell the package."

"Selling the package" meant selling *every one* of the following items to the Crenshaws and adding the charge to the amount to be financed: service agreement, window etching, alarm system, auto club, life insurance, accident insurance, liability and collision insurance. AFF always tried to sell these add-ons in order of profitability. For instance, AFF made $1,400 in profit on the sale of a $1,600 service agreement, but only $800 in profit on the sale of a $1,600 life insurance policy. If they were able to sell only one item, even if the customer needed the insurance, AFF would try to sell the service agreement.

In the Crenshaw transaction, MOPS analyzed 3,758 variable scenarios to find the most profitable scenario for AFF. As Chris Stretch quickly hit keys, MOPS pulled up a split screen. The left side of the screen displayed the institutions by profitability order if the Crenshaws financed a new car, the right screen by the profitability order if the Crenshaws were to finance a used car.

Stretch quickly spotted the single highlighted lending institution on the entire screen, the potential Home Run King in this transaction. "Yum," he quietly said to himself. It was a new lending institution in the AFF family of financing sources, and it was eager for loans—really eager. Chris liked that! This finance company would let the dealership charge the Crenshaws up to 33 percent interest on a current model year used car; the dealership would pay 7 percent for the money. Very nice. The source would finance any add-ons and had not even put caps on the selling price of those add-ons. The company would finance a one-year-old used car for the same months as a new car, *and* they would pay the dealer a "reserve" (an extra profit monthly) on the deal. Stretch laughed out loud. He called eager lending institutions like this

Mr. Hungry—

a dealer's

best friend.

one "Mr. Hungry." Thanks to them, AFF would knock a home run on that nice couple with Buzz!

Selling what's best for the dealership. Stretch sat up with a start. That's if the Crenshaws bought a *used* car. And *if* they financed. But the Crenshaws were driving off the lot in a new car. "Oh damn!" Stretch put his earphones on, keyed in "Buzz-cell" on the computer keyboard, and waited impatiently for Buzz to answer his cell phone in the car with the Crenshaws.

"Good morning," Buzz said, slightly preoccupied.

"How are the Crenshaws enjoying that fine car?"

"Well, we just drove out."

"Hold on a sec. . . ." As Stretch quickly hit three keys, MOPS did more magic. From the two hundred used vehicles on the lot, MOPS selected the *one used vehicle* that the dealership needed to sell the most desperately, which also matched Mr. Hungry's financing guidelines for the Crenshaws. MOPS quickly computed the maximum payment Mr. Hungry would allow the dealership to charge the Crenshaws and also showed the profit that payment would bring the dealership.

MOPS took *everything* into account in selecting the Crenshaws' next vehicle—the customer's variables, the lender's variables, and the dealership's profit goals. It then selected a "special concern" vehicle. The two-door coupe had been bought from a local rental fleet. It had been in the used-car inventory much too long. It had even been damaged to the tune of $7,000 when a drunk lot boy peeling rubber had backed into it. The vehicle's history filled the screen, and right by the VIN number an alert blinked "$1,500" constantly. Any dealership employees involved in selling the vehicle would split a $1,500 spiff—the biggest bonus AFF had put on any vehicle at that dealership this month.

Stretch thought for a minute, then turned back to Buzz on the cell phone. "Don't forget to tell the Crenshaws how many thousands they could save with one of our current-year used cars, Buzz. We've got that really nice dark green hardtop, you know . . ."—the wrecked rental car with the $1,500 bonus—"and management just announced a free trip to the Bahamas to the buyer of that vehicle." Stretch spoke energetically in code.

He'd been taught to do that when calling salespeople who were actually with customers.

Buzz picked up instantly on the real message. Sensitivity training was so fine, he thought as he said enthusiastically to Mr. Crenshaw, "Wow, you may not be interested, but the bosses have approved one of our free Bahama giveaways on a car virtually like this one!"

"What do you mean?" Gin Crenshaw asked skeptically. "Why would they give away a free trip?"

"Oh, I'm in a contest, I told you, I think. And probably the bosses are in some contest, too, and need to meet some goals, you know. The bosses are always doing things like that around here." Buzz kept his tone casual and did not mention that the free trip was a timeshare sales gimmick sponsored by AFF Vacations, owners of the modest timeshare village on Grand Bahama Island. Two seats on a charter plane and one night for free—if you attended the two-hour timeshare presentation, if you paid for your own meals, and if you paid the "administrative expenses" related to the trip. Those expenses covered the cost of the charter.

"What do you mean a car 'virtually like this one'?" Mr. Crenshaw asked warily. "Well, it's the same year and a similar model as this car, and it has an extended warranty, more than this new car, but it also has a few miles on it. An executive of the company drove it. But it's really a *better* deal than this car. The car has already depreciated, *plus* we've fixed all the new-car bugs on it. Our bosses don't put up with any problems on their vehicles, let me tell you."

"Well, isn't that just a used car? We don't buy used cars."

"Mr. Crenshaw, what's a used car? If you buy this new vehicle today, it's going to be a used car tomorrow. Are you saying you wouldn't buy this car, just because of that one day?"

"Well, no, I guess not."

"That's about what we're saying here. It isn't important to me which car you folks get. It's just my responsibility to tell you about nice benefits like the trips, when they happen. It wouldn't be fair for me not to tell you."

Buzz turned this time to Mrs. Crenshaw in the backseat. She seemed more enthused about this idea. "Why don't we at least go drive it?" she said cheerfully, "Shoot, if you can save thousands, and get a better car, and a Bahama suntan to boot, who can beat that?" Mrs. Crenshaw chuckled and Mr. Crenshaw didn't object.

Setting the customers on the dealership's target car. Within minutes the three were on the road again—in the dark green hardtop with the $1,500 bonus, a potential 33 percent interest rate, and $7,000 in damages. Buzz soon drove the vehicle to a side road and "assumed" Mr. Crenshaw into the driver's seat. Rather than ask if Crenshaw wanted to drive, Buzz had simply pulled off the road carefully, jumped out of the driver's seat, and opened Trent Crenshaw's door. Crenshaw headed to the driver's seat without thinking.

"Well, it's pretty nice alright," he commented as the car headed back down the shaded back road, "but it has got 6,800 miles on it, you know."

"But how hard do you work for $5,000?" Buzz had priced the car $5,000 less than the new one. Or, at least that's what it looked like. "And you know, that's going to lower your payments tons and tons."

"How much?"

"Oh, Chris Stretch, our financial adviser, will tell you all about that."

Playing financing hardball that seems like powder-puff ball. The Tracker computer program noted that the Crenshaws returned from their test-drive in thirteen minutes. Buzz led them into "the box," the special closing room recently redecorated with rich, dark green carpeting, old English prints, an imposing desk, and three very comfortable armchairs. A psychological design firm had fussed over this room for weeks as part of the design firm's own beta test for boxes at all the AFF dealerships. The customers' chairs in the box were six inches lower than the chairs of the staff. "This creates a subservient mentality," the design firm psychologist had said. The chairs had been carefully placed so that the customers were farther away from the door than the sales staff. "This creates a confinement mentality," the psychologist happily explained. Customers wishing to leave would have to walk past the sales force.

But the Crenshaws didn't seem anxious to leave at all. They were both excited about the car, charmed by Buzz, and comfortable with Chris Stretch. "Yes, we do like the car," Trent Crenshaw said to him, "plus your man here says we're going to pay $5,000 less than we were on the other one, and get a better warranty. Is that right? Oh, and I want to finance at our bank, First Bank."

Chris Stretch nodded agreement, his mind turning very quickly. First Bank had ranked nearly at the bottom on the MOPS profitability rating for the Crenshaw deal. And if Crenshaw planned to go *directly* to the bank himself, the dealership would get nothing from that. Hell, the bank would "direct" finance Crenshaw for 9 percent if Crenshaw had enough sense to deal with the bank in person. Thank God people didn't have that much sense!

But even if Stretch switched the Crenshaws to "indirect" financing with their bank—which means the dealership would fill out the bank's paperwork for an added profit on top of the bank's rate—Crenshaw's bank would only allow the dealership to charge a 14 percent rate on the Crenshaws' loan. The dealership would only make a 5 percent profit! Stretch wanted to use Mr. Hungry's 33 percent rate.

Stretch smiled slightly and began to work his computer's keyboard. The 20-inch screen, thin as a paperback, finished in a "comforting" matte green, was designed to swivel easily into the customer's view. But Stretch didn't swivel it at first.

"You are a smart man, Mr. Crenshaw," he said, "and we can, of course, handle the paperwork for you right here if you want to go through First Bank. But am I correct in saying you want the cheapest payment?"

"Well, yes, I suppose so. That's how you judge a loan, isn't it? I mean, all things being equal."

"It certainly is. Some of these finance people out there quote you a cheap rate and then load you down with fees. It's ridiculous," Stretch said. "That's why we do a wonderful thing here. Just look at this!" Stretch flipped the screen around to display an imposing chart. At the top was the Crenshaws' name and address. Under their name came a selling price comparison of the new vehicle and the used vehicle. The used vehicle was indeed priced $5,000 less than the new.

A meaningless comparison. The Crenshaws didn't know it, of course, but the comparison was meaningless because the "price" of the new vehicle had been raised nearly $5,000 above the MSRP. The MSRP price is on the window of every new car, and it comes with the car from the factory. But AFF stores, like most dealerships, add their own sticker next to the MSRP sticker. On the new car the Crenshaws had been considering, the AFF sticker had added these charges to the MSRP price: a $2,787 item listed only as "ADP PLAN" and a $2,176 item listed as "Ad, Adm, pop." What did these two items cost America's Family Friend? Nothing. "ADP PLAN" stands for "additional dealer profit plan." "Ad, Adm, pop" stands for advertising, administration, and popularity tax." Both charges are for "air" as the AFF national sales training director is fond of explaining to his acolytes.

Chris Stretch sat quietly for a moment as the Crenshaws studied the computer screen. Under the bold headline "Finance Options for the Crenshaws" were listed seven different finance companies, including both the Crenshaws' bank and Mr. Hungry, the finance company eager to finance their loan at up to 33 percent. Each finance source had a payment listed beside it, and the payment for the 33 percent interest rate approved by Mr. Hungry seemed to stand out just a bit from the others. It was deliberately scaled for slightly more contrast. Stretch let the Crenshaws discover the "cheap" payment among the seven. It was, of course, Mr. Hungry's payment. This screen did not show interest rates, months financed, or down payments—it just showed monthly payments. But Mr. Hungry's monthly payment had been calculated to include a $5,000 cash down payment. AFF knew the Crenshaws could afford that "down stroke" easily—their file showed a savings account of over $60,000; $5,000 down would be a detail. The monthly payment for the other six companies, however, had been calculated without *any* down payment. Of course Mr. Hungry's payment looked cheap.

Hooked by a payment. Trent Crenshaw liked the payment, too. "You know, it is a good bit cheaper than my bank's payment, isn't it?" His bank payment was listed next to Mr. Hungry's payment.

Chris Stretch looked somber. "Buzz, why don't you go get us a drink? Mr. and Mrs. Stretch, do you prefer Coke or iced tea?"

When Buzz had left, Chris started talking again. "Folks, I didn't want to say anything in front of the salesman, but did you have a little problem making payments a year or two ago?"

Both Crenshaws looked stunned. They were responsible people. And they knew they paid their bills on time . . . most of the time. Did those one or two late payments really affect their credit? "Well, uh, there isn't a problem, is there?"

Stretch gave a reassuring nod. "Not a real problem. But the credit report shows some late payments. And, you know, that's probably why your bank's payment isn't as good as this other one. Banks are getting awfully picky about these things. But being a little slow doesn't bother us at all. Shoot, it's even happened to me! Since our store is affiliated with America's Family Friend, we use our enormous power with the lenders to help folks like you two who are just a bit 'credit impaired,' as we say." Stretch just looked at the Crenshaws for a moment. Those lines always worked with people. And usually made them hesitant to go to their bank for a loan, too. Who wants to deal with someone who thinks your credit isn't good?

Reeled in for the kill. Trent Crenshaw raised his eyebrows in a silent question to his wife, then turned to Stretch. "Well, I guess we'll go with your lender." Mr. Hungry. Without a pause, Stretch pushed another button and moved on, "Now, did Buzz tell you about the new services we have been offering since you bought your last car from us?"

"Oh, you mean the life insurance? Oh, yes, I want that. I mean, it's only a couple of dollars a month, right?"

Chris looked at them with his most persuasive expression and said, "Yes, of course, you want life insurance on you, Mr. Crenshaw, and I'm sure health insurance, too. We can put it on your wife, too. But even more important, we have a lifetime service package, and I think it would really help you folks." Chris began to sell the add-ons. And Mr. Hungry had agreed to finance every single one Stretch could sell! He worked quickly. The "lifetime" extended warranty would cost only 79 cents a day. The window etching cost only 3.95 per week, the alarm system cost "less than a Pepsi a day." Collision and liability insurance cost $3 a day, "But we use local agents, you know. We just save you the work of even calling them, and then finance it for you at no charge. We recommend Stricklin Insurance."

"My God," Crenshaw said, "that's who we already use!" Chris, of course, knew that. AFF's new computer synergy with local insurance agents was paying off.

Chris didn't even mention the cost of life and accident/health insurance. The Crenshaws had already told them they wanted it. Such responsible people.

Mr. Crenshaw laughed as Chris Stretch described the Auto Club. "Well, that sounds pretty good, too. So, now, what is all this going to add to the payment?"

Stretch turned the screen back to him, pushed keys again, and started talking casually, "Well, you were going to pay down 30 percent, weren't you? That's what most folks do this day when they don't have a trade. That would be about $10,000."

Conditioning the Customers. Both Crenshaws turned pale. They had been thinking $1,000, certainly not $10,000. "Well, to tell you the truth, that would hurt us a bit. Can you help us with that?"

Of course he would. The $10,000 quote was just "conditioning" them for the down payment Stretch had in mind. He knew he needed only $5,000 down to make his projected profit on this deal. But he wanted every dime of cash he could get. He pushed buttons, continued to talk, and finally said, "We'll if you think you can handle $6,000, I'll get this done for you."

"Okay, we'll do that." Stretch instantly entered the $6,000 in the computer, and just as quickly raised the selling price of the vehicle by $1,000. Bingo! The dealership just made an additional $1,000 in profit.

Stretch frowned, then looked up positively. "Folks, with that down payment, and with all our service items, we are going to have you driving out in that car in about fifteen minutes, for just $979 per month." He didn't say another word, but waited for them to speak. Neither could. That payment was half their house payment and $350 more per month than the payment Chris had shown them less than an hour ago.

"There's just no way, no way!" Crenshaw said. Chris knew that. The actual payment on the amount the Crenshaws would need to finance was only $629 per month, not $979. Chris was just "working them on the payment." During the next seven minutes, he lowered their payment from $979 to $679. They said yes. Bingo! AFF only needed a $629 payment. Chris got $679, an additional $50 per month in profit for the dealership. He pushed a button, and the individual selling prices of the add-ons were raised just enough to eat up that fifty bucks.

Stretch sensed the Crenshaws were in cardiac arrest—running out of patience and money. He made one other slight adjustment. During all this time, the Crenshaws had not asked how many months they were financing. To help cover all this extra profit, without saying a word, he entered a keystroke that raised the number of months financed from seventy-two to seventy-eight. Without a pause he turned to Buzz. Buzz was having trouble not looking too eager just yet. "Buzz, let's get the Crenshaws rolling in that beauty!"

As Chris began to print out paperwork, over fifty-five pages of it, Buzz left the office, walking slowly at first, then nearly running to the break room. "Jesus is Lord! Hallelujah! And his name is Chris Stretch! Guys, how much walking-around money is on that wrecked thing sitting out front!"

"Fifteen hundred dollars."

"Hey, come help me get these idiots' stuff switched out of their old car! Chris just hammered 'em to the wall!"

One of the new saleswomen helped Buzz clean out the Crenshaws' old car and neatly place everything in the one they were purchasing. Buzz set the radio dial to the Crenshaws' favorite station, checked out a bottle of the $7 champagne from the goody room, placed it on the front seat, and drove the car right up to the office window where the Crenshaws were beginning to sign paperwork.

"All this paperwork is just a formality." Inside, Chris "fanned" them through all fifty-five pages of releases, warnings, long-winded verbiage on warranties, deliberately wordy descriptions of dealership customer philosophies, and then moved them quickly through the contract itself. The idea was to wear the customer out with the sheer volume of paperwork, lots of it unnecessary, then casually but very quickly move them through it, just like fanning a deck of cards. The very first sheet in the great pile, the sheet the Crenshaws barely looked at and then signed, was in many ways the most important for the dealership. This sheet alone required *ten* signatures. One of the middle paragraphs said, "I have carefully read every sheet of paper I have signed and understand them." Legal protection in case the Crenshaws actually *did* read all the pages later and wanted to change their minds.

Chris quickly signaled to Buzz, standing at the window, to lead the Crenshaws from the office before they decided to actually read any of the paperwork they had signed. He then folded the paperwork and placed it in a self-sealing envelope. The psychologist had recommended the self-sealing envelopes. "They lessen the chance the paperwork will be looked at anytime soon," he had said lightly. Chris handed the envelope to Buzz. "Here, why don't you put this in the glove box for the Crenshaws? I want to take them down to sign up for the Bahama trip." The trip was such a nice distraction, too!

Chris and Buzz waved happily as the Crenshaws drove off. It had been a nice one hour, twenty-nine minutes, and thirty-six seconds of work, according to the Tracker Computer Program. Chris had not been able to hammer these people with a 33 percent rate, but he had at least gotten them up to 19 percent interest with Mr. Hungry. That made the profit on interest alone $3,124.

The Lifetime Service Agreement netted them $1,400. The profit on the car itself was only $700, but who cared? The car had been *wrecked*. The dealership would have sold it for a massive loss, if necessary. That sucker was just the excuse for making money! The window etching added as much profit as the car, $700; the liability and collision over $1,200; the alarm system, $500; the double life insurance premium netted $1,241; and the accident and health premium, $1,975. Not bad at all.

Chris pushed a button, which quickly "washed" the deal. The computer totaled the profit for the deal, calculated commissions for salespeople, and instantaneously delivered all that information to America's Family Friend Headquarters. The MOPS system began to use these numbers, too, to refine its fuzzy logic, help it do better on the next deal at any of AFF's hundreds of dealerships.

Chris and Buzz knew that but couldn't have cared less. All they cared about was the printout quietly exiting Ronnie's printer. It was the profit and commission summary.

Crenshaw: #13,482

Front-End Gross:	$ 700
Finance Profit:	$ 3,124
Service Agreement Profit:	$ 1,400
Life and Health Insurance Profit:	$ 3,216
Collision and Liability Profit:	$ 1,275
Etching:	$ 700
Alarm:	$ 500
TOTAL PROFIT:	**$ 10,915**

Buzz got on his knees as he looked at that sheet and bowed twice to Chris Stretch. "Thank you, Great Mahatma. Now, what will *I* make?"

"Oh about two grand. Plus half of that $1,500 bonus—I get the other half since I helped you switch them, you know."

More money than Buzz had made in total in the last five weeks. He got up and slapped Chris on the back. "Man, I'll split all my deals with you. You're *supernatural!*"

Stretch laughed and looked at his watch. "Get out of here! I'm the online expert in the chat rooms at three. Gotta go help a few other customers, you know."

Could This Really Happen to You?

Well, let me ask you something: Could you handle paying an extra $4.33 a day, about $133 a month, if you thought you were getting a *good* deal on a car you believed was a *great* car? If you could—if you let a dealership needlessly raise you that $133 a month—you just threw away $10,300 on a seventy-eight-month loan like the Crenshaws' loan. If you finance for only sixty months, as many people do, you would have thrown away $8,000. Would that hurt?

Is the Car Business Really This Relentless in Ripping Every Penny from Even the Poorest Customer?

It's not as bad as I have written here. It's shoddier! You've been reading about the first-rate guys, reading about generally accepted practices, at least in the mind of the retail auto business. For instance, Chris Stretch may have raised the selling price of the Crenshaws' vehicle without them knowing it; he may have raised the interest rate without mentioning that little detail; and he may have upped the months the Crenshaws would finance without saying a word. But when the negotiations were over, Chris Stretch presented the Crenshaws with paperwork and an installment loan contract based on all those price increases, interest rates, and increased months financed. The paperwork made the deal legal, Chris Stretch believes.

A disquieting note about the impact of technology on this practice. In the past, many of the "reworks" of the Crenshaw deal, which raised the profit without telling the customer, would have been traceable for legal purposes. The reworks would have happened on paper at the salesperson's desk, and copies of different versions of buyer's orders and conditional sales contracts might have remained in dealer files, but dealerships are moving quickly away from incriminating paperwork. Now "reworks" happen in the computer many times, and the only version preserved of any deal is the last version. The net result? Consumers will have a much harder time proving they've been defrauded.

"But what about selling a car with $7,000 in damages?" In some states, the seller doesn't have to disclose damage unless it exceeds 50 percent of the value of the vehicle. Think about that! Would you want to buy a used Lexus without knowing it had $25,000 in damages? It could happen to you. And don't expect the insurance companies who allow such abuse to come to your defense, either. One representative of the insurance industry actually stated under oath that a severely wrecked vehicle is better than a nonwrecked vehicle.[2] Makes you want to run your car into a wall, doesn't it?

A very bad trend: secretly reconditioning wrecks for sale. Because of the very loose disclosure laws in many states, some dealerships are actually deliberately *buying* wrecked vehicles from insurance companies for a trifle, repairing them at their collision centers, and then, without disclosing the damage, selling them for very handsome profits to nice persons like you. (Selling reconditioned wrecks without disclosure is also common practice with cars that are "curbed," seemingly sold by individuals who park them in parking lots and driveways.) We'll show you how to prevent being taken in by such deceptions later.

"What about putting the Crenshaws on the highest interest rate?" Perfectly legal anywhere, unless you have a written guarantee that the company choosing the financing source is using the cheapest loan source available based on your credit. And you're going to have to break two arms to get that guarantee. The dealership's goal is to find the best rate for them, not for you.

And I haven't told you about the really bad stuff yet. Wait till you read what the players in the subprime financial market are doing with subprime lending to help abuse the truly poor and credit impaired.

Won't Financing on the Web Save Me from This?

Financing rip-offs are generally *worse* on the Web, unless you are dealing with a very few noncommercial sites or dealing with the Web site of your bank or your credit union. At times, even those sources can hurt you. You are not a human being to most Web businesses. You are an inconsequential response nodule, not even a speck of sand on the beach. Try this experiment: Go to some Web finance sites. Go to a pure finance site and to the finance Web page of a dealership and/or manufacturer. Send an e-mail to those sites using an impossibly stupid name and an impossibly stupid question, and watch what comes back.

For instance, enter your name as I. M. Asucker on one of their friendly forms. Ask if they finance cars if you live on the moon or Mars. Under "special comments," say you're only twelve years old. You will get an answer that takes you seriously. That's because these sites, except for smaller independent dealerships (about as rare as heavy water), are computer driven, not human driven. At least with finance salespersons like Chris Stretch you can look them in the eye, threaten to leave on the spot, and finance directly at your bank—you can duel. You can't do that with the Internet companies.

"What about finance sites that promise to 'shop' your loan for the best rate? Or 'guarantee' the lowest rate?" None of them will meaningfully guarantee that you're getting the cheapest financing and cheapest total loan cost. Please read that again.

Some sites offer you a $100 guarantee that they'll beat any rates. But for that guarantee to be meaningful, you usually must do a lot of legwork—you have to apply for loans at other sites, submit their approvals, and so forth. The guarantee is meaningless. And some Web sites say they'll guarantee you'll get the rate their lending sources quote you. And some say, "Here are the competitive rates in your market." But none tell you what you really need to know:

- **The Web "comparison" sites generally add a layer of cost to a loan you could make directly.** For instance, your local bank may be part of a "comparison" Web site. That costs money. If you have a good relationship with the local branch of your bank, you will probably pay less for a car loan by visiting your branch. Banks *love* direct loans because they make the loan without paying commissions. Take advantage of that.

- **"Convenience" isn't worth thousands of dollars.** How much time do you really save by borrowing online? Six hours? Did you make $2,000 during the last six hours? Convenience is a Trojan horse in the finance business.

- **Rate comparison sites obviously quote only rates from their cooperating sources.** A site might have a thousand sources, but it might not have the one remaining independent bank in your community that just happens to be having a rate sale this week.

- **Very few of the commercial finance Web sites tell you that a credit union may beat their rates.** Credit unions don't exist as far as most commercial Web sites are concerned. Why? The sites don't make any money with credit unions. But a credit union loan may save you thousands of dollars and endless hassle, as we'll see in a minute. And you are probably eligible for membership in one, if you don't belong right now. See page 214.

    An exception and a caution: Some online dealerships list credit unions as potential sources for loans. Although they may quote you a loan rate based on a credit union's lending policies, the dealership will generally try to switch you from that rate to a more profitable rate. Be sure to read the Credit Union portion of this chapter on page 214.

- **Testimonials on Web sites are worthless.** Generally, anyone, including an employee, can submit a testimonial, and specifically testimonials are worthless because they are not statistically based—one tree does not make a forest.

"What's the most basic problem with online finance services?" Because online financial services use a computer program to determine whether or not you will get a loan, because they use a computer program to determine your loan interest rate, your chances of getting the best loan rate and terms are diminished if you have even a hiccup in your credit history. Computers can't "eyeball" you, a process that's still a valuable part of the decision-making process at some banks and most credit unions. Even Chris Stretch is better at times than even the smartest computer.

"Are you saying forget the Web when it comes to financing?" No. Some really great loans are available on the Web, and, at the very least, the Web provides opportunities to compare rates before you actually pick your financing source. But the Web is dangerous because it encourages you to move too fast and too trustingly. *The Web is not the only place to find cheap, smart money.* Don't fall for the "infallibility" of high tech! At the end of the day, your best loan source might be your grandmother's war bonds. Your goal is to look at all potential sources before deciding the best source.

Some Other Creepy Realities You Need to Think About

Your Credit History Isn't What You Think It Is

Some "opinion" on your creditworthiness is flying around the Internet or is dwelling in a gazillion databases right now. That "opinion" may not technically qualify as an unauthorized credit report, but in reality it serves as one.

For instance, even though you pay your bills on time, your request for a limit increase on your charge account at Magic Crystals for You has been denied. Turns out Magic Crystals for You is having cash-flow problems, so it can't extend any more credit. So Crystals sells your account information to a subprime credit card company looking for customers that pay their bills. The subprime credit card company then sells its list to a subprime mortgage broker. Your name and address begin to show up on subprime data lists around the world. Your mere presence on those lists damages your credit rating.

Conversely, you have applied for a car loan in the past year or two and been approved for a very high amount of money. Your name is sold to credit card companies hungry for new cardholders. Your mailbox fills with "preapproved" credit card notices, you accept all the cards, and you're now using one card to pay the other. Pretty soon you'll show up on a subprime database, which leads us to the really creepy reality: **Your credit may not be as good as you think.** Figures published by the major credit bureaus describe more than 40 percent of individuals as having credit scores of C+ or lower (699 and below on the FICO score). Many lenders consider such individuals prime candidates for *subprime* rates. More alarming, several years ago an auto industry insider described 60 percent of the buying public as "credit impaired."[3] That blemish on your perfect credit can be caused by something as simple as one payment thirty days overdue on any bill. Have you ever done that? Or it could simply be that you've changed jobs once in the past year. Or have you moved once? All these things affect your credit in "risk-based computer scoring."

Have you ever accepted a "rate teaser" credit card? Even though you may have made all your payments on time on this card, some rate-teaser credit card issuers have been guilty of deliberately reporting you as being delinquent on a payment or two.[4] Why? If these fine people can ruin your credit a bit, you'll have to stay with their credit card, even when their rates go moon-high, because you won't qualify anymore for a cheaper card from some other issuer.

Dealerships and lenders love customers with "slightly impaired" credit. In fact, they much prefer you to "A" risks. Whether it's an online lender or a "financial counselor" at a dealership, they know they will make much more money on you if you're nervous about your credit—or if they can make you a bit nervous about your credit. Think about how the Crenshaws reacted.

So why not order your federally mandated free credit report to find out your creditworthiness?

About now you're probably asking, "Well, should I just order that free online credit report that federal law allows and see how bad I am?" Unfortunately, even your federally mandated free credit report doesn't tell you the most important number related to creditworthiness—your *credit score*. You'll have to purchase that as I show you below. All the "free credit score" offers you see advertised online or in e-mails are about as useful as an expired credit card. Ignore them.

What is a credit score? Credit scoring is a system of statistically analyzing credit reports that provides a simple three-digit score that compares an individual's past and current credit performance to that of similar consumers. Your credit score provides lenders, or other potential creditors such as insurance companies or landlords, a quick, fairly objective way to assess your creditworthiness—or likely ability to pay back an auto loan or mortgage or pay the rent.

A credit score is often also called a "FICO score," after the Fair Isaac Corporation, which developed the most widely used analytical system and software. It may also be called a "credit rating." Although individual credit bureaus or credit reporting agencies (CRAs) adapt, add to, or modify Fair Isaac models to suit their needs and provide their own credit score, most have used the FICO score or system as a foundation.

The FICO-based systems use a numerical scale from about 300 to 900. These scales are also broken down into alphabetical categories. Each bureau's exact formula for determining that score is guarded closely, but the formulas include such factors as payment history, the amount a person owes, the length of the credit history, the types of credit, and the amount of new credit.

Recently, the "big three" CRAs—Equifax, Experian, and Trans-Union—have introduced a new credit scoring system, called Vantage Score, to compete with the FICO score. The Vantage Score is based on a scale of 501 to 990 and their own letter "grade." For now, the jury is out on whether lenders will buy into the Vantage Score, and the FICO model is still king.(Check www.dontgettakeneverytime.com for the latest information.)

From "prime" to "subprime," how are credit scores ranked? There's not one recognized national standard for which categories of scores represent a "good" credit rating and where the dividing line is between "good" and "bad" or "subprime" credit ratings. Generally, the higher your credit score, the better. The best scores, indicating high creditworthiness, are from the mid-700s and higher. Credit scores below 620 are considered poor. Most people fall in the 600s and 700s. Different lenders will give various scores different weights, but, typically, scoring 680 or above puts you in the category of an average or better credit risk. Here's a typical breakdown:

900 (or 850)–800	13%, "A" tier
799–750	27% "B+" tier
749–700	18% "B" tier
699–650	15% "C+" tier
649–600	12% "C" tier

Subprime Scores

599–550	8% "D" tier
549–500	5% "E" tier
499–300	2% "F–G–H" tier

If your credit score is 750 or above, for example, you are the best prime borrower with an "A" or "B+" credit. In a fair world, you should be given financing rates in line with that excellent credit rating. Your rate and financing terms should be equivalent to others in that 740+ credit scoring category. But "qualifying" for the best rates often doesn't mean actually getting them.

How many lenders use credit scoring to create "bait-and-switch" advertisements? Though the advertisements don't tell you, to qualify for cheapo rates such as 2.9 percent, most national lending companies require a credit rating of 740 or higher—and probably fewer than four in ten of us have that rating. In addition, even if you have that rating, there's still a good chance you won't get the great rate unless you do your financing homework and negotiate. That's why you ought to know your credit score.

Where can you get your credit report and your credit score? Consumers throughout the United States have the right to a free annual credit report from each of the three major CRAs. These federally mandated free reports are available *only online* at www.annualcreditreport.com or by phone at 1–877–322–8228; this is a service run by the three major CRAs. Unfortunately, many scam artists run fake "get your free credit report" Web sites that exist just to "harvest" your personal information such as Social Security number and bank account numbers that they can use to steal your money. At best, even the legitimate "free credit report" sites provide out-of-date information, and their main purpose typically is to sell you expensive "credit-monitoring services." So, get your free credit reports from this Web site or by calling this number.

You may purchase your credit score from any of the major CRAs through this site, too, or you can head right to the Fair Isaac Corporation at www.myfico.com. Whether you like your credit score or are alarmed by it, begin managing it by checking your credit report carefully for errors. Because your credit report provides the primary information used to determine your credit score and your creditworthiness, correct any errors you find immediately.

You can reach the three major credit reporting bureaus online at these Web sites:

www.experian.com
www.equifax.com
www.transunion.com

To reach the three major reporting bureaus by phone or mail:

Experian
1–888–397–3742
TDD 1–800–972–0322

Equifax Consumer Direct
1–888–532–0179

TransUnion LLC
Consumer Disclosure Center
P.O. Box 1000
Chester, PA 19022

*Back to the second most important step in buying a car—
shopping your financing*

All these situations with credit lead us to the second important
step you must take (after shopping the wholesale value of your
trade) if you really care about saving money: *Always* shop for
your financing before you shop for your car.

Whether shopping at a dealership or online, most people find
the car they like, then arrange their budget on the spot to fit the
car. You may say, "Hey, I really like the look of that! What will
it cost me?" That approach is the most expensive approach to
car buying or leasing. A smart shopper finds the cheapest and
best loan source first. A really smart shopper (that's you) then
uses that loan source to drive the rest of the transaction. The
routine goes like this:

- Find the cheapest and best financing source (we do that
  now);
- Develop a car budget based on the amount of money that
  source will give you;
- Do your homework on vehicles that fit your budget;
- Choose the right source for that vehicle (dealerships, Web
  sites, classifieds);
- Buy or lease it;
- Break out the Château d'Yquem.

What Are Your Financing Sources?

At the end of this chapter, we show you how to quickly shop for
the best rate, but, first, consider your options before you shop.
And don't forget that www.dontgettakeneverytime.com has an
up-to-date discussion and our opinions of different types of loan
sources.

1. Uncle Festus or Aunt Bea

There's no shame in a little family help now and then. And lots
of people need to be making $10,000 yearly gifts to tax-shield

their estates a bit. How long since you've been to see those nice people, or at least sent them an instant message?

2. Cash Value in Your Life Insurance

If you're one of the few remaining people with whole-life insurance, you can borrow that cash value for a charge generally less than half of that from any other source. Your insurance will stay in effect, too. Call your agent and ask for a statement of cash value. If you choose to finance by this method, you would be wise to make arrangements to pay monthly sums back into your policy.

3. A Home Equity Line of Credit

If you are a responsible borrower, a home equity loan may have certain advantages for you, particularly from a tax point of view. But don't use this method to finance a car into the twenty-second century—keep the loan as short as you can stand. You may want to check with your tax accountant to see if this option makes sense for you.

Recommended sources: Many credit unions and most banks offer home equity loans. If you have a relationship with a bank or a credit union, go to them first for this type of loan.

"What about online or TV-advertised home equity mortgages?" In my opinion, forget it, especially if you are considering an online mortgage or one hawked on TV because you're worried about your credit or because you already have a high debt-to-value rating on your home or apartment (if you already owe over 75 percent of your property's value). Many of these online services are *very dangerous*. Likewise, the TV hucksters. You've seen the Web banners and television ads with the toll-free phone numbers or online applications: "125 percent of your home's value! Just call 1–800–rip-offs!" These companies, regardless of their claims online or on air, usually charge dramatically

Note: *Because I have consulted extensively with credit unions around the country and have designed an educational program for many of the credit unions that belong to the Credit Union National Association, please hold what I say about the value of credit unions to the highest scrutiny.*

higher rates and fees than conventional banks, and they give you virtually no grace periods before they seize your home.

"Why not get one of our fine credit cards along with your new car and your eviction notice?" Some of these on-line companies will issue you a credit card tied directly to your home equity loan. Be sure to read the fine print on that credit card before using it to take a vacation in your new Ex-penso Gargantula. One lender stated, "You may lose your home if you *miss any of these payments.*"[5] (emphasis added) How would you like to lose your home because you were late on a credit card payment?

4. Credit Unions

With all their faults, credit unions are perhaps the best place to be, and if you don't belong, you probably can.

If you do, I think you will find that in this age of high technology, nanosecond cons, and Internet glitziness, many credit unions are your cheapest and certainly least deceptive source for a loan. Compared to just about every loan source, credit unions are straightforward and positively homey, like comfort food. Good credit unions will give you high-quality, unbiased consumer information, too.

The drawback with some credit unions. Unfortunately, a large number of credit unions with the best of intentions, are probably hurting their members rather than helping them as they try to compete in the Brave New Automotive

World. These credit unions have gone to bed, as they say, with the car dealers themselves. This alliance usually shows itself in a deceptively simple way: You don't have to go to the credit union to get your loan. You do all the credit union paperwork right there at the dealership.

This "service" is called indirect lending, and dealerships are quick to tout its benefits to the buyer. In the perfect world, it should be a benefit, too: You could save a trip to the credit union. But the car business isn't the perfect world; it's a world in which dealerships are looking for new ways to "work" you. And having a relationship with a credit union is a perfect time for a dealership to work you, and work you hard. The end result: You pay more money. "Oh, we're a *partner* with your credit union," a salesperson will say. "They let us do the paperwork for them. And think how convenient it is, too." Instantly your defenses go down, and you begin to believe the Killer Monsoons and Chris Stretches of the world who are just waiting for the moment you become trusting.

And why shouldn't you feel trusting? How could this be a bad dealership if your credit union trusts them? Trouble is, the dealership forgot to tell you one little thing: Your credit union—which is supposed to be saving you money—is probably paying the dealership a fat commission for processing your loan, sometimes up to $1,000. Would you drive to the credit union to save $1,000? Or even a paltry $200?

So, what are the warnings here? If a dealership says your credit union is a "partner" with them, don't drop your guard for a minute during any part of the transaction. That dealership will take you to the cleaners just as quickly as the next. And if the dealership wants, "as a service," to do your credit union loan paperwork, don't do that without first calling your credit union and asking if the dealer fee is paid by you or paid by the credit union. If it's paid by you, do the paperwork directly at your credit union. While you're there, why not find your credit union manager and ask him or her why the credit union had not disclosed their extra charge to you for filling out paperwork at the dealership?

Even with these problems and a few others, credit unions have quite a few pluses going for most of them.

- **Credit unions are nonprofit and member owned.**
  Since credit unions are member-owned cooperatives, a credit union gets stronger because its members get stronger financially, because the members save money, make responsible loans, and so forth. That means a credit union has a vested interest in your continuing financial integrity. They don't want to see you overextend yourself. Many credit unions even have trained staff members or special Web sites that will tell you if you may be paying too much for a particular vehicle. You certainly can't say the same for other financing sources.

- **Some credit unions will finance individuals with little or no credit, particularly if they have been members of the credit union for some time.** Credit unions have been slow to enter the subprime field, but some are entering it now. If you are a first-time borrower or have very little established credit, talk to a credit union first. If you've had problems with your credit, but can explain them ("I was run over by a car dealer and missed work"), many will work with you. And unlike some of the vultures we'll talk about in a minute, a credit union won't use your lack of credit as a weapon against you. Compared with the other subprime sources we're going to tell you about, a credit union rate will generally be dramatically cheaper.

- **Credit unions generally have no selling bias.** Credit unions couldn't care less if you buy a Ford or a Honda. Their advice, therefore, is generally much more impartial when it comes to giving you information concerning the safety, reliability, and resale value of vehicles.

- **Credit union total loan costs generally beat bank and dealership loan costs even during dealership "rate sales."** The key phrase here is "total loan cost," which includes interest, rebates, and fees. Remember, it is only the total loan cost that matters to you. We'll show you how to make this comparison yourself using the Internet, if you want to. But generally speaking, credit unions are a cheaper financing source.

- **Credit unions generally make used-car loans at the same rate as new-car loans.** *That alone could save you thousands.* Do you remember the Crenshaws? The folks who financed the wrecked used car with Mr. Hungry, the finance company that would let the dealership charge 33 percent interest on a used-car loan? Dealerships and some online lending institutions *do that all the time.* How can they get away with it? Because most states allow lending sources to charge ridiculously higher interest rates on used-vehicle loans. How much higher? In some states, *there is no limit on used-car interest rates.* What the traffic will bear is the favorite rate.

   But most credit unions lend money on you, not on the vehicle. If they will finance you at 7 percent on a new car, they'll finance you at 7 percent on a recent-model used car. A dealership or online financing service might charge you 33 percent for the same loan. *Note: If you plan to finance a used vehicle, always check a credit union's rate against your other loan sources.*

- **Credit unions generally charge much less for life insurance, disability insurance, and for service agreements, too.** About 72 percent of all credit unions provide life insurance *at no cost.* On a $20,000 loan, that can save you $800 *on your life insurance alone* compared to the charges at the average car dealership or Web seller. Compared to dealerships and Web sellers, most credit unions charge about half for disability insurance. Most credit unions offer service agreements for under $800, while many dealerships and Web sellers charge you up to $1,900 for virtually the same agreement.

- **"But can credit unions beat those great 2.9 percent rates I saw on the Web?"** Many credit unions generally beat that, too. Just take the rebate (or "cash back" or "cash allowance," the new terms used by the manufacturers now) rather than taking the 2.9 percent. Use that money as a down payment at the credit union or even at a bank. Though the manufacturer's *rate* may be lower, the total *overall* cost of the loan will generally be less. Let's look at this for a moment using a fairly extreme example with a very low dealership rate and relatively high credit union rate:

How 10% APR Can Beat 0% APR

	0%	10%
Cost of new car	$15,000	$15,000
Less equity in trade	$3,000	$3,000
Less rebate	$0	$2,000
Months financed	24	36
Amount to finance	$12,000	$10,000
Finance charge	$0	$1,610
Monthly payment	$500	$322.50
Total cost of financing	$12,000	$11,610
Savings at 10% APR	$0	$390

Even though, in this example, the manufacturer's loan sounds cheaper because of the interest rate, you'll save by financing at the credit union. As we said, you can use the same technique—taking the cash back or rebate rather than the dealer rate—if you want to finance at a bank, too.

- **Credit unions loan money on a simple interest basis.** All credit unions (and banks) lend money on a simple interest basis and determine interest by the declining balance method when a loan is prepaid. Some dealerships, other lending institutions, and many Web sellers still charge interest by the "add-on" method and use the "Rule of 78s" method to determine how much interest you owe when you pay off a loan before its contracted term is over. If you pay your loan off early, this penalizes you because these techniques load the interest to the front of the loan.
- **Many credit unions *really* offer credit counseling and they help build your credit, too.** Some dealerships, many Web sites, and lots of manufacturers like to pretend they give sound financial advice. The key word here is

"pretend." But good credit unions have genuine credit counselors to help you budget and help you dig yourself out of financial holes.

Credit unions build your credit, too, if you do business with them. Unscrupulous lenders like to tell you, "You can borrow money at a credit union, but if you do, you won't be building any credit. You know, credit unions do not report information to credit bureaus." Years ago that was a true statement. It's generally a lie today.

Other funny sellers of money also like to tell you, "Don't use up your credit with your credit union. Save them for important things. We'll handle this little auto loan." Right. Credit unions are eager for all your business. You can't "use up" your credit there any more than you can "use up" your credit at any other financial institution.

Finding a Credit Union If You Don't Have One

Obviously ask at work. If your company doesn't actually have its own credit union, it may have a relationship with one that allows you to join. Failing that, the Credit Union National Association, the largest credit union organization in the United States, provides a credit union locator. Go to www.creditunion.coop/cu_locator/index.html.

Give a Credit Union a Test-Drive

If you'd like to check out a credit union that emphasizes member education, I recommend Digital Federal Credit Union (DCU). For many years, I have worked with them as national spokesperson for their *StreetWise* member education programs. Go to www.dcu.org and click on "StreetWise" for information on car buying and other consumer issues. DCU welcomes non-members to use their information and calculators. Feel free to roam the site and tell them Remar sent you.

Credit Unions on the Web

If you already belong to a credit union, it probably has a Web site and, if so, definitely will have an auto section online. And if you belong to a larger credit union, you can also probably get a pre-approved loan online. Find that credit union newsletter you've been meaning to read and look for the credit union Web address.

5. Brand-Name Prime Banks

Brand-name prime banks, such as Chase, Bank of America, or Citibank, are morphing into odd creatures. As we'll see in a bit, some of them are in bed with some of the toughest people in the auto business, financial services, and e-commerce. Many of these same prime banks have also become as aggressive and deceptive in their loan practices as the worst of them—particularly in their subprime loan area. That's right—the blue-chip banks, keeping up with the captive finance sources such as Ford Motor Credit, are leading the way in making subprime lending "respectable." They are *not*, as we'll see in the subprime section, leading the way in lowering rip-off subprime rates, however.

But a straightforward bank loan can be a very good thing. A bank loan may be your best choice, particularly if you already have a physical relationship with a bank (actually have a branch you deal with), if you have good credit, and if you are dealing *directly* with the bank. But remember, "direct" means you go into the bank to arrange the loan. If you're using an on-line service to buy your vehicle and let that service arrange your loan, you are making an "indirect" loan, and you will generally pay for that privilege. Indirect loans almost always mean the bank is paying the arranger a fee, and it is customary in the auto business to pass all fees and expenses on to you, the customer.

How bank rates compare to "captive" rates. If you are financing directly, a bank is generally cheaper than the "captive" houses used by dealerships (such as GMAC, Toyota Credit, or Ford Motor Credit). It's generally true even if the captive source is offering 2.9 percent financing. Simply take the "cash back" or "rebate" in lieu of the cheap interest rate and use it as a down payment at your bank. **Bank rates on used-car loans are generally much, much cheaper than "captive" rates.**

A no-no: Don't use "indirect" bank financing. *If you plan to finance with a bank, do your paperwork **at the bank,** not at the dealership.* You'll find that the dealership will be happy to "handle the paperwork for you as a service," as the dealership finance salesperson will tell you with a smile, but you'll pay a fat premium to the dealership for that convenience. How much extra could you pay for a little paperwork? On a sixty-month, $25,000, new-car loan, you could throw away $2,500. On a sixty month, $25,000 used-car loan, you could easily throw away $6,000.

How banks determine your interest rate. Obviously, your credit is a factor as well as the number of months you plan to finance. But many banks also give lower rates to customers who already have checking or savings accounts with them. Banks also *negotiate*. Don't be shy in saying, "Well, my credit union beat that rate by 1 percent."

Bank employees, if you're dealing with them in person, and if you're dealing with a real bank versus a subprime bank, are also "low pressure" salespeople, much like credit union employees. Their life and disability insurance is generally cheaper than that offered by dealerships and more expensive than insurance purchased through credit unions.

Surfing your bank online. Bank Web sites are a good place to get rate comparisons, but remember that the site can't bargain on the rate. Your local loan officer might. **A tip:** Some banks are offering online auto specials to build their online business. The specials are supposedly only for the banks "best" customers. But who defines "best?" If a bank is willing to make you a loan, it is able to give you its preferred rate, if it wants to. To find your bank online, look on your monthly bank statement for the Web site address.

6. Online Loan Companies and Services

It seems even morticians will make or help you make online auto loans these days. Almost any site related to cars and trucks

will happily send you to a loan site. They, of course, get a cut.
Check out your favorite search engine or Web portal, such as
Yahoo!, AOL, or MSN—they'll have links to a lender. They get
money for the nanosecond it takes their computer to forward
your click to an advertising lender. LendingTree.com, a rate
shopping search engine, will find you a conventional auto loan,
or a home equity auto loan, or a subprime auto loan, and then
help you find a car! LendingTree.com gets a cut at every branch
of the tree you eventually use.

There's absolutely nothing wrong with any of these people
getting a piece of your pie. But because they get a piece, none
of these sources is likely to tell you that some other source
might be cheaper or better for you. Your strategy here, therefore, is to accept the chirpy words and easy promises of online
lending operations with several grains of sea salt. The average
profit per loan of many online lending services is often dramatically higher than the profit you would pay at a walk-up source
because those online pages lull you in complacency rather than
stir you to high alert.[6]

Getting an ironclad rate quote online. To get an ironclad interest rate commitment online, you will be required to actually apply for a loan. "Estimates" or simple "rate quotes" are
meaningless. Each lender that receives your loan application has
the right to pull a credit report on you. As I've said before, excessive credit report inquiries—even for one loan—used to
lower your credit rating. Even worse, there were lending companies on the Web who deliberately "shotgunned" your loan application in a manner that required every single potential lender
to pull its own credit report. The result was that your credit rating was lowered and the rate at online loan companies went up;
and the company that shotgunned your loan application
achieved its objective—it got your loan. Though many companies still shotgun your application, the damage to you is less
severe these days. Credit reporting bureaus typically distinguish
inquiries about a single loan within a focused time period (such
as thirty days) from a group of inquiries about a variety of new
credit sources. Multiple inquiries within two weeks about an
auto loan or mortgage, for instance, wouldn't necessarily lower

your credit score, but a bunch of applications for new credit cards would. Responsible companies don't do shotgunning, of course. They pull one credit report on you and send that credit report to their lending sources. Those are the only companies to deal with.

How to protect yourself from online shotgun credit inquiries. But you may be dealing with bad guys without knowing it, so do this if you are shopping for a loan online: Before you fill out *any* credit application online—whatever the site, including one run by the Almighty—send an e-mail inquiry that asks the question, *"Does your site pull one credit report and send that credit report to potential lenders, or do your potential lenders each pull a credit report on me?"* If you don't receive a direct answer, or if the source says its sources all pull credit reports, don't use them. If you receive that answer or any other, download it or print it and keep it on file.

We give you search engine keywords and sample sites at the end of this chapter, and at www.dontgettakeneverytime.com.

7. The "Captive" Sources

Captive sources include manufacturer-related companies such as GMAC and FMCC, their relationship with their dealers, and dealership financing itself. (The appendix contains a list of captive financing sites.)

Think you can "shop" dealership financing? Think again. You're going to have a difficult, if not impossible, time "shopping" rates meaningfully at captive sources such as GMAC and Ford, or at a dealership, or a dealership Web site.

The dealership financing sources themselves are as good or as bad as any. Many times, if you know how to ask, and if you have the toughness of an armadillo's shell plus the tenacity of a pit bull, a dealership may actually give you the cheapest as well as best overall loan rather than lose you as a customer.

However, don't expect the dealership's captive financing sources such as Ford Motor Credit, Toyota Motor Credit, and

GMAC to help you in shopping captive rates on the Web. They may provide "applications" for "preapprovals" or for various types of loans at these corporate Web sites, but they actually don't make direct auto loans. Their role is to link you to a dealership. That's what "captive" means—these sources supply loans through the dealers.

Let's play ball! Regardless of your credit, *every* dealership salesperson will give you a rate quote for shopping purposes, that's not the problem. Here's the trouble: The rate quote doesn't mean anything because the dealership generally has no intention of actually financing you at that rate. They're just playing a game called "putting you out on a ball." They give you a rate quote that will beat anyone else's rate quote to get you hooked. Putting you out on a ball is standard industry practice, and it works like this:

You visit a dealership Web site: If you ask for a rate quote, you'll be given a meaningless answer or instantly asked to fill out a credit statement (don't). Or you're feeling courageous and decide to call the dealership directly.

"Yes, I'm shopping around for the best rate, and the bank quoted me 0 percent interest."

"Well, ma'am, if you come in today, we can do better than that! Now, what time did you say you want to come in? Our no-interest-plus-a-trip-to-the-moon sale ends at five o'clock today."

"Well, I couldn't come in today, anyway."

"Oh, they just extended the contest as we speak. And *tomorrow* it's *two* free trips to the moon. Now, what did you say your credit card number was?"

"Well, I've got an appointment at my bank tomorrow."

"Wow, they just made it *four* trips to the moon, just for those folks thinking about going to their bank tomorrow. Does eight or nine tomorrow morning work best for you? I'll just bring the car and the contract to your home."

It really is like that.

Why dealerships have to be that way. The auto loan is the complex, explosive engine that drives the entire dealership sales process. Without the loan, which allows the dealership to mask their shell games in the monthly payment, a dealership has a hard time playing their games with you and your money.

"Yes, I'm a financial adviser. Of course I am. I really *am* a financial adviser. Now, I advise you to give me all your money." Dealership finance salespeople, whether they are talking to you in person or e-mailing you, all neglect to do a very telling thing: they never refer to themselves as salespeople. "Oh, I'm the business manager," is a common phrase, or "I'm the Web coordinator" is another.

In reality, whatever the title, the person that talks money with you at a dealership or dealership Web site is nothing but a sophisticated and highly paid salesperson with little or no interest in your true well-being. The person in the finance office couldn't care less whether or not you can afford a particular car or really need their very expensive insurance or vastly overpriced warranties and protection packages. Job security comes only from selling.

Meet my grandmother. She's a saint, I tell you. And there are some very interesting people in the finance manager's job these days, too. Women are very popular ("not as threatening"); grandmotherly types are the most popular ("they look trustworthy"). On the whole, the people in the job are nice and nonthreatening. As long as you do what they want.

But the moment you don't—for instance, the moment you say no to an overpriced service agreement, or want to go home and think about it, or (God forbid) ask for a copy of a dealership contract so that you can compare hard numbers with other finance sources—the niceness is put away and the tough psychological warfare begins.

"I need to go home and think about it."

"Oh? Didn't you hear me say we're the cheapest? So what do you need to think about? Are you always afraid to make a decision?"

"Well, I don't want that insurance."

"Don't you care about the welfare of your family? Are you saying they're not worth a few pennies a day?"

"Well, I don't want the protection package, then."

"Why not? *Everybody* that's sensible gets this protection. Now, sign right here."

"Well, can I have all the figures to take home and compare?"

"Why would you want to do that? Figures get very confusing, so we can't give them out. Don't you believe me?"

"Well, uh . . ."

The badgering can become endless, if you let it. Try to leave if you're at a dealership and they bring in another manager. Put cash on the table and they'll push it away. Present a check from your credit union, and they'll tell you there will be a special "processing fee" if you pay by credit union check. And I'm only telling you how they do it at the nice dealerships.

Dealerships and your credit report. Dealerships are historically the worst for shotgunning your loan application to a dozen loan sources. Whether you are dealing online or in person, always ask: *"Do you pull one credit report and send that credit report to potential lenders, or do your potential lenders each pull a credit report on me? And can I have your answer in writing?"*

Dealership finance gimmicks on the Web. First, remember that you're generally dueling with dealership finance salespersons even when you're dealing with many of the "non-dealer-type" Web sellers. You are not dealing with nuns. Second, remember that the dealer's objective when you visit their Web site is to make you "sticky"—keep you on the site long enough to "tie you down"—get a deposit. **Don't give a deposit at this stage. And don't fill out a credit application, unless you're ready to be "nailed" by this site and the dealerships related to it.**

When Dealership Financing May Be Useful—First-Time Buyers/College Graduates. If you are new to major installment credit or are graduating from college with no credit but a job in hand—and if you honestly don't want to take the time to join a credit union—several of the captive financing sources have designed financing plans for you. Some will even give you a down payment for starting your credit with them. Why? You are a lucrative target. Unfortunately, you have to put up with special pressures from the sales force if you fit into these categories. A seasoned salesperson drools at the words, "I'm here for that college graduate loan." But we can prepare you for that pressure. Read the section "Dealing with the Finance Manager" on page 337 very carefully.

New Car Dealerships Discover the Ecstasy of "Buy Here–Pay Here" (BH-PH) Loans

If you were a rich new-car car dealer, what should you do in your spare time? How about driving down Main Street, "counting the number of fast-food joints, convenience stores, coffee, and yogurt shops," recommends Don DiCostanzo, vice president of Wynn's Warranty Division in Azusa, Arizona. "Did you ever stop to think," Mr. DiCostanzo continues, "how many of the employees of these establishments could be your customers? Keep in mind that the majority of these workers make minimum wage or slightly more.

"Pick any one of these places and drive around back to see the types of cars being driven by these people," Mr. DiCostanzo suggests. "More likely than not, these so-called working poor are buy here–pay here (BH-PH) customers. This segment of the population continues to grow . . . and someone is selling to them at a handsome profit."[7] Yes they are. The profit on a BH-PH sale to the poorest person can be five times the profit to a person with good credit.

But shouldn't the dealers be worried about collecting those fat profits from these working poor? After all, they probably already have lots of BH-PH loans to pay. Not to worry. Mr. DiCostanzo recommends that dealers consider using Advanced Dealer Systems that can provide the new-car dealers "all the guidance you need . . . including most importantly *how to collect payments before anyone else does.*"[8] (emphasis added)

Well, at least the dealers are going to help the working poor get a good vehicle for those exorbitant prices, right? No. Mr. DiCostanzo recommends the dealers sell these folks the cars the dealers normally would not sell to a retail customer. "How many cars did you wholesale last month," he asks the dealers, "that you think ended up at a BH-PH lot? [It's] time to get serious!"[9]

The absolutely cynical nature of the BH-PH business is typified by a *Dealer* magazine interview with Daryl Moore, special finance manager for Dale Baker Motor Mall. "Everybody who walks in here wants a Corvette, but they should be in a Chevette," Mr. Moore says. "We let them drive the Corvette, fall in love with it, and then tell them they are going to have to buy a Chevette. As soon as we identify them as a subprime customer, *we stop the showing process.* (emphasis added) We bring them to the desk, and the desk will guide them to the appropriate vehicle."[10] That working poor person can't even pick the car they buy.

"The BH-PH business," says Mr. DiCostanzo, "is estimated to be about $60 billion a year. That's *billion* with a *B.* As a new-car dealer, you have a distinct advantage considering that you generate the inventory needed for this business on a daily basis.

"Are you in?"[11] Mr DiCostanzo concludes.

Mr. DiCostanzo and Mr. Moore made these statements in 1999, and, if anything, things have gotten worse since then.

The term used in the automobile business to refer to the working poor, already devastated by the buy here–pay here travesty—the phrase used without shame in the industry—is "subprime cuts." And this "$60 billion" business? It's now more than $100 billion.

8. Stand-Alone Buy Here–Pay Here Used-Car Operations

If anything, they are worse than the buy here–pay here operations at new-car dealerships. Stay away from them.

How the Subprime and BH-PH Industries Justify Fleecing Lower-Income Consumers.

In chapter 4, we told you these bloodsuckers justify it by moaning about high risk. But they generally don't have high risk. Most subprime and BH-PH lots actually have *less* risk on each loan and *less loss* from repossessions than on a prime loan.[12] The great irony is that many of the subprime and BH-PH customers would qualify for a much better loan without an inflated price if they just knew how to apply for it.

Indeed, many persons who finance with subprime operations such as subprime dealerships, BH-PH lots, and small loan houses don't even need to pay these outrageous rates. Subprime lenders are not exactly forthcoming with data about their borrowers, but a study of the whole subprime market suggests that anywhere up to 50 percent of borrowers with subprime loans could have qualified for better rates or nonsubprime loans.[13]

Subprime and BH-PH on the Web

Smiling, oddly spooky cartoons! Guaranteed E-Z Approval! Free $295 credit Repair Kits! As seen on TV! Print this now! Everything that makes the subprime business greasy and slick is on the Web, only magnified in its potential to do harm. The slimeballs who use the Internet to hawk these loans know you're embarrassed, know you'd rather keep yourself hidden behind your computer screen. But don't fall for that. If you have real credit problems, stay away from the Web financers. Go to a credit counselor at a credit union, or go to a legitimate credit counseling service near you.

Many good people with substantial incomes have credit problems these days. Just don't make your problems worse by resorting to the Web's labyrinthine subprime world.

9. Title Loan Operations

To put all these sources in perspective, to make it all seem okay, even righteous, you might want to consider a "title" loan for the down payment on your next auto purchase, or maybe even for the entire vehicle price if you are thinking used, very used. All you do is take the title from some other car you may own to a title loan office, a pawn shop, and they'll give you a loan on the spot, no questions asked! In many states, the interest rate isn't bad, either, typically only 300 percent APR, though it might be as high as 650 percent. And the whole note comes due every month, and you have to roll it.[14]

Ah, the subprime money business! Such fine people.

I've Decided to Pay Cash and I'm Using a Web Service. What Can These Characters Do to Hurt Me?

First, you're going to have to fight to be a cash buyer, particularly if you're dealing with a dealership, and particularly if you don't have a trade. Remember that the sale of the car itself is just the minnow used to hook the whale of a profit a seller plans to make on you. But that big profit won't happen without financing: Without financing there's no interest and insurance and there's no payment in which to mask other profits. That's why sellers usually ask you up front, "Oh, by the way, are you planning to finance this?"

Sellers will therefore do everything they can to convert you to finance. First, they will literally force you to talk to their "business manager" who is craftily schooled in converting cash buyers. Also, expect those fancy computer-driven programs to clearly demonstrate that cash buyers are fools or worse.

If you are a cash buyer who has already arranged financing at a bank or credit union, expect that crafty "business manager" to use computer-driven programs, which demonstrate clearly that *his* financing at 33 percent really is cheaper than your interest-free loan from Aunt Bea.

A smart negotiating tip: Don't tell any seller you're a cash buyer up front. When they ask if you plan to finance, say "I probably will." Then, after you agreed on every single aspect of the transaction, if you're still able to think, say, "Oh, I think I will pay cash."

Should You Buy Credit Life or Disability Insurance?

Definitely yes—if your horoscope indicates imminent death or severe bodily injury within the very near future (and if you believe in horoscopes).

It's not that the protection itself is a bad idea. Many of us do need to insure the payment of debt. But do you want to pay twice what that insurance should cost you? You do that most of the time when you buy credit life or disability insurance through a dealership. The premium is the first rip-off at dealerships. It's very high because up to *60 percent* of it, depending on the state and dealership, is pure profit to the dealer. But that's not the only problem with insurance from your favorite car stores. Virtually all of them conveniently add the insurance premium to your loan, which obviously increases the amount you are financing and the total amount of interest on the loan. Then *they actually insure the insurance.* Nice. If you, for instance, decide to buy only life insurance on a $6,000 loan for forty-eight months, look what happens:

Loan principal	$6,000.00
Interest on the loan	1,725.60
Credit life premium	241.08
Interest *on the premium*	69.33
Total	$8,036.01

The dealership is not going to insure this loan for $6,000—they are going to insure it for *$8,000* at their very silly premium rates. For credit insurance on the loan we've just mentioned, you will pay $6.47 a month for forty-eight months. That doesn't sound like much money, does it? But look what the same amount of money would buy you from about any life insurance agent in town: If you are thirty-five years old, $6.47 per month would buy you almost $50,000 worth of "level" term insurance for *five* years—a lot more insurance for a year longer.

The key word here is "level": The amount of insurance stays the same. If you die during the last month of the fifth year, you would still receive the full amount of the insurance. If you purchased your life insurance from a dealership or lending institution, only the *balance* of your loan would be covered. Die just before the forty-eighth payment, and your $8,000 insurance policy will pay the last payment. Period.

"What about life insurance from credit unions?" If you belong to the 70+ percent of credit unions that provide credit life insurance free, smile. If your credit union charges, you should already know how its costs compare with your other financing options. If you're really smart, call your insurance agent and see what a five-year level-term life insurance policy will cost you. If you're a little lazy, go with your cheapest source.

"What about credit life insurance from a bank?" As we said earlier, it's cheaper than from a dealership but usually more expensive than that sold by credit unions. Banks do seem to have a habit of automatically adding a life insurance premium to their loans by "assuming" your consent. If you're not planning on credit life insurance, watch for this.

"What about credit disability insurance?" Credit disability insurance, also known as credit accident and health insurance, is theoretically designed to make your payments if you are disabled or ill. The concept is great, but the coverage is very expensive—even from a credit union—and always contains a number of exclusions.

For instance, your policy won't pay until you have been disabled and under a doctor's care for at least fourteen days (on some policies, at least thirty days). How many times in the past five years have you been totally disabled and under a doctor's care for at least fourteen days?

Also, preexisting conditions are not covered. If you've had a little bout of something prior to buying your credit disability insurance, that illness won't be covered under the policy.

If you feel you must consider credit disability insurance, shop your sources carefully. Credit unions and banks will offer better rates than dealerships. In addition, some companies have much better ratios of benefits paid to premiums collected (one way consumer service is judged) than others. For example, CUNA Mutual, which provides credit disability insurance to a majority of credit unions, has paid out almost 79 percent in benefits. The average for the rest of the industry in the same year was just under 56 percent. Credit disability insurance provided by dealerships generally has the lowest payout ratio.

"Can you buy credit disability insurance through an insurance agent?" Not very easily, and usually with even more exclusions than through other sources.

"Are either of these types of credit insurance ever a good buy?" If you're in generally, but not specifically, poor health and cannot qualify for other types of insurance, yes. If you're older, yes. Since both credit life and disability insurance are essentially group plans, usually no physicals are required, and persons in their late sixties pay the same rate as twenty-five-year-olds.

But if you fit into any of the following categories, think before you spend extra money for any insurance. You might want to save that money for more car. Remember that insurance eats up your loan cash and therefore your available cash.

Think twice about buying credit insurance if

- you are under forty and in good health. You can buy cheaper insurance from your insurance agent.
- you are single. Insurance should protect survivors. If you die with no survivors, your insurance will be protecting the *lenders*. Let them worry about their own problems.
- you have enough existing insurance to cover your debts. If you're already "insurance poor," why waste the money?
- you really want to beef up your insurance in general. See your insurance agent instead.

"Can finance sources make you take insurance?" An enormous amount of credit insurance is sold because customers feel they must take the insurance in order to receive the loan. But don't fall prey to this subtle blackmail. In most states it is against the law to approve credit on this basis.

Okay, Let's Find the Cheapest and Best Loan

Before you start searching for lending sources online or calling them, prepare a piece of paper with a little form like the sample below. To help you compare rates for credit life and accident and health insurance, ask for their charge for a potential loan of $10,000. (You don't

Go to www.dontgettakeneverytime.com for the latest loan site information.

know how much you will be borrowing yet, but that gives you a good basis for comparison.)

Information from Possible Loan Sources

Cost on new car of:	Source A	Source B	Source C
APR for 36 months			
APR for 48 months			
APR for 60 months			
Credit Life Insurance (on $10,000 loan)			
Credit Accident & Health Insurance (on $10,000)			
Service Agreement/ Extended Warranty			

1. **Find a credit union, either online or in person, particularly if you have any doubts about your creditworthiness.** Apply for an actual preapproved loan. Use this as your control for comparisons. **If you're not going to use a credit union, use your local bank as your "control" source.** In addition to the actual loan cost, ask the credit union or bank the cost of these items:
    - credit life insurance
    - credit accident and health insurance
    - service agreement

2. **If you have had a "satisfactory" loan relationship with a bank** or other prime financing institution (which means you paid "as agreed"), always include that source in your loan comparison. Even if you've been late on a

few bills, an existing loan source is always a good bet for the best loan.

3. **Use an online "rate shopping" company to gather your second loan comparison.** Make sure you find a company that pulls only one credit report for all its loan sources.

    Using your search engine: enter "auto loans"

    Each site gives a one or two sentence summary of their site. Look for sites that shop your credit for the best rate.

    Reminder: Send these sites an e-mail about their policy concerning your credit report and their lending sources.

    Sample site:

    www.lendingtree.com

    An online "loan marketplace." Multiple banks and lenders compete for your business.

4. **If you are attracted to a financing source affiliated with a buying service,** add that source to your rate comparison. You might have fun snooping around the entire site.

    Using your search engine:

    enter "car buying services"

    Sample sites:

    www.carsdirect.com

    This buying service says it works with "top lenders."

    www.car.com, an Autobytel.com company

    This site says it obtains financing through a network of dealers and online finance companies.

5. **If you know you may be credit impaired,** still use this approach to shopping for the best rate. Always assume your credit is better than you think it is.

6. **Fill in the information** on your form as you go along.

Comparing Your Best Loan Source Overall

If you do not plan to buy credit insurance, then the source with the lowest APR for the term you want to finance is probably your best source.

If you do plan to use credit insurance, you will want to determine which loan source (or two) is your best probable source after you learn about Loan Cash and Available Cash in the next chapter. So keep your answers handy.

And a Poke in the Eye, Too

A bank robbery is almost easier than going through all this, ey? Well, it probably is. But bank robberies seldom lead to the peaceful valley where the cows (rather than you) are milked, where the righteous (that's you!) go to count their many thousands of dollars in savings. Taking time now could save you "pennies a day!" (at 99 cents, that's $2,168 on a six-year loan). Saving a paltry 2 percent on interest could make you a dime an hour! (that's $2,200 bucks).

Picking the right financing source leads you right to the hill overlooking that peaceful valley. But before you enter the valley where savings are heavenly, you have to know how much money you've got to spend in the first place. Our next chapter shows you how to figure just that—and (no fooling) it's probably one of the most important chapters in this book.

Chapter 8

How Much Car Can You Afford?

Your budget, not emotion, should drive the car buying or leasing process

The Concept of "Available Cash"

Killer, his tie knotted just right for a change, his hair combed as neat as a schoolboy's at Mass, and his belly sucked in a bit, was sitting in AFF's new Webcam broadcast booth, eyes focused on a Sony ProMaster digital camera. Killer leaned on a desktop that held a built-in touch-screen "chalkboard." The board's screen instantly duplicated any markings on it.

Killer looked tense. "Killer, you look just fine," said Charles Pierce, AFF's Web guru, "but relax your stomach—you look like you're wearing a girdle!"

Killer smiled ruefully, then chuckled. For the first time in years, Killer, the master of nerves, was himself nervous in a car dealership. This was, after all, his national television debut. And the audience was impressive. At 250 AFF dealerships around the country, nearly two thousand rookie salespeople who had never sold a car were getting ready to "Ask the Master" his secrets. "Ask the Master" was a new training program in AFF's national drive to standardize successful selling techniques throughout the AFF system, and Killer was the first VIP salesperson on the debut show. But right then, Killer didn't know whether to thank Charles Pierce or curse him.

"Okay, twenty seconds," Pierce said. "Jeez, Killer, relax. Just imagine you're closing a big, fat deal. I'm going to summarize what the gang has been studying this morning already, and then I'm going to introduce you and open it up for questions from around the country."

Killer quickly reviewed the topic sheet for the just-completed training session:

> *"'Hammerheads!' How to hammer the toughest customer for the biggest finance profit."* Killer knew that subject well.

> *"'TrustMasters!' Putting confusion to work for you."* Shoot, he wrote the book on using trust as a weapon.

> *"'Grinders!'* How to wear 'em down and win 'em over to the BIG DEAL."

Killer finally settled into his chair a little. What was there to be nervous about? After all, he *was* the master on these topics . . .

Killer's debut. *"Killer!"* Charles hissed. Killer looked up from the topic sheet just in time to see his face on a monitor. Showtime. Killer stared blankly, trying to fix the right smile on his face, barely listening to Charles's short introduction. He was totally focused, ready for the questions to start.

"Killer, this is Dollars, a salesman in Memphis. I worked with you a week there before coming here, remember? Well, this morning we were talking in training about the trust thing? Tell everybody about your wall, dude! I've got one here, and it really works."

"Oh, you mean the medals?" Killer smiled at the camera. "Well, none of you are going to have your own closing rooms yet, but this will work for you, anyway. 'Ups' are dying to find someone they can trust at a dealership, someone that will really listen to them. Someone with honor. So, add a little 'honor' to your closing space. Head to the biggest flea market you can find or go to a Web auction online, and buy yourself a medal or two.

War medals are good and are a dime a dozen from the Gulf or Iraq War. Pick ones that fit your age. Even an old 'Appreciation' certificate is better than nothing. Frame them and put them on your wall, or put one in a small frame and move it around with you. Let me tell you, customers just *love* heroes."

"Killer's medals are from the Civil War!" the salesman from Tennessee joked, making everyone laugh, even Killer.

"They may be, but my *paycheck* isn't from that era, I promise you."

The mention of money, of big paychecks, quieted the laughter, and a young woman spoke up in the silence. "Killer, you've seen 'em all. Who's the hardest customer to knock a home run on?"

Killer didn't hesitate. "Oh, that's always the cash buyer. It's real hard to do any damage to those folks."

"But no one really pays cash at our dealerships, do they?" an anonymous voice asked. "I mean, we don't sell Rolls or anything like that."

Killer leaned back and laughed. "How many ups have you worked so far, son?"

"Uh, none yet. This is just my second day of training."

"Well, let me tell you a big secret. *Every* customer is a *cash* customer. Every one. They just don't know it, thank God," Killer said. "And your job is to make sure they don't know they're cash customers."

"Who do you mean? What about all those people that finance, and all those people with trades? They're not cash buyers."

"Oh, yes they are!" Killer insisted, as he warmed to the subject. "People come in here talking payments. But payments don't buy you a car—payments buy you *cash;* then you use that cash to buy a car. *Trade-ins* buy you cash, too. So everybody is a cash buyer."

Killer paused. Were these rookies getting it? He picked up the laser pen resting on the touch screen and began to write as he spoke. "Look at it like this: A person tells you they can afford $400 a month for forty-eight months. What they're really saying is, 'I can afford to buy $16,000 in cash to spend on a car.'" Killer then wrote:

Payments don't buy cars; payments buy cash: $400 a month for 48 months buys $16,000 in cash.

He started jotting again as he continued speaking. "A customer tells you he drives a two-year-old Mustang convertible. He says he owes money on it. This guy doesn't have the slightest idea what his old car is worth, or what his payoff is. But we know both: We find out the sled is worth $23,000, and we find out the customer's payoff is $13,000. So what's the guy really saying to us? *This old sled is worth $10,000 in cash to the dealership.*" Killer nodded at what he'd written on the screen:

Payments and Trade-ins don't buy cars; they buy cash!

$400 a month for 48 months buys	$16,000
2-year-old mustang's wholesale value:	$23,000
Customer's payoff:	($13,000)
Customer's available cash:	$26,000

"Does this make sense? Do you see how everybody's really a cash buyer? Do you see what we do in every deal? We find out how much cash the customer has, based on that customer's assets—his trade-in and his loan."

"Does everybody get it?" Killer stared impatiently at the camera, a little frustrated because he couldn't see the reaction of the rookies, but only hear their jumbled comments.

"Killer," a young guy's voice broke through, "tell 'em why you never tell people how much cash they've really got—why we never explain it like that."

"A good point," Killer answered nodding. "If somebody knows they have only $26,000 to spend, it's going to be hard to get them to spend $36,000. But if they don't really understand their assets—don't know how much money they've got, don't understand the cash value of their payment and the cash value of their old car—well, boys and girls, that's when you smile really big on payday."

Two thousand rookie salespeople clapped wildly at that, then for the next twenty minutes peppered Robert DeMarco with questions about tricks of the trade. Charles Pierce, Web guru, watched Killer, now totally relaxed, enthusiastically sharing his nuggets of gold with the eager proselytes. Just think of it! In one instant, the Web was cloning baby Killers all across America. What a great way to start the day.

Test Time!

Okay, I caught you napping through these last pages. So, let's see if you learned anything.

Which of the following questions is easier to answer?

1. **"I'm trading in a two-year-old Camry.** I don't know what my Camry is worth, but I owe $13,000 on it. I'm looking at a new car that lists for $39,000, and that car has a rebate of $1,000 on it. I can afford to spend only $400 per month for forty-eight months. Can I afford to buy the new car?"

2. **"I have $27,000 in cash to spend on a vehicle, and no more.** I'm looking at a new car that will cost me $35,000. Can I afford to buy the new car?"

Do you agree that question number two is easier to understand? Good. Do you also know that these two questions are based on the same facts and have the same answer? Now you see why Killer doesn't want you to understand the concept of "Available Cash."

Understanding Available Cash means you understand what you're about to spend. Understanding Available Cash makes you a cash buyer. *All cars, always, are bought for cash.* And cash buyers, virtually always get the best deal, if they're careful.

Auto Sellers Want You to Look at the Money Differently

Sellers don't want you to understand Available Cash. Instead, they do their best to convince you that you're one of three types of buyers: a difference buyer, an allowance buyer, or a payment buyer. Because, unfortunately, most of us can be easily placed into one or more of these buying categories, you should understand the terms in order to *avoid* that particular type of buying behavior. Invariably, when you see yourself as any buyer other than a cash buyer, that's when you will be taken. Why? Any method of buying that confuses the total cash price of the car is dangerous. Let's see how.

Difference buyers. Difference buyers care mainly about the difference between the cost of their present car and the cost of the new car. This type of customer will say, "Son, your car lists for $17,000. And I'll be damned if I'll buy it for more than $6,000 plus my car." This man's thinking is logical but flawed.

"Well, sir, how did you arrive at that figure?"

"Well, my car is two years old, and I expect to spend $3,000 a year for each year I drive. *That's* why I'll pay you $6,000!" Or he'll say, "My car cost $14,500 new two years ago. I figure it depreciated about 25 percent the first year and 20 percent the second. *That's* why I'll pay you $6,000!" The man will barely feel the shiv. Both of his arguments are based on his *own* definitions, and neither definition is based on such a minor fact as the current value of his car. A salesman working this guy can: (1) Ignore the value of the man's trade-in. The trade may be worth more than $8,500. (2) Tell the man that people are now trading for $3,500 a year rather than $3,000. After all, inflation takes its toll. If the man agrees, he's just raised himself $1,000. *Magic formulas and percentages just don't work.*

Allowance buyers. These customers aren't concerned with the real *value* of their trade, but with the amount of money they are *allowed in trade*. The allowance buyer typically says, "Give me $5,000 for my car, and you have a deal." A smart salesman can handle this type easily. He'll invariably say, "Well, folks, we can't give you $5,000 for your trade on that Expenso Minutula. But let's take a look at these Expenso Gargantulas." And, of course, the Gargantulas have a larger margin of profit. Switching allowance buyers from a less expensive car to a more expensive one always increases profit to the dealer *if* the allowance stays the same. Allowance buyers never know the real value of their trade or the actual discount on a new car.

Payment buyers—the easiest prey. A payment buyer has only one simple objective: "I don't care about anything else, as long as my payments are low."

"Well, what would be a satisfactory payment?"

"Just as low as you can get!"

Both the salesperson and the customer laugh a little, and then the sales rep goes to work. If you don't have a specific payment in mind, the rep will pick some impossibly high figure out of the air. The payment will be designed to shock you. The salesperson will then lower the payment slowly until you're breathing again. If you have a payment in mind, say $450, the rep might find you a car for a $450 payment, but it will be a car you should have bought for a $325 payment.

What's the flaw in the payment approach? The entire negotiation was never based on the value of your trade or the cost of their car, but on some figure pulled out of the air.

Don't be a victim. The horror stories generated by these methods of buying are endless. One allowance buyer argued for three hours and finally received his allowance. The moment it was agreed to, he slammed his fist on the desk and said, "Now about the financing! I won't pay you a dime over $400 a month for the car!" A very expensive statement. At the allowance figure he had spent hours negotiating, payments should not have run over $365 a month (even at a higher than average rate). But the man raised himself $35 a month for sixty months—he increased the store's profit by $2,100.

And then there's the couple who insisted on receiving $3,500 for their old car. The salesman agreed to give them $3,500 in trade on a new $13,000 tin can, one of the cheapest small cars. He then switched them to a $20,000 midsize car, allowed them the same $3,500 in trade, and increased his profit by $900.

Do you see the danger? Buying a car based on allowance, difference, or payments will only draw your attention away from the three questions that really matter:

1. **How much cash will my old car give me?** That cash is called "equity."
2. **How much cash will the payment I can afford buy me?** This figure is, logically enough, called "Loan Cash."
3. **What is the cost of the car I want to buy?**

If you know the answers to these three questions, you will always be able to get maximum dollar for your old car, and you will always be able to buy their car for the least profit.

All car transactions are based on these questions, and all car transactions eventually come down to two simple questions: How much cash do you have? What does their vehicle cost?

You've already learned how to shop your present car to determine its wholesale value, and you'll learn how to figure the cost of the car you want to buy or lease a bit later in the chapters on shopping. For the rest of this chapter, we'll focus on how to determine the total Available Cash you will have to buy a car.

That Available Cash is always made up of

- the lump sum of cash the monthly payment you can afford will buy you;
- the cash your trade-in may give you; and
- any other cash available to you, such as a rebate, or money from savings.

Developing Your Available Cash Figure Based on Your Own Budget and Assets

Right this minute, you have an exact amount of Available Cash to buy a car, based on your budget and your assets. Our Web site, www.dontgettakeneverytime.com, gives you some useful calculators. Or you can determine it using this book. But don't go any further in the auto adventure without determining it!

1. **Determine what monthly payment you can afford.** Don't think about whether you want to buy new or used; don't think about specific models; just think

honestly about the payment you will be making each month. Deciding what payment is comfortable for you is your *most important decision.* It will determine how much car you can afford to buy regardless of the value of your trade-in.

Most budget counselors say smart people don't spend more than 15 percent of their take-home pay. Other counselors say, "Think about what you're paying right now, and decide if you want to pay more or less." Do you really need to lower your monthly payment? Or are you ready to raise it a bit? Using one of these guidelines, decide what you can honestly afford to spend per month, and write that figure here:

I plan to spend this much per month: _____.

2. **Next, determine how many months you want to pay.**
Killer and others who don't give a hoot about your sanity or financial well-being will try to get you to finance for up to *eighty-four months.* "Easy-payment" plans that stretch your payments over five years or longer are dangerous. Most of the time, extended-payment plans guarantee you'll always be "in the bucket," which means you owe more on your car than it's worth. Know the big problem with that? You won't be able to trade cars again anytime soon. I recommend that you finance for no more than sixty months maximum. If you can manage thirty-six, forty-two, forty-eight, or fifty-four months—the shorter the better—do it.

"And thanks for the extra $6,000." Don't forget that extended-payment plans also allow sellers to make thousands on you by tacking on "just a Pepsi or two a day" to all those payments to pay for add-ons you'd never buy if you had to pay cash for them. Would you fork over $1,800 in cash for an extended warranty? Probably not (hopefully), but tens of thousands of people fork over eighty-two cents a day on a six-year loan and waste that much.

Even worse, extended-payment plans buy you less car for each dollar of payment. For instance, if you buy a car and finance it at an average rate of interest for two years, eighty-six cents of each payment dollar will actually pay for the car; the rest is interest. If you finance the car at the same rate for forty-two months, seventy-eight cents of each payment dollar will be applied to the car; the rest is interest. If you finance the same car at the same interest rate for sixty months, only seventy-one cents of each payment dollar is applied to the car, the rest is interest.

How many months do you want to be making payments? (Try to keep it under sixty.) Write the number of months here: _____.

3. **Determine your Loan Cash.**

    "Loan Cash" is the amount of cash your payment will buy you. If, for example, you decide you can afford to pay $350 for forty-eight months, then that payment will buy you a lump sum of $13,933 (at the 9.5 percent interest rate one of your loan sources offered). The rest of the $16,800 you will lay out in four years goes to interest—$2,867.

    If you want to determine your Loan Cash figure easily online, use the calculators recommended at www.dontgettakeneverytime.com. For an interest rate, use the best rate you received when you shopped your financing (chapter 7). You can also use the pencil-and-paper method located in the appendix (page 427). To calculate your Loan Cash using either method, look at your financing shopping list and choose the interest rate (APR) from the source you are most likely to finance with.

    When you've calculated the figure, write your Loan Cash amount right here:

    My Loan Cash, based on my payment budget, is _____.

4. **Determine your Available Cash.**

    In addition to your Loan Cash, you have more cash available to you to buy a car, right? If the wholesale value of your old car is greater than its payoff, then it will contribute money to your cash pile. You may have some savings you would like to use as a down payment that also contributes to the cash pile. And what about rebates? If you're considering a car with a $1,000 rebate, you can count on that cash, too, can't you?

"Available Cash" is simply all the money you have available right now to buy a car or truck. So that I'll know you're not sleeping, why don't you tell me how much Available Cash you have in this situation:

> Your Loan Cash is $14,000.
> Your old car is worth $6,100, and you owe $3,200 on it.
> You're looking at a new car with a rebate of $1,000.
> You have an extra $750 in savings to put down.
> Your Available Cash figure is _____.

Did you get $18,650? Now, what is that figure? Available Cash is *all the money you have to spend if you plan to stay within your budget.* Please repeat that. In our example, you can go out and spend $18,650 on *anything,* and, for the first time in your life, you're going to have a payment that fits your budget.

How Much Money Should You Finance on a Particular Car? What Down Payment Is Best?

Very good questions that obviously affect your Available Cash and how you figure it. If you listen to lending institutions, down payments are an easy thing to compute. As we mentioned earlier, many financing institutions including credit unions will happily finance 100 percent or more of the selling price. That's nice for them but always bad for you in the long run. Why? You'll always, *always* owe more on your vehicle than it is worth. The result? You can't "step away" from that vehicle under any circumstance. If you can't afford the payments, for instance, you will still be forced to pay them because you won't be able to sell your car.

Well, thanks to this friendly advice, there are millions of folks who don't drive cars—they drive enormous hunks of liability. These people owe more on their cars than any reasonable person would be willing to pay for them. They literally cannot sell or trade their cars without *paying* someone to take them. When they bought their hunks of debt, most of these people made a very small cash down payment; others used only the equity in their trade-in (the amount of its wholesale value over and above the payoff) as a down payment. Some actually allowed the seller to arrange *two* loans—to "dip" them—to make even this minimum down payment.

Financing a car like this with a minimum down payment is dangerous. It means that you will always owe more on your car than it's worth. Try not to put yourself in that position. Turn a deaf ear to all those sucker-come-on offers of "zero down payment." Fight the urge to "overfinance" your vehicle. Pay as much cash down as you can.

How Much Down Payment Is Enough?

If you plan to buy a new car, try to finance less than the invoice cost of the car. If you plan to buy a used car, try to finance no more than its loan value—a specific amount of money, usually 80 percent of its wholesale value. If you use the following guidelines for determining a down payment and computing the amount to finance, your car or truck will never be a true liability—it will almost always be worth more than you owe.

On a new vehicle: Try to finance no more than 80 percent of the invoice cost of a new car.

On a used vehicle. Try to finance no more than a used vehicle's "loan value."

Trade-in equity as down payment. If you plan to trade your current car and have enough equity, you may not need cash to make an adequate down payment. But if it still takes money from your pocket to be 20 percent below actual new-car invoice cost or used-car wholesale value, do your best to find that cash. It isn't easy to part with your hard-earned buckaroos like this, but it is smart, and I've heard you are very smart. If you follow this suggestion, you will usually be in a position to sell your car at any time and receive cash back.

What Is the Minimum Down Payment Possible on a New Vehicle?

If you simply cannot afford these suggestions, you will still have to pay down a sum equal to the following:

- the sum of the profit you are paying on the new car;
- the tax on the sale;
- miscellaneous charges such as titles and other fees.

Because you don't know at this stage the final profit figure or tax figure, be safe: Assume the profit will be $400 on any new vehicle you buy. Assume that tax will be computed on your Loan Cash figure. For example, let's assume that your Loan Cash figure is $13,800 and you live in a state with a 5 percent tax. Your down payment would need to be:

Tax on $13,800:	$690
Profit of $400:	$400
Charges for titles and other fees:	$100
Total Down Payment:	$1,190

What Is the Minimum Down Payment Possible on a Used Vehicle?

On a used vehicle the minimum down payment will need to include

- the difference in the actual loan value of the car and the amount of money you will owe on cost of the vehicle;
- taxes;
- charges for title and other fees.

Because you don't know any of these figures yet, again, be safe: Assume that you will pay at least $500 over loan value for any vehicle. Assume that the tax will be paid on your total Loan Cash figure. For example, if you live in a state with a 5 percent

tax and your Loan Cash figure is $6,500, you would need to pay
the following down:

Tax on $6,500:	$325
Amount you are paying over loan value:	$500
Charges for title and other fees:	$100
Total Down Payment:	$925

Determining Available Cash for Different Buying Situations

*If you're just doodling around—not seriously planning to buy or
lease right now—you can skip this section for the moment and go
to page 225. Then come back when you're really itching to buy.
But if you are seriously planning to buy a car as soon as you can,
read this section carefully.*

Telling you how to put the concept of Available Cash into
action when shopping and negotiating to buy a vehicle is the
subject of the next few chapters. But right now you need to
know how to arrive at an Available Cash figure for specific
buyer situations.

Stop and think, and then actually work out a tentative Available Cash figure for several situations that might fit you as a
buyer. For instance, you might be considering buying a new car
and trading or simply buying a used car straight-out. You should
work out an Available Cash figure for both situations. After
you've done so, note these figures and save them. You'll need
them later.

If You Plan to Buy a New or Used Vehicle and Have No Trade

If you plan to buy a car without a trade, the Loan Cash figure
tells you how much your payment will buy. This figure plus
your down payment is the total amount of car you can buy—
your Available Cash. Your Available Cash must pay for every-

thing in the transaction: the car, tax, tag, and all other extras, such as credit insurance.

Example: Your payment of $220 per month for forty-eight months at 8.5 percent APR gives Loan Cash of $14,793. If you plan to pay $2,000 down, you'll have $16,703 in Available Cash.

If You Plan to Buy a New or Used Vehicle and Have a Debt-Free Trade

In this situation your Loan Cash and the wholesale value of your trade will determine your Available Cash.

Example: You have figured your Loan Cash on $350 a month for thirty-six months at your best financing source with an APR of 8 percent. Your Loan Cash is $11,168. You shopped your current car and know it has a true wholesale value of $4,500. Because you own the car free and clear, it will contribute the whole $4,500 to your Available Cash. So you have a total of $15,668 in Available Cash. If you have additional cash for an additional down payment, you can add that to your total. You may not need to make any down payment other than your trade, but remember that we recommend that you always borrow an amount on the new vehicle that's at least 20 percent under, so you may want to add cash.

If You Plan to Buy a New or Used Vehicle and Owe Money on Your Trade

This situation applies to most of us. Your Available Cash will be determined by

- the Loan Cash you can afford,
- any equity you have in your trade, and
- any cash from savings or rebate.

Remember, equity equals wholesale value minus payoff. Your car has more value to you than debt only if its wholesale value is higher than its payoff. For instance, if your car is worth $6,000 and its payoff is $5,000, then you have $1,000 in equity. But if your car is worth $6,000 and you owe $7,000, then you have no equity. In fact, you owe $1,000 more than your car is worth. You are "in the bucket" or "upside down."

Because you owe money on your vehicle, you need to know which situation applies to you. Call your financing institution and ask them for a "net payoff." The net payoff is the total amount you owe the lending institution minus any rebates for unused insurance and, sometimes, prepaid interest. Now, compute your equity. Subtract your net payoff from the true wholesale value of your vehicle. If the answer is a "plus" figure, then you have that much equity. Breathe easier. Go on to the next section. If the payoff is higher than the wholesale value, go buy a bottle of 100 proof before reading further. Then go to the second section below entitled "*If You Are 'in the Bucket' or 'Upside Down.'*"

If You Have Equity. First, figure your Loan Cash if you have not done it already (page 246). Write that amount down. Then, add the amount of equity you have in your trade. Your Loan Cash and your equity combined determine what you can buy— your Available Cash.

For example, if you have decided to spend $220 per month for forty-eight months at 10 percent APR, you know your Loan Cash is $11,527. If your trade is worth $6,000 and you owe $5,000, you also have $1,000 in equity. Loan Cash of $11,527 plus equity of $1,000 equals Available Cash of $12,527. Unless you add more cash from your pocket, that's all the Available Cash you have to buy a vehicle.

If You Are "In the Bucket" or "Upside Down." If you owe more than your car is worth, you unfortunately don't have any equity. You have what is called "negative equity." That's a nice way of saying you're in the bucket. Negative equity means that you will not be able to trade cars without paying cash down, and without paying a lot of cash down, you will usually end up deeper in that slimy bucket of debt.

Now, before looking at an easy way to determine how much cash you will need to pay down in the situation, please listen to one piece of advice: If you are in the bucket and don't have the cash on hand necessary to trade cars, *don't* trade. Keep your present car for a while longer. High-pressure dealerships and small loan companies—"dip houses"—survive on people who borrow money to bail themselves out of their present car. If a dealership offers to "roll your payoff over" into your new loan, they are simply helping you dig a deeper financial grave in preparation for the inevitable. Thousands of people have their cars repossessed each year because some nice salesperson told them, "Don't worry about the money. We can borrow that extra payment for you." You don't need friends like that.

Sometimes dealerships will dump you deeper into the bucket without appearing to have you borrow additional money. For instance, let's say you are in the bucket but want to trade for a newer used SUV. You want to buy an Explorer for $11,000. You have a car worth $5,000, but you owe $5,800 on it. You're in the bucket for $800, and Killer is waiting on you.

"Mr. Jones," Killer explains carefully, "you have agreed to buy the Explorer for $11,000, and I am going to give you $5,000 for your old car. If you don't mind, however, I'd like to write this sale up a little differently so that we can have you riding tomorrow *without one penny down.*" You slip your tongue quickly over your lips in anticipation.

"What we are going to do is raise the price of the Explorer to $12,000, and raise the amount I'm giving you for your old car to $6,000. Now it will look like your old car is worth more than the $5,800 you owe on it. That's important to the bank, Mr. Jones. They just won't approve any deal if you owe more on your car than it's worth unless you put some cash down, too.

Killer quickly begins to scribble down a small column of numbers. "This is how we'll write up the order. We will deduct the $6,000 I'm allowing you from the $12,000, and that leaves $6,000. Since you owe $5,800 on the old car, the amount remaining to be financed will then be $11,800. And that just happens to be the amount the bank will loan on that Explorer!"

It's one of the oldest tricks in the business. If you think about it, you'll realize that Mr. Jones may be getting a car with no money down. But he is also getting himself even deeper in the bucket on the Explorer. Mr. Jones didn't win in this transaction, he just postponed the time of his defeat.

Every time that you buy a car, new or used, you are simply postponing the pain by not paying lots of money down. That's why most people's cars are liabilities on their financial statements, not assets.

Even if you say, "Hey, I plan to keep that Explorer for at least two years after I pay it off," you will have paid *thousands* more for the "favor" of no down payment.

Depending upon the amount of your negative equity, you may be able to retail your car, sell it yourself, and at least come out even. If, like Mr. Jones, you are in the bucket for only $500 to $1,000, your chances are good on most vehicles that are in good shape.

If You're in the Bucket but Still Plan to Trade Cars and Need to Figure a Down Payment. Here's a good way to know how much cash you will need to pay down. This is extra cash, cash from your pocket. It has nothing to do with Loan Cash.

Cash down payment for a new vehicle. You will need to have cash equal to the total of

- the amount of your negative equity;
- the amount of profit you plan to pay on the new car (over its actual cost);
- the charges for taxes, tag, title, and other fees.

Cash down payment for a used vehicle. You will need to have cash equal to the total of

- the amount of your negative equity;
- the difference in the car's price (excluding your trade) and that specific car's actual loan value (you can call your bank and they will provide the loan value figure; don't use a figure given by a dealership); and
- the charges for taxes, tag, title, and other fees.

As you can see from these items, if you are in the bucket, you will need much more cash than the amount of your negative equity. Even if you come up with the minimum money required, remember that you still won't be financing 20 percent under the new vehicle's true value, you'll be financing the maximum amount. Do you know what that means? You will be in the bucket on this car, too, from Day One.

Next Steps

You're getting smarter by the page, did you notice? You've learned how to determine the true wholesale value of your trade-in, learned how to shop your financing, and can even figure your Available Cash. Most lot lizards don't know how to do that! Maybe its time for you to graduate to the even more serious stuff—like shopping for that four-wheeled, gleaming dream machine in a crafty manner fit for a person of your manifold talents.

Shall we shop?

Chapter 9

The Big Fantasy: Automobile Advertising and Sales Events

J. C. zoomed into the parking spot marked "G.M." Flipping a cigarette in the puddle of water just by the front door to the showroom, he headed to his office, a coffee thermos under his arm, without once looking at any of the sales staff standing around in little clumps, each one of them quickly doing their best to look busy. Damn, things must be slow. It was a Saturday morning, usually one of the busiest days at the store, and J. C. rarely came near the place on Saturdays. The showroom emptied as everyone but the four people assigned to greeting "drive-ups" headed to a computer terminal or phone to begin prospecting.

Killer had already been in his own office—the only private salesperson's office in the entire dealership—for an hour by the time J. C. entered the dealership. Killer was offering all his previous customers "a $200 Cartier notepad" simply for recommending a friend to the dealership. Killer's offer was going out by phone, fax, e-mail, and U.S. mail. The pads, made by Herman Cartier (Killer's local printer pal), cost Killer $2.00 a piece in bulk.

Charles Pierce, Web maestro, had been working more than an hour, speaking by Webcam with Gary Oliver Davies himself! As Pierce had watched Davies on his computer screen, his imagination had conjured up vivid mental images—Davies' yacht, his plane, his island hideaway, and a mountain of Davies' money, *$150 million high!* One day . . .

Pierce shook the images from his head just long enough to preview for Davies the particular Web bait that would lure the most fish into Davies' favorite dealership next week.

The Many Moods of Advertising: What's Your Fantasy?

On this particular morning at Davies Motors, all three men would be practicing their own particular version of the great automobile fantasy: advertising.

One thing was certain: Business had stopped dead at this flagship dealership of the entire America's Family Friend chain—the very home of Gary Oliver Davies himself. It didn't matter that every dealership in the metro area was down in sales. Davies didn't care the least about that. This dealership had *his name on it! Where were the sales?* That's all Davies could say.

Checking newspaper ads. J. C. opened his thermos and took a sip as his attention turned to several items on his desk. A fine Bloody Mary, he thought, as the cool, hot liquid rushed down his throat. He picked up the proof of the ad that was running in Sunday's paper, a four-color spread. The headline read: 100 NEW CARS UNDER $100 PER MONTH! THIS IS *NOT* A LEASE!* The small asterisk by the headline led to lines of copy readable only with "the finest magnifying glass," J. C. liked to joke. *Requires 50 percent down payment; 96 month financing; requires trade-in equity; on approved credit; options extra; offer expires at midnight; requires immediate delivery; provisional contract; includes all incentives; customer inquiry authorizes dealership to pull a credit report; dealership not responsible for mistakes in this advertisement; see manager for details; does not apply to vehicles featured in other specials; not responsible for errors; executive vehicles may be titled to other companies or individuals; rebates may not be applied to deal; customer agrees to statement of dispute; not applicable in all circumstances, requires final equity payment equal to seventy payments; stock-numbered vehicles only; stock-numbered vehicles may be sold.

Promise the moon. Just below the main head were three nice promises. The truck department's ad said: $3,000 DISCOUNTS ON ALL TRUCKS IN STOCK. J. C. scratched through the $3,000 discount figure and raised it to $5,000. Why not? Trucks didn't have fixed MSRP like cars did. Dealerships could raise the price of any truck as much as they wanted to, then slash the inflated price to give the appearance of a true price cut. J. C. sent a quick e-mail to the truck manager telling him to raise the sticker price of all trucks listed in the ad by $2,000 to cover the new "discount" price. Who was hurt by that?

The new-car department's subhead showed a picture of a big "zero" and proclaimed ZERO PERCENT FINANCING AVAILABLE! ZERO CASH DOWN!* Another asterisk closed that heading, too: *With approved credit; 12-month financing; dealer keeps all rebates and incentives; requires equity in trade-in; zero financing not available with zero cash; does not include taxes, tag, title, advertising, and preparation; available on promotion cars only, all cars subject to prior sale; requires same-day delivery; conditional financing contracts only, no terms may be combined with other terms, customers test-driving these vehicles have entered into negotiations as defined by FTC; "cash" is not defined as equity; rebates are not defined as cash. All disputes are subject to arbitration agreement, if conditional offers are made in writing by customer; may imply lease or balloon payment sale.

> *Where's your magnifying glass?*

The used-car department's head was just as enticing: ALL USED CARS FOR SALE AT PRICES GUARANTEED *BELOW* NADA VALUE!* The asterisk here led to an equally long disclaimer that included these words buried in the middle of the disclaimer: " . . . NADA 'Value' defined as clean retail . . ." Very few used vehicles ever sold for clean retail. The guarantee was worthless.

Special enticements. J. C. looked for an instant at the small headline centered on the bottom of the page: WE'RE PROUD TO REPRESENT THIRTEEN CREDIT UNIONS IN THE METRO AREA. JUST SHOW US YOUR MEMBERSHIP CARD FOR SPECIAL SERVICE. For the first time this morning J. C. smiled, then took a blue marker and circled the headline, writing the command, "Make this bigger" in the margin. "Well, *there's* a pile of open wallets waiting to be lightened!" he muttered. "Special Service" virtually always translated into higher profit. He quickly made a note to personally invite the loan managers of the thirteen credit unions who worked with the dealership to the dealership golf tournament.

"Well, damn," he grumbled, searching the ad once more. Though the full-page, full-color advertisement was chockablock with messages and promises, the damn ad agency had left out the award again! The dealership again had been "Selected as one of the Top Ten Dealerships in America in Customer Satisfaction!" And that soothing fact wasn't to be seen. It didn't matter at all to J. C. that the award had been rigged, as most of the "Customer Satisfaction" awards were. J. C. himself had trained the sales force on how to make sure customers ranked the dealer as one of the best. What good was an ad agency that couldn't see the importance of that?

And now for the infomercial. J. C. then picked up a script for the dealership's newest thirty-minute infomercial. Infomercials were a dream medium for the automobile business, particularly for the underbelly of the automobile business—subprime financing. Infomercial content was virtually never monitored by any honesty freaks. Even the worst snake-oil sales pitch sounded believable with the right producer. And airtime rates cost peanuts after 2 A.M., just when the subprime suckers with the worst credit and worst jobs were either coming home from work or heading out to work.

This script for the dealership's newest infomercial was very catchy. It was based entirely on its title, "Even Bankrupts Drive Out *in a Brand-New Car* in Under an Hour!" Well, at least the vehicle, even though it might be a ten-year-old junker, would be brand new to the customer. The script promised a "Free Approval Authorization Number to *every person who calls!*" That was always worth a chuckle. "This number authorizes us to check your credit," was what the script should say if it were accurate, "and you agree to pay us $75 for that credit check if we can get you financed but you refuse to accept delivery of the vehicle of our choice."

J. C. turned from the script just long enough to pull up on his computer screen the average profit made on subprime customers suckered in by the last dealership infomercial. Each infomercial customer cost the dealership $128 to get in the door, but each of those customers made the dealership thousands. The figures reminded him of the axiom of many subprime sellers: *"Always make your money on the poor folks;* that's *why they're poor."* And that objective certainly described the figures on J. C.'s computer screen. While total gross profits on the sale of used vehicles to persons with standard credit were running 30 percent of gross sales profits, gross profits on poor customers with subprime credit drawn in by the last infomercial had run *150 percent of sales.* Enough to draw another satisfied smile from J. C.

What's on the Web? He reached for the phone and called Charles Pierce in the WAR (Web and Resources) room.

"Charles, my man, what advertising magic are you planning to work on our Web sites this week?" J. C. asked, a smile on his face.

"Are you at a screen?" Pierce answered.

"Yeah."

"Well, start punching these keys . . ."

In seconds copy for the week's Web page banners pulled up on the screen. Versions of the specials would appear on all seven Web sites tied solely to this single dealership. "We guarantee an online appraisal of your vehicle in ten minutes," looked believable to J. C., as it did to all those customers who wanted to learn the true value of their old vehicle. The promise was for an appraisal, just not necessarily for an *accurate* appraisal. This dealership, like all dealerships in the America's Family Friend chain, almost always lowered the Internet "appraisal" by hundreds or thousands when each vehicle was actually traded in.

All the bait looked tasty, J. C. thought, from the newspapers to the Web. He took one final sip from the thermos.

Did You Hear the Funny One About Truth in Automobile Advertising?

As J. C. digests his Bloody Marys, let's laugh a little and learn a lot about the biggest joke in the business: dealer advertising. Start by digesting these spicy but very accurate tidbits of info.

All car and truck ads are part of a dealership's track system. The advertising is the first step in the track process: They promise you something enticing and draw you into the dealership or to the Web sites. Of course, there's not a thing wrong with that. Trouble is, auto advertising entices without delivering. Virtually all of it is designed to excite, confuse, mislead; to say whatever it takes to deliver you, breathless, to the dealership or Web site track system. This is even true of simple, text-only ads that say such things as "Forget the hoopla and come to the friendly, low-key place."

You will be taken if you believe sales and "markdowns" automatically save you money. Profits generally are *higher per vehicle* during most sales. Why? You think "sale" means lower prices; vehicle sellers think "sale" means excitement rather than common sense on your part. Deciding to buy a car on the basis of a dealer ad is as foolish as trusting even the most honest salesperson to answer the question, "Is that the best you can do?"

But What About "Truth in Lending"?
How Can They Print Lies?

"If it weren't so, we couldn't say it" has become a motto at many dealerships. "Why, truth-in-lending folks watch us like a hawk!" they say.

Yes, truth-in-lending laws are in place. After an enormous fight by the dealers to prevent them from going into place, I might add. And, yes, the law says the right things. It's there to "assure meaningful disclosure of consumer credit and lease terms so that consumers can compare those terms and shop wisely,"[1] but boy, have the car guys learned to hoist you with that petard.

What the law was intended to do. It was designed to prevent advertisers and lenders from advertising only the most attractive credit terms in an ad. The law says that if you use certain "trigger" terms, you must then disclose enough facts to make that very attractive "trigger" term really understandable.

Here are a few trigger terms:

- the amount of down payment ("10 percent down" or "$150 down" or "95 percent financing")
- the amount of any payment
- the number of any payments
- the period of repayment
- the amount of any finance charge

If advertisers use terms like these, they must also disclose

- the amount or percentage of the down payment,
- the terms of repayment, and
- the annual percentage rate (APR).

Truth in lending's curse. Truth in lending, in many ways, has made it harder to really know what the auto seller is really saying. All that small print exists because of these trigger requirements.

Which probably leads you to the one truth in auto advertising: The *small* type is where you'll find the *honest* information in ads. And the small type generally means the advertisement itself is worthless in delivering its hyped promises to the vast majority of customers.

The ever-present "bait-and-switch" tactic. Truth in lending doesn't prevent bait-and-switch practices, either. The law says that if a dealer advertises certain items, they must be for sale. The dealers get around that very easily by putting "qualifying terms" in their ads. One such "qualifying" tactic, for instance, is putting stock numbers by a really low price. Only one or three or five cars out of hundreds are available at that price, and those are generally cars without engines, steering wheels, or brakes—the cars very few people want to buy or lease. But even these cars have a predictable habit of being unavailable to the average customer. Go down to the dealership even before it opens, be the first one at the door, and nine times out of ten those advertised cars will already be "sold." You, of course, are switched to another, more profitable vehicle.

And were the advertised vehicles really ever available to customers? Of course not! They were either sold to friends or family of the dealership's employees, or used as a "switch" car for a particularly gullible customer. "Well, what car do you want to buy?" "Well, I've only got $14,000 in cash, and I just robbed a bank, so I'm kind of in a hurry . . ." The dealership knows it's not going to gain anything by "working" this customer, sells him the car that will appear in tomorrow's ad, and goes about its business.

But how do you know if the vehicle is really sold at all? You normally don't. Until recently, the salesperson's word has been the law. That, fortunately, is beginning to change, as attorneys general offices around the country undertake investigations of the entire bait-and-switch scam.

The Special Millennium-Edition Bait-and-Switch Scam *(Available today at many of your favorite dealerships or Web sites!).* The auto business is always morphing scams as consumers and law enforcement types catch on to dealer tricks. Most dealerships are aware, for instance, that the days of the traditional bait-and-switch scam are numbered. Most of these dealerships have repackaged bait-and-switch to work like this: The dealership actually has in its inventory dozens or hundreds of advertised cars at impossibly low sales, lease, or payment prices. For instance, the ad might say, THIRTY VEHICLES AVAILABLE FOR $12,999! The dealership indeed has these vehicles and sells you one for $12,999. They make only $100 on the vehicle. They then switch you to their highest financing plan, stretch your loan from forty-eight to eighty-four months ("After all, folks, it's the same numbers, only the order is switched"), automatically add a "protection" package to your loan, talk you into an extended service agreement, and tack on a $200 advertising fee. The dealership now makes $3,700 on you.

Or, you're too smart for that. You tell the seller, "I'm paying cash, and I want that $12,999 price or else." The dealership says yes, makes $100 on the sale of their car, but lowballs you $1,500 on the value of your trade-in, and adds the advertising fee. The dealer now makes $1,700 on you. You have been the victim of bait-and-switch, millennium edition.

Double-dipping for advertising fees—the newest amusing idea. Guess who's now being asked to pay *twice* for all that worthless auto advertising? You, of course. After you've negotiated for a vehicle, many dealerships will automatically tack $100–$300 on your contract for their "Advertising Fund." Now, think about that. They want you to pay for deceptive advertising that hurts rather than helps. Why are you paying extra for the advertising, anyway? Advertising is a cost of doing business.

Asking you to pay an extra charge for advertising is all the more maddening when you realize that in buying or leasing any new vehicle you've *already paid an advertising charge.* It's built into the car's cost and usually adds $100–$350 to the car's total price. When you buy a car, you pay the charge though you don't see it. The manufacturer then sends the money back to the dealer, at times by sending it directly to a dealer advertising fund.

So what do you do when a dealer tries to stick you with an additional advertising charge? Refuse to pay it. Even if you have to break off negotiations, refuse. That's the only way to stop this fast-growing con.

The Special Millennium-Edition Auto Advertising Parlor Game—Yours at No Extra Cost—A Laugh a Minute, Except for Your Pocketbook

Have a Sunday (or Friday) newspaper handy? Pull out the big, fat automobile section, and let's plunge into the thicket of dealer deception. See how many of the following bloodcurdling yet hilarious tricks you can find in your own hometown. As a little cheap entertainment, you might want to make this a regular game with your spouse or significant other as you begin to ruminate about a new or newer vehicle. This game stays topical *forever,* too, because new auto scams and those wonderful morphs of old auto scams keep coming up every day.

Take a look at the general layouts, too. How many advertisements are really designed to provide you honest, easily understandable information?

The universal lie of virtually all advertising is, "Hey, we're the home of the Low Price and the Big Discount! Why, we fire people at sales meetings if they make money!" The tune is the same everywhere, but the lyrics vary a lot.

Note: Although the old-fashioned newspaper still has the convenience of lots of auto ads in one place, you'll find these same gimmicks in online advertisements.

Now, to the Parlor Game

See how many of these tricks, scams, and acts of prestidigitation you can find in your local newspaper, or in any media, including the Web.

The one dollar over (or under) invoice gimmick. Think "invoice" is what a dealer really pays for a car? Think again. Invoices for all domestic and most foreign vehicles are padded hundreds and, at times, thousands of dollars. Remember that padding is called "holdback," an extra, hidden dealer profit paid by you to the dealer. In a magnificent act of self-delusion, a president of the National Automobile Dealers Association once said holdbacks are a "benefit" to the consumer. Right, like the plague is good for crowd control.

The big discount—$5,000 or $6,000. How can they give these great discounts? Easy. New trucks and full-size vans *don't have federally mandated manufacturer's suggested retail price (MSRP) stickers.* Dealers make up their own. Want to discount a van $6,000? Just mark it up $6,000 first. The same gimmick is used on used vehicles. On new vehicles, sellers simply add funny fees to the MSRP. Remember that dealer in California who added a $1,500 "DVF" charge to every vehicle? DVF, we found out eventually, stood for "dealer vacation fund." Other dealers add "popularity" charges for certain models, and for years most dealers in Hawaii have added a "paradise tax" to all their vehicles. Whatever the name, these charges aren't paradise, they are purgatory for your pocketbook; they raise the "asking" price of a vehicle and give you nothing in return.

"We'll pay you $2,000 if you can beat our deal!" Or "We guarantee to beat any deal in town!" Why, shoot, how can you go wrong here? Why, if they guarantee the lowest price, there's no reason for us to even *visit* another dealership!

That's certainly what these nice folks would like for you to think, but you'd be very wrong. First, you would need to find an "exact match" car at some other dealership. "Exact match" cars are rarer than a straightforward car sale because cars can vary in thousands of ways. Even if you find an "exact match" vehicle, you must present the dealership with a completely filled-out copy of a buyer's order signed by a manager at the competing dealership to receive your "guaranteed" lower price. Unfortunately, dealership managers never give out copies of detailed, signed buyer's orders. So what's the outcome? Dealerships never give a cheaper price and certainly never pay off on these worthless guarantees.

"Special purchase" vehicles at "thousands off manufacturer's suggested retail prices." One ad we collected showed a $6,591 discount on a car with an MSRP of $17,588. Wow, you'd better rush down and get one of these! There's only one minor problem, however. The ad is for *used* cars. The ad uses a new-car asking price for a one-year-old used car. Isn't that a bit misleading? But that little bit of fraud is nothing compared to what many dealerships do to you with "Program" or "Executive" cars. More on that later.

"New Minutulas that normally list for $15,000, yours for only $5,000!" Now, here's the type of dealership you've been looking for. But read the fine print on ads like this, and you'll always find the weasel words. Generally, the fine print will say the Minutula is $5,000 *after you pay thousands of dollars down, after you give them a trade worth at least $6,000, and after you give them the rebate.* So, what's the real selling price of this $15,000 car? It's $20,000, not $5,000.

"This once-in-a-lifetime price applies to every single car on our lot!" As long as its stock number is 2331. Another version of bait and switch.

"Double rebates on every new car in stock!" These ads offer to match manufacturer rebates. How do they do that? Real simple. Take a car with a manufacturer's sticker that says $19,000, put up a dealer's sticker beside it that raises the asking price to $23,000 without adding any value, and then knock off a thousand of that $23,000 price as a "dealer rebate." Is there anything deceptive there?

"Brand-new Mosquitoes for $99 per month!" Payment ads are the automobile industry's favorite ads because so many people are suckered by them—and they are also home to miles of tiny print saying why you won't really get that low payment. Payment ads are yet another version of bait and switch.

Imply a low payment at a low rate. This approach is very popular at rate-sale time. It promises low payments on the same page with cheapo interest rates. But if you look closely, you'll see that you can't have both: If you want the low payment, you have to pay lots of money down and pay a high interest rate. If you want the low interest rate, you can't have the low payment without a much bigger down payment.

"One-half" payment plans. For the first year your payment is easy—a couple of hundred for a very expensive car, for instance. But for the next *four* or *five* years, it's really high. Like $1,000. You pay hundreds more in interest for this little "favor," and, if you're like lots of folks, you end up having your car repossessed at the end of the first year. But does the dealership care? Nope. They've already gotten the majority of their profits.

"$129 a month for a Gargantula! This is not a lease!" Before you rush down to this fine establishment, do read the ant print: "83 payments of $129 and one final payment of $21,000." We refer to this as the "Grim Reaper" financing plan. It's actually called "balloon" financing or "deferred payment" financing. These plans emulate leases without giving you even the minimum protection of an actual lease contract.

"Free trip to Mars with every car sold!" This gimmick works one of two ways: The seller either increases the minimum price he'll accept on a car to cover the cost of the gift (which means it isn't "free," doesn't it?) or the salesperson looks you in the eye and says, "Folks, you're such hard bargainers, we just can't afford to sell you this car *and* give you our gift." And what does the customer do? Take the car without the gift, of course.

"Credit problems? No problem! No credit? No problem! Recently deceased? We can resurrect you!" The ultimate and most unfair and bait-and-switch ads. Make sure you've read about subprime lending tactics and sales pitches in detail starting on page 227.

Promotions mailed to your home. "Congratulations!" one mailer said, "We've enclosed a $1,000 check and selected you for a special private sale! No negotiations necessary!" How can you be so blessed?

Salespeople get such a kick out of these "sales." They know the price of every car has been raised by a thousand to cover the phony "check." They also know anyone who falls for "private" sales is prime sucker game and therefore target these suckers for extra special sales pressure.

Throw direct-mail dealership promotions in the garbage, where they belong.

"You don't have to deal with those nasty dealers when you deal with our Web site or buying service!" These offer the great dream of all customers: a transaction without dealer involvement or deception. But the dream is just that.

Virtually all dealer chains and large dealers either now own or control portions of buying services. How do you know if the service is controlled by dealers? You don't!

The ever-present use of weasel words. How many times in your local ads have you seen wording like these:

- "With approved credit" or "for qualified buyers." Who determines the criteria for approval?
- "All units subject to prior sale," and, boy, are these cars sold before you can get there!
- "Dealer participation/contribution may affect consumer cost." The dealer was required to give up some of his normal profit to offer this, and you can bet he's going to get it back from you and then some.
- "Invoice may not reflect true final cost to the dealer." You remember that one, don't you?
- "No reasonable offer refused." Who determines "reasonable"?
- "Savings *up to* . . ." What does that mean? On which cars?
- "Starting at . . ." Of course, there's only one car starting at that price.
- "On selected models." And do you really think the model you want is of one of them?

Whew! How Can You Find a Rose in All That Garbage?

Simple: Forget automobile advertising. Never rush down to sales. Laugh at their funny promises. Great prices don't come from sales, they come from doing your homework.

What About Ads from Individuals Selling Their Own Cars? Or Classified Ads Online?

If you are planning to buy a used car, classified ads—particularly the online ad services—can be a very productive source for locating a car, but not a price. Many classified ads, particularly online, are also placed by salesmen, not individuals. We've talked about this in detail on page 62.

Killer had a copy of Sunday's ad, too. The ad was on Killer's desk, by an open phone book turned to the name "Smith." Killer cleared his throat as the phone rang. "Hello, Mrs. Smith, this is Robert DeMarco. I just wanted to tell you that your new car arrived yesterday and will be ready for delivery on Monday morning. Would ten o'clock be a good time for the two of you to come down?"

Killer had never talked to these people before, and certainly there was no car waiting for them, either. The voice on the other end of the phone confirmed this. "I'm sorry, but you must have the wrong Smith. Were you calling Allen C. Smith?" The voice was a little surprised but friendly, so Killer continued.

"Oh, ma'am, I'm sorry. I was trying to reach Allen *D.* Smith. I sure hope I didn't bother you."

"Oh, no," she volunteered, "I wish we *were* getting a new car, our old one is honestly on its last legs."

Killer liked the sound of that. "I'm sorry to hear that. What type of car do you have?" His tone was that used more frequently by morticians.

"Oh, it's a three-year-old VW bug, the new style."

"Mrs. Smith! I think someone up there is really watching after us today. I have a customer looking for a used Volkswagen right now. Even though you may not be interested in trading right now, I might be able to *sell* your car for you at a retail price. And then you *could* afford to buy a new one, especially on Monday. You know, we're having this special sale then; after you buy a car, we give you back $300 in cash and a color TV. . . ."

Not all of the "wrong numbers" proved so productive as this one. But the Smiths did come in on Monday, and Killer immediately gave them a demo to drive for the morning while he "showed" their car to his imaginary prospect. They spent three hours driving the demo and didn't even seem upset by the fact that Killer's "prospect" had, of course, already purchased some other car. After spending several hours in a shiny new car, the Smiths would just trade in their sparkling VW, anyway. Killer made a really nice deal. And think how many Smiths are left in the phone book!

Do Car People Ever, Ever Have Real Sales?

In an odd way, they never do and they always do. If "sale" means a low price, you can have that any time—if you've done your homework, as we said. If "being taken" means paying more than you have to for a specific car, people are taken at every single sale in this country. Car people, regardless of the circumstances, are going to attempt to make a *maximum* profit on you, even if the car you're looking at is marked down to dead cost. To do this, they may give you less than your trade is really worth, sell you add-ons, or simply raise their financing rates. By some method, they'll try to make more money.

Sales *may* be a fun time to shop, as we discuss in the next section, but you would do well to forget about sales. Forget about easy payment plans and low-down-payment plans. Definitely forget about consumer lease come-ons. Your objective should be to get the lowest price on the car you are buying, the highest dollar for your car if you trade, and the most advantageous financing. Do it like we tell you, and you'll always be purchasing a car at a *true* sale price.

Is There an Easier Time to Buy?

It was two days before "showtime," the intro date for the store's newest models, and J. C. was chairing the sales meeting again. Or, at least, he was chairing this special meeting at closing time on Saturday, and every salesman had been told to be there or *else*. J. C. had also passed the word that all the service mechanics and writers, even the parts men had to be there. Every single one of these people was nervous, especially after catching one quick glance at the boss. He was nearly frothing at the mouth, standing up in the front of the room next to one of the dealership's 60-inch flat plasma computer screens.

No one needed to call the meeting to order that day. Everyone was dead still and silent as J. C. began to thunder. "Sloppy! This place is the damnedest bunch of pigs I've ever seen in my life, and I'll be damned if we're going to Intro Day without being a tight place. Every single one of you is going to know what really interests our customers, and know how to provide them that! Now, I'm going to show you a presentation on our customers put together by our computer maven, Charles Pierce. If there's anyone in this room who doesn't watch every second of it, memorize every fact, I'll be damned if that person will be working here long. Killer, pass out these pads."

Killer took the yellow legal-size pads and started passing them down each row as J. C. continued. "And one other thing. Starting tomorrow morning, *no one* is to put a date on any of their deals. And *everyone* is to tell their customers all new cars will take three days to get ready for delivery. I'm talking about all the deals on current cars, not the show cars." No one said a word, though few knew the significance of J. C.'s request.

The front row of lights was turned off, and as Charles Pierce keyed in some commands on a computer keyboard on the desk next to J. C., the screen came to life. It took about three seconds for most of the people in the room to catch on. They were watching a tabulation of Web sex sites visited by each customer who had visited a dealership Web site in the past few weeks. J. C. liked a good joke every now and then.

Delaying the paperwork—a tactic as tricky as Web tracking. In the midst of this amusing violation of privacy, one important piece of information was actually passed out in the sales meeting: the matter of the dating of buyer's orders at "showtime." When the next year's cars are introduced, the vast majority of manufacturers give their dealers an extra 3 or 4 percent profit on all leftover new cars in stock from the previous model year. Called a carryover allowance, it is important to the dealers, to put it mildly.

But many dealerships like to cheat just a little bit. Why should they sell a car a few days before show date, before it earns that extra percent profit? So what do these dealers do? They fudge the paperwork. If a deal is written on a car four or five days before show date, the paperwork on that deal, including the buyer's order, isn't processed until show date. The actual computer files that are supposedly sent to the manufacturers the day a car is sold are held to show date, too. Yum. Dealers just love this little sleight-of-hand.

Though this carryover allowance is meant to be an incentive for dealers to stock more cars at the end of the model year and then sell them for less money, don't expect to see any of this money in your pocket. Dealers are very jealous of both this end-of-the-year "holdback" and their normal holdback, and they seldom share this profit with their salesmen, much less their customers—though they love to ballyhoo "end-of-the-year" savings and "secret hold-back sales" in their promotions. They ballyhoo, but of course don't give them to you. If you are aware of the largess, however, you will be in a stronger position to negotiate your deal.

"Is it a good idea to wait until year-end to buy a car in the first place?" As with most things in the business, the answer is yes and no. During the course of a year, most manufacturers generally raise their prices on every car line by hundreds of dollars. These price increases are usually much larger than any savings you may earn by waiting. But if the year-end is the time you plan to buy anyway, you can certainly buy a leftover for less money than the new models just appearing, and *if* you trade cars for another leftover two or three years down the road, you won't be hurting yourself. Many people will make the mistake of trading cars during the last month of a model year, then trading cars again in thirteen months. On the used-car market, that thirteen-month-old car is *two* years old. If the same car had been traded during the twelfth month, it would have remained a one-year-old car and been appraised as that.

So, Are There Any "Best Times" to Buy a Car?

If you remember that car people will always make more if you let them, and if you guard against that, timing can be important. Here are a few times when you may do better.

Everyday sales. The prices are not really lower at sales, but the pressure to sell is greater. For instance, advertising and promotional expenses need to be recouped, and sales managers are continually under the gun of gaining "extra deals"—more sales than usual for the time period to pay for the added expense. At sale times a good bargainer may not get a better deal but may have an easier time negotiating that deal.

Before Christmas. Most people's minds are on other things at Christmastime, and many dealerships' sales drop dramatically. Managers are more inclined to take small profits during this time.

When car sales in general are low. When the economy and other factors depress the car business as a whole, competition is at its fiercest for those few customers who do buy *new* cars. As we've discussed, used-car sales are usually highest at times like this.

At monthly "pressure" times. Car salespersons are under two great pressures. One is the pressure of the dealer, who expects his salespeople and managers to sell every day. When business is slow—when it's pouring down rain, for instance—the sales manager's neck is under the guillotine, and you would be surprised how much money some people save. Sales personnel refer to rainy-day buyers as "fairies," weird folk who only come out in the rain, invariably with a pad in hand. That's okay, though. You can afford to put up with this contemptuous attitude for enough bucks, right?

Another good time to buy a car can be the last few days of the month. Dealerships keep profit-and-loss statements on a monthly basis, and salespeople can get a little desperate toward the end of the month if forecasts aren't being met. Even if the month has been a successful one, you will probably come out better—any deals made then are pure gravy.

If you really want to be mean, go down to a dealership thirty minutes before closing time on a rainy night on the last day of the month. You'll either get a really great deal or a really black eye.

Remember: A really smart car buyer can usually get the same deal any day of the month. It's just easier to negotiate during pressure times.

Part Two

Battle Time

Chapter 10

Battle Time or Dueling with Killer

A Moral Tale, Sort Of

"Damn it!" The bright blotch of blue ink had spread over six inches of Killer's shirt before he noticed it. "Why is it always a new shirt?" He said it out loud. Not that anyone was listening— saying it out loud just seemed to let out more anger. Killer pulled his car off at the first exit and headed back home. Maybe he should have stayed there, too, but he didn't. After all, he was supposed to meet some lady and her husband, a lady who was definitely going to buy a car—at least that's what she said. Dana Wright had called him the night before and setup an appointment for ten this morning.

Hell, I'll sell them a car and buy *two* new shirts, he thought, as he headed once again to the store, speeding just a little bit more than usual. About a mile from the store, Killer flipped open the glove box and grabbed one of those small liquor bottles airlines dispense regularly. The tasty juice was down his throat in a swallow. Killer didn't know it, but even three of those liquid tranquilizers would not make this day any better.

He didn't really like the Wrights from the beginning, from the moment Trey Wright sat down comfortably in Killer's office and pulled out his personal organizer. Hell, the guy was probably a pipe smoker, too. Everyone in the business knows that pipe smokers, those thoughtful, nonemotional SOBs, are some of the hardest people to make money on. And every single one of them seems to have a notepad or a PDA glued to his palm.

Killer also didn't like the Wrights' attitude. These people didn't let Killer lead them by the nose the least little bit, but knew exactly which cars interested them. As a matter of fact, they knew the *one* car that interested them, and the damn thing didn't even have a bonus on it!

Checking out the Wrights. Killer excused himself just long enough to quickly search the entire America's Family Friend Master-Minder Prospect Database. MMPD could usually show any employee in the AFF dealership chain what Web sites any "up" had visited and quickly list everything about their past dealings with any AFF dealership. But a search of the Wrights' name and license tag number had pulled up little information other than their registered address. According to the tracking file, they had visited two dealerships but expressly forbidden the dealerships to pull their credit reports, had even *walked out* when the salespersons had tried to "T.O." them to a closer! Jerks! Killer should have known these two were the types who had disabled their computer's cookies and been very careful about giving out any information on their previous dealership visits.

He headed back to the office. "Folks, sorry about that, but that particular vehicle you liked? I was just checking with our service manager to be sure," Killer blithely lied, "and, you know, we've been having a lot of trouble with the transmission on that model. Let me show you something that could be a lot better value for the money," Killer said. Like a car with a "spiff," a cash bonus: *That* was Killer's idea of value.

But Mr. Wright answered just as quickly, "Thanks, Mr. DeMarco, but we've researched that model very thoroughly. We've even rented one for a weekend, and quite frankly we're satisfied with our choice. Now, why don't we get to business. We have an appointment with another salesman at noon."

Killer makes a move. Damn, this guy was going to be a pain. He probably *did* have an appointment with someone else. Killer grabbed a pad of "Offer to Purchase" forms and began to fill out each line with information about the vehicle the Wrights seemed determined to discuss. This normally was a good tactic. Before talking price, he liked to have the entire order completed except for the trade allowance. Then, after discussing price for a few moments, Killer would fill in the allowance "offer" acceptable to his customers, turn the pad around, and simply say, "Why don't you okay these figures for me?" Most people would sign without thinking, very easy. But hell, the Wrights didn't let him write one line!

The Wrights counter Killer's tactic. Dana made the point. "Mr. DeMarco, it isn't necessary to fill that out just yet. Why don't you take our car and have it appraised? We may be just wasting your time until we know how much you'll give us for our car, don't you agree?" She smiled, a friendly smile. Killer smiled back as he took the keys, a brittle smile, and headed out the door.

"Oh, Mr. DeMarco?"

"Yes, ma'am?"

"If you don't mind," Dana said with a pleasant firmness, "please bring the keys to our car back to us when you come back. We'll want them in our hand before we go any further."

Where did these people come from? Killer exited the office with a brief smile and a quick, "Of course."

"Trey?"

"Yeah, honey?"

"Should we have told the man our highest offer?"

"Shhh!" Trey pointed to his ear. Dana nodded quickly and smiled. She took a small spiral ring notebook from her purse and started scribbling furiously. *Oops! I nearly forgot they may be listening! But shouldn't we tell them the highest offer we've gotten on our car, the $12,500 from that place down the road?*

Trey grabbed the pad and scribbled as furiously. *No, let's not tell them yet. Maybe they'll give us more—anyway, I want to see if the guy lowballs us!*

The Wrights were beginning to enjoy this; they were the drivers rather than unwilling passengers, for a change. Killer, on the other hand, was on the high side of simmer. He'd dialed his office's intercom extension and listened to the Wrights' silence—he knew what that meant. Even the special Web camera, discreetly built into the edge of his office's computer monitor, hadn't helped gather any intelligence! Most of the used-car staff watched over Killer's shoulder, standing in the used-car manager's office, as the monitor showed a clear picture of the Wrights continuing to scribble notes to each other, grins on their faces. But it did not show what they were writing.

"I *told* Charles Pierce we should have more than one camera," Killer muttered as he stood up and handed the Wrights' keys to an appraiser. Killer let out an exasperated laugh, "Oh, and give 'em back to me when you finish looking at the car. These jerks want their keys before they go any further."

Killer makes a second move. Killer returned within ten minutes, sat down, and began to write figures on a blank sheet of paper on the desk, seemingly preoccupied with the magical figures. Then he looked up, smiling his most sincere smile. "Mr. and Mrs. Wright, I've got an excellent appraisal on your car! We have normally been taking in cars like yours for $11,500, but let me ask you this: If I could allow you $13,000 in trade, $1,500 more than usual, would you buy that car? Of course, the boss will have to approve something like this, it's so much higher, but would you buy the car today?"

The Wrights nearly fell for it. But as the word "allow" exited Killer's mouth, alarm bells began to ring in the Wrights' ears. Dana turned to Trey, and both of them began to speak at once, the echoes of a miniature Tower of Babel filling the room. All three laughed, but Killer's laughter didn't match the slightly quizzical look on his face. Why had they reacted so quickly?

Countering Killer again. "Mr. DeMarco," Trey said firmly, "thank you for the generous offer, but we are not interested in allowance—we asked you to have our car appraised. Now, what wholesale value did you put on our car, if you don't mind telling us? We'll talk about the discount on your car after we discuss our car, if that's okay."

Killer froze for a second, all the little cubbyholes up there in his mind opening wide, ready to throw out answers that worked every time. The real big cubbyhole, the one containing sarcasm, was trying to open, too, but Killer mentally pushed the door shut and locked it. So what if they didn't want to do it the right way, or rather the dealership's way? There were many ways to lighten a customer's wallet.

Killer tries flattery. "Trey and Dana—I hope it's okay if I call you that—let me tell you something. I can see that you are very intelligent car buyers, and that's refreshing. So many people don't know the first thing about buying cars." That line always worked. Get their attention with a compliment, and then do a number on them. Killer continued, "And of course we can discuss the value of your car first, the real value. As you probably know, our buyer's orders aren't designed to show a discount on a new car and then actual wholesale value on your car—Mr. Davies, our owner, doesn't want to make it too easy on customers, you know—but I'll handle that." Another good line. The owner was the enemy, and Killer was the good guy, a lamb in wolf's clothing, of sorts. Right. *All* selling systems use some lines like this.

"Now, about the wholesale value of your trade," he continued. "Our used-car manager personally drove the car and placed a wholesale value of $11,800 on it." Killer forged on before anyone else could speak, confident he was heading in for the kill. In truth, he was speeding toward the ground, tail high in the sky. The car had been appraised for $12,200; he was just lowballing them a little. Everyone could be taken just a bit; he was sure of that. But Killer, of course, didn't know the Wrights' already knew their old car was worth $12,500.

"And, Trey and Dana, let me tell you: That's really more than the car is worth. The used-car man put such a high figure because he has a customer for the car." Killer smiled.

The Wrights start to leave. But the Wrights weren't smiling at all. "You know, Mr. DeMarco, maybe we are just wasting your time. You see, we already have a much higher offer than $11,800 on the car," Trey Wright said.

"How much higher?"

"Well, that's not important. If you don't think your people can do much better, we'll just sell the car ourselves; I've done that many times before."

"Jim, why don't we do that?" Dana added. "And, anyway, it's about time for us to head to that other dealership. Mr. DeMarco, if we don't buy at the other dealership, we might buy from you some other time."

Killer sacrifices a pawn. To the experienced ear, Killer's voice now betrayed a little impatience. Customers weren't supposed to be talking like this. "Ma'am, before you do that, let me go back up to the used-car lot. Maybe they can do a little better than eleven-eight on your car . . . like, maybe twelve-two?"

"I'm sorry, that just won't do it," Trey answered quickly.

"Well, let me see what I can do. You folks just make yourselves at home."

At home? Hell, they were more comfortable than Killer at the moment. He headed back to the used-car lot and grabbed Timothy Raxalt. "Rax, I need another two or three hundred at least on this car. The people say they have got it sold to someone for more than $12,200. They won't say how much more. What do you think?"

Rax didn't look at the car but at Killer. He had heard that line so many times from Mr. DeMarco. "Killer, I'm going to rename you Chicken Little. It's a damn nice car, but I am not going to put another dime in it just to make *you* a higher gross. Now, go trade the thing at $12,200."

"Damn it, I'm telling you the straight! Now, do you want me to send them on their way, or do you want the car at $12,500?"

"What's got into you, man? Can't you allow them a little more?"

"Hell, no! The damn people won't talk allowance. I'll tell you what, though. Let me try one more thing. But then if they don't agree, can I go ahead and figure the deal from $12,500?"

I don't think up to now the Wrights had noticed how much their approach to buying a car was messing up the mind of our number one salesman. But they might have had some hint when Killer returned. His shirt pocket was again stained in that same blue ink, and not once did Killer notice it. He was talking as he entered the door.

"Folks, the used-car department is going to call me in a minute—they are trying to do a little better—but do you really want to sell your car to someone else? After all, the paperwork can be pretty tricky, and . . ."

"Mr. DeMarco," Wright interrupted in midsentence, "we've handled the paperwork before, as I said. You don't need to worry about that. Plus, we will be selling the car to a dealer just down the road. They'll be doing the paperwork this time."

Killer attacks from another direction. Killer was hanging from the cliff of calm with one hand, and even those five fingers were beginning to slip. He agreed to give them $12,500 for their old car and without a beat began to discuss the new car. *That's* where he would stick them.

"Now folks, on the car you're buying . . ." Killer laid a stock card for the particular car on the desk, pushing the card around with his finger until it faced the Wrights. As they looked at the stock card, Killer glanced at the coded cost figure in the corner. Or rather, the packed figure. The dealership still used these phony "cost" cards as much as possible. The "cost" figures contained an extra $500 profit. "Now, as you can see, this beauty lists for $29,600. But let me show you something. See this figure in the corner? It's the coded cost of the car. We are *never* supposed to show that figure to customers, but since you are knowledgeable people, why don't we simply add a profit to that figure?"

This ploy usually worked. Killer was sure the Wrights would say yes, add a small profit to that inflated figure, and—ka-*ching!*—pay that profit plus the $500 pack.

Wright nodded his head yes, and, for the first time, Killer smiled a real smile. "Mr. DeMarco, that certainly sounds fair to us. Would a $200 profit be acceptable?"

Bingo—he had them! "Well, I can't say for sure what my boss will accept, but why don't we write it up, and I'll go argue with him a little. After all, I won't make any money if you don't buy at some figure, isn't that right?" Another standard, logical question. Wright nodded again, and Killer started to write.

The Wrights execute a countermove, foiling Killer. "Oh, Mr. DeMarco . . ." Killer looked up just in time to see Wright consult his PDA. "If you don't mind, we've calculated the true 'cost' of that exact car ourselves using the *Consumer Reports* Web site. We stopped by the lot a few nights ago and copied down the price information from the window sticker. So, we'd like to check our figure against the card's figure and the figure on their Web site." Wright's words were as calm and self-assured as Killer's usually sounded. Killer ran his right hand through his thinning hair and pulled his tie loose. His other hand? It was in the cookie jar, so to speak.

Wright compared the three figures, looked off into space, then spoke. "You know, Mr. DeMarco, I'm afraid your bosses are pulling the wool over your eyes. If my figures are correct, and I'm sure they are, the 'cost' listed on this card is about $500 or so higher than the actual invoice." Wright looked at Killer without blinking and just sat there. "But I'm sure you don't know about that mistake, do you?" Killer lifted his eyebrows and shrugged, doing his best to look surprised, nod agreement, and disavow any guilt simultaneously. He, instead, looked like the smoking gun itself.

Wright continued, "But since we seem to have agreed on a $200 profit, why don't we just take *my* figure and add $200 to that? As you can see, we have the cost of every single item on the car, and our manufacturer's suggested retail prices for these items match your figures." Wright laid his PDA in front of Killer and then turned the stock card back around.

Killer tries for a deposit. Killer didn't touch either object but gazed at them for a moment. "Mr. and Mrs. Wright," he dropped the first-name bit. "My company will look at any offer. If you are saying you *will* buy a car at that figure, I believe the total would be $26,835. Let's write up your offer and I'll take it to the manager. But Mr. and Mrs. Wright . . ." Killer looked at Dana, hoping to find a little moral support there; instead he found a firm smile, "the manager will not even consider an offer this low without a deposit. It's a policy, and I can't do a thing about it. If you will give me a deposit, I'll go in there and fight for *us*." What a guy! The Wrights had found a friend in the car business.

Dana's expression didn't change, but amusement crept over Trey's face. "You know, I've read so much about the tricks all you folks play. And I really do think you've tried to play them all on us. Including the 'deposit' trick. I keep waiting for you to tell me you're in a contest!"

Killer nearly bit his tongue off. He *was* in a contest but knew better than to say so right then. He swallowed as Trey Wright went on. "But, whatever you say, Mr. DeMarco, we're not going to give you a deposit just yet. We didn't come to this dealership to waste your time or ours, so we don't need to give you a deposit to 'show you we're serious.' We're very serious. And, quite honestly, I am not interested in an hour of offers and counteroffers, and I'm certainly not going to have you turn me over to some other salesperson. That's of course the real reason you want that deposit—to keep us here while you try to wear us down."

Trey Wright leaned forward in the chair as he continued, "But I'll tell you what. I'll be happy to sign the buyer's order right now, saying I'll buy at my price. But there will be no deposit of any kind until your management agrees to *my* price."

As soon as Killer left the office, Dana pulled out her notepad and began to scribble furiously again, a look of concern on her face. *What if they won't approve it w.o. a deposit? I really do like this car . . . even if we did have to pay a little more, we could . . .*

Trey shook his head no, then scribbled back, *Weren't you telling me not to get emotional?!!* He laughed, while continuing to write, *Look, we've gone this far w.o. messing up. Let's keep with the plan!* His words made sense. After all, Killer was emotional enough right then for all three of them.

Killer brings in more artillery. Killer sat down in the manager's office, looking like some forlorn puppy. Don had been watching the Wrights on his monitor as they scribbled and laughed. Don had seldom seen the Master like this. "Killer, what is wrong with you? I mean, did they bite you or something?"

"Screw you! I'm telling you, I haven't seen anyone like these people in months!" Killer threw the signed buyer's order on the desk. "Here's what the guy will do. And he says he'll walk if I try to 'bump' him. He won't give me a deposit, either, until you sign the damn thing." Killer glanced at the monitor as the Wrights laughed again and continued to communicate via the pad. "These damn people! Don't they trust anybody?"

Don grinned. "Killer, I know why you're giving this car away. You're worried about your shirt."

Killer looked down and saw the patch of blue ink, and started laughing. "Oh, man, I just *knew* this wasn't going to be my day. Hell, I'm going home as soon as these jerks leave. Well, come on, tell me what you want to do."

"What's their trade like; can we make any money on it?"

"Hell, yes, it's a cherry from the word 'go'."

"Well, will Rax put any more money in it?"

"No, I already got him up $300, and he's strong in the car."

"Well, are you going to get any financing? Have you tried to sell them a Motor Club membership or a warranty? Killer, you know you can knock them dead on something."

"Don, I'm telling you, the people won't discuss financing or anything until you lock the deal down at their figures. Now, what do you want me to do, put their asses on the road or sell them the car? Hell, *you* could bounce them around some, if you want."

During his four years at the dealership, Don Burns had never been asked to go in on one of Killer's deals. There had really been no need to go in, either. Killer didn't leave money on the table, and Burns would have normally taken the deal, despite the paltry profit, just to get the cherry trade-in.

But this was a good chance to show the master a few tricks. Burns picked up the buyer's order, looked at the $200 profit figure, and headed out the door with Killer in lukewarm pursuit. Dana was flipping through a brochure for another manufacturer's vehicle as they entered, and Trey Wright stood up, shaking Burns's hand, returning his smile. "Folks, Don just wanted to have a chance to meet you. Why don't we all sit down?" Killer's voice betrayed as much enthusiasm as a man meeting his shotgun in-laws for the first time.

Don began to speak, a replay of countless other T.O. situations. This time he was using the "logical and fair" approach, which seemed to work best on people like this. "You know, Mr. and Mrs. Wright, I believe you are fair people, am I correct?"

A big slice of baloney, compliments of Don Burns. As both nodded slightly, Burns continued. "Let me tell you a little about what it costs to run a dealership this size. We have a hundred and twenty employees here. All of them receive benefits over and above their earnings. We also have nearly $10 million worth of cars sitting here, and, as I'm sure you know, we pay interest on every one of them just to sit here. For instance, the car you folks like so much, costs, as you said, $26,635. Our interest on that car runs just about 1 percent over prime, or about 1.5 percent of its cost per month. That particular car started costing the dealership interest payments about two and a half months ago. As you can see on the stock card, the car has been here about three months. During the past two and a half months, we have paid on this specific car approximately $421 in interest."

Burns wrote the figure on a pad and continued. "Now, you have offered to pay us a profit of $200. If we sell you the car for that profit, we're really losing money on this transaction from the beginning. But there's more. I have to be paid something. Bob here has to be paid something. The title clerks in the office have to be paid for doing your paperwork. My point is simple— your offer isn't really a fair one, is it?"

The expression on Don's face would have reminded you of Saint Peter as he sat there at the pearly gates, gently asking each petitioner, "Now, are you *really* a nice person?" Killer looked equally sincere. During this entire sermon the Wrights simply sat there, good members of the flock listening patiently to the shepherd.

Standing firm against pressure. Trey Wright cleared his throat and responded, "Mr. Burns, you are a convincing man." Don had him, Killer thought. "But even at that figure, you know you are making money." Don's mouth couldn't move fast enough to keep Wright from continuing, "Now, before you interrupt, let me tell you what I mean. I know the 'cost' figure, the real invoice figure, has at least $450 extra profit built into it. I also know you are going to sell my trade and make at least

$1,000 profit on it. I am willing to let you have my trade, even though it would be easy for me to retail it. Mr. Burns, I'm also willing to pay you the $55 'title and documentary fee,' even though that little bit of work certainly doesn't cost $55. You're making $50 on me right there." Trey Wright raised his hands, palms up. "Now, if you don't think I am paying a fair profit, that is certainly your right. We have an appointment down the road, as I mentioned to Mr. DeMarco, so perhaps those people will think my offer is fair."

The dealership's last volley. Burns had only four more bullets in his gun, but they were wasted before the trigger was pulled. "Mr. Wright, what you say may be true. I don't really know. The dealer doesn't tell us those things. And I'm not saying we won't sell you the car at your figure, either. But before I check, has Mr. DeMarco told you about the other services we can offer you?"

"Oh, you mean the protection package? And the special service agreement and all that?" Wright said noncommittally.

"Yes. And our special alarm system package, too." Burns started figuring on a pad. "Let's see, all three items are on sale now for just $1,895 total, and . . ."

"Sir, don't waste your time discussing that junk," Wright interrupted. "Now, what about our offer on your car?"

"Oh, yes," Burns said, "and how many months were you planning to finance with us?"

"None, thank you," Dana answered, even though Burns was looking at Trey. "We've already checked the various sources, and our credit union will be handling the transaction. As a matter of fact, the money is already in our checkbook, right here." Dana laid the checkbook on the table. It was the stripper's last garment. Killer's tongue slipped by reflex over his lips as Don responded.

"Well, what I will do is talk to J. C. Hollins, our general manager . . ." Don paused. "But there is probably one thing you can do to ensure Mr. Hollins will accept your offer. You see, he really does want to know that offers like this are serious. I believe what we should do is this: Let me figure up the total cost of the car, including tax. If you will give me a check for the entire amount, I'm sure the sight of that check will convince my boss to approve your offer. I know it sounds silly, but money does talk in this business."

The Wrights stay in control of the bargaining. "Mr. Burns, you're sounding like Mr. DeMarco, who already tried that on me. I not only won't give you a check for the full amount now, I won't give you more than a $100 deposit, at most, *if* our offer is approved. I prefer to give you all the money only *after* I check out the car before we pick it up. If you accept our offer, we'll pick the car up tomorrow.

"And, quite honestly, I'm not interested in talking to anyone else, though your boss may be a nice man. That would be a waste of his time and ours."

Killer and Don Burns were probably thinking the same thing, slowly savoring how nice it would be to choke these people, to pull their fingernails out one by one. The two of them left the office with the buyer's order showing the same $200 profit— supposedly to visit J. C. They didn't have any deposit, either, much less a check for the full amount.

"Well, Don, what do you think?" Actually, Killer wasn't feeling all that bad at the moment. At least Burns hadn't sweetened the deal, either.

But Burns was feeling lousy. He really did need the deal, even though the gross was nothing. Business was slow. And the used-car boys needed the trade, too. He signed the order quickly and said, "Here, take the damn thing back in there and get me their deposit," pushing the paper into Killer's hand.

Killer returned to the office, another one of those plastic smiles glued to his face, and concluded his little visit with the Wrights, shaking both their hands and finally saying, "Now, folks, we'll have the car ready for you by six tomorrow evening. And I look forward to seeing you then."

Was that ever a lie!

Wouldn't you like to do it like that, whether you buy from a dealership directly or just take delivery of your Web purchase? Would you like to be ready to meet variants of the same ploys when you negotiate on the Web?

The Wrights were such champs in beating the system because they did their homework: They took the time to shop their own car and learned its true value, using the steps outlined in chapter 6. They shopped their financing sources, too, just as we outlined in chapter 7, and figured out their Available Cash, as outlined in chapter 8. They ignored the lure of fantasy-based advertising and sales events, as discussed in chapter 9.

The Wrights also shopped carefully. They spent a good deal of time on the Web finding a couple of specific cars that fitted their needs, and then computed the cost of those cars. That's why Killer couldn't fool them with artificial "cost" figures.

That's what we are going to look at next: where to shop and how to compute the accurate cost of any vehicle. Then, we'll take you step by step through the negotiating process of buying a vehicle at the dealership or on the Web, and leasing a vehicle. This is a full-service book, you understand, but we have to check all these services first with our manager. And would you mind giving us a deposit?

Chapter 11

Shopping for a New Car the Right Way Whether You Plan to Buy at a Dealership or Online

Even if you plan to do all your shopping and buying on the Web, *read this section!* You'll learn

- the "secrets" about dealer "cost,"
- the pros and cons of ordering a car,
- the shocking secret no seller wants you to know about trucks and full-size vans, and
- other good and wacky stuff that applies to shopping both online or at the dealership.

This nifty section also tells you a simple way to check out a nearby dealership's service department. Even if you're buying a vehicle through a "no dealer" Web outfit or some other buying service, you'll still need to have a dealership "home" to service your new wheels. You'll want to check out an online seller's arrangements with a local dealership to maintain your vehicle *before* you do business with that online seller or with any other buying service.

What Do Vehicles Really Cost?

Dealer Invoice, "Cost," MSRP, and Dealer Stickers. What's the Difference?

Dealer Invoice and "Cost"

The amount of money a dealer pays the factory for a vehicle is the "Cost." The invoice figure, however, isn't what a vehicle really *costs*. The invoice includes kickbacks to the dealer, hundreds of dollars on virtually every car sold. These kickbacks are sent back to the dealer in a separate check—a nice bonus account filled with your money.

Kickbacks come in several flavors. They include

- 2 to 4 percent in extra profit (the "holdback") hidden in the "cost" of the car;
- charges for putting gas in the car and for servicing the car (though many dealers try to charge you again for this); and
- an advertising charge.

On a car with an invoice cost of about $20,000, the kickback to the dealer might look like this:

Actual cost of car:	$18,600
Holdback (extra profit):	$720
Gasoline:	$35
Make ready (servicing):	$85
Advertising fund:	$135
Invoice cost:	**$19,575**

The salesperson can now look a customer in the eye and say, "Hey, this car cost me $19,575, so you've got to pay me a profit over that." Most customers fall for this trick. Then in a few months the dealer will receive $975 *back* from the manufacturer. He's happy, too, because that's your money.

Even though you'll seldom negotiate a dealer out of his kickback on any car, you can negotiate harder simply knowing it's there, can't you?

Manufacturer's Suggested Retail Price (Also Known as MSRP or Simply the Manufacturer's Sticker)

You'll find the MSRP sticker on the window of every new car sold in America. Or at least you'd better find it, particularly if the car is sitting in a showroom. Federal law says it has to be there.

MSRP is the "suggested" retail price for a particular car. It includes a nice profit for the dealer, but dealers are free to raise the MSRP as much as they want, as we'll see. But for the purposes of determining what a specific car *costs a dealer,* this sticker is what you need to find on the specific car you like.

Dealer's Sticker

The dealer's sticker is usually placed right beside the manufacturer's sticker. It's very easy to identify because its total is so much higher than the manufacturer's sticker.

The philosophy behind the dealer's sticker is simple. Take an already handsome profit and bloat it as much as you can. What the dealer's sticker does is raise the *asking price* of a vehicle without raising the *value* of the vehicle a comparable amount.

For instance, do you remember the dealer's sticker we showed you earlier? Here's another one for a really inexpensive import. And you could actually find all of these items on the windows of cars around the country.

Manufacturer's Suggested Retail Price:	$15,000
Special value package:	$1,800
Protection package:	$1,200
Striping and special tires:	$795
ADP:	$1,000
DVF:	$1,500
Total price:	$22,295

The dealer, in this instance, has raised the asking price of this vehicle by $7,295. And how much has he increased the value of the vehicle? *Virtually none.* The $1,800 special value package cost nothing—it's simply extra profit. The $1,200 protection package (rustproofing, undercoating, glazing, fabric conditioning) cost $150. The $795 striping and special tires cost $150.

ADP simply stands for "additional dealer profit." Nice of them. And the $1,500 charge for DVF? I had to go to a local salesmen's bar the night I first saw this charge on a window and buy many rounds of drinks to finally find out what DVF stood for: "Hey, don't tell anyone, okay?" said the salesman finally, "but that stands for 'dealer vacation fund'."

So what has this upstanding dealer done by putting all these items on the dealer sticker? He raised the asking price of the vehicle by $7,295 but only raised the value of the car $300. How would you like to make money like that? And oh, did you catch the little mistake in addition on this dealer's sticker? Like every car on the lot of this particular dealership, the dealer's sticker has a thousand-dollar *error in the dealer's favor.* The add-ons total only $6,295.

I can hook you up with this dealer, if you're a financially masochistic type.

Dealerships are constantly finding new ways to ask you for more moola. Recently, dealers have begun adding several hundred dollars to the dealer's sticker or sometimes the buyer's order for "national advertising fees." It's another way to try to boost profit at the customer's expense. Don't pay it. An advertising fee is already hidden in the cost of every vehicle.

The moral of this story. Cackle, snort, or chortle at the sight of a dealership sticker. For our purposes, pay attention only to the manufacturer's sticker.

And what if a dealership says they can't remove their dealer "add-ons"? Tell them to give them to you free or find you a car without them. What if they say, "Oh, we have to write this up from the dealer's asking price"? Tell them that won't do. The only way to negotiate for a new car is to negotiate *up* from what a dealer paid—never down from what the dealer is asking.

"Do Little Cars Have Less Markup Than Big Cars?"

Though dealers will still try to tell you to the contrary, the profit margin on smaller and/or less expensive cars is now very close to that on larger and/or more expensive ones. For instance, a Cadillac might have an 8 percent markup, while a smaller Chevy might have a 7 percent markup. Salespeople will try to tell you smaller cars just don't have any markup at all. Not so. The actual dollar amount of profit may be lower on a small cheapo car versus a large luxury car with the same markup, but you can't count on that. The only way to be sure of the actual cost to the dealer of the vehicle you want is to do the research. We'll show you how in a moment.

Finding One of the Good Guys: Choosing Dealerships for Shopping, Buying, and Service

Does dealership location matter? Does wasting time matter? If it does, consider dealerships close to your home or work. Some people purchase a new car a hundred miles from home and then spend much more in gas having the car serviced under warranty than they saved in the actual purchase—if they saved anything.

Your warranties add to the importance of dealership location, too. Don't think you can automatically buy a car far from home and then have it serviced at the dealership next door. Most cars are sold with two separate warranties. The "adjustment" warranty is usually for ninety days or so and includes problems such as squeaks and rattles, air leaks, and alignment. Since adjustment warranties are generally the responsibility of the *selling* dealer, the expense is paid by the selling dealer. Obviously, other dealers will not incur expenses for your selling dealer.

Your car's regular warranty has some restrictions, too. Generally, other dealerships are not required to honor regular warranty work if your selling dealer is located closer than fifty miles from the dealership at which you wish to have the work done.

Some service departments will honor anyone's warranty work, but don't count on it. Warranty work, even regular warranty

work, is relatively unprofitable for the dealer because most manufacturers limit the number of hours a dealer can charge for each
specific repair. For instance, a manufacturer might allow only
three hours for a mechanic to make a warranty repair on your
transmission, even if the work takes four or five hours.

Tips for Choosing a Dealership

In many ways, you're getting ready to "marry" a dealership.
(That's actually a terrible thought, isn't it?) Why not make sure
you're courting one from the right side of the tracks, not one
recently released from lockup.

1. **Look at the quality of the employees roaming
   around the dealership.**
   Believe it or not, many dealerships, particularly around
   large metropolitan areas, still employ sales forces that
   look like they came from the Goons Are Us employment
   service or, worse, direct from a prison bust-out. If the
   people themselves give you a chill on your first visit to
   a dealership, get out of there.

2. **If the people look okay, take the emotional temper-
   ature of the joint.**
   I've told you never to trust a smiling salesperson, but
   courtesy does count. Are the people that talk to you nice
   after you let them know you're only looking? (Which is
   all you're going to do on the first visit. More about that
   in a minute.) Do they try to force you, at that point, to
   talk with someone else, or force you to enter an office?
   If they do, get out of there.

3. **Talk to a few people waiting to have their vehicles
   serviced.**
   In the long run, a good service department is as important to you as a good seller of vehicles. It makes sense,
   therefore, to know what type of service department
   you'll be dealing with after you take delivery on your
   vehicle. If you talk to service customers who generally
   like the dealership's work and attitude, you're in luck.

But if you find nothing but complaints, strike that dealership off your list.

4. **Don't rely on "quality" ratings.**

Virtually all manufacturers really do care very deeply about how you are treated at a dealership. If an individual dealership's CSI (customer service index) is consistently rotten, it can ultimately cause a manufacturer to "pull the franchise"—put that particular dealer out of business. Because CSIs are so important, many of the worst dealerships either falsify customer questionnaires or train their sales forces to "coach" customers on the importance of rating even the most nightmarish sales experience as dreamy.

Why Can't I Skip Dealerships *and* the Web Entirely and Just Use a Buying Service?

You could. You'll certainly have less hassle. Most car-buying services provide you a printout of car cost, and most will also buy you a car at a price less than sticker price. Those appeals are alluring and have made buying services very popular. But most services won't save you money if you're a good bargainer. For instance, they can't buy you very popular cars cheaply— dealerships have a right to hold out for big profits on those models and certainly aren't going to cut their profits for buying services.

If you have a trade-in, services can't help you much, either. Most of the dealerships involved with these services will be happy to take your trade-in as an "accommodation"—they claim they are just providing you a service, you understand. They're happy, however, because they're probably giving you less for your trade-in than it's really worth.

Dealerships that work with services invariably will still try to sell you unwanted add-ons and will work hard to switch you to their financing plans.

"I still want to use a service. How do I protect myself?" If you just can't stand the thought of negotiating, use a service, but use it with your eyes wide open. Know the value of your trade before you give it to a dealership. Don't be switched to dealership financing without carefully comparing it to other financing sources, as we show you in this book. And don't be pushed into useless add-ons.

Finding a good buying service. On your computer, search "Automobile Buying Services" or talk to your credit union or even AAA. One nonprofit, fee-based service you might want to take a look at is CarBargains. CarBargains is part of the Center for the Study of Services Consumers' Checkbook program. This nonprofit organization was founded in 1974 with the help of funding from the U.S. Office of Consumer Affairs. The organization runs a great consumer information center for many products and services. The center's CarBargains program charges you about $190, but takes over the entire bargaining process for you. Take a few minutes and go to their nonprofit, advertising-free Web site: www.checkbook.org/auto/carbarg.cfm.

Either Online or at a Dealership, Does It Make Sense to Order a Car Rather Than Buy from Stock?

Ordering at a Dealership

Dealers would always rather sell you an in-stock vehicle, so you'll find some resistance when you bring up the "order me a car" scenario. And if a dealer is overrun with inventory, you'll probably buy an in-stock vehicle as cheaply as you will an ordered vehicle.

But if you are buying straight-out—not trading your car—it can make sense to order. First, you'll have the exact car you like. But, more important, you will generally pay less; dealers don't pay floor-plan interest on ordered cars. Because of that, most sellers will accept smaller profits.

Rapid-order. Some domestic manufacturers are beginning to encourage ordered vehicles, and promise delivery within weeks, not months. Some of the sales pitches may be very high-tech, flashy, and fun, but don't put your guard down. Behind most flashy innovations is another gimmick to increase profit.

If you are planning to trade your car, ordering can be a little more complicated. The seller will appraise your trade at the time your new car is ordered but will insist it be reappraised when your new car arrives.

Many dealerships will write or stamp the phrase "subject to reappraisal" on their contracts and tell you, "Hey, your trade could drop in value before your new car comes in." That's true. But, as with most things at the dealership, these guys have found a way to make a little extra money. When your trade is appraised again—even if it's *gone up in value* (and that happens)—some dealerships will tell you, "Sorry, folks, but that car of yours has become so unpopular we can't even give them away." And you lose hundreds of dollars unnecessarily without knowing.

How to protect yourself. If a seller wants the right to have your trade reappraised when your new car comes in, make a manager write this on your contract: "Customer has the right to have car appraised by another source." Make the manager sign the statement. If the dealership's appraisal doesn't suit your fancy when the new car comes in, shop it at other dealerships or used-car lots.

Ordering a Vehicle Online

Most "indirect" online services (those that don't manufacture their own vehicles) discourage ordering vehicles, and require a very hefty deposit if you do order. The services have learned that many people who order a vehicle end up buying a vehicle from someone else. Most of the "direct" services, which include both dealership Web sites and manufacturers' Web sites, are quickly moving toward the aggressive marketing of ordered vehicles. The idea is to "nail you" quickly with the pleasant experience of designing your own vehicle online, then try just as quickly to lock you into a selling price that is much higher than sane people should pay. If you are planning to order online, follow all the steps in this book to determine the actual price you'll pay for your ordered wheels.

What About Buying "Demos," "Demonstrators," "Executive," or "Program" Cars?

"Demos," or demonstrators, are new cars driven by salesmen, managers, and other employees of a dealership or manufacturer. All of these cars are "new" in the legal sense only—they have not been registered to an individual but are still the property of the dealership or floor-planning institution.

Many customers actively seek out demos because they believe these cars are less expensive than new ones. Nine times out of ten this is false. The average dealership's profit on demos is just as high as its profit on new cars.

Other folks seem to prefer demos because they believe the "kinks" have been removed. These people assume dealership employees baby demonstrators—another dangerous assumption. Many dealership employees treat demos like bumper cars. And why not? They don't own them and drive them for only a few months.

So, what's the advantage of buying a demo? There is none.

Fraud at the Factories and Dealerships: The Selling of Rental Cars as "Special Vehicles"

Are you driving one of those "Program," "Executive," or "Brass Hat" vehicles the dealers were pushing for years? Would it bother you to know that your "special" vehicle was simply a rental car from Hertz, Avis, and other rental agencies rather than a car maintained by some fancy executive? Or would it bother you that you paid $1,000–$3,000 too much for that rental car?

It bothered lots of state attorneys general who successfully brought suit against the perpetrators of this formerly favorite selling ploy. That's why the majority of dealerships have stopped their "special vehicle" sales. If you're unlucky enough to be at one that hasn't, walk out the door and call the office of your attorney general.

Thinking About a Truck or Full-Size Van?

Remember that all new *passenger* vehicles must have a federally mandated MSRP sticker slapped on the window at the factory. This sticker ensures you that two vehicles equipped with exactly the same equipment will have the exact same "suggested retail price."

To the dealers' delight, this rule does not apply to trucks and full-size vans, which are classified as commercial vehicles, not passenger vehicles, thanks to a nice loophole in federal pricing regulations. Dealers, therefore, get to make up their *own* stickers, adding thousands of dollars to a vehicle's asking price and then slashing some of those thousands of dollars supposedly to give you a deal.

If you plan to buy a truck or full-size van, simply ignore the prices on the dealer's sticker and determine the true "cost" of the vehicle using our online recommendations.

Determine your offer for one of these vehicles as you would for a car: Negotiate up from cost; *never* negotiate down from list price. What's the most important thing to remember about advertising as it relates to trucks and full-size vans? *Ignore the advertising.*

Researching Vehicles That Fit Your Budget

You've eaten your vegetables and now it's time for dessert— you're finally going to start thinking about the car or truck that fits your fancy and your budget. This foray is the same whether you plan to purchase your new wheels online or at the dealership. Here's the plan:

1. **Make sure you've determined your Available Cash figure.**

   You might want to rewrite it here: _____. If you haven't determined it, stop right now and go back to chapter 8 and do it.

2. **Do your homework on what vehicle best fits your Available Cash and your needs.**

   Whether you plan to buy in person at the dealership or online, I highly recommend that you use the resources of the Internet for this step. I'll give you tips for using print resources in a moment, but you can find reams of info on the Web. If you aren't wired to the Web yet, try your local library, work with a friend, or rent some Internet time at a Kinko's or the like. The idea here is to relax, so put some Scott Joplin on the stereo and start surfing. Look for vehicles that have an MSRP within your Available Cash range. If you can't find a new vehicle in that range, find a used one.

3. **Disable your cookies on your Internet browser or make them visible.**

   Aside from protecting your privacy, disabling cookies dramatically lowers your spam (unsolicited e-mails and offers). Page 37 tells you how to cook your cookies.

4. **Start with a vehicle type you've been considering.**

   For instance, do you want an SUV or a convertible? If you want an SUV, do you want the bare-bones model or a fancy one? After deciding on the type of vehicle you want, gather basic information on two or three models. Gather information on more than one manufacturer's vehicle. You can collect general information from dealerships, from run-of-the-mill car magazines, or from the Web.

5. **For quick information gathering, go to at least two manufacturers' Web sites.**

   Remember that manufacturers' Web sites only give you the good news about their products and not the news you really need. Enter the manufacturer's name (like GM) or the make of vehicle (like Chevrolet) rather than simply the vehicle model (like Suburban) or you'll pull up lots of useless sites. Simply add the "www" prefix to any manufacturer's name, or use the Web addresses in the appendix.

- **For instance, visit www.gm.com.** Then go to the Chevrolet Suburban SUV. Most sites will give you a virtual tour of any vehicle and will also let you "build" a vehicle to your own specifications. Play around on these sites. Why not build a vehicle that best fits your needs, and print out the specs for that vehicle, including the vehicle's MSRP or retail "asking" price? Ignore the pop-ups and enticements to spend money with the click of a mouse.

- **Now, do the same search for comparable vehicles from other manufacturers.** For instance, visit www.ford.com, then go to the Ford Explorer or Expedition SUV, and repeat the process. Or visit www.toyota.com, then go to the Toyota 4Runner or Toyota Land Cruiser SUV.

6. If at all possible, use *Consumer Reports* online to gather objective information on these vehicles.
You can do library research to gather your objective information, or you can buy *Consumer Reports* magazine, but using this one site alone makes fooling with the Web worthwhile. Manufacturer and other commercial sites don't provide objectivity, but the *Consumer Reports* site is your best, most objective source for hard information about specific vehicles and pricing. Though *Consumer Reports* makes mistakes at times, it virtually always errs on the consumer's side rather than on the seller's or manufacturer's side. You need a friend like that online.

ConsumerReports.org will cost you if you use their very thorough services. The best deal is to join *Consumer Reports* online. For $5.95 a month or $26 a year, you get their reports on all products (not just vehicles). Vehicle reports include safety, maintenance, and reliability ratings. **Note:** Subscription services are continuous and will renew automatically each month or annually unless you cancel.

Whether or not you are a member, *Consumer Reports* also offers a New Car Price Service for $14; reports on additional vehicles are $12 each. This excellent service includes current rebate figures, unadvertised dealer incentives and holdbacks, accurate dealer "invoice" (cost) prices, MSRP (retail price), latest vehicle safety ratings lifted from *Consumer Reports'* vehicle tests, and a list of alternative vehicles. To take advantage of this service, visit www.consumerreports.org or call toll free 1-800-693-9582.

7. **Do additional research and reading on vehicles.**

The number of automotive Web sites providing a great variety of information has proliferated. Sites such as Edmunds.com or the auto channels of ISPs such as Yahoo!, MSN, or AOL have lots of useful information. All of these sites, however, have multiple affiliations with auto businesses, so exercise your common sense. You can find links to news stories and dozens of other resources at sites such as www.theautochannel.com. Again, be aware of automotive business affiliations. Bankrate.com provides some good, independent information. And if you like car buff magazines, don't forget their online versions.

8. **Always exercise caution while surfing for information.**

There are hundreds, even thousands of enticing automotive Web sites. For instance, most of the auto magazines you like browsing through at the newsstand have Web sites. Enjoy as many as you like, but remember, leave those offers for financing or come-on-and-buy-now alone. Don't click on those banner offers unless you wish to offer yourself as today's sacrificial lamb.

9. **Get "hands-on" experience in the vehicle you like the most: Rent one.**

Investing $100 for a weekend rental is far better than any test-drive at the nicest dealership, and safer for your wallet in the long run, or rent one for the day. Look at rental car advertisements and you'll generally find a list of the makes of vehicles each company rents.

10. **Print any information you'd like to have from any Web pages as you go along.**

On most Web sites you simply have to click PRINT on your menu bar. Some may also offer downloadable files.

11. **Take a break.**

Look at your options and narrow your choices down to one or two models before you get ready to hit the dealership for the first time or go further online.

Are You Planning to Buy on the Web and Skip Dealing with the Dealer?

If you are, you can skip ahead to page 362. But if you're planning to duel with the dealerships yourself, read on.

Dealership Shopping If You Plan to Buy a New Vehicle

Oh yes! You are getting ready, finally, to darken the door of a dealership. But on this visit, you're not going to buy. On this visit, you're going to gather intelligence. Here's a summary of your plan:

1. **Choose two dealerships.**

Once you have determined the specific vehicle that interests you the most and fits your Available Cash figure, locate two dealerships that sell that vehicle. Why two dealerships? You'll get bug-eyed if you go to six. Choosing two dealerships lets you more easily play one dealership against the other.

If you can, find a small, locally owned dealership as one choice. Small, locally owned dealerships like to make money like any other dealership, but you generally have a better chance of getting a fair deal from these folks. Unfortunately, "local" dealerships are as rare as hen's teeth, and many small "independent" dealerships are really wolves in sheep's clothing—they've been bought by the megachains but deliberately don't tell you that. They want to appear "small town" while in reality they're big-time and very impersonal.

Car stores have personalities just like the rest of us. Usually an independent new-car store's personality and ethical standards are determined by the dealer. You need the option of comparing similar stores' attitudes and tactics. One store may have a friendly, laid-back way of taking you to the cleaners, and a similar store six miles away may emulate the tactics of Vlad the Impaler, the true-life model for Dracula. Good old Vlad was famous for having troublesome villagers boiled alive at his dinner table.

"Can you use the Web to choose your two dealerships rather than visit them in person?" You can, but you probably shouldn't. Virtually every dealership has a Web site, but few of these sites really give you the true personality of the dealership itself. A personal visit would be wise. If you are buying new, it's not important to worry about a specific store's profit policies or its trade-in policies at this stage. For shopping purposes, assume that you will get the best deal from any store.

One possible exception. If you live in a large metro area, you may not know the location or number of dealerships close to you that carry the makes and models in which you're interested. Conversely, if you live in a very rural area and have your heart set on an Expenso Gargantula, you may not know where the nearest dealership is. In those cases, use the manufacturer's Web site or go to www.dealernet.com to locate a dealer near you. Use this site for that purpose alone.

2. **Slip Benny Goodman's "You're Not Going to Pull the Wool over My Eyes" in the CD player and visit the two dealerships. Find one vehicle at each dealership that best fits your needs.**

Objectively look at the vehicle; drive the vehicle; let the sales force wine and dine you with hot dogs and wine spritzers, but don't discuss price. Don't be "iffed" to death. Don't, under any circumstance, buy a car on this visit. Your objective on this visit is to find the best vehicle for you. Expect lots of pressure to buy on this visit, but don't succumb to it. You'll save yourself a lot of hassle if you'll tell the salesperson up front at each dealership that you are definitely a buyer, but you're not going to buy on this visit.

3. **Copy down the price and model information from the manufacturer's window sticker.**

There will probably be two or more stickers on the window of the vehicle, but pay attention only to the manufacturer's sticker. (Ignore the dealer's sticker.) Copy down the name and price of everything—base car, all options, freight (transportation), and so on. Note the code numbers for the options by their price. Ask your salesperson to give you the stock number of the vehicle. Write that down by the name of the dealership and the name of your salesperson. Ask the salesperson to give you the amount of any miscellaneous charges, such as title fees. Ask how tax is computed. For instance, is tax paid on the total price of the new car or on the difference figure?

4. **Ask the salesperson to let you see a copy of the actual dealer invoice for this vehicle.**

Some dealerships are finally providing this information, but most aren't. It doesn't hurt to ask, however. If the salesperson will show you the invoice, copy down the invoice cost of the vehicle.

5. **Leave the dealership.**

Don't be talked into anything during this visit. Just thank your salesperson and leave. Your sole purpose during this visit was to find a car you like and copy down the price and model information about that vehicle.

6. **Go home and have a stiff drink, or go for a jog.**

You've survived your first dealership visit, and your pocketbook and sanity are still in place. Listening to "Let's Get Away from It All," the Tommy Dorsey/Frank Sinatra duo, is a grand way to start your break.

What Do Those Pretty Rides Cost the Dealer?

What the Dealership Actually Paid for the One Vehicle You Liked at That Dealership

After all is said and done, isn't that what you need to know? Here's how to figure that amount. If the salesperson or Web site actually gave you this figure, you should probably check that figure, anyway. Unfortunately, some dealerships show phony invoices to customers.

Several times in this book, I've recommended *Consumer Reports* as your best source of accurate information on cars and trucks. It's also your best source of accurate cost information. To get *Consumer Reports'* pricing information, you can join online at www.consumerreports.org or you can order a report on a specific model for $14; reports on additional models are $12.00 each. If you're feeling extra, extra frugal, you can use another reputable pricing service called Edmunds (www.edmunds.com). For many years they provided pricing guides that gave you the "dealer cost" and MSRP of the base car and every option of every car sold in America.

In recent years, however, Edmunds has gone into business with the manufacturers and therefore with many dealers on the Web and with lending institutions. In all likelihood, you are going to be "data-mined" if you visit their Web sites and haven't disabled your cookies. But the car pricing guides themselves remain a valuable resource. Follow the steps outlined here, and you will determine the exact cost of just about any car. But don't automatically accept the Edmunds ads as gospel.

1. **If you visited the dealership, take out the paper on which you listed the MSRP of the car and all its options.**

    If you created a car you liked on a manufacturer's Web site, get your printout of its cost and options.

2. **Go to *Consumer Reports* (if you've joined), Edmunds, or other pricing guide, and find the exact make and model car you've selected. Print out all the pricing**

information for base car and options. If there is information on rebates and incentives, print that, too.

3. **Compare the list price/MSRP you copied down (or printed) with the MSRP of the vehicle.**

These should match. Determine the total cost of the car by adding these up:

- the base cost of the car
- the cost of any options
- an estimated charge for advertising
- a charge for gas and oil (usually $50 or less, so use $50)
- the charge for transportation or freight (listed on the manufacturer's sticker)

A few unknowns . . .

- Manufacturers include in the base cost of their cars a charge for dealer preparation and handling. Many dealers will try to charge you for preparation again and will insist on adding an additional $100 or $200 to the list price of their vehicles. Don't fall for it.
- If you are considering a "leftover" new car (a new car left over from the previous model year), the dealer's profit margin will usually be 3–5 percent more than the margin listed in the general pricing guides. *Consumer Reports* usually gives you the straight on these.
- Automotive manufacturers periodically give their dealers other "incentives" on slower-moving cars. These are usually unadvertised bonuses to encourage dealers to lower their prices. Of course, they don't, preferring to retain these bonuses as additional honey for the pot. You and I don't know which cars may have these incentives either, but we can assume slow-moving, unpopular cars may have them. How do you know a slow-moving car? They usually receive the most sale advertising.

- Don't forget the normal dealer "holdback." All new cars have an extra 2–4 percent profit built into their invoices. Neither you nor the salesperson ever sees this money, but remember it's there when you begin to bargain.

Why We Put You Through All of That

Because of your intelligence, of course. If you're planning to buy in person, this figure is priceless in helping you control the negotiations when you get down to the final negotiations. If you're planning to buy on the Web, you'll use the cost of the model you've developed to help you judge the "deals" you are being offered online.

Now, Let's Duel!

If you're buying at the dealership, proceed to chapter 13. If you're buying on the Web, skip ahead to chapter 14.

Chapter 12

Shopping If You Plan to Buy a Used Car or Truck at the Dealership or Online

In the past twenty-six years, I've only bought one new vehicle for my personal use. All the others have been used, from my fiberglass, electric-blue Gurgel convertible (now serving as a scuba-diving site off Grand Bahama Island, and please don't ask me how that happened) to my silver Lincoln Town Car (twenty-four years later still a stately, finely tuned land yacht, happily transporting friends and family along the byways of Long Island, New York). So, you don't have to convince me that you're a very smart person for deciding to buy used. It's a very clever move, with one enormous "if": *if* you realize that *shopping* for a used vehicle is *not* like shopping for a new one.

Virtually every new car is as good as it looks. Every part, nut, and bolt is new. Close your eyes, pick any new vehicle, and you're usually guaranteed many happy miles without major hassle or major expenses for repair or maintenance.

Virtually every used car, however, is not as good as it looks. Every part, nut, and bolt has had some portion of its useful life used up. Some portions, like the exterior metalwork (how most of us judge a used car), can appear new for decades, particularly with a little expert touch-up—even though the metalwork may be eaten alive with rust. Other portions, like the bolts that hold the sheet metal to the frame, or the sensitive calipers that determine whether or not you can brake to a stop, can be at the point of failure or able to last for years, based entirely upon the use that individual vehicle has had.

It's this uncertainty that makes used vehicles cheaper than new ones. On the plus side, this uncertainty allows a careful person either to buy a lot more car for the same money or to save a lot of money. For instance, you can buy that used Lexus rather than a new Camry, or spend $20,000 on a used Grand Cherokee rather than $40,000 on a new one. Supply and demand and high technology are on your side these days, too, if you're beginning to think used. The "pre-owned" market is filled with clean, late-model vehicles, and anyone can locate a specific used car with relative ease.

Even with all these good reasons to consider buying used, stay away from used cars and trucks if you're not a thorough and careful shopper. The used-car universe makes the new-car universe look pristine and innocent. Each year, literally millions of people pay too much for used vehicles and, even worse, saddle themselves with endless repair bills and junk rather than dependable transportation.

It happens because most folks don't understand that neither the surface appearance of a used vehicle, its price, nor the reputation of the seller are the most important factors in buying a good used vehicle. You may find a car at a great price, and you may be buying it from the mother of the president of the Better Business Bureau, but if the internal organs of your bargain vehicle—the things you cannot see and cannot judge easily—are junk, you are sunk.

That's why the overriding factor in choosing a used vehicle is the condition of that specific vehicle. If it is sound mechanically, it's worth more money than a bargain vehicle. If it really checks out thoroughly, *who* sells it to you isn't important—a good used vehicle from a stranger or even the local fly-by-night lot is better than an average vehicle from your Mercedes or Lexus dealer.

Preparing to Shop

We're going to discuss the whole used-vehicle hunt and purchase in detail, but, first, think about these few "givens"—

practices that savvy used-vehicle shoppers have employed since the combustion engine replaced mules.

1. **You must put away your shyness.**

    The only safe approach to buying a used vehicle is assuming that you have a *right* to know everything about that vehicle before agreeing to price or terms. If the seller doesn't agree with this approach, go somewhere else. Many sellers will imply that only amateurs check out a vehicle, or they will imply their used-vehicle warranty makes close inspection unnecessary. Not so.

2. **You'll need a pencil and pad or PDA and a checklist.**

    Two checklists are provided in the appendix. The first checklist, "Personal Checklist for Used Vehicles," will help you take the emotion out of the buying process. It outlines sixteen easy points to check on any used vehicle. This checklist will help you determine if a specific used vehicle is probably beautiful enough under the skin to be worth having it checked out further if you're thinking seriously about buying it.

    Smart used-vehicle sellers (including many individuals) make the exterior and engine compartment of their vehicles sparkle. They make the skin as beautiful as possible in order to take your mind off the condition of the vital organs. This checklist will be your first protection from the thousands of junkers sitting hopefully on lots across the country. (The second checklist is for your mechanic or diagnostic service.)

3. **You will need to wear old clothes.**

    Fashionable, but old. If you are really going to check out a used vehicle—even if you use a diagnostic service to eventually check out a used vehicle—you may get a bit of dirt or a spot of grease on your duds. So what? Would you get a little dirty to save $1,000 in repairs the moment you buy a used vehicle?

4. **You will need a mechanic or the services of a diagnostic center.**

    Our checklist will tell you many things about a vehicle, but unless you have a shop in your backyard with the latest diagnostic computers, you really can't check most of the important and less obvious problem centers in a vehicle. Choose your diagnostician before you begin to shop for a specific used vehicle.

Who should check out your potential new wheels? Diagnostic centers can do a fine job. Car-care centers and tire shops often provide this service. Your area may also have a good mobile diagnostic center that will go to the vehicle to perform the inspection. Enter "prepurchase used auto inspection" into your browser to search for possible services.

A great value for the money. You might have to pay up to $200 for a really good used-vehicle physical, but, hey, what did *your* last physical cost? The money you spend on checking out a used vehicle will be the smartest money you'll spend in your used-car lifetime. In addition to revealing problems and potential problems, the mere fact you plan to have a vehicle checked by a mechanic will lessen the seller's natural desire to stick you with a piece of junk (though the seller may not admit that).

Extra bargaining power. You will also be in a much better position to negotiate price on a specific vehicle if you know what's wrong with it. You'll know how much to budget on repairs *before* you spend all your money on the vehicle itself, too. Which brings us to the final given.

5. **Expect things to be wrong with every vehicle.**
As they say, wear and tear *is* the reason used vehicles cost less. But, if you know that a really nice one needs a brake job for $600, the vehicle might still be the best buy if you plan that expenditure as part of your purchase price. If a specific one you like needs a dozen things fixed at a cost of $1,700, that vehicle might be a good purchase, too, if you plan that expenditure as part of the purchase price.

   If you will accept these pointers as a given, you will validate the nice things I said about you at the start of this chapter, and you will probably be rich beyond your wildest dreams, or something like that.

Money! Why All This Work Is Worth It

Unless you plan to keep a vehicle for a long time, a *new* car is probably one of the worst investments in the world. As a matter of fact, as noted earlier, 99 out of 100 new ones will depreciate *40 percent* in value the day they're driven home.

But if you purchase a used vehicle wisely, you won't face such drastic losses. The only depreciation you'll face the moment you drive off the lot will be the amount of profit you've paid. For instance, if you pay $6,500 for a used vehicle with a wholesale value of $6,000, your vehicle will be worth $6,000 the moment you own it, a depreciation of less than 10 percent. If you maintain it well and drive it for a year, it will probably depreciate only another 10 percent. So even at the end of those twelve months, you'll still be far ahead of the new-vehicle game.

Why Not Buy a "Certified" Used Vehicle and Skip the Work?

Over the last few years, sales of "certified" late-model used cars have skyrocketed. They currently account for about 40 percent of dealership used-car sales. Many consumers are attracted to certification programs because they think the programs guarantee the quality of the vehicle and therefore offer greater peace of mind when buying used. Dealerships just love that kind of reasoning because certified programs also boost dealership profits by hundreds or thousands of dollars per vehicle. That must be why no manufacturer or dealership ever calls these wheels "used"—oh no, they are "pre-owned." Well, driving a "certified, pre-owned" car can cost you several hundred to several thousand dollars more than buying a similar model used car that's not "certified."

Just what is a "certified" vehicle? Would it surprise you to learn that the term has no specific legal definition and no laws or regulations apply? Any seller can slap a label on their used vehicles and call them "certified."

The best "certified, pre-owned" programs (CPOs) generally are those backed by automotive manufacturers. Almost all manufacturers offer some type of CPO, but the terms vary widely among manufacturers. Vehicles eligible for certification are typically newer models (no more than five years old) that have no more than 60,000 to 80,000 miles. Dealerships inspect and condition the vehicle, and the manufacturer offers a warranty.

A 2006 survey by Edmunds.com indicated that about two-thirds of consumers felt that the warranty was the most important factor in their consideration of purchasing a certified car, and only 20 percent felt that the inspection was most important.

If you are interested in a certified vehicle because of the warranty, you might want to consider several facts. First, warranties vary widely from program to program, and you have to look at the fine print. One ad's headline, for instance, screams "100,000-mile warranty," while the ant type says, "from original date of service." If you purchase a vehicle with 50,000 miles, that 100,000-mile warranty is really a 50,000-mile warranty, isn't it? Second, if you are thinking of buying certified for the warranty, you can purchase an extended warranty independently on most later-model cars, even those you buy from a private seller.

If you're thinking of buying a certified vehicle because you don't want the hassle of getting the vehicle inspected yourself, think again. I agree wholehearted with *Consumer Reports*' recommendation that consumers shop for certified used vehicles in the same way they would shop for any used vehicle. That includes having the vehicle independently inspected no matter how extensive the "multipoint" check the certification program promises.

What's the bottom line? Only you can decide if a certified vehicle is worth the extra money you'll pay. And if you wish to consider a certified pre-owned vehicle, stick with manufacturers' programs and shop for the vehicle using the same techniques and same caution you'd use for any used vehicle.

Why Buying Used Is Harder

From Web sites on the Internet to road hogs to small independent lots to new-vehicle dealerships to the new mega used-car operations owned by blue-chip companies, the used-vehicle business is still tainted with questionable tactics from top to bottom. Many road hogs give the pig a bad name; they are as disreputable as ever. A new-car dealership's used-car department may rip you off in retail pricing and financing. Even many of the mega used-car dealers (who like to claim their operations are run by a new breed of car person) are in reality run on a day-to-day basis by recruits from some of the toughest, meanest dealership chains in the country.

Five Discomfiting Variables About a Used Vehicle

Aside from the people you're dealing with, buying a used vehicle also presents you with more ways to make a mistake. Being smart, you know some of these variables, but it's worth taking a minute and thinking about them again.

1. **Each used vehicle is an original.**
   Don't think you'll find an identical one down the road. You'll certainly find the same year and make and model, maybe even the same color, but these very similar-looking vehicles can be as different as lightning and a lightning bug, to paraphrase Mr. Twain. Used-vehicle dealers continually use surface similarity to their advantage. They may, for instance, advertise a nice low-mileage vehicle for $7,000, and then sell you a virtually identical one with high mileage and hidden body damage.

2. **Used vehicles don't have fixed wholesale values or asking prices.**
   It's harder to "shop" the price on a specific used vehicle. Asking prices change with the wind. They invariably go up if you plan to trade in your old car. They invariably go down if you look like you are going to walk.

3. **A great vehicle may be found at the worst sales venue.**
   And vice versa. You can't automatically assume that the fly-by-nighters sell only junkers, and you certainly can't assume new-vehicle operations will always have the most dependable vehicles.

4. **It takes time to properly check out a used vehicle.**
   Cursory evaluation is the friend of the seller and the enemy of your pocketbook.

5. **Financing rates vary tremendously on used vehicles.**
   In automobile lingo, the "spread" is much greater. On new vehicles, for instance, the percentage spread between the cost of money and the highest legal rate that can be charged for money (the profit on the money) might be 6 percent. But the spread (and profit) on a two-year-old vehicle loan can easily be *20* percent. If you plan to finance a used vehicle, you must shop for the lowest rate for that particular *year* vehicle. We show you how to do that in chapter 12.

The Importance of "Loan Value"

Used cars and trucks obviously don't have set "invoice" prices. Vehicles of the same year and roughly equal condition can vary in value by hundreds or thousands of dollars, depending on mileage and color or even on the time the vehicles were traded in. For instance, minivans normally trade at a premium before the summer begins. Many folks trade for vans then, planning on a nice family vacation in their newer tub. But in the fall, buyers seem to look for smaller vehicles, hardtops, and four-cylinder jobs to use for work and short trips. Station wagon and minivan wholesale values can drop dramatically at that time.

The value of a used vehicle can also be affected by a seller's current used-car inventory and financial situation. If a dealership already has a dozen used minivans in stock, that dealership probably won't put top dollar in the next minivan they appraise. If the dealership is already having a cash-flow problem, it may put even less in a vehicle.

This variation in wholesale value poses a problem for lending institutions: What would be a generally safe amount of money to loan on a used vehicle? Lending institutions have historically wanted to loan less than the true wholesale value—a nice way to protect their loans—but have not had the manpower to actually determine the wholesale value of individual vehicles.

"Loan value" defined. Over the years, lending institutions developed a "loan value" formula as a safe compromise for setting loan limits. They began to loan about 80 percent of the "average clean wholesale" price for all vehicles of a particular make sold at auctions. For instance, if the average clean wholesale figure for all three-year-old Expenso Compactas last month at used-car auctions around the country was $5,000, lending institutions would loan $4,000 on those cars. Loan value is affected by a vehicle's general condition, mileage, and options.

Because it may be impossible for you to know the true wholesale value of a particular used vehicle, the loan value figure can at least give you a conservative indication of its worth. We will be using loan value as our benchmark in the examples in chapter 14 on "Negotiating for a Used Vehicle at the Dealership." However, because some vehicles are actually worth *less* than their loan value, we don't mind at all if you offer *less* than the loan value, raising your offer slowly from that figure. Your financing source will determine the loan value of specific vehicles for you. When you are thinking about what used vehicles might fit your Available Cash, you can use some of the average loan values for various models/years found in online or print pricing guides such as *Consumer Reports* or Edmunds, but when it comes to buying a specific vehicle, you must use the loan value provided by your financing source.

Used-Vehicle Sources: From the Internet to Aunt Wilma and Her Neighbor

Why go trekking through countless used-car lots or continually risk rear-end collisions trying to get close enough to read phone numbers on little red FOR SALE signs in the back window of speeding cars? Use the Web right and you can spend your extra time enjoying the latest copy of *The Paris Review*. The Web offers an easy, stress-free, and reasonably accurate way to locate specific used vehicles near you. It's probably one of the best uses of the Internet this side of e-mail. And these tools are available at your library, even if you're not Web savvy. We'll give you lots of good advice on this in a minute.

Whether or not you use the Web, lots of used-vehicle sources are accessible to you. The first two sources, in my opinion, are even better than online sources and certainly better than dealerships.

Dealers, of course, don't like any suggestions that they might not be the best source for a vehicle. Dealerships will tell you never to buy a vehicle from a friend or neighbor or stranger—they'll argue it won't have a warranty, you will lose a friendship, and in all likelihood you will be "cheated" by your erstwhile buddy. Or they'll say the paperwork for a private sale is tricky. Chicken feathers. Pretty good warranties are now available for private sales, and the paperwork, though something of a hassle, isn't tricky.

But maybe you're one of those people who savor dealership visits. That's fine. From good to not-so-good, here's a look at all your used-vehicle options.

Remar's First Choice: People You Know

This is generally the safest and most overlooked used-car source. Do you have neighbors who trade regularly? All of us have friends who trade every two or three years. Wouldn't it be better to consider offering that person more money for his vehicle than any dealership will give him? If you can find a friend or neighbor who is planning to trade, show him how to determine his vehicle's true wholesale value (all a dealership would have given him for the vehicle; let him read chapter 6). Then offer him a profit. Both of you will be better off—your friend will receive more than wholesale, and you will acquire a nice, newer used vehicle with little or no hassle. Some smart used-vehicle buyers regularly buy the same person's trade year after year. Could that make sense for you? You'll still want to have this vehicle (*any* vehicle, regardless of the source) checked out by a mechanic or diagnostic center.

Second-Best: Bulletin Boards at Work

Your chances of finding a nice car by reading those little notices posted on bulletin boards (or on your company's Web site, or in your company's credit union office) are just as good or better than your chances of finding a nice vehicle on some lot. Unfortunately, many people who attempt to sell their vehicles like this are in the bucket—they owe more on them than their actual value. But that's the seller's problem, not yours. Once you have agreed on the wholesale figure plus a fair profit, the seller is obligated to pay off his vehicle.

Fair Warning: Ignore any friend, bulletin board notice, or any other ad that says "assume payments" or "$500 down and assume payments." These sellers are generally deep in the bucket: They owe much more on their vehicle than its worth, and can't sell to some used-car operation because they would have to pay an operator to take their vehicle. These folks can't sell to an individual for a lump sum of cash for the same reason. "Assume payment" sales are also generally not legally recognized sales, unless they are made by the entity actually holding the installment loan on that particular vehicle. Don't fall for any "assume payment" offer—that crafty soul wants you to pay his way out of the bucket. Walk on by.

The same warning goes for any cars parked in a parking lot or beside a highway with a FOR SALE sign in the window. The practice of "curbing" (so-called because these vehicles are sold on the street) of formerly wrecked and totaled cars is rampant in some metro areas. Quick buck artists get a wrecked car that's been reported totaled, patch it up, give it a forged title, and get some individual to sell it off the curb as if it's his or hers. Drive on by.

Third Choice: Used-Vehicle Sites on the Web

I recommend that you use the Web as the third-best used-vehicle source—particularly if you want to find a very specific vehicle. For instance, if you must have a three-year-old white Toyota wagon with leather seats rather than any wagon in any color with any interior, the Web is your marketplace. Rope in a Web-wise friend to help you make this search, or head to the library, or rent Internet time at Kinko's or a similar establishment.

The good, the bad, the very ugly online. The World Wide Web's great power in the used-vehicle arena is twofold.

First, it pulls together tens of thousands of small used-vehicle inventories into a few easily searchable inventories. Second, the Web allows individuals to enter the used-car arena, as either a seller or a buyer, without the murky involvement of commercial sellers. You can duel mano a mano with an individual without the overhead, inflated profit objectives, and deception of many professional sellers. This is the good.

Enter the dealers. Virtually all used-car sellers, including the slimiest, have realized that most people like shopping for used vehicles online precisely because they think they can avoid dealers. For the dealer, that, of course, won't do. Used-car profits are the beating heart of the auto business. The dealers, therefore, en masse have slipped on a perfect Web-suit of sheep's clothing. In many cases, they present their used-car inventories on classified used-car Web sites as if the vehicles belong to *individuals* rather than to dealerships.

You, for instance, find a nice Web site ad for a white Toyota wagon, and call "Tom," the person who listed the vehicle. You're comfortable, thinking you're dealing with an individual. But Tom is actually a salesperson or manager at Nail 'Em to the Wall Used Cars. You'll pay the dealership's overhead if you buy from Tom, have to put up with the dealership's electroshock sales tactics, and have to put up with Nail 'Em to the Wall's patented "Suck the last drop of blood from the Suckers" Master Deception Plan, too. The better used-car sites may have rules that require dealers to identify themselves, but some will always try to get around these requirements.

Enter big business. And don't forget that many of the players in the used vehicle–Internet alliance include the titans of big business, e-business, and the media. Prick a tire on many of the used vehicles listed online, whatever the Web site, and you'll find a company interested first in its stock price, not in you as an individual. You'll also find a company interested in gathering information on you and in selling you something beyond a used car.

Which leads us to an important warning: Know who and what you're dealing with on the Web and, in any

dealing, always watch your backside. If a dealership has the only used vehicle that fits your specific needs, by all means deal with that dealership. But don't be deceived. For instance, as part of your contact with any online seller not clearly identified as a dealer, it is important that you e-mail the person this question: **"Is this vehicle being sold by an individual or a dealership?"** If it's being sold by a dealership, you'll need to be wary. Follow all the precautions throughout this book about dealership sales tactics. And if the vehicle is being sold by an individual? Be cautious and you'll probably have an easier time when it comes to negotiating for price.

Used-Vehicle Sources on the Web

For our most current list of used-car classified sites, along with our comments, visit www.dontgettakeneverytime.com or enter "used-car classifieds" in your search engine. Hundreds of sites will come up, including independent, commercial sites, dealership Web sites, newspaper Web sites (more on that later), and Web sites put up by consumers solely to sell one vehicle. Many of the sites have the same vehicle inventory listings. All these sites are free, and most of them will give you pictures and data on each specific vehicle. Keep in mind that few of these sites are written by monks—they're written by people who want to sell you something. So, don't believe everything you read on any site.

   A Web Tip: Try to find six or seven vehicles that interest you, and print out the page for each of these vehicles.

Some examples of the types of sites you may wish to surf:

- **AutoTrader.com** claims to list over 2.8 million vehicles from approximately 40,000 dealers and 250,000 private individuals. They have partnerships with other sites to provide used-car listings. Such sites include Yahoo! Autos, AOL, and Edmunds.com.

- **Autoweb.com, Car.com, and Autosite.com**, three of Autobytel.com's subsidiary sites, offer used-car listings from dealers and private individuals.
- **Cars.com** is a site maintained by major newspaper chains and offers ads from dealers, individuals, and different media outlets.
- **Your local newspaper's classifieds/Web site** typically lists local ads from dealers and individuals.

What About Shopping or Buying at a Web Auction Site?

The largest and most well known of the auction sites is probably eBay Motors, but there are many others. In my opinion, stay away from purchasing cars at online auctions. Regardless of the guarantees and safeguards these sites may offer (if any), they can't really protect you from the fatal flaws of virtually all auto auctions aimed at the everyday consumer rather than at professional appraisers. These auction sites draw many unsavory characters who try to sell junk vehicles no purchaser in their right mind would normally buy. These characters are banking on the fact the Web will mask the junky nature of their vehicles.

Online auction sites also make it even harder for you to check out a used vehicle before purchasing it. Use online sites to try to sell your vehicle, if you'd like. But stay away from them for shopping purchases.

Other Offline Sources for Your Used-Vehicle Search

Classified ads and free "shoppers." Many people don't list their old cars on Web sites because they don't use the Internet, period. So, you may more easily find the right car for you in that familiar old throwaway shopper than on a slick Web site. As they do with Web sites, many used-car operations disguise their inventories in shoppers, or pay individuals a fee to act as "curbstones" for a particular vehicle. Don't be shy if you plan to search the classifieds. Ask the party specifically, "Is the vehicle titled in your name?" Ask to see the title if you are uncomfortable with the person's answer. **A good rule:** As with shopping online, be especially careful if the vehicle isn't in the seller's name. In fact, I'd give it a miss.

Mega used-car dealers. Though these national and regional chains will happily let you spend more money than you need to, and though, contrary to their advertising, you must use real diligence in dealing with them, mega used-car dealers may still be a good source of late-model, generally very clean, and dependable used cars. Most of the mega used-car dealers also have a service department, which can come in handy. But ponder these points before pulling out your checkbook:

- Most of their cars are rental or lease cars. This makes it practically impossible for you to talk with previous owners—which means taking one of these cars to your mechanic (or having a mechanic come to the car) is more important than ever.
- All of these chains say they won't negotiate. They will, however, if you are serious about buying.
- Though you'll experience very little pressure at their fancy places, you will still be subject to subtle pressures to both finance with them and buy extra options from them. Don't fall for those spiels. Follow all the normal steps we give you in this book when buying and/or financing a used car.
- Most mega used-car dealers offer some type of "money-back" warranties, usually for a very limited period of time, such as for thirty days. But these warranties are generally not offered on all cars, and the money-back guarantee *does not normally include add-ons* such as what you may have paid for extra warranties or for insurance. If you're looking at a car with a money-back guarantee, carefully review what parts of the transaction are really 100 percent "money back."
- Unfortunately, some of the worst mega new-car dealers are now entering the mega *used-car* business regionally. These dealers are generally taking the used vehicles from all their dealerships in one area, putting them on one lot

and, *voilà!* they say they've created a mega used-car dealer. But you can expect these bad guys to use all their bad techniques at their fancy new used-car lots. How do you know if you're at a bad guys lot? You won't. That's why you must always follow the steps we outline here. For instance, *never buy a used car from even the fanciest mega used-car dealer on your first visit.*

New-vehicle dealers. Most of the used cars on their lots were trade-ins, a positive fact in itself. New-vehicle dealers can also be held more accountable than many independent used-vehicle sellers. Their operations are more visible in the community, and the caliber of their salespeople may be just a shade above the strictly used boys.

As with all used-car operations, it will be important for you to select the vehicles that interest you rather than letting a salesperson lead you by the nose to a specific vehicle. Sales personnel are not interested in selling you one particular model that might fit your needs; they are interested in selling the vehicle with the highest likely profit or bonus for *them*.

New-car dealers also offer you the advantage of their own service departments. You certainly won't receive any price breaks on service, but you might have a better chance of buying a vehicle with fewer problems if you are dealing with a lot that has an in-house service operation.

Independent used-car dealers. Look for large lots that have been in business for years. Once you've found a few with nice selections, call your local Better Business Bureau. The bureau will tell you if complaints have been lodged against those particular lots. If the complaints have been numerous, either forget that lot or plan to have your mechanic check their vehicles twice. Many independent lots purchase virtually all of their vehicles from new-car dealers and "road hogs," wholesalers who travel from city to city peddling individual vehicles. Such a vehicle may be a fine piece of merchandise, but shy away from it unless you can locate the previous owner. Road hogs make their living by taking dying vehicles from one market and giving them a new life in another.

Rental agencies. These people must have good public relations organizations working for them. Countless articles have praised them as the used-vehicle-buyer's salvation. These articles enthusiastically tell you how helpful their selling procedures are and, of course, how rental car sellers pioneered the "one price" method of selling. The rental car company sellers are also fond of saying, "Our vehicles are cheaper because there are no middlemen. We already own the vehicles." Incorrect. Rental agencies generally determine the true wholesale value of a vehicle and then add their profit to that figure, as all used-car sellers do. Rental agencies also tout their "twelve-month warranties." It's the same warranty offered at most used-car lots these days.

Rental agencies are no better or no worse than many other sources. Shop them carefully. Decide if you really want a vehicle that's been driven by several dozen people, too.

A Used-Car Source to Ignore: "Retail" Used-Car Auctions

"Retail" auctions, as with online auto auction sites, are one of the main dumping grounds for junk vehicles and worse. Don't consider them an option as you shop for a vehicle, and certainly don't buy from one. No matter how fancy the auction locale, you have no time or opportunity to carefully check out these cars mechanically. Also, you have no time to consider and negotiate price. Do you really want to buy a car in the heat of a bidding battle? Stay with our other sources.

Another Source to Ignore: "Buy Here, Pay Here"-Type Dealerships

You'll pay thousands more for a car at these places than it's worth.

Checking Out a Used Vehicle

Most people's idea of checking out a used vehicle is simply to walk around it slowly, kicking each tire vigorously in the process—an evaluation that usually results in nothing more than a sore foot. Some people are a little more thorough in their inspection: they will blow the horn, turn on the radio, or lift the hood.

How professional appraisers do it. Professional appraisers at most dealerships are never quite this casual when putting a figure on a vehicle; their job is the real essence of the automobile business. And Rax, Killer's favorite man on the used-car lot, knows that, too. His ritual is always the same. "First, I determine if anything needs to be spent on the car's drive train—the engine, transmission, and so forth. I crank it up and let the engine idle for a few minutes, listening for clatter or other unusual noises in the engine. Then I slip the transmission into neutral, then reverse, then neutral, then reverse. If there's any motion there, clanking, you've got transmission problems, at least in that gear. Then I do the same thing, from neutral to drive.

"I've also got a road that serves as my 'drag strip.' After the vehicle is warm, I bring it to dead still, kick the accelerator to the floor, and look out the rear window. If there's smoke back there, she's burning oil. And valve jobs are expensive. An easier way to check for that, especially if it's dark, or on a busy road, is to simply rub your fingers inside the exhaust pipe. If there's oil there, you know the same thing. If I find anything mechanically wrong with the car, I make a little note on how much it'll cost to fix it. I make the same type of notes about the outside, too. If the paint's dull, will it buff out or will it need a new coat? If there's body damage, can it be hammered out or will the piece need to be replaced? I also look very carefully for rust. Usually, the best places to look are leading edges under the hood and around the doors, really any place where water or salt can accumulate. Then I add up all the money it'll take to put the vehicle in shape and deduct that from the fair wholesale value when it's ready to go on the front line." Of course, if Rax has real doubts, he can have one of his mechanics run a quick computer diagnostic, too.

Computer diagnostics are probably beyond you, but you can use most of Rax's techniques and some others we share with you in the "Personal Used-Car Checklist" in the appendix on page 449. Anyone who plans to trade an old vehicle should be familiar with at least some of the factors Rax has been talking about. If you plan to trade for a new vehicle, you'll need the information to prepare for the battle surrounding the value of your trade.

Researching Specific Used Vehicles That Fit Your Budget and Needs

Online at the dealership, here's the plan:

1. **Make sure you've determined your Available Cash figure.**

    You might want to rewrite it here: _____. If you haven't determined it, stop right now and go back to chapter 8 and do it.

2. **Do your homework to determine what vehicle best fits your Available Cash and your needs.**

    Whether you plan to buy in person at the dealership or online, I highly recommend that you use the Web for this search. If you aren't wired yet, try your local library, work with a friend, or rent some Internet time at a Kinko's or the like. The idea here is to relax, so slap in Freddie King's "Living on the Highway," and get ready to do some serious window-shopping in a huge virtual mall, minus the lot lizards.

3. **Disable your cookies on your Internet browser or make them visible.**

    Aside from protecting your privacy, disabling cookies dramatically lowers your spam (unsolicited e-mails and offers). Slip Lazy Lester's classic "I Hear You Knockin'" into your music box as you do it. (Instructions on how to cook your cookies are on page 37.)

4. **Use *Consumer Reports* magazine or, better yet, go to their online site to gather objective information on the used vehicles that interest you.**

    The *Consumer Reports* site is one of the best, most objective sources for hard information about specific used vehicles. Though *Consumer Reports* makes mistakes at times, it virtually always errs on the consumer's side. You need a friend like that online. ConsumerReports.org will cost you if you use their very thorough services. The best deal is to join *Consumer Reports* online. For $5.95 a month or $26 for a year, you get all their product reports (not just autos). Vehicle reports include safety, maintenance, and reliability ratings. Though *Consumer Reports'* evaluations are generally made on new vehicles, the conclusions apply to used ones as well. Go to www.consumerreports.org to join and receive individual reports.

5. **Use the Center for Auto Safety's Web site for the best, most objective and most timely safety check on virtually any make and model (www.autosafety.org).**
The site is free and priceless. It has links to crash reports and other information on the National Highway Traffic Safety Administration Web site, as well as to other good sources.

6. **Do additional research on used vehicles.**
The number of automotive Web sites providing a great variety of information has proliferated. Sites like Edmunds.com or the auto channels of ISPs such as Yahoo!, MSN, or AOL have lots of useful information. You may enjoy reading reviews posted by owners of various models. All of these sites, however, have multiple affiliations with auto businesses, so exercise your common sense. You can find links to news stories and dozens of other resources at sites such as www.theautochanncl.com. Again, be aware of automotive business affiliations. And if you like car buff magazines, don't forget their online versions.

7. **When you've settled on a specific type of vehicle, find several sources for that type of vehicle.**
I won't be obvious and say look in your classifieds and pick up your local "shoppers," but I will be obvious and say use the Web. The Web is a stunning resource for locating specific used buggies. Search as many online

sources as you want to find a specific vehicle that appears to fit your Available Cash and your fancy. But choose vehicles that are in a location *close enough to you to get to for a physical inspection*. Virtually all the used-vehicle selling sites are free.

8. **When you've located a few potentially good vehicles on the Web or in a shopper, determine the "loan value" of these vehicles.**

   Consider the loan value figure the "cost" of any used vehicle. Your objective is going to be to buy the vehicle as close to the loan value figure as possible. Either call your bank or credit union and ask them the loan value of the specific vehicle, or go to www.edmunds.com.

9. **Physically inspect and drive your favorite choices.**

   Bunny Berigan's "The First Time I Saw You" would make nice background music for this foray. Whether you're looking at dealerships or at a vehicle owned by an individual, don't be conned into buying on the spot. If you're at a dealership, do not tell the salesperson you are trading. Used-car operations raise the prices of their cars if they feel you are going to trade. Do not tell them your Available Cash figure. As you find cars with asking prices close to your Available Cash figure, take time to drive them.

10. **Using our checklist (page 449), look for obvious problems with the car.**

   If you still like the car after a test-drive, write down
   - the stock number (if it's at a dealership);

An important tip: Download or print information about each vehicle that interests you. You can then compare them at your leisure when you sign off. Look for vehicles with asking prices up to $400–$1,000 over your Available Cash figure.

- a description of the car;
- the asking price;
- the name and phone number of the person you are dealing with;
- the miles on the car; and
- any option(s) that may add to loan value, such as a vinyl roof, air-conditioning, power windows, or cruise control.

11. If the car is at a dealership or not represented by the person who owns the car, insist on the name and phone number of the previous owner of the vehicle.

If you're at a dealership, many sellers will try to tell you that information can't be given out. Don't accept that answer. If you can get the phone number of the previous owner, call that person and ask them what was wrong with the vehicle. Former owners love to talk about their old vehicles, so don't be shy about this. Make a list of the owner's problems.

12. If the seller says the vehicle was a lease vehicle, insist that they, in writing, state that it was a lease vehicle and not a rental vehicle. Lease vehicles generally had one driver. Rental vehicles, as we've said, could have had hundreds, or had me, which is worse than hundreds.

13. Pry the seller's clinched fist from your elbow and go home.

You've earned yourself a break. Plug Duke Ellington's "I'm Just a Lucky So and So" into the CD player and relax. You've survived your first venture into the mad arena.

Once you've recovered, move right on over to chapter 14 if you'll be hitting the bricks to buy your vehicle at a dealership or from an individual. Hit chapter 16 if you plan to click your way to a happy ride to Nirvana entirely on the Web.

Chapter 13

Negotiating for a New Vehicle at the Dealership

You're ready to buy a new vehicle, and you've decided to duel with the dealership directly. That's a first-rate decision, actually. We're going to walk you through specific tactics for that buying foray. But first, put Slim Harpo's "Blues Hangover" into your CD player, paying particular attention to Slim's plaintive declaration, "I don't have change for a grasshopper, and that's two crickets. . . . " That's about how poor you'll feel if you skip this chapter and go to a dealership posthaste. So, contemplate more than your navel, like this question, for instance:

"Just What Is a Fair Deal? How Do I Know When to Say Yes?"

One of the most successful general managers I know says and believes this definition of a fair deal: "If the customer is happy and the dealership is happy, *that's* a fair deal." Unfortunately, there is a problem with his logic. The seller always knows how much money it makes on a customer, but the customer seldom knows how much unnecessary profit he or she really paid. Would you be happy if you knew you'd paid even $100 more than you needed to pay? How about thousands? If you would, have I got some dealerships for you!

It's a cruel world out there. You've worked hard for your money, and all those dealers are living in fancy houses, so let's define "fair" in the buyer's terms, for a change. *A fair profit is the least dollar amount any particular seller will take for a specific car.* That figure may include a $100 profit or a $1,000 profit—or that figure may mean the dealer is actually losing money on an individual sale. A dealer will lose money on an individual sale anytime that particular sale qualifies the dealership for bonus money on other sales. A dealer will sell at a loss for other reasons, too. Happens all the time.

You won't know if you're lucky enough to be buying a loss leader until you do your research and bargain a little. But you can always assume a dealership will say yes to your deal only if the deal benefits them. A dealership won't say yes unless they need your deal, loss leader or not. This chapter on negotiating the sale assumes that fact. It will show you how to negotiate price until the seller says yes, however reluctantly.

It's important to approach "fair" from this point of view rather than from a fixed percentage of profit. Aside from hidden dealer bonuses and incentives, supply and demand, cash flow, and other factors mean a dealership may accept different levels of profit on the same vehicle at different times. Today a dealership may happily sell a specific car for less than $100 profit; tomorrow it may refuse to sell the same car for less than $1,000 profit. A fair deal is always the least a dealer will take right now for that car.

"What if I don't want to bargain that hard?" If you are the type of person who absolutely refuses to dicker over price, if you are determined to offer one firm price only, offer the seller a maximum profit of 2 percent of the list price. If the dealer absolutely refuses to take your offer, raise it a percent if you like, but don't go above that figure. Go to another dealership. Car dealerships survive on churning their money and turning cars quickly.

"But how can those poor dealer types survive on a 2 or 3 percent profit?" Easily. If you are looking at a car with a $20,000 retail sticker, remember that the dealer didn't pay

$20,000 for it, or even the invoice cost of $16,400. The vast majority of new-car automobile dealerships floor-plan their cars; they do not own them outright. Most dealerships' new cars are owned by their financing institutions, such as Ford Motor Credit or GMAC. When the dealership orders a new car from the factory, that car is shipped to the dealer on consignment. The dealer in essence rents the vehicle until a customer buys it. In our example, a car with a list price of $20,000 and an invoice cost of $16,400 might cost the dealer $3,600 a year in interest, or $300 per month for each month the car sits on his lot.

Let's say you decide to pay the dealer a 3 percent profit based on the list price of $20,000. The dealer starts out by grossing $600. Add to that profit the hidden "holdback" profit of at least $600, and the dealer's gross is up to $1,200. Add to that profit the dealer's profit on "fees" and other add-ons, and the gross profit is up to $1,500. Now, let's subtract the dealer's costs. We'll assume the car has been sitting on the lot three months. The dealer has to pay $900 in "rent." Then the dealer has to pay a commission to the salesperson, about $140. On an investment of $1,040, the dealer made a gross profit of $460 *in three months*. Can you do that?

So, what's a fair deal? When you know the seller is taking the least amount of money, *that's* a fair deal.

Handling High-Pressure Techniques

As you know by now, dealerships are masters at using sophisticated, high-pressure sales techniques. Sales staff wear you down, curse you behind your back if you really bargain, are voracious with your money, and generally don't give a damn about you once you've bought a car from them. Because most of us have felt many of these pressures before, it's hard to imagine a vehicle transaction that is simple, clean, and to the point.

But that's exactly what your next transaction can be, if you've read this book reasonably carefully and if you'll stick to the basic ground rules for dueling with the dealerships as summarized here:

1. **Slow down.**

    Indecisiveness and a deliberate, koala-like pace are anathema to the Indianapolis 500 pace of dealerships who survive on speed and winning at any cost.

2. **Have all your facts in writing when you go to the dealership.**

    Having a detailed map keeps you from being lost and eaten alive. If you know the true wholesale value of your car, the amount of your Available Cash, the cost of their car, and your financing terms *before* you shop, sales personnel won't be able to lead you on some mini-safari around their lot back to that gloomy space called the slaughterhouse of financial calamity.

3. **Don't fall for "if" questions.**

    It may not sound like a high-pressure technique, but remember these questions represent the highest-pressure technique. "If" questions are designed to suspend logic. For instance, anyone would be inclined to say yes to, "If I can sell you a $10,000 car for $5,000, will you buy it?" Of course you would. But logic, if not suspended, tells you that no dealership can do that—the math's too good to be true. When salesmen use the "if" approach, *take control of the conversation* and don't commit. Simply smile and say, "I don't know."

4. **Insist on straight answers.**

    If you ask the wholesale value of your trade, don't accept some vague answer about "allowance." If you ask for the keys to your car, don't accept some vague, delaying comment.

5. **Don't be "worked."**

    All selling systems are based on working you. The salesperson brings in reinforcements, or the salesperson keeps leaving and coming back with sincere-sounding notes written by his boss, or the salesperson keeps picking up the phone as if he or she is carrying on a sincere conversation with his manager. *Don't put up with any of it.* Break the system. Don't be intimidated; demand quick answers or get out of there. There's another dealership just around the corner.

6.   Do things in your sequence, not theirs.
In order to understand a vehicle transaction, you will have to control the order in which information is gathered. Many salespeople will tell you, "Oh, no, before we have your car appraised, we always fill out the buyer's order." Say no. I'll take you through all the action steps of negotiating in a minute.

7.   Don't be beguiled by the dealership finance manager (a.k.a. the "business manager" or "financial counselor"). As surely as hours follow minutes at a car dealership, you're going to be forced to visit with this high-pressure salesperson—even if you've arranged your own financing or are paying cash. Don't forget that this oddly friendly yet insistent soul will generally do anything, including lie, to switch you to a dealership financing source or to sell you add-ons. So, how do you handle the pressure? If you want to be tough, refuse to listen to the sales pitches at all. Tell the person you're not interested in talking at all, and if they pressure you, leave.

"But what if they say I have to fill out my paperwork there, even if I don't want to?" Listen very politely, and expect some of the nicest, most believable lies you've ever heard, as they try once more to switch you to their financing. Then tell the person this: "I'll be happy to consider your financing if you'll give *me* an exact copy, filled out, of the finance contract you want *me* to sign so that I can compare *it* with *my* other source." That's a very simple request. When they hem and haw and eventually refuse, remember how readily your bank and credit union provided you their figures, then refuse to discuss financing with the dealership any further.

What if the dealership actually gives you a fully filled-out contract to take home before you sign it?
Take the dealership contract to your other loan source, and ask them to print out their contract for the same

amount of money. Choose the financing source that's actually cheaper.

8. Don't fall for "spot" delivery.

But if you really want to take it home today, refuse to sign any document that says the seller has a right to change any terms on your contract.

Facing the Fan: Signing Documents

Most dealerships are very smart when it comes to the moment of signing. They invariably pick the very second your heart is beating wildly, your lips are smacking in anticipation, and your common sense is visiting in a neighboring state; *then,* and only then, will your salesman or finance manager stealthily slide the large mound of papers under your quivering hand and say, "Sign here, and here, and here." We told you about the "fanning" of documents earlier. Though the routine may vary a bit, we also told you that the first two documents you will be asked to sign are usually the most disquieting.

- The first sheet normally states, "I have read all of the documents put before me very carefully before I signed them." Don't you think that's an interesting document to put in front of you *before* you sign anything?
- The next document says, in effect, "I agree that the dealership may have made mistakes on these papers. I also agree that, even though the dealership has told me I am financed, they could be telling a little white lie. So I agree that none of this paperwork means anything if the dealership wants to change its mind. I'll be glad to pay more." That's the fabled "yo-yo" technique (read all about it on page 100.) Stay away from these problems by shocking the dealership and carefully paying attention to every document you're asked to sign. Here are some tips on what to pay attention to on some key documents:

1. The buyer's order. This is the conditional sales contract you sign before you actually sign the finance contract. A buyer's order shouldn't be a scratched-up piece of paper; it should be a clean, neat sheet of paper with every important piece of information filled in. Look at those figures to make sure they are the figures you've agreed to pay. Also, make sure the buyer's order figures match those on the actual installment loan contract if you're financing at a dealership. Though it sounds corny, and you're in a hurry to drive off in your new wheels, carefully paying attention to this document can save you lots of grief down the road. Many customers have been taken because the major record of their sale was too scratched over and through to stand up in court. Remember, this is a *contract*. If you are not financing at the dealership, it is the *only* contract. If you are financing at the dealership, it is the only record containing important information about warranties and a few other tidbits. Make sure your buyer's order contains the following information. Take this list with you to the dealership, if necessary.

- **a.** The date
- **b.** Year of cars (yours, too, if you're trading)
- **c.** Make and model of cars
- **d.** Vehicle identification numbers (VINs)
- **e.** Asking price
- **f.** Trade allowance (if you're trading)
- **g.** "Difference" figure (if you're trading)
- **h.** Amount of your payoff
- **i.** Taxes
- **j.** Amount to be financed
- **k.** Other fees
- **l.** Complete warranty statement (if a used car, if no other warranty statement is provided)
- **m.** Number and amount of payments (if you are financing at the dealer)
- **n.** APR (if you are financing)

2. Mileage statement. You will be asked to sign a mileage statement for your trade-in. The statement should be completely filled out, *including* the mileage. Many salesmen will leave the mileage blank and happily inform you the figure will be filled out later. Say no. Your mileage statement makes *you* liable for the actual mileage on your trade. If you let the salesman leave this figure blank, a sneaky salesman or store could run the miles on your car back, enter the false figure, and sell the car. If the new buyer should discover this, *you* can be sued, not the dealer—because you signed it blank, dummy. The seller will also provide you a mileage statement on his car. If you are buying a new car, the mileage should obviously be low. It should also match the figure on the odometer. Again, insist that the statement be filled out completely. If you are buying a used car, the seller is obligated to give you a copy of a statement signed by the previous owner. If there is no mileage statement from the previous owner, *don't* buy the car. Insist that copies of both mileage statements be given to you.

3. Powers of attorney. You will be required to sign "limited powers of attorney." Normally, you will be asked to sign two of these: one for the car you are purchasing and one for the car you are trading. These powers of attorney simply give the seller the legal authority to change titles. If you have already signed the buyer's order, it's okay to sign the powers of attorney. Many dealerships must type these up to satisfy state law—but insist that they be filled out before you sign, especially if the people you are dealing with make you feel a little uneasy.

4. Finance contracts. All finance contracts, especially those used by dealers, will remind you of *War and Peace.* The back of every single page is just loaded with all types of unusual protection for the financing institution. For instance, most contracts say your car can be repossessed even if you pay your payments on time—the institution simply needs to feel that their loan is in jeopardy. Most of these contracts also state that your car cannot be driven or "domiciled" out of your state without the permission of the financing institution. Unfortunately, you can't do much about all this fine print, but you do need to make sure the typed-in portions of the finance contract match the fiures and other entries on your buyer's order.

Your Hour upon the Stage: The Importance of Play-Acting

Remember when you met that person you really didn't like but managed to be passably nice, anyway? Remember when you said the "right" thing to your mother rather than the thought really on your mind? You'll need to call on those impressive acting skills again at the dealership. But this time, its going to be easy! Dealerships are the world's greatest arena for lay actors. Salespeople do it every day—like Joe Girard, "the world's number one car salesman," as he's fond of claiming in his book. Girard, who sells more cars than many manufacturers, proudly proclaimed in a *Newsweek* article that he would "do anything to make a sale. I'll kiss the baby, hug the wife. It's nothing but an act."

Customers do it every day, too. Even the most intimidated Casper Milquetoasts usually forget to tell their salespeople the little things that might adversely affect the value of their trade-ins.

Rather than condemn the process, however, why not accept it for what it is? Car negotiations are unforgiving turf battles for lucre. If that dealership has an economic right to make-believe, you certainly do, too. Put away the guilt. Put on that mask. You're the star in the hit Broadway production *Keep Your Tires Off My Greenbacks!*

Doing It by the Numbers If You're Buying New

Here's this charming book in a nutshell, the whole process in outline form. We're using the most common buying situation for the vast majority of people:

- You are going to finance.
- You're trading your old vehicle rather than selling it yourself. You owe money on that trade-in, and (unfortunately) you don't have much equity in that trade-in.

In the appendix we outline other buying scenarios. For instance, if you have no trade-in or are paying cash for your new vehicle. *But please read through this process even if you are using a different scenario.* You'll have an easier time when you enact your own scenario. And there's a hidden prize in here, anyway. . . .

Here's the Scenario

You and your better half are handsome, upwardly mobile people admired by everyone for the neatness of your home, your gift for cooking, and those beautiful haiku poems, in addition to your overall discernment as well as your calm brilliance. Oh, and you are very modest.

You haven't been seduced by the thought of tricentennial finance terms and therefore want to finance for the fewest months, not the most. You laugh at dealership advertising, and though you love a sporty new set of wheels, you love your money more. You want to conserve much of your hard-earned money right now, too, for *really* important things like a trip to Bali. A few of your less intelligent acquaintances laugh at your cautious deliberation, but you slough off the laughter and run a tab on all the money you're saving. Heck, you and your other half can buy Bali with all that moola! You turn up Bob Marley's "You Can't Do That to Me" and steadfastly continue your brilliant work, starting with a quick review.

1. **You've already determined the wholesale value of your trade-in, your payoff, and the equity in your trade.**

   "Wholesale value" is what your old car is worth in cash to a seller who plans to resell it. Wholesale value is a fixed value, not a variable value based on the price of the vehicle you want to buy. You shopped your old car to get its most accurate value (page 166). You subtracted your payoff from this wholesale value to determine the amount of equity you have (page 171). Write those figures here:

   Wholesale value: _____
   Less payoff: _____
   Equals equity: _____

   If you don't have equity, you're "in the bucket," as they say. I'd slip Paul Whiteman's "Muddy Water" into the player (try the Whiteman/Bing Crosby rendition), and then read "If You're in the Bucket" on page 252. If you have equity, why not hum along to William DeVaughn's "Be Thankful for What You Got."

2. **You determined your Loan Cash and Available Cash figures.**

   "Loan Cash" is the sum of cash your payment will buy. "Available Cash" is the total of your Loan Cash, your equity, and any other cash you're bringing to the transaction. It tells you the maximum amount of car you can buy including tax, tag, title, and all other charges (page 244). Write your figures to determine Available Cash here:

   Equity in trade: _____
   (If no equity) Cash from your pocket: _____
   Loan Cash: _____
   Equals your Available Cash: _____

3. **You shopped financing sources for the best overall loan.**

You used the best source to determine your Loan Cash, right? List your first and second choices for financing right here:

Finance source one: _____
Finance source two: _____

4. **You've shopped and selected two convenient dealerships that sell the vehicle you like and you've figured what each vehicle cost the dealer (page 308).** Write those figures here:

Dealership one: _____
Vehicle stock #: _____
Dealer cost: _____

Dealership two: _____
Vehicle stock #: _____
Dealer cost: _____

Excellent! All your facts and figures are in one place now. Stick a new battery in the PDA and let's march forth.

5. **If you have not yet actually applied for a loan yet, do it.** You want the cheapest overall loan, right? Then apply for an actual loan at your two best sources. Use your Loan Cash figure as the amount you want to borrow. When the loan is approved, double check that your payment amount is consistent with what you budgeted.

6. **Determine your maximum offer on each vehicle.** You have determined the true cost of each vehicle. Remembering our definition of "fair profit," determine what your maximum offer will be. Write the figures here:

Total cost of vehicle: _____
The maximum profit you will pay: _____
Your maximum offer will be: _____

7. **Compare your offer on each vehicle to your Available Cash figure.**

Put those two comparisons here:

Dealership one: _____
First vehicle stock #:   _____
Available Cash figure: _____
Cost of this vehicle: _____
Over or under Available Cash: _____

Second vehicle stock #:   _____
Available Cash figure: _____
Cost of this vehicle: _____
Over or under Available Cash: _____

Dealership two: _____
First vehicle stock #:   _____
Available Cash figure: _____
Cost of this vehicle: _____
Over or under Available Cash: _____

Second vehicle stock #:   _____
Available Cash figure: _____
Cost of this vehicle: _____
Over or under Available Cash: _____

8. **Now compute your "difference" figure.**

"Difference" is the final selling price of their car (your maximum offer) minus the wholesale value of your trade-in. You'll need this figure later during the negotiations or you'll probably be bamboozled. Do this for each vehicle, like so:

Your offer on the new car: _____
Subtract the wholesale value of your car: (_____)
Difference figure: _____

9. **Take a day off.**

"Let's Get Away from It All," from the Tommy Dorsey/ Frank Sinatra duo, is a grand way to start your break.

Dealing with the Store

Have you ever heard Billie Holiday going at it on "Havin' Myself a Time"? Well, get it, because that's you, the educated car buyer. Or, mostly you: "I mean, I'm having what I want, wanting what I have, and liking what I do, and I'm having myself a time . . . I'm certainly in my prime. . . ."

That's you because you probably have more information at your fingertips than the salesperson at either of your "buying" dealerships! Now, keep that calm but wary confidence, and let's go buy a new set of wheels.

1. **Make an appointment with the salesperson that waited on you at the dealership that's home to your favorite new vehicle.** These folks work hard, make no money, and deserve your sale, if they are nice. As you enter the dealership, remember that you have a car you like just as much at another dealership. You don't have to buy here. Don't forget to take all your buying facts, from the information on your Available Cash to the information on their vehicles.

2. **Let the salesperson show you the two cars you priced at the dealership.**
   Make an emotional decision on which car you really like the best. This is one of only two times it's safe to be emotional in the car process, so enjoy! And this is the only time your heart rate should affect your negotiation. *But don't let the salesperson know you really like the vehicle!* If you betray enthusiasm at this point, all the work you've done to protect your pocketbook will fly off the lot. If you show any outward emotion, make sure it's indifference, and consider muttering something like, "Well, I really like the one at the other dealership better. . . ."

3. **Once you have decided on *the* particular car, lead the salesperson to his or her office.**
   You take control of the buying situation. Be nice. Smile and laugh. But remember that *you* must control the order of the next few minutes. Take the following negotiating steps.

4. Tell the salesperson to have your car appraised.

You know the true wholesale value of your old car but don't tell them that wholesale figure, even if they won't bring you a free hot dog. Remember that many dealerships will say they won't appraise your car before knowing what you're going to buy. Don't accept that answer. If a dealership won't do the transaction in your order, go to the other dealership.

5. Ask the salesperson for the appraisal on your car.

Let the person know you want a wholesale offer, *not* an allowance figure. If the figure is lower than your wholesale value, say so. But don't say by how much; give the dealership room to come up in their offer as much as they will.

If their wholesale figure is higher than your figure, don't say a word. You must become the well-known cat that swallowed the canary. You are going to make money on your old car!

If the dealership offer never equals yours, tell them your figure. At this point, even tell them who gave you the buying figure on your old car. If necessary, remind your salesperson that his used-car boys can sell your car to the same people you would sell it to. If they finally agree to your figure or offer you more, write their offer on your pad. If the dealership just won't accept your figure, go to your other dealership.

6. Make your offer on the new vehicle.

If you are feeling particularly testy today, offer *less* than your figure; give the dealership room to dicker a little. But don't go over your maximum figure. In fact, I recommend bargaining up from dead cost as your first offer.

7. Write down the agreed selling price of the new vehicle when the two of you have agreed on it.

Put it by your original offer for that particular car.

8. Stop and check your difference figure.

Deduct the dealership's offer on your trade from the agreed price of the new car. If this difference figure is more than your difference figure, you are losing money. If the figure is lower than your figure, you are making money. If the figure is an acceptable one to you, go to the next step. If it is not acceptable, continue to negotiate or go to your other dealership.

9. **Tell the salesperson to write it up.**

Once the buyer's order is completely filled in, *look at the difference figure.* If you don't see it, ask the salesperson to point it out to you. That figure must agree with your difference figure. Most buyer's orders are not designed to show cash offers (which is what you're really making) on a new car and the true wholesale figures on used cars. Your salesperson will probably indicate, for instance, that you are buying the new car at sticker price but receiving more than wholesale on your trade. That's okay *if the* difference figure is the same.

10. **If the difference figure is the same, sign the buyer's order, but *do not give a deposit.***

Tell the salesperson you will give a check when the deal is approved by a manager. The salesperson will probably insist on a deposit. *Don't give it.* Remember, a deposit before you have an approved deal is the dealership's way of keeping you there while they "work" you. While the salesperson is gone, loudly play Maxene Andrews's "Show Me the Way to Go Home" on your iPod. That's exactly what you're going to do if these folks send in a bunch of burly men to try to raise you.

11. **If the salesperson returns with a signed order, give a deposit.**

If the dealership tries again to send in someone else to grope for more money, crank up Jimmy Anderson's "Naggin'," and tell them again that you will not be raised. If you're so inclined, and if you have room in your Available Cash budget, raise yourself a little or a lot. It's your call. If you are determined not to be raised at all, don't be shy about vamoosing. Head to your other dealership.

12. **If you're not financing at the dealership, be prepared for tricks to convert you to dealership financing.**

Every self-respecting dealership just has to try to convert you to their financing. If a seller insists they are actually cheaper than the source you've already chosen, require the seller to give you a copy of the completely filled-out finance contract and physically compare that contract to your primary source's contract.

13. **Arrange the time to pick up your car. If you are financing the car at the dealership, be prepared to talk with the finance manager.**

Remember, *you* already know the number of months and the interest rate. You have already made a decision on insurance. *Don't let the finance manager change your terms.* Before you leave his office, confirm the amount to be financed, and take that figure home with you. If the amount to be financed is not exactly the same as your projected Loan Cash, compute the payment when you get home either using our charts in the appendix or the payment calculator at www.dontgettakeneverytime.com, and take that figure with you when you pick up the car.

14. **If you are financing with the seller, be prepared for "add-on" pitches even when you go to pick up your chariot.**

Many sellers will even add additional charges and "services" without your permission. Mr. Louis Armstrong's "Don't Jive Me" is your answer to that.

15. **Gaze upon your magnificent chariot, slip behind the wheel, and crank Benny Goodman's "You're a Heavenly Thing"** as you drive into a rainbow-hued sunset. You've survived!

16. **When your envious neighbors ask how you negotiated such a fine deal,** slip Sinatra's "I Did It My Way" in the CD player, and crank it!

Chapter 14

Negotiating for a Used Vehicle at the Dealership

We established in chapter 12 ("Shopping If You Plan to Buy a Used Car or Truck at the Dealership or Online") that used-car buyers are much, much smarter and more handsome than new-car buyers. This chapter will establish also that we have lower cholesterol, don't suffer from nervous prostration, and are generally the type of people everybody wants to hang out with. Oh, and we are better bargainers.

We are better bargainers because we *have to be* to keep from being eaten alive by all those used-car people. But that's what natural selection is all about, isn't it?

Here, you'll find a reasonably concise summary of the most common used-vehicle transaction for the vast majority of very smart people: You are going to finance, you have a trade-in, you owe money on that trade-in, and (unfortunately) you don't have much equity in that trade-in. In the appendix we outline other buying scenarios. For instance, if you're buying used but have no trade-in or are paying cash.

Before we get to the specifics, do think about this little matter:

"Just What Is a Fair Deal? How Do I Know When to Say Yes?"

One of the most successful general managers I know says and believes this definition: "If the customer is happy and the dealership is happy, *that's* a fair deal." Unfortunately, there is a problem with his logic: The seller always knows how much money it makes on a customer, but the customer seldom knows how much *unnecessary* profit he or she really paid. Would you be happy if you knew you'd paid even $100 more than you needed to pay? How about thousands? Sophisticated well-turned-out men and women don't make mistakes like this.

It's a cruel world out there, too. You've worked hard for your money and all those dealers are living in fancy houses, so let's define "fair" in the buyer's terms, for a change. *A fair profit is the least dollar amount any particular seller will take for a specific car.* That figure may include a $100 profit or a $1,000 profit—or that figure may mean the dealer is actually losing money on a used vehicle. Maybe it's been sitting around too long or isn't a popular color. Dealers sell used vehicles all the time at a loss.

You probably won't know if you're lucky enough to be buying a vehicle at a loss, but you can know if you're buying it as cheaply as possible if you do your research as we showed you in chapter 12, then follow our guidelines and bargain a little. You can also bet your life that a used-car seller will say yes to your deal only if the deal benefits the dealer. A dealer won't say yes unless he needs your deal. This witty and charming chapter assumes that fact. It will show you how to negotiate price *until* the seller says yes (a very reluctant yes, if you've bargained correctly).

Handling High-Pressure Techniques

As you know by now, dealerships are masters at using sophisticated, high-pressure sales techniques. Used-vehicle dealers are generally even worse, particularly if the dealership isn't a part of a new-vehicle franchise. Sales staff wear you down, curse you behind your back if you really bargain, are voracious with your money, and generally don't give a damn about you once you've bought a car from them. Because most of us have felt many of these pressures before, it's hard to imagine a vehicle transaction that is simple, clean, and to the point.

But that's exactly what your next transaction can be, if you've read this book reasonably carefully and if you'll stick to the basic ground rules for dueling with the dealerships, as summarized here:

1. Slow down.

Indecisiveness and a deliberate, koala-like pace are anathema to the Indianapolis 500 pace of dealerships that survive on speed and winning at any cost.

2. Have all your facts in writing when you go to the lot.

Having a detailed map keeps you from being lost and eaten alive. If you know the true wholesale value of your car, the amount of your Available Cash, and your financing terms before you shop, sales personnel won't be able to lead you on some mini-safari around their lot that leads to the slaughterhouse of financial calamity.

3. Don't fall for "if" questions.

It may not sound like a high-pressure technique, but remember these questions represent the highest-pressure technique. "If" questions are designed to suspend logic. For instance, anyone would be inclined to say yes to, "If I can sell you a $10,000 car for $5,000, will you buy it?" Of course you would. But logic, if not suspended, tells you that no dealership can do that—the math's too good to be true. When salesmen use the "if" approach, *take control of the conversation* and don't commit. Simply smile and say, "I don't know."

4. Insist on straight answers.

If you ask the wholesale value of your trade, don't accept some vague answer about "allowance." If you ask for the keys to your car, don't accept some vague, delaying comment.

5. Don't be "worked."

All selling systems are based on working you. The salesman brings in reinforcements, or the salesman keeps leaving and coming back with sincere-sounding notes written by his boss, or the salesman keeps picking up the phone as if he or she is carrying on a sincere conversation with his manager. *Don't put up with any of it.* Break the system. Don't be intimidated; demand quick answers or get out of there. There's another dealership just around the corner.

6. Do things in your sequence, not theirs.

In order to understand a vehicle transaction, you will have to control the order in which information is gathered. Many salespeople will tell you, "Oh, no, before we have your car appraised, we always fill out the buyer's order." Say no.

Your Hour upon the Stage: The Importance of Play-Acting

Remember when you met that person you really didn't like but managed to be passably nice anyway? Remember when you said the "right" thing to your mother rather than the thought really on your mind? You need to call on those impressive acting skills again at the dealership. But this time, its going to be easy! Dealerships are the world's greatest arena for lay actors. Salespeople do it every day—like Joe Girard, "the world's number one car salesman," as he's fond of claiming in his book. Girard, who sells more cars than most dealerships, proudly proclaimed in a *Newsweek* article that he would "do anything to make a sale. I'll kiss the baby, hug the wife. It's nothing but an act."

Customers do it every day, too. Even the most intimidated Casper Milquetoasts usually forget to tell their salespeople the little things that might adversely affect the value of their trade-ins.

Rather than condemn the process, however, why not accept it for what it is? Car negotiations

If you did not read chapter 13 on negotiating for a new vehicle, be sure to read the sidebar on signing paperwork on page 338.

are unforgiving turf battles for lucre. If that dealership has an economic right to make-believe, you certainly do, too. Put away the guilt. Put on that mask. You're the star in the hit Broadway production *Keep Your Tires Off My Greenbacks!*

Doing It by the Numbers If You're Buying Used

Here's this charming book in a nutshell, the whole process in outline form. We're using the most common buying situation for the vast majority of people:

- you are going to finance;
- you're trading your old vehicle rather than selling it yourself; and
- you owe money on that trade-in, and (unfortunately) you don't have much equity in that trade-in.

In the appendix we outline other buying scenarios. For instance, if you have no trade-in or are paying cash for your new vehicle. *But please read through this process even if you are using a different scenario.* You'll have an easier time when you enact your own scenario. And there's a hidden prize in here, anyway. . . .

Here's the Scenario

You and your better half are seasoned rock climbers, tackle class-five white-water rapids with ease, and were both awarded the Mayor's Award for heroism that time you single-handedly stopped that roving band of muggers. You bought stock in Hotmail when it was a penny a share, and you collect rare books. Though you try not to let it change your natural modesty, your friends, naturally, envy you, particularly your business acumen (why else would you be buying used?).

You are amused at lesser personages who finance used vehicles for years on end, and you plan to finance for the fewest months, not the most. You consider used-car advertising in particular to be great fiction reading, and you chortle at the most amusing ads.

You want to conserve as much of your hard-earned money as possible for *really* important things like your collection of rare thimbles. A few of your less intelligent (and ultimately poorer) acquaintances laugh at your studied pace when it comes to negotiating to buy anything, but you slough off the laughter and run a tab on all the money you're saving. On this used-car purchase alone, you're planning on saving enough to finance a veritable thimble orgy on your next trek to Ladakh. You carefully raise the volume as Gluck's "Dance of the Blessed Spirits" begins to spin on your 500-CD player and steadfastly continue your brilliant work, stopping for a moment to review past research:

1. **You determined the wholesale value of your trade-in, your payoff, and your equity in the trade.**
   "Wholesale value" is what your old car is worth in cash to a seller who plans to resell it. Wholesale value is a fixed value, not a variable value based on the price of the vehicle you want to buy. You shopped it to get its most accurate value (page 166). You subtracted your payoff from this wholesale value to determine the amount of equity you have (page 171). Write those figures here:

Wholesale value:	_____
Less payoff:	(_____)
Equals equity:	_____

   If you don't have equity, you're "in the bucket," as they say. I'd slip Paul Whiteman's "Muddy Water" into the player (try the Whiteman/Bing Crosby rendition), and then read "If You're in the Bucket" on page 252. If you have equity, why not hum along to William DeVaughn's "Be Thankful For What You Got"?

2. **You determined your Loan Cash and Available Cash figures.**
   "Loan Cash" is the sum of cash your payment will buy (page 246). "Available Cash" is the total of your Loan Cash, your equity, and any other cash you're bringing to the

transaction. It tells you the maximum amount of car you can buy including tax, tag, title, and all other charges (page 244). Write your figures to determine Available Cash here:

Equity in trade: _____
(If no equity) Cash from your pocket: _____
Loan Cash: _____
Equals your available cash: _____

3. You shopped financing sources for the best overall loan.
You used the best source to determine your Loan Cash, right? Remember that a credit union is almost always the cheapest place to finance a used vehicle—if that credit union uses the same interest rate for loans on new and used cars. List your first and second choices for financing right here:

Finance source one: _____
Finance source two: _____

4. You've shopped around and found a used vehicle you like at two convenient sources—dealerships or individuals. You've determined the loan value of each vehicle (page 318).
If the vehicles are at dealerships, write the stock number and loan value of each vehicle here. Also note each vehicle identification number (VIN):

Dealership one: _____
Vehicle stock #: _____
Loan value: _____
VIN: _____

Dealership two: _____
Vehicle stock #: _____
Loan value: _____
VIN: _____

If an individual owns the vehicle, note its model, year, loan value, and VIN number.

Dealing with the Store

Disc 5, Andrés Segovia, begins to play as you sip a fine fruit-flavored wine (well, you can't do everything right, you know). Gagging slightly, you continue.

1. **Use a service such as www.carfax.com to check the history of your favorite vehicle.**

These services won't tell you if a vehicle has had major damage, regardless of their advertising claims, but they can tell you other important facts about almost any vehicle using the vehicle identification number (VIN).

2. **Call your financing source and tell them about your favorite vehicle. If you have not yet applied for the loan, do it without delay.**

Do not pass Go, do not go any further until you are approved. Get the specific interest rate, total amount of money, and number of months your source will give you on this vehicle. Put that information in your PDA or notepad.

3. **Compare the seller's asking price to the loan value of the car.**

We'll assume you've found a car with an asking price of $10,000 and a loan value of $8,000. The spread is their *probable profit*—in this instance, $2,000. Chuckle. A person as smart as you know you are laughs inwardly at such a lofty profit.

4. **Compute your "best probable" difference figure.**

Subtract the wholesale value of your old car from the loan value of the seller's car. For instance, assume the wholesale value of your old car is $3,000, and the loan value of the seller's car is $8,000. Your best probable difference figure is $5,000. When you begin to negotiate, you will be trying to be close to this difference figure or below it. Determine the "best probable" difference figure for your situation, and write it down; it's your most important figure this side of a winning lottery ticket.

5. **Go back to the lot and tell your salesperson you have decided to trade your car.**

   Tell the person you want the actual wholesale value of your car, *not* an allowance figure. He'll probably be surprised you know the difference.

6. **At this point, announce you would like to have your doctor give the vehicle a physical.**

   Danger! Some used-car sellers will try to palm off "reports" on used vehicles or call in their own diagnostic wizards. Forget it! Use your own, independent mechanic or diagnostic service for this physical. You're getting ready to find out whether that beauty is a "Tulip or Turnip," which is precisely the reason you are listening through your Labtec earphone to Duke Ellington's rendition of that immortal classic.

7. **Deduct any estimated repair bill from your Available Cash figure.**

   Let's assume your Available Cash figure is $12,000. Let's assume your mechanic says you need to spend $2,000 on the vehicle to put it in dandy condition. That's fine, if you really like the vehicle. So, deduct your repair bill from your Available Cash. In our example, you're now left with $10,000 in Available Cash. Make this calculation for your vehicle, and write it down.

8. **Head back to the lot.**

   Don't let your salesperson do the figuring when you return, but do ask how much the dealership is giving you for your car. Subtract that from the dealership "asking price" and determine the difference figure. Now, compare this difference figure to your "best probable" difference figure. The balance will be how much more money the dealership wants for the vehicle than you are planning to spend.

9. **If by some act of the divine powers, the difference figure is the same as yours, don't automatically**

agree to buy the car. Every salesperson's first offer, regardless of how low it is, has a cushion in it. Offer them hundreds less. You should be smiling on the inside, too. If their figure is close to your figure, only $200 or $300 above, tell him that the figure is $400 or $600 away. Always compromise and split the difference on any offer.

10. At some point in the discussion, your salesperson isn't going to budge.

When he reaches that point, check these things:

- his probable profit. Subtract your difference figure from his.
- his final difference figure. Compare that to your "best probable" difference figure.

Can you afford it? Add these items together and determine how much you will owe the seller.

- his final difference figure,
- the payoff on your old car,
- tax.

You will owe the seller: ─────────────────

Subtract what you will owe the seller and the repair estimate from your Available Cash.

11. If you're really ready to buy, discuss warranties.

A review of warranties on page 432 is in order.

12. If the seller's final offer fits your budget and the warranty is satisfactory, have him write it up!

Tell him you'll take the car at that figure.

13. Once the salesman has completely filled out the buyer's order, look at the difference figure.

If you don't see it, ask the salesman to point it out to you. That figure must agree with your final difference figure. Make sure the warranty is written.

14. If the figure is the same, sign the buyer's order, but *do not give a deposit.*

Tell the salesperson you give deposits only when the deal is approved by a manager. The salesperson will probably insist on a deposit. Tell him it's your way or no way at all. You wisely remember that a deposit before you have an approved deal is their way of keeping you there while they "work" you. If the salesperson returns with his boss or insists your offer is too low, don't be raised without a fight. If you are determined not to be raised, say good-bye.

15. **Don't be beguiled by the dealership finance manager** (a.k.a. the "business manager" or "financial counselor"). As surely as hours follow minutes, at a car dealership you're going to be forced to visit with this high-pressure salesperson—even if you've arranged your own financing or have decided at the last minute to pay cash. Don't forget that this friendly but insistent soul will generally do anything, including lie, to switch you to a dealership financing source or sell you add-ons.

So, how do you handle the pressure? If you want to be tough, refuse to listen to the sales pitches. Tell the person you're not interested in talking at all, and if they pressure you, then you're outta there.

But if you're curious about the dealership spiel, listen very politely and expect some of the nicest, most believable lies you've ever heard, then tell the person this: "I'll be happy to consider your financing if you'll give me an exact copy, filled out, of the finance contract you want me to sign so that I can compare it with my other source." That's a very simple request. When they hem and haw and eventually refuse, remember how readily your bank and credit union provided you their figures and refuse to discuss financing with the dealership any further.

What if the dealership actually gives you a fully filled-out contract to take home before you sign it? Take the dealership contract to your other loan source, and ask them to print out their contract for the same amount of money. Choose the financing source that's actually cheaper. Page 212.

16. **If you are already financing with the seller, be prepared to be "worked" again.** Remember, you already know the number of months and the interest rate. You have already made a decision on insurance. Don't be talked into changing your mind. Before leaving, confirm the amount to be financed, and take that figure home with you. If the amount to be financed is not exactly the same as your projected Loan Cash, refigure the payment when you get home and take that figure with you when you pick up the car. It should be within pennies of his payment.

17. If you're not financing at the dealership, give the final figures to your financing source and make sure the source will approve your loan for this specific vehicle.

18. If you are financing with the seller, be prepared for "add-on" pitches.

After agreeing to a price on the vehicle and financing, many sellers will add additional charges and "services" without your permission. Refuse to take them.

19. Pick a fancy restaurant for dinner.

A place with parking spaces right at the front door. Slip Frank Sinatra's "For Once in My Life" into the ol' 8-track, and smile as you drive away. You've bought a used car right!

Chapter 15

Negotiating Online for a New or Used Vehicle

A Tangled Web

Charles Pierce, chief Web maestro for all of AFF's nearly two hundred dealerships; possessor of an office next to God himself, Gary Oliver Davies; Charles Pierce, easygoing man-about-town; admired by countless lot lizards and lesser Web jockeys—Charles Pierce was shivering in his smoothly tanned skin, Killer thought, and Killer felt for him.

"You say *What?* . . . Say *that* again for the group, and please don't tell me *these guys* agree with that last proposal!" Gary Oliver Davies punched the air three times in no particular direction, his eyes first drilling Pierce, then the four men who sat opposite him in honey-smooth leather armchairs at Davies' magnificent conference table. Everyone at the table felt the unexpected shock wave of Davies' outburst. Except for Killer, of course, who was used to the master's roar when people said really dumb things.

But this was the first meeting of the Web Integration Task Force, Davies' baby. As a consequence, the (now) minority owners of Cars Without Dealers (CWD) were getting their first bleak view of what lay ahead. Any thoughts they may have had of independence as part of a national auto chain run by Davies had evaporated as quickly as Davies' calm.

Cars Without Dealers, the massive car-buying service formerly owned by the four, was being "integrated" into the America's Family Friend dealership chain. Although each of their bank accounts was richer by $2 million from the sale, and millions more in AFF stock options were in their grasp, at the moment, neither the money nor the options seemed to protect them from Davies' ire.

Cars Without Dealers had been a good, consumer-friendly buying service, a household name. Even consumer groups had applauded CWD's efforts to give customers the actual appraised value of their trade-in, to publish actual vehicle cost figures rather than inflated costs that hid extra dealer profits, and to deal in a straightforward manner with financing matters. CWD *had actually let people finance with the cheapest financing source!* Killer found that funny, even naive. Sure, CWD had taken a cut from each financing source, but they had also let the customer actually choose the best finance company from the CWD list of finance sources.

Sure, CWD had relationships with lots of dealers around the country. Because the manufacturers had caved in to the dealerships' massive pressure not to cooperate with buying services directly, and because the state legislators had kowtowed to the dealers as usual, how else could any buying service get cars?

But Cars Without Dealers, with all their good intentions, had lost millions in their first six years of business. They had been struggling through their first year of "peanut profits," as Davies called it when he approached them on behalf of America's Family Friend. "Oh, we won't call it a buyout," Davies assured them, "we'll just become a 'consumer partner' with Cars Without Dealers. The customers don't have to know much. We'll just be the people that conveniently deliver cars to their door, and conveniently take away their trade-ins. You'll hardly notice the difference in the way you do business, either. But you *will* notice the difference in your bank account and blood pressure! Do you guys have offshore accounts yet?"

Gary Oliver Davies had been a charmer before the deal was done, but that charm was gone now, washed away by the first tentative suggestions just presented by the four former owners and agreed to by Davies' own Web maestro, Charles Pierce. The suggestions, Davies knew, showed why CWD had been a peanut operation. These guys wanted to allow Web customers using the Cars Without Dealers buying service to have the right to "shop" the value of their trade-ins! They wanted to *sell a used car to people with bad credit for the same price the car would be sold to people with good credit!*

Where did these people keep their brains? But these whacko ideas hadn't set Davies off. He was actually amused by them, calling them "Jesus thinking," the babbling of do-gooders who would change the world. No, what brought on the meltdown was the simple statement made by Charles Pierce on behalf of the former owners that "we feel all our buying service Web sites should emphasize Cars Without Dealers consumer legitimacy above every other selling point." Davies had just stared at Charles Pierce: these four men *and even his own Web maestro* didn't get the Great Web Gimmick! They didn't understand that *the Web made customers feel safe and move fast! And they had left out the most magnificent, most lucrative improvement to The Great Gimmick in history:* **the online signing of vehicle purchase and finance documents!**

The ultimate impulse act was just becoming a reality, thanks again to the lobbying of the auto industry. The fine senators and congressmen had passed an innocuously worded bill that said facsimile signatures were as legally binding as real signatures. No longer would sales or finance contracts have to be overnighted to customers for their signatures. No longer would customers be able to take their own sweet time to actually *read* the damned documents. No longer would they have hours to become infected with buyer's remorse—or, worse, shopping-itis. Davies had already heard the horror stories of other dealership chains, even more advanced than AFF in Web selling, who were losing customers constantly to other dealerships and shopping services when the customers actually took their paperwork and used it to shop other dealerships! Who did these customers think they were?

The potential for all that consumer foolishness— brought on by the ugly reality that actual paperwork

had to be signed by customers—had been erased with barely a wink of Congress's eye. Billions of dollars in extra profits would flow from that simple piece of legislation—Gary Oliver Davies himself had calculated that gross profits per online sale would rise 30 percent thanks to the legislation, and had already calculated that the "closing" rate of prospects online would skyrocket because of it. Hell, once consumers were induced into signing online, they'd have no choice but to do what the dealership wanted! Wallets could soon be grabbed online in a more financially devastating fashion than any customer would want to imagine! And not one customer could weasel out of these contracts!

Gary Oliver Davies swept the conference room again with his unassailable stare, then turned to Killer. "Killer! Did you hear what these guys left out of their little master marketing plan? They didn't make 'instant online agreements'—the key marketing strategy! What type of idiot would do that? Don't they know consumers want speed more than any damned consumer folderol? Who, tell me, doesn't know that in this business?" Davies was right, of course. Given the choice of carefully buying a vehicle and saving money or quickly buying a vehicle and unknowingly spending more money, the majority of customers still preferred speed. The auto industry thrived on that premise, and "Signatures Online" was the last great extension of the "speed and convenience are more important than thinking" premise. It would ruin tens of thousands of unwary consumers, but make Davies' stock options worth hundreds of millions of dollars, he was sure.

"*That's* why we're going to weld instant online agreements to every online marketing strategy," Davies decreed. "Link it to the consumer stuff all you want, link it to our toilet paper, but *link it!*"

Davies turned to Killer. "So, you see why I wanted you in this meeting and the rest of these damn meetings, Killer? What the Web needs is more people like you, not more moon-eyed consumerists. Now, why don't you tell our Web genius here"—Davies jerked his head in the direction of Charles Pierce—"and his four disciples how the Web and the auto business should really work."

Killer knew he needed to stay modest in manner and thought right then. Even a millisecond of the wrong smile could further embarrass all the new boys and Killer's pupil, Charles Pierce. And Killer planned to make as much money as anybody on the Web. He had his *own* master Web plan. So he notched his smile carefully into the "I'm a small cog and what do I know?" position and began to speak. "Well, Gary, these men know a lot more than I do about the Web and all those Web sites. But, you know, we might have several opportunities here to 'help' our customers. . . ."

Killer's arched eyebrows and tone began to lighten the atmosphere around the table. "And believe me, we want our customers 'helped' by the likes of Killer," Davies chimed in, with a short laugh. "So why don't you help us with a little consumer advice à la Killer Monsoon?"

It did not escape Killer that, for the first time in his automobile career, he was the focus of Gary Oliver Davies and the center of attention in a marketing meeting that might impact a $6 billion business, the AFF chain of dealerships. Killer was both excited and unnerved at the thought.

Types of Web sites. "Well, as I understand it, AFF has six types of Web sites up and running. First, we've got the direct dealership sites, one for each dealership in the chain. They provide us the cheapest prospects and easy profits—especially since Charles here has started our 'special pricing' for Web customers." This time, everybody in the room laughed. "Special pricing" had for years been an automobile industry code word for higher profits from groups like credit union members or others who thought they had special arrangements with auto industry businesses.

"The second type of site out there," Killer continued, "is the indirect site that provides us 'ups,' for a fee or a piece of the profit. These guys just collect names with their fancy advertising, add on their profit, and send 'em to us for slaughter."

"They are *cheap* sources for prospects for us," Davies interjected, "since we just add the site's charge for each customer to the customer's bill. I like that."

"Believe me, your salesmen like it, too," Killer added with a quick smile, nodding as he continued his soliloquy.

"Then our third type of Web site includes the ones we bill as 'consumer' sites. They look and sound a lot like the real consumer sites, have the same window dressing. I personally find our consumer sites a lot of fun when I'm online as the consumer expert." As the laughter broke out, Killer pushed ahead, maintaining his "sincere" facial mask, never acknowledging the good-natured jibes of the men around the table. "Well, if they can't trust me," he added quickly, "who can they trust? Our finance managers?"

"They had damn well better pay attention to our outside 'consumer experts,' I tell you that," Davies said sharply. "Those guys are costing megabucks."

"That's because of all those PhDs they've got, Gary," Charles Pierce said. "We can counter just about any safety concern or reliability concern anybody brings up by using these guys. It's worth it. Did you see that online piece on the safety advantages of the titanium brake calipers on the new sport-utes? Who cares about the failure rate of the brake lines themselves, as long as those titanium calipers are out there?"

Targeting youth—even before they can drive. The meeting was very quickly degenerating into bursts of unexpected laughter, a shift in emotion that both surprised and relieved the new players around the table. At the shift, Web maestro Charles Pierce decided to seize the mood to talk about his favorite new Web deception.

"Gary, that brings up our fourth type of site, our new teen site, speaking of trust," Charles Pierce said. "We've developed it, you know, with some of our manufacturers. We're thinking about calling it Tails Out—you know, the shirttail thing with young people."

"A damn good name."

"I actually thought that up in a meeting with the manufacturers' psychological mining committee, you know," Pierce said, beginning to feel in control again, "and our beta test is already showing us what we can learn from these kids—about their parents and about their own buying habits."

"Like, what can we learn about their parents? How much probing are we doing with the kids?"

"Oh, it's more than probing, we're getting *permission* from the parents to probe the kids. No one's done that, and does that ever make this site a gold mine!"

At this, one of the four men from Cars Without Dealers asked, "How did you get permission from the parents? I mean, everyone's so paranoid about that."

Sneaking in a back door for information. "We teach the kids about driving safety, and we preach against smoking and about the dangers of drinking and driving. Hell, we got a liquor company and a cigarette company to help underwrite the site because of that. Part of their 'penance' thing on underage smoking and drinking, you know. The parents love it! We require them to fill out a questionnaire before their kids can belong to the site. And it doesn't hurt that we have ten keywords listed for Tails Out with the major portals and search engines, and we've just enabled the site so kids can join in from their cell phones. We're not first in doing that, but we've got the best system."

"So, exactly what does that damn site do? It sure costs a pot of money." Davies was growing grumpy again.

"Well, the kids talk about any subject they want to in the chat rooms, from their music to school problems to their parents' sex habits to the cars their folks like and don't like." Charles Pierce looked amused. "Did you know that in the beta test, the kids said parents worry about money and sex more than safety and reliability! We're using a computerized word-tabulation program that tabulates every repeated topic online, from first kiss to four-in-the-floor.

"Our 'moderators' are also specially trained to raise interesting questions or topics. Like this week, we're probing what issues parents might sue about. You know, are they really concerned about safety as much as the Nader nuts think they are? Does a hundred bucks matter to the parents? If it doesn't matter that much, that information makes it easier for us to raise freight charges, for instance." Charles Pierce turned to the four new men. "Everybody thinks freight charges aren't profit items, so, at Mr. Davies' suggestion, we're really working on raising them and having that profit passed on to us by the manufacturers."

Instant online agreements. "What about instant online agreements? How can you pump that on the site?" Davies asked.

"Oh, well, we're doing two things," Pierce said eagerly, relieved that the Web marketers had at least worked on instant online agreements, even though they hadn't emphasized it in the marketing plan. "First, we're getting the kids to explore all our other Web sites and to encourage their parents to explore them, too. We're finding that looking at cars online can be a real bonding experience for kids and their parents—especially for boys and their dads. Girls aren't pulling their mothers to sites that much, yet.

"And then we're doing this great rote response program to get the kids comfortable with signing online, then showing their parents how easy it is. What we're doing is so 'bad' as these kids say! We get them to facsimile sign to join our free 'Hero' page, where we let them e-mail a list of celebrities on AFF's payroll. Flashing banners designed around our 'Sign-Up-in-a-Sec!' motto really suck them to the 'lockdown' page. Then we get the kids to chose a hero their parents talk about, and we tell the kids their parents will get a real e-mail from the hero, if the kids will just give us their parents' e-mail address."

Everyone in the room nodded approvingly as Charles Pierce, as excited as a kid in a room full of free CDs, continued. "*Then,* we really get to work! We pull profiles on the parents based on their e-mail addresses, using all our AFF data banks. We can pull together any information on any purchase they've made with any AFF company, any other questionnaire they've filled out, *any* information at all.

Secret tracking. "And then—this is where it gets fun—we e-mail the parents, offering to send their kids a free T-shirt if the parents will give us their opinion on the convenience and safety of signing online for purchases. To give us their opinion, the parent has to go to our Web site about signing online. When they go to the site, we install a cookie on their machine and track just about anything we want."

Davies chortled, "Yeah, I heard about your little session with the sex-tracker cookies. You know I don't officially approve of that type of misuse of our intelligence capabilities," he said with a wink.

"That was all in the name of science, you know," Killer chimed in, as Charles Pierce, without missing a beat, nodded and went on. "What we really track, unless I hit a wrong key or something, is what auto dealership, or finance, or manufacturer sites the parents go to other than our own. If they've been hitting wrecked credit sites, we add them to our data bank for subprime borrowers; you know, that type of stuff. . . ."

Pierce grinned. "And in the midst of all of this, we've got our new Mind Reader profiler software, developed right here. Gary, we used *lots* of your ideas on this. Based on the kid's answers to our questionnaires, Mind Reader tells us which kids can really influence their parents' purchase, and which can't. It tells us which parent is the decision maker—we get that information by using psychological cue questions provided by our new AFF behavioral psychologist. Let me tell you, all this is damn valuable information. It's a knockout 'service' we provide kids from ages fourteen to eighteen! That whole teen thing is something the manufacturers actually did right for a change," Pierce said, quickly adding, "though they're still idiots, those factory guys."

Dealer relationship to manufacturers' sites. "Damn straight!" Davies added at the mention of the fifth type of Web site in AFF's arsenal, the manufacturers' sites. For his entire career Davies had believed that manufacturers couldn't tell a convertible from sport-ute. He knew that many of the manufacturers would just as soon see dealers eliminated entirely. Some damn manufacturers had actually wanted to open "service centers" independent of dealerships! Virtually every damn manufacturer had quietly lobbied to sell cars directly to buying services *and even to consumers!* Davies had organized the dealer rebellion that put a stop to that type of thinking! Now, all manufacturers' Web efforts were facades, shills for their individual dealerships. Virtually all of them simply collected "ups" and passed them on to the dealerships. The manufacturers' Web sites also did a great job of showcasing products, which helped the dealerships, putting the best spin on the worst products.

"And that . . ." Killer quickly picked up the conversation as Davies glanced impatiently at his watch, "brings us to the real reason we're here, our sixth and most important Web presence, our 'independent' buying service, Cars Without Dealers . . ."

". . . A knockout buying service," Davies finished Killer's sentence. "Killer, if you were running my damn buying service, what would you do to goose it up? How can we make our dealerships the ruling force in the buying service world without the customers knowing it? I mean, I want to make some money here, folks."

A new treasure trove. Killer broadcast a nearly evangelical conviction. He'd used that same persona many times with customers. "Gary, let me tell you, this is exciting stuff! I think these guys are all loaded for bear, loaded with good information. Shoot, the most important thing I've learned from these guys is the fact most customers actually feel safer dealing for a car on the Web than they do dealing in person. That's a license to print money! We just need to focus a little better. So, my suggestions are really based on their thinking and your experience, to make that buying service even better for us."

Brilliant! Killer had conquered the room as surely as he conquered the most contrary customer. He continued, without missing a beat. "We've got to remember why we're really here." Killer pulled his wallet out and laid it on the table. "It's money. Plain and simple. I've met plenty of customers who *want* to pay us a bigger profit, and *want* to give us their trade-ins for thousands less than they are worth." Killer spoke convincingly. "And, I'll tell you, I think we've got a right to squeeze every dime of profit we can from our grandmothers, if they'd let us. Heck, we'll probably end up spending that profit on them anyway, down the road, you know."

"Killer, I wish I could clone you, son," Davies joked.

"Just adopt me," Killer retorted as he continued. "Well, anyway, none of our profit motives change just because we're on the Web. None of our sales techniques change just because some 'up' comes to us from Cars Without Dealers. But *all* of our sales techniques have to get smarter as we interact with those Web ups."

"First, remember that a Web up's trade-in offers the easiest opportunity to make money, like falling off a log. All of our sites already 'guarantee' the value of the up's old sled, and we know how customers fall for the word 'guarantee.' They put their guard down in an instant and quit worrying about the value of their trades! All we need to do now is get the word around to the appraisers to consistently lowball the trades when they actually see 'em. I don't care if we send the appraisers to the ups' homes to see the sleds, or draw the ups to a dealership, let's just make lowballing a command."

Killer's words energized Davies. "Hell, if we lowball every AFF trade just a couple hundred dollars, we'll move *$32 million to the bottom line!*"

What a bottom line! Killer licked his lips. "Second, remember it's easier to lock 'em down when a customer thinks they're dealing with an independent buying service like Cars Without Dealers. If we can get only a hundred bucks deposit, they're not going anywhere! Believe me, they're nailed down."

"And we can offer 'em all a 100 percent money-back guarantee on any deposit," Charles Pierce added quickly, "since we really don't have to give any money back. Gary, did you see the new statistics on money-back guarantees on the Web? They're virtually worthless! Consumers don't sue over a hundred bucks, and our research is showing that 90 percent of the people walk away from the money rather than fight for it or go to all the trouble to contest a deposit with their credit card company. So, we can't lose! The deposit keeps their attention while we try to sell 'em, and we keep their deposit if they don't buy. The deposits become a profit center. It's easy money! So, why not offer a money-back guarantee on all deposits?"

"Son, what do you mean they 'won't' sue over a hundred bucks? They *can't* sue!" Davies asserted. Even Killer laughed at that knowing comment. Simply by signing on at any AFF dealership Web site, the consumer was agreeing to one of the toughest binding mandatory arbitration clauses in any auto contract in the country. Nobody sued an AFF dealership!"

Davies looked at his watch for the second time.

The glance prompted Killer to speed up his presentation. "These new guys are already doing a really good job of making sure that nothing we do on Cars Without Dealers comes over with a lot-lizard mentality. And they're doing everything they can to make the whole transaction happen before the ups take delivery of their wheels."

Killer focused on Davies again. "Uh, that's about all I can see we need to do right now, Gary," Killer said as Davies' attention went for the third time to his watch, a stormy look clouding his face. The meeting ended with a quick, dismissive nod from Davies and a final word of warning: "Hey, don't really think we're in the consumer business around here," he said curtly, "we're in the money business."

How to Buy a New Car, Click by Click, on the Web

Okay, you love the Web, which is a sign of your shrewdness. You love your money, which is very brainy. Here's a summary of the entire new vehicle buying process, if you're making the Web the battleground for your wallet.

We're using the most common buying situation: You are going to finance, you have a trade-in, you owe money on that trade-in, and (regrettably) you don't have much equity in that trade-in. In the appendix we outline other buying scenarios. For instance, if you have no trade-in or are paying cash for your new vehicle.

If you're buying a used car, skip ahead to page 379.

The page numbers refer to where you can turn for more details.

1. Oh, about your trade . . .

They're pretty easy to sell on the Web, you know. Not to be a nag, but shouldn't you think about doing that? This message is brought to you by your budget. See page 172. If you're not planning to sell it, you might want to slip Charlie Daniels's "Uneasy Rider" into the CD player.

2. Slow down!

Speed on the Web, as we've said, is a very dangerous thing.

3. **Disable your cookies or make them visible, unless you want to be naked to the world.**

   Aside from protecting your privacy, disabling cookies dramatically lowers your spam. Page 37 in chapter 1 helps you do this. We recommend a listen to Clint Black's "Until Santa's Gone (Milk and Cookies)."

4. **Download or print all of your contact in both directions.** Why not open a special directory? Don't worry about the casual visit to a site, but save and print records of all contact as you become serious about buying—particularly all contact from the one source you'll eventually use to purchase your new wheels.

5. **Determine the average wholesale value of trade-ins like yours.**

   Go to www.kbb.com. Write the figure here: _____. Kelley Blue Book and other used-car sources give *average* values, not the specific value of your individual trade-in. Page 166.

6. **Slide "Armed and Dangerous" in the music box. That's what you'll be when you "shop" your trade-in and determine its exact, specific wholesale value.**

   You'll be armed with the most specific fact you need to protect your budget. Drive to three used-car operations and see what they'll pay you to buy it outright. The highest offer is your car's real wholesale value. Page 163.

7. **Determine the payoff on your trade-in.**

   Either multiply your remaining payments, check your payment book, or call your lender directly.

8. **Determine your Loan Cash and Available Cash figures.**

   Go to www.dontgettakeneverytime.com and click on the Available Cash calculator. Page 244. Write your figures here:
   - Loan Cash: _____
   - Available Cash: _____

9. **Choose your financing source.**

   For the purposes of finding the cheapest loan source, apply for an actual loan at two sources. Use your Loan Cash figure as the amount you want to borrow.

- **If possible, always use a credit union as one potential source.** Call your credit union if you are already a member, or go to www.creditunion.coop if you need to join a credit union. Page 214.
- **For your second loan source,** your options are virtually limitless: Every site has lending links to financing sources, from GMAC to your bank to independent finance companies. But don't reinvent the wheel. If you've had a satisfactory loan with a bank, for instance, make that bank one of your comparisons rather than automatically going to an unknown source. Page 220.
- **Use a lending search engine such as LendingTree.com** if you don't want to actually "shop" for your own loan. Downside: You may not get the cheapest rate. Page 221.

10. **Use the manufacturers' sites to find vehicles that fit your Available Cash and your needs.**

For instance, do you want an SUV or a convertible? If you want an SUV, do you want a cheap one or a fancy one? After deciding on the type of vehicle you want, go to the manufacturers' sites to gather general information on these vehicles. For comparison purposes, go to more than one manufacturer. Remember that these sites give you only the good news, not the news you really need. Enter the manufacturer's name (like GM) or the make of vehicle (like Chevrolet) rather than the vehicle model (like Suburban) or you'll pull up lots of useless sites. Simply add the "www" prefix to any manufacturer's name, or use the Web addresses in the appendix, page 429.

For instance, visit www.gm.com, then go to the Chevrolet Suburban SUV. Most sites will give you a virtual tour of any vehicle and will also let you "build" a vehicle to your own specifications. If you build a vehicle that best fits your needs, print out the specs for that vehicle, including the vehicle's MSRP, or retail "asking" price.

Now, do the same search for comparable vehicles from other manufacturers. For instance, visit www.ford.com, then go to the Ford Explorer or Expedition SUV, and repeat the process. Or visit www.toyota.com, then go to the Toyota 4Runner or Land Cruiser SUV.

11. **Use *Consumer Reports* online to gather objective information on these vehicles.**

Manufacturer and other commercial sites don't provide objectivity, but the *Consumer Reports* site is your best, most objective source for hard information about specific vehicles and pricing. Though *Consumer Reports* makes mistakes at times, it virtually always errs on the consumer's side rather than on the seller's or manufacturer's side. You need a friend like that online.

ConsumerReports.org will cost you if you use their very thorough services. The best deal is to join *Consumer Reports* online. For $5.95 a month or $26 for a year, you get all their product reports (not just auto). Vehicle reports include safety, maintenance, and reliability ratings. Whether or not you are a member, *Consumer Reports* also offers a New Car Price Service for $14. This excellent service includes current rebate figures, unadvertised dealer incentives and holdbacks, accurate dealer "invoice" (cost) price, MSRP (retail price), latest vehicle safety ratings lifted from *Consumer Reports'* vehicle tests, and a list of alternative vehicles. You want to join and you want the New Car Price Service if you love your pocketbook. Go to www.consumer reports.org.

12. **Use the Center for Auto Safety's Web site for the best, most objective, and most timely safety check on virtually any make and model (www.au tosafety.org).**

The site is free and priceless. The Center for Auto Safety has links to crash reports and other information on the National Highway Traffic Safety Administration Web site, as well as to other good sources.

13. **Do additional research and reading on vehicles.**

The number of automotive Web sites providing a great variety of information has proliferated. Sites like

Edmunds.com or the auto channels of ISPs such as Yahoo!, MSN, or AOL have lots of useful information. You may enjoy reading reviews posted by owners of various models. All of these sites, however, have multiple affiliations with auto businesses, so exercise your common sense. You can find links to news stories and dozens of other resources at sites such as TheAutoChannel.com. Again, be aware of automotive business affiliations. And if you like car buff magazines, don't forget their online versions.

14. **Get "hands-on" experience in the vehicle you like the most: Rent one.**

Investing $100 in a weekend rental is far better than any test-drive at the nicest dealership, and safer for your wallet in the long run. Or rent one for the day.

15. **When you've settled on a specific type of vehicle, settle on two potential sources for the actual purchase.**

Here are your choices:

- **Manufacturers' Web sites.** They can't sell you a vehicle. They simply forward you to a local dealer.
- **Dealership Web sites.** Search your local dealership's name or, on the manufacturer's site, use your zip code to locate the dealership nearest you. Many manufacturers' sites will now allow you to choose a dealership near you and browse the dealership's actual inventory. **The pros of dealership sites in general:** A savvy bargainer can get a very good deal—dealerships negotiate; most Web sites don't. You'll also have a local dealer for service. **The cons:** Regardless of the Web site window dressing, expect a wolf under the sheep's clothing at the vast majority of dealership sites. Even with all the downsides, if you are a careful shopper with steady nerves, I recommend that you select a dealer Web site that sells your favorite vehicle as one of your shopping choices.
- **"Independent" Internet buying services such as www.carsdirect.com.** These services act as brokers,

finding a specific vehicle for you and generally handling all the negotiating and paperwork. **The pros:** No in-your-face pressure. **The cons:** Not necessarily the cheapest price, regardless of the guarantee; be careful with your trade-in.

- **"Prospect Aggregators" or Agents, such as Autobytel.** Sites like these generally provide you as a prospect to a dealer. **The pros:** Some of these sites supposedly allow you to submit a "bid" and create a bidding war. Don't count on it. **The cons:** Most of these sites simply add another layer of overheadonto the buying situation, and some of them require extra caution when it comes to your trade-in.

16. **Follow each source's online process, but do not give a deposit yet.**

For each source, use exactly the same vehicle. Require binding price quotes on a vehicle at each source. If the sources insist upon a deposit before giving you a binding quote, don't give the deposit unless you are ready to purchase the vehicle at that price. Don't give a deposit on more than one vehicle!

17. **If you're dealing with a "bidding" service, be cautious.**

Bidding services are famous for implying a price, requiring a deposit, and then raising that price with exorbitant fees and/or other charges. Many also lull you with promises of "money-back" deposits to lock down their price. The deposits can be hard or virtually impossible to get back in a timely manner, so don't automatically fall for this gimmick. In my opinion, stay away from money-back guarantees unless the seller agrees in writing to credit your money back, no questions asked, within twenty-four hours.

18. **Be prepared for tricks when it comes to your trade.**

Even the best seller may try to steal your old car. Many sellers will try to change their "appraisal" after you have agreed to buy their car. Don't deal with these sellers.

19. Be prepared for tricks when it comes to financing.

Everyone is going to try to convert you to their financing. If a seller insists they are actually cheaper than the source you've already chosen, require the seller to give you a copy of the completely filled-out finance contract and physically compare that contract to your primary source's contract.

20. If you are financing with the seller, be prepared for "add-on" pitches.

After agreeing to a price on the vehicle and financing, many online sellers will add additional charges and "services" without your permission. Refuse to take them.

21. Have a drink or go for a jog!

You've survived an online purchase with your pocketbook intact.

Negotiating for a Used Vehicle, Step by Step, on the Web

We established in chapter 12 that used-car buyers are much, much smarter and more handsome than new-car buyers. This chapter will establish also that used-car buyers who click rather than brick are niftier by a power of ten: We listen to the most righteous music and are generally people everybody wants to hang out with. Oh, and we are better bargainers.

We are better bargainers because we *have to be* to keep from being eaten alive by all those used-car people. But that's what natural selection is all about, isn't it? Yep, we are so fine, and our friends are very lucky to have us. We're giving you a summary of the entire online process right here, for negotiating a used-vehicle purchase precisely to give you more time and money to spend on your friends.

This is the statistically most likely scenario for the vast majority of Web mavens: You are going to finance, you have a trade-in, you owe money on that trade-in, and (unluckily) you don't have much equity in that trade-in. In the appendix we outline other buying scenarios, for instance, if you have no trade-in or are paying cash for your new vehicle.

The page numbers refer to where you can turn for more details.

1. **Slow down!**
   Speed on the Web, as we've said, is a very dangerous thing. When you rush, you don't think and you don't compare. Use the Web to educate yourself, and feel free to buy there, but don't let it rush you into buying without thinking.

2. **Reread** the chapter on shopping for a used vehicle starting on page 311.

3. **Disable your cookies or make them visible, unless you want to be naked to the world.**
   Aside from protecting your privacy, disabling cookies dramatically lowers your spam. Page 37 in chapter 1 tells you how to cook your cookies.

4. **Download or print all of your contacts in both directions.** Don't worry about the casual visit to a site, but save all contact as you become serious about buying—particularly all contact from the one source you eventually use to acquire your vehicle.

5. **Determine the average wholesale value of trade-ins like yours.**
   Go to www.kbb.com. Write the figure here: _____.
   Kelley Blue Book and other used-car sources give *average* values, not the specific value of your individual trade-in. Page 166.

6. **If you're thorough, "shop" your trade-in and determine its exact, specific wholesale value.**
   Drive to three used-car operations, and see what they'll pay you to buy it outright. The highest offer is your car's real wholesale value. Page 163.

7. **Determine the payoff on your trade-in.**
   Either multiply your remaining payments, check your payment book, or call your lender directly.

8. **Determine your Loan Cash and Available Cash figures.**

Go to www.dontgettakeneverytime.com and click on the Available Cash calculator. Page 244. Write your figures here:

- Loan Cash: _____
- Available Cash: _____

9. Sell your current vehicle yourself.

Either wholesale it to a dealer, which is easy but not as profitable, or retail it yourself. Start that process right now. I know you don't want to do this, but do it. The Web isn't a friendly place if you actually plan to "trade" your vehicle—use it physically as a portion of your payment for a newer vehicle.

10. Choose your financing source.

The greatest financing rip-offs are in the used-vehicle arena, as we've said, so be alert. For the purposes of finding the cheapest loan source, apply for an actual loan at two sources. Use your Loan Cash figure as the amount you want to borrow.

- **A good credit union is virtually always the cheapest place to finance a used vehicle—if that credit union finances used vehicles and new vehicle rates.** If possible, always use a credit union as one potential loan source. Call your credit union if you are already a member and ask whether they finance used vehicles at new-vehicle rates. If you don't belong to a credit union yet, go to www.credit union.coop to find a credit union. Page 214.

- **Use a lending search engine such as LendingTree. com** if you don't want to actually "shop" for your own loan. **Downside:** You may not get the cheapest rate. Page 221.

11. Use *Consumer Reports* online to gather objective information on the used vehicles that interest you.

The *Consumer Reports* site is one of the best, most objective sources for hard information about specific used vehicles. Though *Consumer Reports* makes mistakes at times, it virtually always errs on the consumer's side. You need a friend like that online.

ConsumerReports.org will cost you if you use their very thorough services: The best deal is to join *Consumer Reports* online. For $5.95 a month or $26 for a year, you get all their product reports (not just auto). Vehicle reports include safety, maintenance, and reliability ratings. Though *Consumer Reports'* evaluations are generally made on new vehicles, the conclusions apply to used ones as well.

12. Use the Center for Auto Safety's Web site for the best, most objective and most timely safety check on virtually any make and model (www.autosafety.org).
The site is free, and priceless, and if you think about it, the Center for Auto Safety knows the nitty-gritty on used vehicles better than new vehicles. Safety problems don't show up on undriven vehicles; they show up on cars with miles.

13. Do additional research and reading on vehicles.
The number of automotive Web sites providing a great variety of information has proliferated. Sites like Edmunds.com or the auto channels of ISPs such as Yahoo!, MSN, or AOL have lots of useful information. You may enjoy reading reviews posted by owners of various models. All of these sites, however, have multiple affiliations with auto businesses, so exercise your common sense. You can find links to news stories and dozens of other resources at sites such as TheAutoChannel.com. Again, be aware of automotive business affiliations. And if you like car buff magazines, don't forget their online versions.

14. When you've settled on a specific type of vehicle, search as many online sources as you want to find a specific vehicle that appears to fit your Available Cash and your fancy.
Also choose vehicles close enough to you for a physical inspection. Virtually all the used-vehicle selling sites are free, so make your search broad enough to give you lots of choices. I strongly recommend that you try to buy from an individual rather than from a dealership. You'll have an easier time bargaining. Whatever the source, the Web makes it relatively easy for you to find a specific

used vehicle by make, model, color, and year. Very nice. Chapter 12 gives you methods to do this. **An important tip: Download or print out information about each vehicle that interests you.** You can then compare them at your leisure when you sign off.

15. **When you've located a few potentially good vehicles, determine the loan value of these vehicles.**

   Consider the loan value figure the "cost" of any used vehicle. Your objective is going to be to buy the vehicle as close to the loan value figure as possible. Either call your bank or credit union and ask them the loan value of the specific vehicle, or go to www.edmunds.com.

16. **Decide if you need an escrow service or other help with your paperwork and financing.**

   If you're financing with a dealership, your credit union, or a bank, they'll do the paperwork. If you're financing with an individual close by, you can probably do the paperwork. If you're buying a car long-distance, you may need a service. Page 184.

17. **Physically inspect and drive your favorite choices.**

   Don't buy a used vehicle on the Web without making the effort to see it yourself.

18. **Have your favorite vehicle inspected by a professional.**

   Either arrange to take the vehicle to a diagnostic center or arrange for a used-vehicle diagnostic service to go to the vehicle. Page 313.

19. **Use a service such as www.carfax.com to check the vehicle history.**

   These services won't tell you if a vehicle has had major damage, regardless of their advertising claims, but they can tell you other important facts about virtually any vehicle using that car's vehicle identification number (VIN).

20. **Use the necessary repairs to negotiate down the price of the vehicle.**

   Your objective: buying as close to loan value as possible.

21. **Discuss warranties.**

   Page 432.

22. **Give final figures to your financing source, and make sure the source will approve your loan for this specific vehicle.**

23. **If you're buying from a dealership Web site, be prepared for tricks when it comes to financing.**
Everyone is going to try to convert you to their financing. If a seller insists they are actually cheaper than the source you've already chosen, require the seller to give you a copy of the completely filled-out finance contract and physically compare that contract to your primary source's contract.

24. **If you are financing with the seller, be prepared for "add-on" pitches.**
After agreeing to a price on the vehicle and financing, many online sellers will add additional charges and "services" without your permission. Refuse to take them.

25. **Give that beauty a silicone treatment!**
You've survived an online purchase with your pocketbook intact.

Chapter 16

Leasing a Vehicle

To celebrate their fiftieth wedding anniversary, the Grants decided that buying a new car would be a grand idea, even though their current set of wheels was only two years old and fully paid for. They had the cash for a big down payment, too. Though the couple were by no means rich, they were comfortable and very proud of their independence and good business sense. Mr. Grant had owned his own small construction company, and Mrs. Grant had been their bookkeeper.

Both Grants felt they were good judges of people's character, too, which is why they had been so comfortable with Peter Kiever, known as Buzz. His disarming manners and solicitous questions were the mark, they felt sure, of a truly helpful sales "consultant." Peter just loved the stately ring of the title.

And he *really* loved the Grants. Within an hour, he'd set them on a new car that had been on the lot for *thirteen months* without selling! He'd given the best test-drive of his career, making sure to drive by the church "where I've been a deacon for five years"—fiction, but delivered with conviction. Peter had even pulled out a dozen charming pictures of his sweet wife and handsome children, a neat trick, since Peter wasn't married and certainly didn't claim any children. He'd "chosen" his wife and kids from a box of pictures his friend at the sixty-minute photo store had lifted from customers' print folders in a neighboring city. Mr. Kiever was zooming, particularly in the profit department!

Peter had lowballed the Grants $2,000 on their immaculate trade-in and quoted them a full-boat deal—list price plus all those wonderful add-ons. Let's see, that was a total profit of $5,000 so far. Peter had also gotten them to agree to a payment that would generate a $2,500 finance profit. That got the deal up to $7,500.

But Peter had "seen Jesus." He muttered that under his breath whenever a sucker showed up who could at least temporarily provide Peter salvation from his perpetual cash-flow dilemma. That's why he decided to "flip" them.

Peter excused himself, leaving the Grants with his "Customer Testimonial album" overflowing with glowing letters. The whole album, including letters, had cost only $30. He walked past one finance manager's office and instead chose to seat himself across from Mickey, the newest finance manager. Peter leaned forward, a conspiratorial smile on his face.

"How would my new best friend like an extra $500 in cash?" Mickey nodded his head toward the door, then leaned forward himself as Peter tipped the door shut with his hand. "So, what've you got?"

"Two old geezers who are just begging to be flipped."

"So, what do you need me for?"

"They've got $14,000 to pay down, Mickey. And one hell of a trade. I've already lowballed them a couple of thou on that, and they didn't blink. I thought you might just want to bounce 'em around a bit with me. We need your magic on the computer, you know." A little fraud was needed.

Mickey kept his face expressionless. These people were probably so old they'd be dead before they could cause any trouble. But the dealership had already received six letters from attorneys about his deals. Although the dealership normally didn't blink at the threat of legal actions, Mickey didn't want to push his luck. And, anyway, he needed to "work" Peter Kiever a little bit before he agreed to work the customers.

Mickey grimaced. "Peter, I've reformed, you know. I mean, what's $500 to my reputation?"

Going for a record "flip." "Well, how about a thou? That's if we 'swallow' it all: the trade, the cash, their rebate."

Mickey laughed, "Man, you must really think we can knock those suckers to the moon."

"I'm telling you, they think I'm their long-lost son! This is going to be a mega-flip!"

Within minutes the Grants were in the "delivery" office, the corner office with an expansive glass window that framed a solitary parking spot, lushly landscaped and lit with theatrically appropriate lighting. The couple had entered the room excitedly, holding hands—good buying signs that made Peter Kiever actually salivate. Paperwork for a lease transaction, completely filled out, lay on the desk. The stack of documents was a dense inch high—fifty-seven items requiring thirty-eight signatures from both the Grants. Mickey had very carefully put the documents in a particular order before the couple had entered the office. He had also made the monthly lease payment $10 less than the regular installment loan payment Kiever had quoted the Grants. Mickey always thought this a nice, disarming touch in a major flip.

Let's take care of the paperwork. As a lot boy pulled the sparkling new sedan into the delivery spot, just outside the window, Mickey sat between the Grants. "Folks, I want to go over this paperwork with you to make sure you really understand it all. It's important you know. You folks are smart businesspeople, I can tell. You know the importance of contracts and all that."

"Oh, we sure do," Mrs. Grant said brightly. Good. Under oath both Peter Kiever and Mickey could swear that they had talked to these people about the importance of contracts.

"Well, then, let's work our way through this," Mickey said. He began with the most unimportant piece of paper—a sheet saying that Peter had thoroughly shown them the features on the vehicle. Mickey went over the sheet as if it were a will, then had both sign it. Next, he went over the tire warranty in great detail. They signed that. He continued at tortoise pace until he came to the sheet that stated, "I have had each of these documents thoroughly explained to me," chuckled slightly, then said, "Well, we certainly can't say we didn't review these documents, can we?" Everyone laughed as the signing continued.

Wearing down customer caution. By the thirty-third signature on the fifty-first document, the Grants were impatiently urging Mickey onward, and by the final three sheets, they would have signed anything. Why, any dealership this thorough couldn't be doing anything wrong! That's when Mickey laid out a rewritten buyer's order showing that the price on the vehicle had been raised $10,000 as he quickly commented, "Oh, and this is just a copy of the buyer's order," his hand slightly blocking the new selling price. "And this is a worksheet thing," he added in his most studied tone. The words "LEASE WORKSHEET" were clearly written across the top of the page in bold type. But the Grants signed the bottom of the sheet without once looking at the headline. "And here's the contract itself and, boy, do I have a great surprise for you: I've gotten the payment *lower* than the one Peter mentioned. Look here!" Mickey completely ignored the headline across the top of the document that clearly stated the Grant's were leasing a vehicle, and pointed to the one line that showed the payment. They signed it without protest and without noticing that their trade-in allowance had gone from the $17,000 Peter had mentioned to $8,000. They also didn't notice that the number of months on the contract was for sixty rather than the thirty-six they had requested. The Grants and left the dealership a few minutes later, absolutely glowing. Their paperwork, however, did not leave with them. Peter, at the last minute, had said, "Oh, I'll send that along when the clerk notarizes it, you know how all that paperwork is!"

Jacking the profit by $10,000. Peter and Mickey were absolutely glowing at that moment, too. The piddling $7,500 profit on these people had grown to $17,500, and the couple didn't even know they had leased!

They wouldn't know for two months, either, until the Grants' son happened upon their paperwork. When the Grants saw the enormity of what had happened to them, they first attempted to get the dealership to help them. "My dad just wanted out of the lease," Mr. Grant's son said. "The car had less than five hundred miles on it and was less than three months old." The dealership said fine! "Just pay us the early termination penalty written right in the lease, plus an excess wear-and-tear charge."

Sure, you can end the lease early—for $34,000. Let's see, the early termination penalty takes a calculator and an amortization table to calculate. It is not written in language any consumer or leasing expert can easily understand. Not to worry! The dealership lease manager quickly figured the penalty, $34,000 for sixty days and five hundred miles. Oh, and then there's the excess wear-and-tear charge, $2,500 (even though the three-month-old car had no damage, no wear). Perfectly legal, the dealership said calmly.

The Grants decided to sue with the financial help of their son. At best, their chance of success is questionable, for three reasons. First, the dealership had created a wonderful (but deceptive) paper trail showing (on paper at least) clearly that the Grants should have known what they were doing. Second, both Peter Kiever and Mickey swore on a well-worn Bible how carefully the least paperwork had been explained to the nice old couple. "Shoot, we even talked about the importance of contracts!" Such a shame, Peter said, when people get confused like that. Third, the dealer doesn't plan to lose, even if he loses. He has been quoted as saying he'll keep the case going until the people die, if need be. You can't have those damn customers taking advantage of dealerships!

That's really what he said in this true story.

The Good and Oh So Bad of Leasing

Over sixteen million people drive leased vehicles right now. Undoubtedly, millions of those people are happy lessees and will remain so—at least until they bring their car back and are handed their bills for excess wear and tear. In the history of the automobile business, there has seldom been an abuse of the consumer to match leasing abuse. The Florida Attorney General's Office said it best: "The technical and complex language, and the greed of some car salesmen, cause car leasing to be an option that is fraught with many pitfalls for the average consumer."[1] And is that an understatement! Between 1993 and 1999, for example, the Florida Attorney General's Office alone received 19,000 phone calls and written complaints about leasing fraud, and 40 percent of those complaints eventually proved to be actual fraud. According to Terry O'Loughlin, lead automotive investigator at the Florida Attorney General's Office, a typical customer was overcharged $1,500, and one was overcharged $10,500.[2]

Those 19,000 complaints encompassed instances of "flipping" as in the Grants' case, "disappearing" trade-ins, swallowed down payments and rebates, tacked-on fees, excessive wear-and-tear charges, misrepresented mileage terms, and thirty-four other specific types of leasing fraud. Think about that! Forty types of leasing fraud, just in the good ole Sunshine State. Such abuses continue to this day.

Combating abuse. Rampant abuse in auto leasing is one reason Ralph Nader and I founded the Consumer Task Force for Automotive Issues (CTF-A) some years ago to attack leasing industry problems head-on. About twenty-three state attorneys general, hundreds of consumer groups, and many plaintiff law firms joined us in that attack. CTF-A continues to monitor leasing and to support national consumer class actions as we discover new or recurring lease abuses.

New government action on leasing. The Federal Reserve's tightening of lease disclosure requirements several years ago helped the informed and very cautious consumer a lot, too. The new requirements mandate that dealers itemize on the front page of every lease the components of the monthly lease payment, the trade-in allowance, and any down payments (or "cap cost reductions"), including rebate money. Before these requirements took effect, these items didn't have to appear at all or were spread out in tiny print throughout the lease.

But as the Grants learned, simply having the correct paperwork doesn't keep you from being destroyed in the leasing minefield. That's why this chapter asks you to heed the warnings outlined here, take your time, and then decide if leasing is right for you. Despite all the negative things you've read in the past few pages, leasing done right isn't a bad way to finance a vehicle. We're going to show you how to know if leasing might be for you and then show you how to do it, and even do it relatively easily by using the Internet.

Just What Is a Lease?

In one way, leasing is similar to renting a car. You pay for the use of someone else's vehicle. In a lease, you *use* the vehicle, you don't *own* it.

Leasing has one major difference from renting, however: When you rent a car, you can normally bring it back to the renter early, if you'd like to. It's okay to rent a car for two weeks, for instance, but return it in one week. But leases severely, *severely* penalize you for bringing a car back early. Ask the Grants.

Why do lease payments seem so cheap? The general answer is simple: You're renting rather than buying. The specific answer is more complex, but worth understanding if you're the detailed type.

What Happens When You Buy?

Let's say you're looking at a $21,600 car. It's a very popular car, so the dealership has refused to discount it even one cent. You've decided that's okay since your aunt Matilda has agreed to finance it for you at no interest for three years. Your payments are simply going to be the cost of the car divided by the number of months you finance: $21,600 divided by thirty-six months equals $600 per month.

At the end of thirty-six months, you have spent $21,600 but you *own your car.* It's an asset, like cash. Let's say the car's worth $8,000. This means your net investment in buying the car is $21,600 minus the car's value of $8,000; you really have only $13,600 invested.

Leasing the Same Car

Let's say Aunt Matilda has agreed to *lease* you that car instead for thirty-six payments. She writes a check for $21,600 to buy the car. Matilda, a CPA, also knows it will be worth $8,000 in three years. Her net investment, like yours, would therefore be only $13,600. And since Matilda is a sweet and fair lady, she decides to base your payments on her *net investment* rather than the cost of the car itself. Your payments are now going to be $13,600 divided by thirty-six payments, or just *$377 per month versus $600 per month for buying the very same vehicle!* Well, let's see ... $377 per month to lease versus $600 per month to buy the very same car! Put this book down and lease a car right now!

But wait a minute. That lease *payment* is lower than your purchase payment for the same car, *but the lease isn't cheaper at all.* If you look again, you'll see that your total investment is *exactly the same* in our example whether you lease or buy. The lease payment is lower simply because, in the lease, you receive credit for the end value of the car *before* the payment is calculated. When you buy a vehicle, you receive "credit" *after* you've finished making the payments—you own that beauty.

Enter the Real World

In the real world, lease or buy, you're going to pay a profit. There's nothing wrong with that, either. But two factors usually mean you will pay a dramatically bigger profit if you lease a vehicle rather than finance it with a conventional installment loan. In fact, because leasing companies aren't putting any bargain leases out there anymore and because leasing companies generally rip your knickers, lease payments are beginning to approach the payment you'd pay to buy. When you could have a $350 lease payment rather than a $600 purchase payment, that was enticing. But if the lease payment is $550, why bother?

What's the moral of this story? A lower lease payment doesn't mean your *cost* is lower. Just because a lease payment is lower doesn't mean you're getting a better deal than if you were to buy the very same car.

Why Leasing Companies So Easily Rip Your Knickers. First, you're not used to negotiating leases, and, second, leasing contracts still don't disclose the real facts, figures, and terms you need to make sensible decisions.

Leasing companies just loved this, of course. For years, leasing was far and away the most lucrative profit center at every dealership precisely because consumers didn't have the vaguest idea what they were doing. To make matters worse (for the consumer), all leasing outlets presented leases as "done deals," seemingly carved in stone, that required absolutely no bargaining. That's what attracted customers, along with payments that *looked* cheaper than buying.

Who's Making the Big Profits Here: the Leasing Companies or the Dealerships?

Both, although, in general, the massive rip-off profits in leasing are ebbing somewhat except for subprime leasing and used-car leasing. But the way dealerships and leasing companies work together is still a nice lesson in free enterprise gone a bit amok.

Because many lawsuits are now rumbling around out there against dealerships and/or leasing companies, neither really likes to talk about their relationship except under court order, but if you are a student of business, you might enjoy this peek.

Dealerships are the most interesting place to peek first. A dealership, as we now know, is interested in only one thing: how much money it can generate from the sale of a vehicle. As we also know, that money includes profit from the sale of the car itself, from the trade-in, from financing, and from dealer add-ons and extras. When a dealership thinks of leasing a car rather than selling it, the same juicy thought is on its mind: how much profit can be made.

That profit will be determined by how easy the customer is to "work," and in leasing, customers are easy to work. But profit will also be determined by how much money the dealership can get *financed* on that lease customer. It won't do any good if a dealership "writes someone up" on a $5,000 lease profit, for instance, if they can't get some company to allow that much profit on the lease.

Enter the leasing company. Dealerships have dozens of leasing companies to choose from, and guess what criterion they use to choose their favorite? Do you think they look for the one that gives the best terms to the consumer? Of course not! Time and again, dealerships choose the leasing company that will lend the most lease money on every part of every transaction.

Let's say Loving Leasing Inc. has been writing leases for Happy's Expenso dealership. They've been loaning 100 percent of manufacturer's sticker, plus tax and title and a little extra profit, and up until now Happy's Expenso has been happy.

But then the field representative for another leasing company stops by for a visit. His company, he cheerfully announces, will go 110 *percent* of the manufacturer's sticker, or 10 percent more of the sticker price. On a $20,000 car, that raises the dealership's profit by $2,000 in one stroke. Which leasing company do you think Happy will use now? And who is hurt by that little competition? You.

The competition goes beyond percentages of list price, too. Leasing companies compete to offer dealers the highest "participation"—a cut on the financing charge. Some of them still compete to offer the most generous "add-on" guidelines. Until recently, most leasing companies would allow dealerships to charge whatever they liked for rustproofing, striping, service agreements, and the like. The leasing companies would then gladly finance that charge. Why not? More finance income.

But in a little poetic irony, the leasing companies themselves started being victimized by the dealerships' enthusiasm in this area. Dealerships would charge unsuspecting customers $2,995 for rustproofing and undercoating. The customers wouldn't yell because the salesperson had simply said, "Oh, we've added our special environmental packages: it's only twenty-nine ninety-five," implying $29.95. Since such add-on charges didn't at that time have to be shown separately on a leasing form, the customer never knew the true price. That $2,995 charge didn't add any value to the lease car, but it did raise the lease loan by nearly $3,000. And if a lease customer defaulted on his lease, that money would, as likely as not, be eaten by the leasing company.

These days, therefore, most leasing companies limit dealerships to specific amounts for add-ons. The leasing company will finance only the true cost of an add-on radio, for instance, not its selling price. The leasing companies' interest there was to protect themselves, not the consumer. Self-interest rules throughout this business.

Lease Terminology Adds to the Budget Carnage

In addition to the self-interest mentality of leasing, lease terminology itself doesn't help you. It's different from the familiar terms you use in buying a car and at times is very confusing. What would you negotiate in a lease? How about the "capitalized cost" or "cap cost reduction," or the "money factor"? Do you negotiate those? Heck, what's the payment based on? Leases don't clearly tell you the selling price or cost of a vehicle, so just how do you know whether or not you're leasing that proverbial pig in a poke?

By contrast, in a normal purchase situation, even the most unskilled person probably knows a few terms like "sticker price" and knows some negotiating tactics; for instance, simply saying "you're not giving me enough for my old car." Most of us know to shop for a cheap interest rate for financing.

The Deliberate Lack of Understandable "Back-End Clauses" Compounds the Carnage

Even with the new disclosure requirement, leases still don't protect you from the most insidious lease danger: the obfuscated language that leads to massive financial penalties years down the road. When we buy a vehicle rather than lease it, there are no direct financial penalties tied to the condition of the vehicle when you've finished making your payments. You own it without penalty, regardless of the condition of the vehicle.

But all leases contain potential penalties related to early termination and wear-and-tear clauses, and (I don't know why this should come as a surprise) virtually all leasing companies are trying their darnedest to turn these clauses into profit centers. For instance, guess who usually determines how much wear and tear is normal on a leased vehicle? The very people who would profit by overcharging you for that wear and tear. If a lessor (the parent leasing company), for instance, estimates true wear and tear on your vehicle at $500 but has the unquestioned right to say wear and tear is $2,500—and has the right to force you to pay that $2,500—the lessor just made an additional $2,000 profit. Excellent! You didn't need that money as much as they do, anyway.

Another "back-end" surprise. Most leases gloss over other hits on your pocketbook. How much would this clause (buried three pages back, in ant print) bother you, if you saw it at all? "Lessee or his assigns are responsible for all mandatory expenses related to this lease." That clause says the dealership has not paid the property tax on this vehicle and plans on sending you that bill for payment when they receive it—even though in many states the dealer is legally responsible for that expense!

Would an unexpected bill for $1,000 ruin your day? Leases are filled with time bombs like this.

Then There's "Flipping"

Matters go from worse to ridiculous when you realize many people who lease a car hadn't planned to lease at all. According to an article in *Automotive News,* many people don't even consider leasing as an option until they're at the dealership. According to the survey, taken several years ago, less than 6 percent of the people who lease planned to lease when they entered a dealership, but about 25 percent ended up leasing before they had left the dealership. They were "flipped!" With no opportunity to do their "homework," they were either talked into leasing or switched to leasing without even knowing it.

That figure is higher today. Flipping older people to leases without their knowledge has, in fact, become one of the top two causes for litigation, according to my survey of attorneys who belong to the National Consumer Law Center auto fraud e-mail group. The story of the Grants is echoed thousands of times around this country.

"So, are all those '$199 per month' lease payments a bad deal?" Not at all, if you can actually lease a vehicle even close to that rate. You'll still see the promotions, sure, but most of those rates are pure come-on, barely legal bait and switch. In reality, the bloom is off the rose of truthfully cheap lease promotions. Years ago, many manufacturers offered truly fantastic leasing deals on specific vehicles both to push the sale of that vehicle and to establish their dominance in leasing. To offer those fantastic rates, the companies had to "jimmy" the lease-end value of those vehicles—artificially raise the value of the vehicle at the end of the lease.

For instance, even though a vehicle three years down the road would realistically be worth $14,000, leasing companies decided to base their lease rates on a value of $16,000 for that vehicle—ergo, a cheaper monthly lease payment. Everybody was happy for a while: the consumers for once in their lives got genuine bargains, and the leasing companies made millions of loans.

But at the end of three years, the party was over. When those lease cars were returned to the leasing companies, the company was stuck with a loss of about $2,000 on each vehicle. A few years ago, leasing companies lost money on *71* percent of all leased vehicles that went for the full term of the lease. The actual average loss was $1,878.[3] For once, the car people took the bath, not the consumer. Shortly thereafter, cheap leases disappeared, probably along with the managers who approved this idea in the first place.

"Assuming Leasing Can Still Be a Good Deal at Times, How Do I Know If It's Made for Me?"

You ask very good questions, a sign of your astute mind and charm. So, let me ask you a few questions:

1. **Do you generally continue to drive a vehicle after you've made the last payment, and enjoy that feeling of "free" driving?**
   If so, you're generally not a good candidate for leasing. You'll do better to negotiate carefully and buy the car you like. After that last loan payment you'll own an asset (your car) that goes on providing transportation.

   Well, why can't I just lease a car to get that low payment and then buy the car at the end of the lease? You can. All leases give you that right. But, generally speaking, you will have to pay more than the vehicle is actually worth in wholesale dollars. We tell you about this later. But even if you decide to buy your vehicle at lease-end, you'll need another loan right then to buy it, unless you have cash stowed away for the purchase. Rather than having a paid-for car, you'll have more monthly payments on an even older car.

2. **Do you always trade for a new car before the old one is paid for?**

    Are you the type of person who always has car payments? If so, and if you have carved out a monthly vehicle payment in your budget for the foreseeable future, you're a good initial candidate for leasing. If you're always making payments anyway, it makes sense to make your payment as low as possible.

3. **Just how stable is your job situation? And how healthy is your general financial situation?**

    If you buy a car and have trouble making the payments, you have a perfect right to sell that car for as much money as you can to pay off your loan. If you lease a car and have trouble making the payments, you don't have the same rights. In fact, you'll have your legs broken financially if you try to break a lease early. Leasing is therefore safest for those who hold down a secure job and are in good shape financially.

    *   **Well, my budget is so tight I barely break even each month. Should I lease?** First, if you're having budget problems, you probably shouldn't trade cars at all. Think about fixing up your old car. Maybe your credit union or bank can help you with a "fix it" loan. If you don't want to fix up your old car, think about buying a carefully checked-out used car. Don't lease a car if you're barely meeting your budget.

    *   **What about those leases for people with poor or nonexistent credit?** They're very popular now because they are the hot, new profit darling of the leasing industry. But stay away from leasing if you have credit problems. These "subprime cut" leases, as they are called, will ruin you and provide you a junker, to boot. Virtually all of these leases are on junker used vehicles.

4. **How many miles do you drive a year?**

    Whether you buy or lease, the number of miles you drive will dramatically affect your vehicle's value. But mileage considerations are particularly important when a person leases. Most lease payments are based on the fact you will drive no more than 12,000–15,000 miles a year during the lease. Some rip-off leases (usually a "sale" lease payment) are based on a paltry 10,000-mile yearly driving mileage allowance. You put that on a car going up and down your driveway.

So, imagine what's going to happen if you are a high-mileage commuter who drives 40,000 miles per year. On an average three-year lease, do you know how much cash you would need to hand over to the leasing company because of those extra miles? From $5,000 to $11,000! We'll talk more about mileage and smart leasing later, but, generally speaking, if you're a high-mileage driver, leasing may not be for you unless you make absolutely sure the lease is based on the actual miles you'll drive.

5. **Are you stable financially but yearning for more car for the payment?**

If you are comfortable with constant payments but want more car for the same payment, then leasing may be an option. Maybe you need a bigger car, for instance, because the family has grown, or simply like the looks of that electric-red convertible. If you're careful, leasing can be just right for you.

Are There Tax Advantages to Leasing That Make It a Good Option?

If you use your car primarily for personal use, there are generally no tax breaks. And if you do use your car primarily for business, there may be tax advantages whether you buy or lease. Talk to your tax preparer.

Are There Many Leasing Companies Out There?

If you loosely define a leasing company as a "sales outlet," a place where you can get a lease filled out, there are thousands:

credit unions, banks, car dealerships, independent leasing outlets, subprime used-car lots. Many sales outlets offer leasing
through more than one company. For instance, many GM automobile dealerships can offer leasing through GMAC, a bank, or
some other leasing company.

Are There Different Types of Leases Out There?

Leases have lots of variations, all based on these two types:

- **Closed-end or "walk-away" leases.** This is the type of
  lease virtually all consumer leasing companies use. A
  "closed-end" lease means you're not responsible for the
  value of the car at the end of the lease beyond a specific
  amount of money. That amount of money is always
  defined in a lease document itself and is called "residual
  value." More on that term later.
- **Open-end leases.** This is the type of lease you generally
  want to stay away from. An "open-end" lease can mean
  you have virtually unlimited liability when you turn the
  vehicle in. Open-end leases are seldom used these days for
  the general consumer.

**"If there are different types of leases, what about the
difference in leasing companies? And how do those
companies really work?"** To understand the dynamics of
leasing, you really have to understand that the leasing transaction can involve two, and at times three, participants. If you can
stand a little confusion in your brain, these participants can be
separate companies or the same company.

The Three Participants in a Lease Transaction

1. **The parent leasing company itself, called the
   "lessor."**
   This company actually provides a leasing form and the
   money to fund the lease. Lessors include well-known

firms like GMAC and Ford Motor Credit and firms you've never heard of. These companies really determine the terms of your lease itself: for instance, what the effective interest rate on the lease will be and what the terms concerning breaking your lease early will be.

The lessor also has to buy a vehicle for you to drive. And they generally buy it from an automobile dealer or at times from the factory itself, if the lessor is a dealership selling those brands of cars.

The lessor doesn't normally make a profit on the vehicle itself. Instead, the lessor charges the leasing customer a monthly profit and certain other items (we'll talk about them later). They have no incentive to pay a large profit on a vehicle. In fact, lessors generally have an incentive to pay as little as possible for a vehicle. Why? The less money owed on a car, the less risk for the lessor. For instance, if a car's wholesale value is $12,000, a leasing company would much rather loan $12,000 on that car than $14,000.

2. **The company that sells the vehicle to the leasing company.**
That's always a dealership. And dealerships of course have a great incentive to make as much money as possible on the sale of the vehicle to the leasing company: that's what they do for a living.

3. **The company that actually fills out your lease forms.**
That company is usually called an "originator," a "leasing representative," or a "sales outlet." Automobile dealerships, banks, or entirely separate companies can be sales outlets. Sales outlets can be as fly-by-night as your worst nightmare can conjure up—and about as bad as some of leasing's own language. So, let's look at that foreign tongue.

Leasing Terminology— Chinese Would Be Easier

Memorize these. Just kidding. But at least look them over pretty carefully.

Lessee That's you.

Lessor That's the leasing company, the company that legally owns the vehicle a person plans to drive.

Originator The people who actually fill out the paperwork. They're also called "sales outlets" and "leasing representatives."

MSRP The manufacturer's suggested retail price of a new vehicle.

Used Cars, which can also be leased, don't have MSRPs. Some new recreational vehicles and trucks don't have MSRP stickers from the factory, either.

To refresh your memory, the MSRP sticker is placed on the window by the manufacturer and contains an amount of profit that is exactly the same for identical vehicles. This sticker allows you to compare the actual price you will pay for a vehicle at one dealership versus the price at another. For instance, if the MSRP for a car with certain options is $15,000 at two dealerships, but one dealership offers to sell it to you for $14,000 rather than $14,500, which dealership would you buy from?

The MSRP is a "fair" price for that vehicle, according to the law, but any seller can charge more than that, if you allow them to. MSRP is not a legal "cap" on vehicle cost. But you also have a right to negotiate that price down as much as possible.

Dealerships use MSRP when they're talking to the leasing company itself to define how much profit the dealership is making on the sale of the vehicle itself. For instance, let's say a vehicle has an MSRP of $15,000. If the vehicle is sold for $15,000, that sale is referred to as "100 percent of MSRP." If the car is sold for $16,500, that is referred to as "110 percent of MSRP."

Acquisition Fee The lump sum of money a person agrees to pay the leasing company for arranging "financing" on a vehicle. It's what they charge to "acquire" the lease. Not all leasing companies charge an acquisition fee.

Capitalized Cost The total "selling price" of the vehicle to be leased, including these items: the total cost of the vehicle; taxes, title, and license fees; any acquisition fee; any optional insurance and warranty items. Using the capitalized cost figure is one way to compare the costs of more than one leasing sales outlet.

Interestingly enough, all leasing companies and their sales outlets refer to capitalized cost in their internal documents in a very easy-to-understand way. They just don't generally share that information with the consumer.

Cost of Money You won't see this important phrase much on leases. The "cost of money," when it's presented in an understandable way, really tells you the effective interest rate you are paying for the right to lease a vehicle.

On many leases, this cost is referred to as a "monthly lease charge," "service fee," or "service charge." Whatever it's called, most leases don't list this cost as an effective interest rate—they list it as a monthly amount. That makes it much harder for a person to compare cost of money from lease to lease or to compare the cost of money on a lease compared to a regular "purchase" contract.

"Why don't all leases clearly list something equivalent to an interest rate?" The Federal Reserve doesn't require them to. The Federal Reserve, as a matter of fact, agreed with the leasing companies and outlets that leases didn't have "interest" charges since the consumer technically wasn't financing ownership of a particular vehicle—the consumer was just using someone else's vehicle.

That loophole allowed some leasing companies to take advantage of the uneducated consumer by charging very high usage fees.

"Well, how much should a person pay for money?" Since the "service charge" you pay each month for the right to lease a vehicle isn't technically "interest," there generally is no limit to what a leasing company can charge you. And you can certainly pay as much as you want.

But you also have a right to pay as little "interest" as you can negotiate. Free enterprise rightfully drives the car buying-financing-leasing process. But you can't negotiate correctly unless a lease very clearly tells you what the use of money really will cost you.

Capitalized Cost Reduction Sometimes called "cap reduction," it's generally any nonrefundable down payment.

Residual Value "Residual value" is the amount of money the leasing company says your leased vehicle will be worth when your lease ends. The figure is important for two reasons: the leasing company uses it to help determine your lease payment and also uses it in determining any penalties should you break your lease early.

The leasing company normally develops a residual value figure based on the projected wholesale resale value of the vehicle at the end of the lease. They're in essence making a long-term guess.

Many leases now clearly show you the residual value of a vehicle at the end of a lease. But very few make it possible for you to know a vehicle's residual value if you terminate your lease early. Most leases use complex formulas rather than simply list value at a particular month.

"Since the residual value affects the lease payment, would it make sense to pick a car that has a high resale value?" It would indeed. Leasing a car with a high resale value should lower your potential lease payments.

"How do I know if a particular vehicle will have a good residual value?" Chances are, a car that is popular now will be popular at the end of your lease.

Gap Insurance "Gap insurance" makes sure you don't owe any money if your leased vehicle is wrecked, totaled, or stolen. This coverage is in addition to your normal collision insurance and is *not* automatically included on all leases.

Some leasing companies provide gap insurance for free, and virtually all leasing companies offer it for a fee. But, paid or free, no one should lease a vehicle without it.

Early Termination All leases have "early termination" clauses that define how much money you will have to pay the company if you terminate your lease early. Unfortunately, most leases make it virtually impossible for the average consumer to determine how much that penalty will be. The figure is determined by a complicated formula.

It's important for you to understand, therefore, that *early terminations can be extremely expensive*. If you should break your lease during the first year of a three-year lease, for instance, your penalty could easily be thousands of dollars. What's the moral here? **Never enter into a lease unless you plan to keep the vehicle for the full term of the lease.**

"Excess Mileage" As we mentioned earlier, leases offer a certain number of "free" miles a person can drive over the course of a lease. Beyond that, you pay extra. The "excess mileage" portion of your lease will tell you how many cents per extra mile you must pay.

Most leasing companies allow you an average of 12,000–15,000 "free" miles per year for the length of the lease. On a three-year lease, for instance, you might have 45,000 free miles.

Unfortunately, some leasing companies have been known to make a lease payment appear inexpensive by deliberately understating the miles used to determine the payment. The consumer then pays that heavy penalty we discussed earlier. **"Since mileage is important, should I have my lease based on the actual miles I drive on average each year?"** Absolutely! Every smart leasing customer should realistically determine how many miles he or she will drive over the course of a lease, and *insist* that mileage is used in advance to determine the lease payment and contract.

For instance, if your present car is three years old, and it has 60,000 miles on it—and if you plan to have the same driving habits—you would want your lease figured on that mileage. While using the higher figure will make the payment higher now, it will also prevent a multi-thousand-dollar penalty at the end of the lease.

Insurance and Warranty Items Items such as credit life and disability insurance, extended warranties, and vehicle maintenance agreements are offered by virtually all leasing companies.

"Excess" Wear and Tear Virtually all leasing companies charge extra for any wear and tear they consider above and beyond "normal" wear and tear.

Security Deposits These are generally refundable under certain conditions.

Purchase Option Fee A few leasing companies still try to charge this fee, but most reputable companies don't. The "fee" is simply additional profit.

Disposition Charge Leasing companies say this fee covers their cost involved with selling your old lease vehicle after you have turned it in. Many consumer groups say it's simply extra profit.

Leasing the Right Way:

If you already drive a leased vehicle and want to maximize your next lease transaction, skip to page 416 before you read this.

1. **If you haven't read the rest of this book, you should.**
   All of the exciting horror stories and much of the valuable information contained in the other chapters applies as well (or more) to leasing as it does to buying.

2. **If you have a trade-in, consider retailing it yourself rather than trading it.**
   The trade-in is the Achilles' heel of leasing. Selling it yourself could make you a thousand or two, plus it makes it much harder for a leasing company to confuse you or steal your trade as you begin to negotiate the lease. Page 172 tells you how to sell your old vehicle yourself.

3. **Disable your cookies or make them visible, if you're using the Web for research or for actually leasing, unless you want to be naked to the world.**
   Aside from protecting your privacy, disabling cookies dramatically lowers your spam. Page 37 in chapter 1 helps you do this.

4. **Remember to download or print any information you may want later.**
   Don't worry about the casual visit to a site, but save all contact as you become serious about leasing—particularly all contact from the one source you eventually plan to use to acquire your new wheels.

5. **If you're planning to let the leasing company take your old car as a trade, "shop" it to determine its exact, specific wholesale value.**

In a lease transaction, this step is as vital as air. Drive to three used-car operations, and see what they'll pay you to buy it outright. The highest offer is your car's real wholesale value. "Lowballing" is the powerful engine that drives the leasing world, particularly on the Web. You can throw away thousands and barely feel those bills flying out of your pocket, if you don't determine your old vehicle's true wholesale value accurately. Unfortunately, you cannot determine the actual wholesale value of your specific trade-in using the appraisal services or wholesale sites associated with virtually every leasing organization. At best, you'll get an "average" value of vehicles like yours, which is relatively worthless. At worst, you'll be robbed. Page 166 shows you how to determine the value of your individual trade-in to the dollar. It's about the most important homework you can do if you plan to lease. After determining the value, write your wholesale value here: ————————————————————— .

6. **Determine if your old vehicle is going to cover your up-front costs on a new lease:**

- Your wholesale value: ————————————————— .
- Payoff (call your financing source): ———————— .
- If the wholesale value is at least $1,500 more than your payoff, you should be able to lease a vehicle without paying any out-of-pocket expenses. Don't be conned by the leasing agent into forking over any cash.
- If your payoff is greater than your old vehicle's wholesale value, you will probably need to provide cash in your lease transaction equal to two lease payments plus the amount you're "in the bucket." Determine the amount you're in the bucket by subtracting your wholesale value from your payoff and write that figure here: —————————————————— .

7. **Determine how many miles you will probably drive your leased vehicle each year.**
Excess mileage charges can run thousands and ruin hundreds of thousands of people's budgets each year. Part of your homework is to prevent that from happening.

Divide the current miles on your present vehicle by the number of months you've driven it. If your past driving experience is going to be similar, we're going to use that average to determine your lease. If you think you may drive more miles, add miles to your average. Write the number of miles you plan to drive your leased vehicle here: ——————————————————————— .

8. Do your homework on your budget, but don't use the leasing company as your budget counselor.

Leasing companies just love to help you determine what you can afford to pay per month. Lots of the online companies even provide "calculators" to assist you, and, likely as not, these calculators will have you spending about 200 percent of your take-home pay per month, happily calling this their "prepaid bankruptcy" plan. Decline their kind offer of help. Remember that the leasing gang makes more money if you pay higher payments, regardless of the damage to your budget, credit, or sanity. Use our budgeting process in chapter 8, or go to www.dontgettakeneverytime.com and use our recommended budgeting calculator. Or follow this quick tip: Can you afford the monthly payment you're making now? Can you afford to pay more? How much more? Or would you rather pay less than you're paying now? Use your current payment to come up with a comfortable lease payment. Whatever budgeting process you use, determine a lease payment that rationally makes sense for you. Write the maximum amount you want to pay per month on your lease here: ——————————————————————— .

9. Determine how many months you want to lease a vehicle.

If you're smart, don't lease for more months than a particular vehicle's bumper-to-bumper manufacturer's warranty. That usually means limiting your lease to thirty-six months, unless you really like to gamble. Go longer than that, and you may be stuck with the cost of major repairs on a vehicle you don't own. Want to spend $1,000 fixing the A.C. of someone else's vehicle?

In determining months, think about how many miles per year you drive. High-mileage driving increases the cost of leasing dramatically. If you drive more than 20,000 miles per year, don't lease for more than thirty-six months at the maximum. Lease-end vehicles with more than 60,000 miles on them are relatively worthless.

10. Let the lease payment and months determine what vehicle you lease.

A thirty-six month lease at $400 a month buys more car than a thirty-six month lease at $100 per month. If, for instance, you can only afford a $100 per month payment, you're probably going to have to limit your choice of vehicles to used Tonka toys. If you can afford $400 for thirty-six months, you can probably get something nice. "Determining Available Cash" on page 244 will help you easily see how much car you can afford, regardless of the lease payment. Write down the Available Cash figure for your lease payment here: _____. This figure tells you how much vehicle your budget will let you "buy."

11. Do your homework on the vehicles that fit your lease budget using nonprofit, consumer sites first.

Safety and dependability matter even more if you plan to lease. Since you're not going to own the vehicle, you actually have less rights than a purchaser. Lease a lemon or the most dangerous vehicle sold in America, and you may be stuck with it. Page 301 leads you through some great Web sites and other sources for checking out the safety and mechanical reliability of the vehicles that fit your lease budget.

12. Read up on current leasing news.

Consumer Reports and Bankrate.com usually post excellent and unbiased "insider" articles on auto leasing.

13. Use the Web to "shop" vehicle leasing companies.

You're not spending on these visits, just having an entertaining and educational foray. What's out there?

- **Go to the Web site of the "captive" financing source of your favorite vehicle.** Always use a captive site as one of your lease comparison options. Like Chevrolets the best? Go to www.chevrolet.com or to www.gmacfs.com and click to their lease or finance page. Play around, design a vehicle you'd like to lease, and keep an eye out for lease "specials." Print a rundown on the vehicle you'd like to lease the most.

- **Go to some independent leasing sites.** If you've had bank loans, go to your bank's site. Look at "broker" sites such as CarsDirect.com. If you belong to a credit union, go to its Web site. If you're considering a specialty or luxury car, go to sites such as NVLeasing.com. Specialty sites may not save you money, but may provide you easier access to certain vehicles. Also search "Automobile Leasing." Virtually all of these sites, wherever they are located physically, operate by buying a car for you to lease from a local dealer, or by sending you to that dealership themselves. But don't go there, just yet. Your task is to become familiar with the many types of sites and leases out there.

- **Using your budgeted monthly lease payment, let several sites develop a lease quote for you.** Always specify the exact same vehicle and equipment at each site. Print out these quotes.

- **Take your time and have some fun on this Web-shopping foray.** You'll notice some sites require a deposit to give you a "guaranteed" lease payment or terms. Scratch these sites off your shopping list.

14. Get "hands-on" experience in the vehicle you like the most: Rent one.

Investing $100 in a weekend rental is far better than any test-drive at the nicest dealership, and safer for your wallet in the long run. Or rent one for the day.

15. Choose two leasing companies.

I recommend the "captive" source that manufactures the vehicle you like the best (which means you'll be dealing with a local dealership) and an independent source. Your independent source can be your bank, a leasing broker such as CarsDirect.com, or a "click" source on the Web. I know you don't want to visit the dealership, but do it! You're not going to know if you're throwing away thousands if you're not willing to make this trip. Think of it as inoculations before a wonderful, exotic vacation. You may not like the shots, but they're worth the pain. Make sure you've printed out a vehicle quote, based on your budgeted payment, for each of these sources.

16. Find an actual vehicle through your captive leasing source that fits your needs and budget.

This means you're going to a local dealership! We're going to use this vehicle to allow you to "work" your leasing companies and get them to the best deal. The captive leasing company's Web site will lead you directly to your closest local dealership.

17. Visit the dealership and find the one vehicle that fits your needs.

Deal only with the leasing manager. Let the dealership appraise your trade-in. Tell the manager in advance the true wholesale value of your trade-in, and let the manager know you're not leasing with his company if they don't meet that wholesale value. If the manager refuses to deal with you or your trade-in before discussing the lease, leave the dealership and find another source.

18. When you agree on the true wholesale value of your trade, drive the new vehicle that interests you the most, and then let the lease manager write up a detailed lease quote.

Make sure the quote includes these tidbits, at the minimum:

- A lease based on the *actual number of miles you will probably drive over the lease term*. You figured that number of miles in step seven. Insist that your lease is computed using this mileage. If a leasing company won't do this, then don't lease from it.
- The MSRP of the vehicle
- Your trade-in's true wholesale value

- Total "rent" or "service charge" or "cost of money"
- Itemized breakdown of capitalized cost. Note: Leasing companies are now *required* to give you a breakdown of capitalized cost.
- Number of months and monthly payment
- Vehicle identification number (VIN)
- Residual value of vehicle
- The amount required as an initial cash payment, including deposits and any other cash payments whatsoever. (Hey, this becomes important in a minute!)
- Excess mileage charge.

19. Plot your escape!

Tell the manager you'll get back to him after talking with your other lease source. At that point you'll notice the manager may begin to cut his lease payment. Sit patiently if this happens, write down the new figures, and then leave. At this point, the manager is probably going to call in reinforcements. Don't fall for it! Get outta there and head home.

20. Compare the monthly payment and lease terms to your budget figures.

How are you doing? If the payment and months fit your budget, you're doing fine. Now, let's get that payment down some more.

21. Contact your other leasing source.

Provide them with the information, including dealership name and vehicle indentification number (VIN), of the vehicle you've just visited, but don't tell the source what payment and terms the dealership gave you. Ask your source to provide you the exact same information on the exact same vehicle, if possible. **Make sure the company uses your actual miles to develop their lease.** Many times, this source will actually get you information on the very same vehicle—excellent for you. At other times, they will get information on a similar vehicle. That's okay, too, as long as the vehicle is relatively similar. If the dealership lease payment quote, for instance, is for a loaded Expenso Gargantula with the thirty-six-cylinder Ozone Eater engine, don't let your other independent or Web source quote you a payment on the piddling, gerbil-powered Gargantula.

22. Compare item for item your out-of-pocket outlay for each leasing source's charge for deposits, registration fees, and any other charge you're required to pay in cash.

Any financed document charge, such as an "origination fee," will have already been accounted for in the lease payment for each source. But cash outlays can skew your comparison. For instance, if both sources agree to a $400 payment, but one source requires a nonrefundable $1,000 payment for *any* reason, that source just lost the contest for your lease.

23. Compare payments and months between your online, independent, and dealership sources.

In leasing, the payment and months you finally pay are the test of truth, all things being equal. The cheapest payment will be the cheapest leasing source of the moment.

24. Call up your dealership source and negotiate on the phone for a lower payment.

Dealerships, or brick-and-mortar independent leasing companies, virtually always have room to negotiate. And don't be shy. Your leasing company is probably making a "full boat" profit on their first lease quote (a list-price sale)—thousands of dollars in profit, as a matter of fact. If the dealership had agreed to $400 per month, try for $350 per month, and tell the dealership you are going to lease from some source within twenty-four hours. Leasing companies know that 80 percent of the people who don't lease at this point, won't. Use this for pressure.

25. If you're being really stingy with your money, go back to the alternate company and try to negotiate the monthly payment down, too.

Purely online leasing companies are trying to learn how to negotiate on the Web. They just hate it. But if you're insistent, you may see their price drop, too.

26. Make your choice. If your choice is an online lease company, be certain that company agrees to the

wholesale figure on your trade-in before agreeing to lease with them.

Most Web-based companies will weasel on all online appraisals, unless the appraisal is so low the company knows it's stealing your old car, regardless of the figure. For instance, if the "average" wholesale value of the car (the value quoted by Edmunds, for instance) is $4,000, the company probably won't need to look at your vehicle if you will accept $3,000 for it sight unseen. By e-mail, tell the Web company you'll be glad for them to appraise your vehicle in person, but you won't lease from them unless the figure matches its true wholesale value. Many of these companies will send an appraiser to your home or business.

27. Regardless of the source, do not be talked into evaluating the condition of your trade-in.

Don't fill out any self-appraisal forms. You are not a mechanic and are in no position to guarantee its reliability. As we mentioned, companies are using self-appraisal forms to obligate you down the road for financial liability.

28. Be prepared for an "add-on" pitch.

"Initial here if you want your airbag to be full of fresh Aspen air, instead of gravel. Only $600" Scott Adams memorably intones that perfect "add-on" sales pitch in a memorably accurate *Dilbert* cartoon.

29. If you are leasing a vehicle for more months than the vehicle's 100 percent warranty, you might want to consider purchasing a service agreement.

Trouble is, you'll probably have to pay for more coverage in months than you need. You decide. *If you're dealing with an online company,* some of these folks will at the last minute try to add service agreements, accessories, or other "special value" packages to the paperwork package they normally send you. Don't fall for it.

30. Actually read the lease paperwork.

Important figures change magically at dealerships and online sources alike. *Vehicles* have been known to

change—and if you don't catch the change, you're stuck.
31. Take that beauty for a ride!
You're home free—until that first payment comes due.

What About Leasing Used Cars?

If you need a car for only a couple of years, and if you're not planning to put many miles on a car, leasing a late-model used car can make a lot of sense. Negotiate your lease payment as you would for a new vehicle. And then after you've negotiated your payment, insist that you have the vehicle checked out by a mechanic. If your mechanic says the vehicle needs work, have the work done before you sign any contracts. And don't let the lessor raise your monthly payment to cover the repair.

If Your Present Car Is a Lease Vehicle

If your lease term is about up, you want to make sure that the leasing company doesn't rip you off in two areas related to your current vehicle: lease-end value and "normal" wear and tear. You also want to decide if you should lease from the same company again. People who lease with the same company without carefully negotiating their lease pay a heavy sucker tax.

Lease-end value. Your current company is going to do everything short of breaking your legs to get you to buy your old vehicle rather than turn it in if that vehicle *is not* worth the lease-end value figure in your lease. Your current company is going to do everything short of breaking your legs to *keep* you from buying your old vehicle if it's worth more to them than the lease-end amount in your contract.

Use these two little cues to decide what to do with your old vehicle. If they want to sell it to you, don't buy it at the lease-end figure. If the company won't sell you the vehicle for less than the lease-end (which they can do), walk away from it.

If the company doesn't want to sell it to you, start smacking your lips. The vehicle may be worth thousands more than its lease-end value. **How to know:** Shop it to determine its true wholesale value as if you owned it. If the wholesale value is at least $1,000 more than the value you can buy it for, consider buying it and then simply selling it. You can either wholesale it to the company that appraised it and make $1,000, or retail it and perhaps make a couple of thousand. Nice!

"Normal" wear and tear. Many leasing companies have made wear and tear a profit center. Don't be caught in that trap. You have a right to shop any leasing company's estimate for normal wear and tear. Demand that the leasing company give you a detailed written estimate concerning wear and tear. Take your vehicle and that estimate to a body and/or service department of some other dealership that sells the same brand of vehicle, and ask for a written estimate on repairing wear and tear. Use this repair estimate to defend your leasing company's estimate, and don't be afraid to argue. "Wear and tear" has not been clearly defined by the courts and generally isn't clearly defined in your contract. Stand up for your rights. If you still believe you are being ripped off, contact a consumer attorney and your state attorney general's office.

Should you lease with the same company again? If you don't shop their lease quotes as if you've never leased from them before, most leasing companies are going to charge you a hefty premium for that trust. Generally speaking, virtually all leasing company profits go up on the second lease. Don't fall prey to these statistics.

Chapter 17

Lomax

It began as the sweetest of dreams. Killer had fallen into bed, rolled on his back, and sighed, his fall rocking the bed like some giant jelly bean making hard contact with a bowl of Jell-O.

"Honey, are you okay?" Killer's better two-thirds asked.

"Lilly, I feel fine, just fine. Guess what?"

"What?"

"I've decided to open my own auto buying service on the Web. I'm going to call it LOMAX—Low Prices, Maximum Service! What do you think? I'm tired of the rat race. And I hear those online customers are awfully nice people."

Killer's definition of nice is "easily taken," but Lilly didn't know that. She is much like some Mafia don's wife who thinks her husband sells olive oil for a living. Lilly was used to Robert DeMarco's crazy schemes, too. Killer had bought the first Invisible Ion Cleanser franchise in the state, years ago. And Lilly was well aware that Killer had been spending lots of time at the new computer in his garage "office."

"That's fine, honey, but do you really want to work at home all day? Isn't the Dead End closer to the office than to here?"

"Lilly, that isn't fair! You know I work there."

"Yes, honey. Sweet dreams," Lilly said lightly. In moments, they both had drifted off. . . .

LOMAX CONSUMER AUTOMOTIVE—Robert DeMarco, owner! Killer's dream took him quickly to the big new office conveniently attached to the kitchen. He eagerly opened the first of dozens of e-mail messages, the result of his first Web ad, and as he began to read, Killer broke into a smile. This was going to be so easy!

"I'm a bit nervous," the first e-mail started, "since I'm a woman, and this is the first time I've bought a car by myself. I hope it won't bother you that I'm a rookie buyer."

"Oh no, ma'am, that won't bother me at all," Killer muttered to himself as he quickly began typing a response, glancing for a moment at her name. Jo Wright. At that point in the dream, Killer should have awakened, but he didn't. He continued to type, "Jo—I hope it's okay if I call you Jo—I'll tell you what. You are one of our first customers at my company. And I *personally* want you to know that you will be treated fairly. If we don't, I'll *give* you the car!"

Killer quickly found the perfect car for the lady—a new car that had been sitting on a friend's new-car lot for months. Killer bought it below cost. Jo herself had gone to look at the car. "Oh, Mr. DeMarco, I just love it!" her e-mail had said. "I am such a lucky customer! What do we do now?"

We get nailed right now, Killer thought. He wanted the money. Killer began to type with the speed of a demon, "Well, why don't I appraise your vehicle online, and we can finish this transaction in a blink.

"Jo, I'm going to give you a really enormous allowance on your car: $2,500!" The car was worth $5,000. Killer smiled as he waited for her response. Such a nice lady!

But at that instant, his computer announced angrily, "You've got mail, and you're not going to like it one bit!" Before Killer could react, an instant message filled his screen: "Allowance! Mr. DeMarco, I'm not interested in allowance! Do you think you can lowball *me?* What are you going to do next? Try to fool me with the 'cost' figure of your car?"

Killer was stunned. He looked back at the message sender line, and this time the name Jo Wright took his breath away, sending a dagger to his heart. Killer tried to clear the screen, but the message wouldn't clear. He unplugged the modem, but it had no impact. He lunged for the power pack, but even unplugging that didn't clear the screen.

The door flew open to his office, and before Killer could react, a dozen strangers began storming into his office. What was going on? How could these strangers invade his private space? Who did they think they were! And then Killer looked harder at the couple leading the stampede in the office. They looked too familiar. He stuttered, "You . . . you . . . are you. . ." Killer knew the answer. Jim and Gloria Wright! Followed by Trey and Dana. The one family Killer had not been able to bamboozle in years of trickery! Killer let out a loud, piercing scream.

Lilly DeMarco opened her eyes and listened. Killer, still sleeping, was emitting the moan of some wounded animal. Beads of sweat were popping on his forehead. "Bob? Bob!" Lilly reached over and shook him gently. But the dream was not to end that quickly.

"*Mr. DeMarco!*" Jo Wright said, "do you remember these people? My aunt and uncle? My cousins?" She was smiling now, but the eyes that had appeared so beautiful moments ago were red and glaring, her teeth sharply pointed. "Do you remember these people, MR. MONSOON?!"

Killer's office quickly filled with perhaps twenty customers, and suddenly Killer remembered them all: the only buyers during Killer's entire career who had really defeated him in car transactions. Each carried a placard emblazoned K.O. KILLER or KILL HIM! KILL HIM! All were chanting, "Killer! Killer! Killer!"

"We know your name, Killer Monsoon! We know your game! And we all have cookies living in your computer forever!"

Killer's moans sounded like the dying rumbles of an army of evil, and Lilly began to shake him violently, a shake that coincided with the joggling Jo was giving him at that moment in the dream.

"A free car! A free car!" Jo yelled, grabbing the keys for the new office. Killer tried to run, too, but he was blocked by the twenty maddened buyers, and then his own salesmen, who were yelling, "Rotten geek! Rotten geek! Rotten geek!"

"Stop!" Killer bounced awake in the bed, sweat pouring from his body as from a broken pipe. He rubbed his neck.

"Honey, are you okay?" Lilly asked.

Killer looked around the room, slipped his feet to the floor, and headed to the door. "Yeah, yeah, I'm okay," he said over his shoulder. "Lilly, forget what I said about the buying service, okay? That computer stuff can be pretty dangerous, you know, now that I think about it." Like to Killer's sanity.

Scraps of the nightmare roiling in his head, Killer with great trepidation opened the darkened garage door, mortal fear momentarily keeping him from turning on the light and looking at the computer monitor. Surely *that* hadn't been the last image he'd seen on the monitor in the nightmare. Surely it hadn't said, "All of your customers from now on, click or brick, are going to be as smart as us!"

Endnotes

Chapter 1

1. Yahoo! press release, "Ford and Yahoo! team to serve cunsumers online," January 9, 2000. http://docs.yahoo.com/docs/pr/release 450.html.
2. GM News for Investors press release, "General Motors and America Online announce major strategic alliance," January 9, 2000. http://media.gm.com/news/releases/g000109c.html.
3. www.edmunds.com/dealers/index.html (accessed September 23, 2006).
4. Autobytel Inc. Backgrounder. www.car.com/content/home/help/pressroom/index.cfm?id=24093;ccom&action=backgrounder (accessed August 10, 2006).
5. James Nastars, V.P. Lending, University Federal Credit Union, Austin, TX. Memo. March 13, 2000.
6. TargetLive.com. Online live training. March 2000. http://207.192.67.17/dls/courses/firstarchive/slide001.html.
7. Ibid.
8. Ibid.
9. *Automotive News*, "Manufacturers enter e-pricing arena."
10. Consumer Conference, Beltway group, Ralph Nader's office.
11. E-mails and telephone discussions with Silvia Gambardella and press coverage of the firings.
12. www.junkbusters.com/cookies.html.

Chapter 2

1. www.car.com/content/home/help/pressroom/index.cfm?id=24093 ;ccom&action=backgrounder (accessed August 11, 2006).
2. www.autobytel.com/content/home/help/pressroom/pressreleases/ index.cfm/action/template/article_id_int/1752 (accessed August 10, 2006).

Chapter 3

1. TargetLive.com online training seminar.
2. TargetLive.com online audio training.
3. Ibid.
4. Ibid.

Chapter 4

1. Comments to author in conversation with dealer.
2. Donna Harris. "One-price is a winner in Houston, but Sonic won't go all the way." *Automotive News* online, January 4, 1999.
3. Author. E-mail poll. NCLC group. March 30, 2000.
4. Author's notes. National Association of Consumer Advocates Annual Conference. 1999.
5. Ken Hylton, "Mel Farr Auto Dealership Sued over Payment Timer." AP netwire.
6. Ibid.
7. Tom Domonosky. E-mail to author. March 1, 2000.
8. AAEFCU newsletter. March 17, 2000. "FTC warns dealers: Hold off on credit report checks."

Chapter 5

1. TargetLive.com online training.
2. TargetLive.com online training.
3. Registered to author.
4. "Holdback" is an extra dealer profit we'll tell you about in chapter 11.

Chapter 7

1. Registered to author.
2. Dianne Craft, insurance article.
3. Paul Snider in *Dealer* magazine online. "Selecting the Best Candidate for Your Special Finance Department, Part 2." www.theautochannel.com/mania/industry/dealeronline/issues/adm19907–20.htm.
4. Information about credit rating practices obtained in author's conversation with David Szwak, Fair Credit Reporting Act Plaintiff Attorney. April 18, 2000.
5. www.povertylaw.org.iwn/aug98/aug98_6.htm.
6. Center for Poverty Law article, CUNA file, online research material.
7. Don DiCostanzo. July/August 1999. "Sub-prime cuts: Should new car dealers do buy here pay here?" *Dealer magazine* online.   www.theautochannel.com/mania/industry/dealeronline/issues/adm199907–30.htm.
8. Ibid.
9. Ibid.
10. Interview by Mark Hafner. July/August 1999. *Dealer* magazine online.
11. DiCostanzo, ibid.
12. BJT Auto Sales.
13. Most available and accessible studies on the subprime market look at mortgage lending. Often cited estimates from the quasi-governmental agencies Fannie Mae and Freddie Mac are that 35 to 50 percent of borrowers with subprime mortgages could have qualified for lower-rate conventional mortgages. Extrapolating from these data and other studies related to auto lending suggests that a significant portion of subprime auto loan borrowers would also qualify for lower rates.
14. "Driven into Debt: CFA Car Title Loan Store and Online Survey." Consumer Federation of America. November 2005. http://consumerfed.org/pdfs/Car_Title_Loan_Report_111705.pdf (accessed August 21, 2006).

Chapter 9

1. Federal Trade Commission. *How to Advertise Consumer Credit*, p. 3.

Chapter 16

1. Tips from Florida Attorney General's Office.
2. www.bankrate.com/brm/news/auto/19990120.asp.
3. Lucy Lazarony. August 30, 2000. "Lenders get tough on new auto leases." www.bankrate.com.

Appendix

How to Figure Loan Cash from a Payment

Payments don't buy a vehicle, they pay for a lump sum of cash. Using the chart in this section, it's easy to figure how much cash a payment will yield at various interest rates. Using a calculator will save you some time and long division, but it isn't necessary.

First, I'll demonstrate how the process works using an example. Let's say that you have decided that you can afford a payment of $300 per month for four years (forty-eight months) and that your best interest rate is 7 percent. How much loan cash will that payment buy?

To begin, look at the chart and find the payment per thousand borrowed at the APR (7 percent) and term (four years) you selected. That figure is $23.95. To determine how much cash your payment will buy, divide your payment of $300 by the payment per thousand of $23.95 as listed on the chart. In our example $300 divided by $23.95 yields 12.526 thousands, or $12,526. (To convert the answer into dollars, you multiply by $1,000—just move the decimal three places to the right.)

Using the chart and this simple math, you can find out how much cash any payment at any interest rate will buy.

Chart for Use in Figuring
Loan Cash or Monthly Payments

Monthly Payments for $1,000

	3%	4%	5%	6%	7%	8%	8.5%
2 yr	42.98	43.42	43.87	44.32	44.77	45.23	45.46
3 yr	29.08	29.52	29.97	30.42	30.88	31.34	31.57
4 yr	22.13	22.58	23.03	23.49	23.95	24.41	24.65
5 yr	17.19	18.42	18.87	19.33	19.80	20.28	20.52
6 yr			16.10	16.57	17.05	17.53	17.78

	9%	9.5%	10%	10.5%	11%	11.5%	12%
2 yr	45.68	45.91	46.14	46.38	46.61	48.84	47.07
3 yr	31.80	32.03	32.27	32.50	32.74	32.98	33.21
4 yr	24.89	25.12	25.36	25.60	25.85	26.09	26.33
5 yr	20.76	21.00	21.25	21.49	21.74	21.99	22.24
6 yr	18.03	18.27	18.53	18.78	19.03	19.29	19.55

	12.5%	13%	13.5%	14%	14.5%	15%	15.5%
2 yr	47.31	47.54	47.78	48.01	48.25	48.49	48.72
3 yr	33.45	33.69	33.94	34.18	34.42	34.67	34.91
4 yr	26.58	26.83	27.08	27.33	27.58	27.83	28.08
5 yr	22.50	22.75	23.01	23.27	23.53	23.79	24.05
6 yr	19.81	20.07	20.34	20.61	20.87	21.15	21.42

	16%	16.5%	17%	17.5%	18%	18.5%	19%
2 yr	48.96	49.20	49.44	49.68	49.92	50.17	50.41
3 yr	35.16	35.40	35.65	35.90	36.15	36.40	36.66
4 yr	28.34	28.60	28.86	29.11	29.37	29.64	29.90
5 yr	24.32	24.58	24.85	25.12	25.39	25.67	25.94
6 yr	21.69	21.97	---22.25	22.53	22.81	23.09	23.38

	19.5%	20%	20.5%	21%			
2 yr	50.65	50.90	51.14	51.39			
3 yr	36.91	37.16	37.42	37.68			
4 yr	30.16	30.43	30.70	30.97			
5 yr	26.22	26.49	26.77	27.05			
6 yr	23.66	23.95	24.24	24.54			

Using the Chart to Determine Payments When You Know the Lump Sum

You can use this same chart to determine what the payments will be on a lump sum of money. Why do you need to know this? If you are lucky, you may negotiate a final price on a vehicle that is less than your Loan Cash. If you do, this technique will provide a quick way to compute your new payment. It will also allow you to check the other guy's figures—that's handy and protects you.

The technique will also give you flexibility. If, for instance, you decide to spend $16,000 on a car, but then find a red dream machine for $16,800, the chart will let you quickly determine your new payment. And, finally, it can bring you to your senses should you accidentally fall in love with some beauty $3,000 or $5,000 over budget.

Here's how to use this simple technique when you know the lump sum you must pay plus the term you want to finance and the interest rate (APR). For an example, let's say you need to know what the payment will be if you borrow $15,000 at 7 percent for four years. First, using the interest rate and term of your loan, locate the monthly payment per $1,000 figure on the chart. In our example, that figure is $23.95. Now divide your lump sum by $1,000 (just move the decimal three places to the left): $15,000 divided by 1,000 is 15.000 or 15—that's the number of thousands in the lump sum. To find the monthly payment simply multiply $23.95 by 15. The answer is $359.25.

This approach works as easily even when you don't have a nice round figure. Let's say that you need to know the payment for borrowing $15,627 at 7 percent for four years. Divide $15,627 by 1,000 to get 15.627. Then multiply that figure by $23.95. The result: 15.627 x $23.95 equals a payment of $374.27 per month.

Web Site Addresses for Automotive Manufacturers

Acura Division, American Honda Motor Co. Inc.   www.acura.com
Adam Opel AG   www.opel.com
Alfa Romeo Automobiles   www.alfaromeo.com
American Honda Motor Co. Inc.   www.honda.com
American Suzuki Motor Corp.   www.suzuki.com
Aston Martin Lagonda Ltd.   www.astonmartin.com

Audi AG   www.audi.com
Audi of America Inc.   www.audiusa.com
Automobili Lamborghini S.p.A.   www.lamborghini.com
Automobili Lamborghini USA Inc.   www.lamborghini.com
Automobiles Citroën   www.citroen.com
Automobiles Peugeot   www.peugeot.com
BMW AG   www.bmw.com
BMW of North America LLC   www.bmwusa.com
Buick Motor Division, General Motors   www.buick.com
Cadillac Motor Car Division, General Motors   www.cadillac.com
Chevrolet Motor Division, General Motors   www.chevrolet.com
Chrysler Division, DaimlerChrysler   www.chrysler.com
Daewoo Motor Co. Ltd.   www.dm.co.kr
Daihatsu Motor Co. Ltd.   www.daihatsu.com
DaimlerChrysler AG   www.daimlerchrysler.com
DaimlerChrysler Canada Ltd.   www.chryslercanada.ca
DaimlerChrysler de México, SA   www.chrysler.com.mx
Dodge Division, DaimlerChrysler   www.dodge.com
Ferrari North America   www.ferrari.com
Fiat   www.fiat.com
Ford Division, Ford Motor Co.   www.ford.com
Ford Motor Co.   www.ford.com
Ford Motor Co. Ltd.   www.ford.co.uk
Ford Motor Co. of Canada Ltd.   www.ford.ca
General Motors   www.gm.com
General Motors de México SA de CV   www.gm.com.mx
General Motors of Canada Ltd.   www.gmcanada.ca
Honda Division, American Honda Motor Co. Inc.   www.honda.com
Honda Motor Co. Ltd.   www.honda.co.jp
Honda North America Inc.   www.honda.com
Hyundai Motor Co.   www.hyundai.com
Infiniti Division, Nissan Motor Corp. USA   www.infiniti.com
Isuzu Motors America Inc.   www.isuzu.com
Isuzu Motors Ltd.   www.isuzu.co.jp
Jaguar   www.jaguar.com
Jeep Division, DaimlerChrysler   www.jeep.com
Kia Motors America Inc.   www.kia.com
Kia Motors Corp.   www.kia.co.kr
Land Rover   www.landrover.com
Lexus   www.lexus.com
Lincoln Mercury, Ford Motor Co.   www.lincolnmercury.com
Lotus Cars   www.lotuscars.com

Mazda Motor Corp. USA   www.mazdausa.com
Mercedes-Benz   www.mercedes-benz.com
Mercedes-Benz USA Inc.   www.usa.mercedes-benz.com
Mitsubishi Motor Sales of America Inc.   www.mitsucars.com
Nissan Canada Inc.   www.nissancanada.com
Nissan Motor Corp. in USA.   www.nissanmotors.com
NUMMI   www.nummi.com
OpelEisenach GmbH   www.opel.com
Paccar Inc.   www.paccar.com
Pontiac-GMC Division, General Motors   www.pontiac.com
Porsche   www.porsche.com
Proton   www.proton.com
Renault V.I.   www.renault.com
Rolls-Royce Motor Cars   www.rolls-roycemotorcars.com
Saab Automobile   www.saab.com
Saab Cars USA Inc.   www.saabusa.com
Saturn   www.saturn.com
Subaru of America Inc.   www.subaru.com
Suzuki Motor Corp.   www.suzuki.co.jp
Toyota Canada Inc.   www.toyota.ca
Toyota Motor Manufacturing North America Inc.   www.toyota.com
Volkswagen AG   www.vw-online.de
Volkswagen of America Inc.   www.vw.com
Volvo Canada Ltd.   www.volvocanada.com
Volvo Cars USA   www.volvocars.us

Web Site Addresses for Captive Financing Companies

You can usually reach the Web sites of the financial services of the automotive manufacturers that offer them from the home page of the individual company's home page as listed above. Here are the addresses of the
financing companies of several big manufacturers.

Chrysler Motors   www.chryslerfinancial.com
Ford Motor Credit   www.fordcredit.com
General Motors, GMAC Financial Services   www.gmacfs.com
Honda Financial   www.hondafinance.com
Toyota Financial Services   www.toyota.com, then click on the EXPLORE
FINANCIAL TOOLS button

Warranties, New and Used

Here's a rundown on warranty issues, whether you're buying new or used or leasing new or used.

New-Car Warranties Three specific "free" warranties apply to just about every new car sold or leased in America.

Adjustment Warranties are provided by the selling dealer, not the manufacturer, and supposedly cover items such as squeaks and rattles, air leaks, alignment, and other minor annoyances. Because the selling dealer provides this warranty and pays for the work himself, many dealers are loath to spend much time correcting those little problems that affect most new cars.

Dealers also limit the time period for minor adjustments—usually to no more than ninety days. If you are concerned with rattles, you should talk with a dealership's service department before purchasing a car. Ask the service manager specifically if *all* problems with your new car will be fixed for free. Note the time limit on these repairs. Smart car buyers keep a small notepad in their new cars and list each problem the moment it develops. You would be wise to do the same and provide your service department with a written list of all minor adjustments.

The Manufacturer's Warranty protects the major components of each car for a specified time period. The common minimum is twelve months or 12,000 miles. At the high end, some manufacturers offer up to five years or 100,000 miles or longer. Should your car need repairs under the manufacturer's warranty plan, these repairs will be paid for by the manufacturer—and that's the rub. Most manufacturers allow fewer repair hours for warranty repairs than the service department says the actual repairs require; consequently, the service department makes less money on this work. So, which cars normally are serviced first? Those of the paying customers, of course. Warranty work is shuttled to the end of the line, and you are left sitting in "the customers' lounge"—at many of the older dealerships still an imitation of the black hole of Calcutta—reading a six-year-old copy of *Dental Collectibles*.

How to prevent that? Shop your service department before you choose a dealership, page 295.

Secret Warranties are another "free" warranty no dealer will volunteer to discuss. Secret warranties are provided by virtually all manufacturers. Dealers and manufacturers even deny that such warranties exist, but they do. Called "policy adjustments" or "goodwill service," they apply to most cars, including the best. Dealers and manufacturers like to keep these little free perks from the general public to save money, as usual. But should you have a major problem with your car after the normal factory warranty expires, be loud and visible in your complaints. If your selling dealer refuses to help you with a problem, write the manufacturer's customer service office. The addresses of these offices are located in the owner's manuals for cars produced after 1979.

A hot tip: The National Highway Traffic Safety Administration (NHTSA) maintains a really useful toll-free number if you want to know about recalls, want to report a problem, or even want to know about "secret" warranties. The menu on this service is always changing, but call if you're thinking about a *used* car: 1–888–327–4236 (for the hearing impaired, TDD 1–800-424-9153). You can also check out NHTSA's information online (www.nhtsa.gov).

What About New-Car Service Contracts?

Service contracts, a.k.a. extended warranties, have replaced life and disability insurance as most sellers' favorite trinkets. They have replaced life and disability insurance because they can be sold to cash and finance customers alike, and because they are much more profitable than life and disability insurance since, unlike real insurance, the prices of service contracts aren't regulated by state insurance commissioners.

For instance, an insurance provider might sell you life and disability insurance that costs $2,000 over the course of your loan. The provider's maximum profit on that sale is generally limited to "only" 55 percent of the insurance's gross cost. That would be $1,100 in our $2,000 example.

Service contracts can cost thousands, too. But guess what an average service contract costs the average dealer in claims? Under $100. The rest of the sales price is pure profit. Let's see: if a seller charges you $2,000 for a service agreement, that makes the seller's profit $1,900 on the sale of the service agreement. Nice.

The profit for the dealer is so great because claims are very small and coverage is generally limited. For instance, if you read the average policy carefully, you'll find a version of this language: "Though we say this is a five-year contract, this policy doesn't go into effect until your car's regular warranty expires in three years." This limitation means you're in reality paying a fortune for a two-year warranty, not a five-year.

Many dealers get rich on these agreements for another reason: Rather than sell you a national service agreement such as one offered by GMAC, they sell you a questionable agreement from no-name companies located in states with few consumer protection laws. Why? The dealers generally own the companies.

So, should you buy a service agreement? Unless you're absolutely sure you're going to keep a car for years beyond the manufacturer's warranty, service contracts on new vehicles are a waste of money for most people. If you buy one, insist on a contract from a national brand and negotiate that price down to around $450. If you're financing through a credit union or bank that obviously can't sell you a GM or other manufacturer's warranty, make sure the warranty company is a national company. Generally speaking, banks and credit unions use reputable companies.

If you are buying a used car from a dealership—whether on the Web or in person—negotiate a proper free warranty *before* you sign anything but *after* you have agreed on a price for the vehicle. If you insist on a good free warranty before agreeing on the vehicle's price, you'll probably (and secretly) be stuck with a "service pack." For instance, if you insist on a 100 percent ninety-day warranty before you agree on price, your seller will be happy to provide it but will probably charge a higher price for the car to cover the potential risk of repairs. The seller will sell you a $4,000 car for $4,400 and bank the extra $400 as "insurance" against future repairs. Since the seller has neglected to tell you he's raised the price, he is covered on both ends. If the car needs repairs, you have paid for them in advance; and if the car doesn't need repairs, he has an extra $400 in profit. You want to buy that car for $4,000 *and* receive the best warranty.

Used-Car Warranties, from Best to Worst

After agreeing on a vehicle's price, begin your battle for a free warranty by asking for the best of the following warranties first; negotiate downward to less valuable warranties only after long and intense discussions.

1. The 100 percent warranty on all mechanical parts

This warranty won't cover your radio, squeaks and rattles, or leaks, but it will cover just about everything else. Try for a ninety-day, 100 percent warranty. Be happy if you get a thirty-day or sixty-day warranty. If your used car has major problems, they'll usually show up within thirty days. This is a hard warranty to get any seller to agree to, but try for it. The mere fact you are just asking for the best warranty means the seller will be less likely to offer you some of the really rotten warranties.

2. The 100 percent drive-train warranty

The drive train encompasses your engine, transmission, and drive axle (rear or front). It does not include your braking system or air conditioner. Drive-train warranties are fairly common in the business, but most sellers will try to give you a fifty-fifty drive-train warranty. Say no; it's usually a worthless option, as we'll see in a second. Aim for a 100 percent drive-train warranty as your minimum coverage. Again, try for ninety days, but accept thirty or sixty.

3. Fifty-fifty warranties

If sellers were honest, fifty-fifty warranties would be acceptable under most circumstances. But many dealers will agree to split your repair bills fifty-fifty, then simply double the price of each repair. Voilà! You are left paying the full bill. Another version of the fifty-fifty warranty is the "parts and labor" split: You agree to pay for the labor, and the seller agrees to pay for the parts. In most instances, the price for labor is conveniently raised far above its normal cost. Because labor is the largest portion of most repair bills, you are doubly stuck. Nice! Providers of this warranty can do this because they require you to have service work done in their shops or in places of their choosing.

If a fifty-fifty warranty is your only option, consider doing this before actually taking your car to the seller's shop for repair: Take the car to some other shop and ask for a written estimate for the same work that needs to be done. Then take your car to the seller's shop and ask for an estimate before the work is done. If there is a substantial difference in the two estimates, you are being taken again. Confront the service manager with your other estimate. If he or she refuses to meet the other repair estimate, consider making a protest to your local help line or Better Business Bureau. If you're dealing with a new-car dealership, consider writing the factory. On any fifty-fifty warranties, insist on coverage for at least ninety days.

4. Repairs "at cost."

This type of warranty is worthless because who defines "cost"? How can you check the definition of "cost"? Don't accept this favor.

5. "As is" warranties

The majority of used-car sellers these days post "As Is" stickers on the windows of their cars to protect themselves when they sell you a junker, to discourage you from asking for a proper free warranty, and to force you to buy a used-car warranty—even if the vehicle they're trying to sell you costs tens of thousands of dollars. Many dealers will actually attempt to make you sign a statement acknowledging that you know that you are purchasing a vehicle "as is." Your signature waives virtually every single right of recourse, even if the car blows up *before* you drive it off the lot. Some of these same dealers (the most unscrupulous) even try to get you to waive your "implied" warranties (coming up next). Don't go along with any of these tricks. *Unless you are deliberately buying a junker out of some masochistic yearning, don't buy any car "as is" from a licensed used-car dealer.*

Regardless of the type of warranty you finally negotiate, insist that the full conditions of the warranty be placed in writing, either on the buyer's order or on a separate sheet of paper signed by the manager, not by the salesman. Salesmen can promise you anything, even sign their personal guarantee in blood, but they cannot obligate the seller to honor their promises.

6. Implied warranties

For both new and used cars, many courts are beginning to enforce the principle of "implied" warranties. New cars are more strongly protected by the principle, but you should consider *any* car to be covered by implied warranty. This principle states that any car you buy can be safely purchased on the assumption that it is roadworthy and will perform for a reasonable amount of time without undue expense or trouble on your part. Some states have developed specific implied warranty definitions, but most are developing guidelines slowly.

Should you purchase a car that honestly fails to give reasonable service, first have a talk with your seller. Mention the implied warranty concept. If the seller is uncooperative, tell him you are filing a written complaint with your state consumer office, attorney general's office, and Better Business Bureau. Normally, a seller will help you with your problem rather than enter into sticky ethical battles with the various agencies responsible for consumer protection.

Used-Car Service Agreements

Here's a quick summary of these agreements, including service agreements available on the Web. A good, nationally recognized used-car service agreement bought cheaply enough can be a very smart idea if you plan to keep the used car for years. But the purchased service agreement should never replace the seller's own warranty; it should supplement it. In all likelihood, the seller will tell you this is a duplication of warranty and will not be inclined to provide his own protection. Don't accept that answer. If the seller's warranty does duplicate your service agreement, he will be protected. But if problems should develop that are not covered by the service agreement, you may still be protected.

Checking out a used-vehicle warranty: Those sold by credit unions and banks are usually relatively good. Used-vehicle warranties underwritten by the major manufacturers are usually good. But the used service agreement business is dominated by fly-by-night companies, and many dealerships sell the fly-by-night variety. Stay with brand names, and pay attention to other lending institutions that use the same warranty company. For instance, if the particular service agreement isn't also sold by a local bank or credit union, I would avoid it. You shouldn't pay more for a used agreement than you pay for a new agreement: try to bargain the price down to under $450.

A Note on Deposits

Regardless of the car, don't give the dealer a big deposit. Car people are like the rest of us: they need incentive. Let's assume you signed up last night for the perfect car and gave the man a check for the total purchase price. You return to the dealership the next day to pick up your car and notice a funny noise in the thermostatically controlled automatic mirror heater and a small scratch on the genuine wood dash hand-carved from extinct trees. The salesman says they will, of course, take care of both, but the rare-wood shop is busy for two years, and the mirror repair experts are busy right now, too. Can you bring the car back at six in the morning sometime next month? What can you do? You've paid for the car. If you had paid a $100 deposit instead, your car would be in the shop before the eye can blink, and talented repair persons would be swarming over it like bees over a queen. To car people, a car isn't sold until all the money is paid. Keep your deposit low, and turn over the rest of your hard-earned dough or sign that contract when you are satisfied the car is right.

Negotiating for Vehicles in Other Buying Scenarios

The most common buying situation is discussed in detail in chapters 12 through 15: you are going to finance, you are trading your old vehicle rather than selling it yourself, and you owe money on that vehicle. The steps given in detail in those chapters apply to other scenarios with some minor modifications. So be sure that you read them carefully. Then use these outlines to prepare for your specific situation.

If You Are Financing and Buying a New Car Without Trading

1. Determine your Loan Cash.
2. Determine your down payment.
3. Compute your Available Cash (Loan Cash plus down payment).
4. At the dealership, copy down all information on the particular cars that interest you.
5. At home, develop the cost and your maximum offer for each car.
6. Check your budget: compare your Available Cash to your maximum offer.

Dealing with the store: Take the following information with you:

- the location, stock number, and color of each car
- your maximum offer on each car
- your Available Cash figure

7. Go to the dealership that is home to your favorite car.
8. Take the salesperson to his or her office.
9. Tell the salesperson you are prepared to make a firm offer.
10. Make your offer and insist that it be taken to management.
11. Check the buyer's order. Compare the figure on the order to your Available Cash. If the figure is satisfactory, sign the order, but do not give a deposit.

12. Give a deposit when your offer is approved. Compare the final accepted offer to your Available Cash, if necessary.

13. If you are financing at the dealership, check the amount to be financed and the APR.

14. Expect finance pressure.

If You Are Paying Cash and Buying a New Car Without Trading

1. Determine your Available Cash.

2. At the dealership, copy down all information on the particular cars that interest you.

3. At home, develop the cost and your maximum offer for each car.

4. Check your budget: compare your Available Cash to your maximum offer.

Dealing with the store: Take your Available Cash and maximum offer figures with you.

5. Go to the dealership that is home to your favorite car.

6. Take the salesperson to his or her office.

7. Tell the salesperson you are prepared to make a firm offer.

8. Make your offer and insist that it be taken to management.

9. Check the buyer's order. Compare the figure on the order to your Available Cash. If the figure is satisfactory, sign the order, but do not give a deposit.

10. Give a deposit when your offer is approved. Compare the final accepted offer to your Available Cash, if necessary.

11. Expect pressure to finance even when you are paying cash.

If You Are Paying Cash, Buying a New Car and Trading the Old

1. Compute your Available Cash (your car plus the equity in your trade).

2. At the dealership, copy down all information on the particular cars that interest you.

3. At home, develop the cost and your maximum offer for each car.

4. Check your budget: Compare your Available Cash to your maximum offer.

5. Compute your "best probable" difference figure (your maximum offer minus the wholesale value of your trade).

Dealing with the store: Take the following information with you:

- the location, stock number, and color of each car
- your maximum offer on each car and "best probable" difference figure on each car
- the wholesale value of your trade
- your Available Cash figure

6. Go to the dealership that is home to your favorite car.
7. Take the salesperson to his or her office.
8. Have your car appraised.
9. Agree on the wholesale value of your trade.
10. When you have agreed, make your offer on their car.
11. Check dealer's difference figure (their offer on your trade minus the agreed price on the new car); compare it to your "best probable" difference figure.
12. Let the salesperson write up the buyer's order. Check it for accuracy.
13. If the figure is satisfactory, sign the order but do not give a deposit.
14. Give a deposit when your offer is approved. Recheck your difference figure if necessary.
15. Expect pressure to finance.

If You Are Financing and Buying a Used Vehicle Without Trading

1. Determine your Loan Cash.
2. Determine your down payment.
3. Compute your Available Cash (Loan Cash plus down payment).
4. Decide on two or three used-vehicle sources.
5. Look for vehicles with asking prices higher than your Available Cash figure.
   Drive each vehicle. Use your checklist to inspect each car. Write down all items that may affect loan value. Go home.
6. Call your credit union or bank and ask for (a) the loan value of the vehicles and (b) the lowest interest rate and number of months each vehicle can be financed.
7. Determine the dealership's "probable profit." Compare their asking price to the loan value of the vehicle.
8. Determine your maximum offer for the vehicle.

Dealing with the store: Take the following information with you:

- the location, stock number, and color of each vehicle
- your maximum offer on each vehicle
- the loan value of each vehicle
- your Available Cash figure

9. Go to the dealership that is home to your favorite vehicle.

10. Take their vehicle to your mechanic. Give your notes on the vehicle and the Mechanic's Checklist to your mechanic. Ask your mechanic for an estimate to repair the vehicle to your satisfaction.

11. At the lot, offer your salesperson less than loan value. Negotiate.

12. When the salesperson will not budge, compare the dealership's final offer to your Available Cash figure. Determine their "probable profit" figure: subtract the loan value of the car from his final offer.

13. After agreeing on price, discuss warranties.

14. Let the salesperson write up the buyer's order. Check the buyer's order, sign it, but don't give a deposit.

15. Negotiate. Compromise. Give a deposit when your offer is approved. If necessary, compare the final figure to your Available Cash figure.

16. If you are financing with the seller, check the amount to be financed and the APR.

17. Expect finance pressure.

If You Are Paying Cash, Buying a Used Vehicle, and Trading Your Old Vehicle

1. Compute your Available Cash (your cash plus the equity in your trade).

2. Decide on two or three used-vehicle sources.

3. Look for vehicles with asking prices higher than your Available Cash figure.

  Drive each vehicle. Use your checklist to inspect each car. Write down all items that may affect loan value. Go home.

4. Call your credit union or bank and ask for the loan value of the vehicles that interest you.

5. Determine the dealership's "probable profit." Compare their asking price to the loan value of the vehicle.

6. Compute your "best probable" difference figure (loan value of their vehicle minus the wholesale value of your car).

Dealing with the store: Take the following information with you:

- the location, stock number, and color of each vehicle
- your "best probable" difference figure on each vehicle
- the loan value of each vehicle
- the wholesale value of your trade
- your Available Cash figure

7. Take their vehicle to your mechanic. Give your notes on the vehicle and the Mechanic's Checklist to your mechanic. Ask your mechanic for an estimate to repair the vehicle to your satisfaction.

8. Subtract the repair estimate from your Available Cash figure and write the figure on your pad.

9. At the lot, offer your salesperson less than loan value. Negotiate.

10. When the salesperson will not budge, compare the dealership's final offer to your Available Cash figure. Determine their "probable profit" figure: subtract the loan value of the car from his final offer.

11. After agreeing on price, discuss warranties.

12. Let the salesperson write up the buyer's order. Check the buyer's order, sign it, but don't give a deposit.

13. Negotiate. Compromise. Give a deposit when your offer is approved. If necessary, compare the final figure to your Available Cash figure.

14. If you are financing with the seller, check the amount to be financed and the APR.

15. Expect finance pressure.

If You Are Paying Cash and Buying a Used Vehicle Without Trading

1. Decide on your Available Cash.

2. Decide on two or three used-vehicle sources.

3. Look for vehicles with asking prices higher than your Available Cash figure.

Drive each vehicle. Use your checklist to inspect each car. Write down all items that may affect loan value. Go home.

4. Call your credit union or bank and ask for the loan value of the vehicles that interest you.
5. Determine the dealership's "probable profit." Compare their asking price to the loan value of the vehicle.
6. Determine your maximum offer.

Dealing with the store: Take the following information with you:

- the location, stock number, and color of each vehicle
- your maximum offer on each vehicle
- the loan value of each vehicle
- your Available Cash figure

7. Take their vehicle to your mechanic. Give your notes on the vehicle and the Mechanic's Checklist to your mechanic. Ask your mechanic for an estimate to repair the vehicle to your satisfaction.
8. Subtract the repair estimate from your Available Cash figure and write the new figure on your pad.
9. At the lot, offer the salesperson less than loan value. Negotiate.
10. When the salesperson will not budge, compare the dealership's final offer to your Available Cash figure. Determine their "probable profit" figure: subtract the loan value of the car from his final offer.
11. After agreeing on price, discuss warranties.
12. Let the salesperson write up the buyer's order. Check the buyer's order, sign it, but don't give a deposit.
13. Negotiate. Compromise. Give a deposit when your offer is approved. If necessary, compare the final figure to your Available Cash figure.
14. Expect pressure to finance.

Glossary

Add-Ons: High-profit items added to cars by the seller, not installed at the factory.

Affinity Relationships: For the automotive business, business agreements between automotive manufacturers and businesses and Internet service providers or Internet portals such as AOL, Yahoo! and Greenlight.com.

Allowance Buyers: Customers who care only about the amount of money given them for their trade. Also referred to as weenies.

Asking Price: The maximum amount of money sellers wish to attain; an imaginary figure used by sellers to snare imbeciles.

Available Cash: The total amount of money available to an individual buyer, including equity, Loan Cash, and out-of-pocket cash.

Baitfish: New floor salespersons at dealerships.

"Be-Backs": Customers who tell a salesperson, "Oh, don't worry, I'll be back tomorrow." Sure.

"Best Probable" Difference Figure: The lowest price a customer will probably pay when trading.

Bird Dogs: People who send customers to a particular salesperson, usually for money.

Bonus Cars: Slow-selling cars that pay extra commission to salespeople.

Bumblebees: Folks who flit from dealership to dealership, looking at every new car in sight but never buying.

Bumping: Getting a customer to raise his offer on a particular car. Also called "raising."

Captive financing: Lending institutions owned by automotive manufacturers.

Car Queers: People who dream constantly about buying a new car and enjoy hanging out at car stores.

The Chart: When a customer is paying the highest interest rate for financing allowed by law and also buying life and accident and health insurance.

Chopped Car: A car reconstructed from two wrecked and/or stolen cars. This procedure, also called clipping, is a specialty of "chop shops."

The Christmas Club: A technique designed to convince the customer his or her first payment is being paid by the dealership when it is actually being paid by the customer.

Clocking: Turning the car's speedometer back to register lower mileage.

The Close: When a customer is finally convinced to sign the buyer's order.

Closer: A dealership employee whose only job is getting customers to sign a buyer's order.

Cookie: A file placed on your computer by a Web site that you log on to which allows the Web site owners to track what you view on their Web site and sometimes beyond.

Cream Puffs: Extremely nice used cars; also referred to as cherries.

Curbing: The practice of selling used cars by placing them in a parking lot or area beside a street. Most of the vehicles sold in this manner are represented as being sold by individuals when they are usually owned by a dealership or another party. Many "curbed" cars have also been wrecked, so avoid these.

Curbstones: A person paid by a used-car dealership who tells potential buyers that he or she is the owner.

Demos: New cars driven by salesmen and other dealership employees. Seldom a good buy.

Detail Man: A person who cleans new or used cars, especially a person who "doctors" minor problems with cars.

Difference: The selling price of a new or used car minus the actual wholesale value of a trade-in.

Difference Buyers: Customers who care only about the difference between their present car and the newer car. Also referred to as jerks.

Dipping: Borrowing a down payment for a customer, usually from a small loan company.

Double-Dipping: Borrowing a down payment for a customer from two lending institutions. Persons who are double-dipped are also referred to as spastics.

Down Stroke: The total amount of the down payment, including cash and equity in your trade.

Equity: The amount of value left in a used car when the car's payoff is subtracted from its true wholesale value.

"Financial Counselors": By any name, high-pressure salespeople for loans and add-ons.

Finance Charge: The total of all charges customers incur when they finance a car rather than pay cash; includes interest, documentary stamps, insurance, and credit fees.

Floor-Planning: When cars are owned by financing institutions rather than dealerships. The vast majority of automobile dealerships floor-plan their cars.

Floor Whores: Also known as lot lizards. Salespeople who don't work by appointment but simply tackle any unattached customer on the lot.

Geek Masters: Computer-friendly automotive salespeople trained to look like order takers rather than skilled salespeople.

Gross, Back-End: The profit to the dealership on the sale of financing, insurance, and add-ons, such as rustproofing.

Gross, Front-End: The profit to the dealership on the sale of a new or used car.

Holdbacks: Profits built into each new-car invoice but considered "cost" by the dealership.

"In the Bucket": When a car owner has a net payoff that is higher than the true wholesale value of that car, he is said to be "in the bucket."

Lepers: New or used cars avoided even by the salesmen due to their physical condition or length of stay at the dealership.

Loan Cash: The lump sum of cash an installment loan will buy; the actual sum of an installment loan that is applied to the purchase, not interest.

Loan Value: The average amount of money lending institutions will lend on a particular car; usually refers to used cars.

Negative Equity: When you owe more on your car than its true wholesale value.

Net Payoff: The amount owed on a car minus any prepaid interest or insurance premiums.

Nickel: Five hundred dollars.

Nickels: Small dents and scratches on a car.

The Pack: Extra profit added to the invoice cost of cars by dealers; packs are used to confuse both customers and salesmen.

Paper Men: Used-car sellers who finance their own cars regardless of the credit of the buyers.

Payment Buyers: Buyers who care only about their payment. Also referred to as suckers.

Peacocks: Persons who must drive the newest cars, regardless of the price penalty they must pay for the privilege.

Prospect Aggregators: Web sites that direct potential buyers who surf their sites to specific dealerships.

Retail Value: The wholesale value of a car plus the anticipated profit gained from reselling the car.

Road Hogs: Used-car wholesalers who travel from dealership to dealership peddling their wares.

Skating: When a salesman deliberately sells another salesman's customer.

Spiffs: Cash bonuses paid to salesmen—tax free, of course.

Spot delivery: The practice of selling and delivering a vehicle to a customer as quickly as possible on the first visit. Spot delivery prevents you from doing your homework to protect your pocketbook.

The Store: The dealership.

Switching (the automobile version of sadism): convincing a customer to buy a car with a larger profit margin; convincing a customer to buy a car with a bonus to the salesman.

Tanks: Unpopular cars or station wagons.

Tissue: The actual invoice price of a new car.

T.O.: To turn a customer over to another salesman or manager in order to close or raise the profit on a sale.

Trading Down: Buying a smaller or less expensive car than your present one; trading a newer car for an older one.

Ups: Customers.

The Up System: When ups are assigned to salesmen by numbers, viz., "Okay, Killer, you're up next."

Upside Down: See "In the Bucket."

VIN: Vehicle identification number.

Walking-Around Money: Spiffs, cash bonuses paid to salespersons.

Water: What remains when the value of a used car is less than the amount the seller has in the car. For instance, if a seller has $1,000 in a car with a true wholesale value of $600, the dealership has $400 in "water."

Web: The World Wide Web, part of the Internet.

Web Dogs: People who send customers to a particular automotive Web site or Web "consultant," usually for money.

Wholesale Value: The value of a used car to someone who plans to resell it.

Write-Downs: When the value of a used car is lowered on a dealership's book.

Checking Out a Used Car or Truck

Objectivity and honesty aren't qualities you'll find very often when you talk with used-car people about their wares. Used-car dealers will tell you their vehicles have "been checked out from top to bottom," place fancy stickers on many car windows proclaiming their top-notch condition, and then head for the hills the moment you drive back in with your first problem. Invariably, your problem just isn't one of the things their "service specialists" checked out. Tsk, tsk.

If you will adhere to the first checklist carefully yourself, and have your mechanic adhere to the second, you won't need these folks' help, and you will discover just about every skeleton in any vehicle's closet. The first checklist will require some judgment calls and a good amount of objectivity on your part. Copy the items and take them with you as you shop. Take a flashlight, too.

Personal Used-Car Checklist

1. **The name of the previous owner.** Insist on a name and number. If the seller resists, ask to see the title. If he still resists, don't buy. The previous owner's name and address should be on the title. Call the owner and ask specifically, "What were the major problems with the vehicle when you owned it?" Don't ask the owner *if* he or she had problems; assume there were problems. You'll get a more direct answer. Note the problems, if any, and add them to your Mechanic's Checklist.

2. **Check the exterior.** Kneel down by each front fender and look down each side. Look for ripples in the metal or dull paint. Either could indicate that there's been body damage. If the ripples or bad paint cover an area larger than twelve inches, make a note for your mechanic to check the frame. Also look directly at the damaged area and check for the match of the paint. Are you satisfied with the paint job? When you call the owner, ask him, "How badly was the car wrecked?" Again, don't ask him *if* the vehicle was wrecked. If it had damage to the frame or engine compartment, you would do well to look for another vehicle. If you are still interested in the car, plan to drive it at least half a day.

3. **Check the moldings around the bumpers, grill, wheel wells, and windows.** Are any missing or damaged? Cosmetically, is the vehicle well-kept? Are there signs of small paint bubbles accumulating around the moldings? If you see these small rust bubbles, ask the seller to punch through them firmly with a screwdriver. If the screwdriver continues through the entire piece of metal, the body is rusting from the inside out and will probably require major work. If the bubbles are only surface bubbles, repairs will be less costly. *Any* rust indicates the presence of salt. Be conscious of other rust as you check the vehicle.

4. **Open and close all doors.** Do they open and close properly? If a door needs to be forced to close, the door may have been hit in an accident. Look carefully at all metal on the bottom and inside of the doors. Are paint bubbles present or are other signs of rust evident? Many doors begin to rust through along the bottom first. If rust is present there, ask the seller to use his screwdriver again. Normally, doors with rusted-through bottom edges will continue to rust even after repairs. If you buy

such a vehicle, you may eventually need to replace the doors. Look at all rubber moldings on the doors and adjacent surfaces. Are they brittle or cracked? Rubber moldings are expensive to replace. Make a note.

5. **If it's a car, open the trunk.** Look carefully at all inside edges. Is there rust present? If so, check it with the screwdriver. Look at the interior walls of the trunk. Are there stains present? Stains are an indication of leaks. If possible, lift up the trunk mat and check for rust. Check the spare tire. Does it match the other tires—e.g., is it a radial if the others are radials? Or, is it the proper small spare for that vehicle? Will the tire make a satisfactory spare? If the tire doesn't match or is barely serviceable, make a note and insist on a different spare. Make sure a jack is in the trunk.

6. **Check the wheel wells and undercarriage.** Turn the steering wheel completely to the right and look in the left well. Do the opposite for the right well. Are there signs of rust? Are there signs of fresh undercoating? Many sellers will simply spray over rust. Take a screwdriver or knife and scrape away a small portion of the undercoating. If rust is mixed in with the undercoating, don't buy the vehicle—you are probably dealing with a shyster. Check the rear wheel wells, too. Then look under the car with your flashlight. Check the muffler system with the engine running. Are fumes escaping at any point along the system? Are the holes larger than a pinpoint? If so, the system will probably need to be replaced rather than repaired. Has the underside been freshly undercoated? If so, forget the vehicle or plan to spend an hour or so scratching undercoating from the various surfaces. Used-car sellers have absolutely no incentive to undercoat their vehicles other than to hide things. Most rustproofing and undercoating companies won't guarantee or perform their work on used models because the product actually seals in rust; it does not stop it.

If the vehicle is a front-wheel-drive model, look for welding seams along the frame or underbody. Welds can indicate a wrecked vehicle or, worse, *two* wrecked vehicles. Some less-than-reputable dealers are actually taking two wrecked cars and welding them together—and not telling the potential customer. Don't buy a vehicle with extensive welding seams *unless* it's checked out first by a body shop. If the seller has failed to inform you of welding work, do the rest of us a favor and report the incident to your local Better Business Bureau.

7. **Check all glass and plastic.** Is any broken or cracked? In many states, a cracked front windshield must be replaced. The seller should be responsible for the expense. Check the headlights, parking lights, and taillights. Are they cracked or broken? All broken light covers will need to be replaced.

8. **Check the wiper blades.** Are they cracked or pitted? They are cheap to replace, but make a note and determine who will replace them.

9. **Check any vinyl roof for lumps.** Under every lump is a mountain of rust. If the lumps are really numerous, don't buy the car unless the seller will pull the roof and repair the rust. Rust under vinyl roofs can be serious and can actually rust through the roof of the vehicle quickly. Check for tears in the roof. Do they appear large enough to allow water to enter? If so, they must be repaired. Note this and determine with the seller who will bear the expense.

10. **Check brake lights, turn signals, hazard lights, parking lights, interior lights, and headlights.** Have someone sit in the vehicle and use each one as you watch. Note problems. If any systems are not working properly, don't just assume that a bulb is burnt out. Have the bulb replaced then and check again. Bulbs are cheap to replace. Repairs to electrical systems are normally very expensive.

11. **Check for ease of starting.** Start the engine cold, and then start it several times after you test-drive. Race the engine under both circumstances, and look for blue smoke shooting from the exhaust. Many sellers will tell you that smoke "simply means the carbon is burning off the rings." Don't believe them. Make a note for your mechanic to test to determine the cause.

12. **Open the hood and check the following with the engine off:**

   A. ALL BELTS AND HOSES. Look on the inside of the belts, not the outside. Are they cracked and dry? They will need to be replaced. Make a note.

   B. LOOK FOR CORROSION AND RUST ON THE RADIATOR. If there is any, the radiator probably leaks. Make a note for your mechanic to check it.

   C. LOOK AT THE RADIATOR COOLANT. If the coolant is rusty, the cooling system has probably not been maintained. Make a note for your mechanic to determine if the radiator needs to be recored or replaced.

D. LOOK AT THE BATTERY. Are the terminals corroded? Are the wires wearing through? If so, the battery probably has not been maintained. Check the battery case. Is it cracked? If so, the battery will probably need to be replaced. Look at the battery levels. If even one of the cells is dry, the seller obviously doesn't service his vehicle—or the battery is definitely in need of replacement.

13. **Leave the hood open and have someone start the engine.** Have him push the accelerator down gently, slowly increasing pressure. Do you hear knocks? Knocking sounds can indicate valve problems. Make a note. Do you see any signs of leakage on the engine block or attached parts? Leakage can indicate bad seals. Do you hear any clicking or grinding? Both can indicate problems. Let the engine idle for at least five minutes, and then pull the vehicle forward. Are there pools of liquid? Many sellers will tell you, "Oh, that's on the air-conditioner condensation." Likely story. Rub your fingers in the pools. If they are red or brown or clear and slippery, you have problems with the transmission, engine seals, or block. While the engine is running, walk back to the exhaust. Is it pulsing? If so, you could have a bad valve. Check this by holding a dollar bill over the end of the exhaust pipe. If the bill is pulled to the pipe, you have *serious* valve problems. Rub your finger inside the pipe (before it gets hot). Is there oil on your pinkie? If so, the engine is burning oil.

14. **Check the interior:**

A. LOOK UNDER MATS AND CARPETS. Are there signs of rust or excess wear? You can live with the water, but rust indicates both leakage and rust coming through from the underside, which is very expensive and at times impossible to repair.

Again, look for welding seams on both sides of the floorboard. Seams can indicate a wrecked vehicle at best, two pieced together at the worst.

B. LOOK UNDER THE SEAT COVERS. Are they just soiled or are the seats tearing apart?

C. LOOK ALONG THE WINDOWS AND AT THE HEADLINER. Are there signs of stains? Stains always indicate leakage.

D. LOOK FOR MISSING DOOR HANDLES OR CONTROL KNOBS. Are the missing parts important to the operation of the vehicle?

E.   CHECK THE HORN, RADIO, WIPERS, AND OTHER ELECTRICAL GADGETS, SUCH AS POWER WINDOWS AND SEATS. Are any inoperative things important to the operation of the vehicle? If so, make a note.

F.   START THE ENGINE, CHECK THE OPERATION OF THE AIR CONDITIONER, HEATER, AND DEFROSTER. CHECK ALL GAUGES. If any systems are inoperative, make a note for your mechanic.

G.   CHECK THE BRAKES. Don't move the vehicle, but apply strong pressure to the pedal and hold it for at least thirty seconds. If the pedal continues toward the floor, you probably have leakage in your braking system.

H.   CHECK THE CLUTCH (for standard transmission). Start the engine, set the parking brake, put the transmission in first gear, and let the clutch out as you slowly press on the gas pedal. The engine should stall when the clutch pedal is one-half to three-quarters of the way up. If it doesn't, you probably need clutch work. Make a note.

I.   CHECK THE AUTOMATIC TRANSMISSION. With the engine idling and your foot on the brake, slip the transmission from neutral to reverse. If you hear a loud "clunk," the transmission bands probably need tightening, at the minimum. Make a note. Slip the transmission from neutral to drive, and listen for the same sound.

J.   LOOK AT THE SPEEDOMETER. Are the miles reasonable for the age of the vehicle, no more than fifteen thousand miles per year? If the miles are unreasonably low, ask the *owner* what the mileage was when he traded the car in. If the vehicle has a conventional odometer, see if the numbers line up evenly; if they don't, the mileage may have been altered. If the vehicle has an electronic speedometer, you will have to rely on the previous owner to confirm its true mileage.

15. **The test-drive.** Tell the seller you will be happy to buy the gas, and you will be happy to have him go with you, but that you would like to drive the vehicle thirty to forty-five minutes. Plan to drive on crowded streets and on uncrowded ones; on bumpy roads and smooth; up and down hills, if there are any in your neck of the woods. Don't be satisfied with a drive around the block. Too many problems with used vehicles don't surface during quick test-drives.

A. CHECK THE ENGINE PERFORMANCE. The vehicle should be responsive when cold and warm. There should be no grinding or humming sounds in the rear end or transmission. If there are, make a note for your mechanic.

B. CHECK THE BRAKES. The brakes should stop you without pulling, fading, or making unusual noises. Listen for a grinding sound when the brakes are applied. Grinding can indicate worn-out brake pads or worse. At an appropriate place on the highway, slow the car to five miles per hour and apply the emergency brake. If the vehicle does not come to a complete stop immediately, the emergency system is faulty.

C. CHECK THE STEERING. Is there lost motion when you turn the wheel back and forth? The vehicle could have linkage problems. Does the steering wheel jerk and resist when you turn it? There are probably power-steering pump problems.

D. CHECK THE TRANSMISSION. *If the vehicle is an automatic,* speed up gradually until the gears shift. Is there a clunking sound or a second hesitation before shifting? Hesitation or jerky shifts could indicate problems with a gear mechanism. Slow down to ten miles per hour and then press firmly on the accelerator. Do the gears shift quickly? If you are driving a three-speed automatic, the vehicle should shift two times. If it doesn't, this could indicate gear problems, too. *If the vehicle is a standard shift,* shift several times through all gears from a standstill. Are some gears hard to enter? Is there a grinding sound? Either could indicate linkage problems.

E. CHECK THE SUSPENSION. Drive over bumpy roads at slow and fast speeds. At a safe point on the road, veer hard right and left. If either action causes a large amount of bouncing or sway, your shocks may be defective. Make a note for your mechanic. Now, drive back to the lot and check under the hood again. Is there any fluid on the engine? Is steam or any other vapor rising from the engine? Is the radiator hissing? Make notes.

16. **Finally, check the tires.** Do they match, four radials or four polyester? If they don't, the tires will have to be changed. Driving with mixed tires can cause excessive tire wear and heating, handling problems, and accidents. Are the tires worn evenly? Look at the rear tires. Are the edges of the tires badly or unevenly worn? If so, your seller has probably placed the front tires on the rear. That's okay, but if any of the four tires show unnecessary wear along the edges, your vehicle is probably out of alignment. Make a note.

These sixteen steps obviously take a good deal of time and attention, but take the time. And don't be self-conscious. Look over each vehicle as if you were going to marry it. If you buy it, that's what you will be doing: living with the thing, warts and all.

Now, look over your checklist. If there are many minor things wrong with the vehicle, don't scratch it from your list. If there is an indication of major things, make sure each of those items is added to the following checklist for your mechanic. Make out a clean, neat sheet for him, and leave room for his notations concerning each item. Leave room also for his cost estimate to repair the car to your satisfaction.

Mechanic's Checklist

1.   Check the Engine

inspect transmission fluid
check points, condenser, and rotor
check spark plugs and ignition wire

2.   Check Fan and Belts

charging system
power steering
air conditioner

3.   Check Cooling System

radiator
heater
bypass hose

4.   Check Battery

5.   Check Braking System

lining
wheel and master cylinders

drums and front disks
hoses, bearing, grease seals

6. **Check Exhaust System**

7. **Check Suspension**

ball joints
tie rod end
idler arm

8. **Remove Differential Plug and Check Lubricant**

9. **Test-Drive Vehicle**

In Your Opinion

- Should engine compression be checked with gauge?
- What are the specific problems, if any, with this vehicle?
- What is your estimated repair cost?

Index

equity, 171, 244, 252, 355–56, 445
as down payment, 248
negative, 252–54, 446
escrow services, 185, 383
ethics, 33–35, 62, 102, 306, 436
executive cars, 266, 300–301

F

fair deal, defining, 333–35, 351
fairies, 274
Fair Isaac Corporation, 209, 211
Farr, Mel, 107, 424
FICO score, *see* credit reports, scoring numbers on
finance charge, 445
finance contracts, 18, 24, 337, 339, 340–41, 349, 360, 364, 379, 384
finance managers, financial counselors, 225, 337, 360, 445
financing, 24, 25, 27, 70, 120–21, 188–236, 343–45, 356, 357, 360–61, 374–75, 379, 381, 383, 384
balloon payment, 91–92, 153–54, 268
from banks, 220–21
buy here-pay here, 227–29, 327
buying services and, 298
captive sources of, 223–28, 431, 444
credit and, *see* credit; credit problems; credit reports
credit unions as source of, *see* credit unions

dealership, 223–25, 297–98
dipping and, 119–20, 248, 445
down payments and, 247–50, 253–54
extended-payment plans and, 245–46
family sources of, 212–13
finding the cheapest and best loan, 233–36
home equity loans, 213–14
from "independent" buying services, 63–64
invoice cost and, 248
life insurance as source of, 213
"no hassle" selling and, 98–100
sources of, 212–29
spot delivery, 100–102, 338, 446
subprime borrowers and, 107–8, 227–28
title loans, 229, 425
of used vehicle, 121, 249–50, 318, 325
Web sites offering, 67, 205–7, 221–23, 226, 229
see also payments
Firmin, Michael, 39
flipping, 390, 397–98
floor-planning, 56, 57, 298, 300, 335, 445
floor whores (lot lizards), 9, 49, 445
Ford Motor Company, 21, 28, 34, 303, 423
Ford Motor Credit Company (FMCC), 66, 67, 110, 220, 223–24, 335, 402
foreign cars, 142–43

lowballing and, 28, 63, 65, 66, 113–14, 160–62
making it worth more, 155–58
mileage of, 158–59
and ordering a new car, 298–300
popularity of, 157–58
retail value of, 162
shopping for value of, 124–25, 163–65
trading down and, 143–44, 447
Web sites and, 63, 89, 100, 161, 162, 166–70
wholesale value of, 159–72, 343, 346, 355, 374, 380, 447
see also car, currently owned
trading down, 143–44, 447
trucks and vans, 301
TRUSTe, 185
turnover system (T.O.), 3, 71, 94, 96, 278, 286, 447
20/20, 31

U

underallowing, *see* lowballing
"ups," 447
upside down ("in the bucket"), 117–18, 120, 121, 144, 171, 245, 252–55, 321, 343, 355, 408, 446, 447
"up" system, 447
used vehicles:
  assuming payments on, 321
  auctions and, 324, 327
  bulletin board notices on, 320
  buying from people you know, 320–21
  checking out, 313–14,
327–29, 331–32, 358, 382–84, 447–55
down payment on, 249–50
and drop in value of new cars, 141
financing and, 121, 249–50, 318, 325
honest-salesman ploy and, 83–84
independent dealers of, 326
leasing and, 403, 416
loan value and, 121, 248, 249, 318–19, 332, 356, 383, 446
negotiating for, at a dealership, *see* negotiating for a used vehicle at the dealership
negotiating for, online, 379–84
from new-vehicle dealers, 326
new vs., 135–42, 315–16
online market guides for, 169
preparation for shopping for, 312–18
problems in buying, 317–18
researching, 329–32
shopping for, 311–32
sources of, 319–27
warranties on, 325, 434–36
Web sites dealing in, 66–67, 141–42, 158, 321–24, 330

V

vans and trucks, 301
vehicle identification number (VIN), 183, 193, 339, 356–57, 383, 413, 447
VeriSign, 185